Oxford University Press

Oxford   New York
Athens   Auckland   Bangkok   Bombay
Calcutta   Cape Town   Dar es Salaam   Delhi
Florence   Hong Kong   Istanbul   Karachi
Kuala Lumpur   Madras   Madrid   Melbourne
Mexico City   Nairobi   Paris   Singapore
Taipei   Tokyo   Toronto

and associated companies in
Berlin   Ibadan

Copyright © 1996 by Oxford University Press, Inc.

Published by Oxford University Press, Inc.
198 Madison Avenue, New York, New York 10016

Oxford is a registered trademark of Oxford University Press

Library of Congress Cataloging-in-Publication Data
Haliczer, Stephen, 1942–
Sexuality in the confessional : a sacrament profaned /
Stephen Haliczer.
p.   cm.   Includes bibliographical references and index.
ISBN 0-19-509656-8
1. Confession—Catholic Church—History—16th century.
2. Confession—Catholic Church—History—17th century.   3. Catholic
Church—Spain—Clergy—Sexual behavior—History—17th century.
4. Catholic Church—Spain—Clergy—Sexual behavior—History—17th
century.   5. Spain—Church history—16th century.   6. Spain—Church
history—17th century.   7. Inquisition—Spain.   I. Title.
BX2263.S7H35   1996
264'.020862'09460903I—dc20   94-47094

1 3 5 7 9 8 6 4 2

Printed in the United States of America
on acid-free paper

Sexuality in the Confessional

A SACRAMENT PROFANED

Stephen Haliczer

New York   Oxford
OXFORD UNIVERSITY PRESS
1996

Sexuality in the Confessional

A SACRAMENT PROFANED

Stephen Haliczer

New York   Oxford
OXFORD UNIVERSITY PRESS
1996

Oxford University Press

Oxford   New York
Athens   Auckland   Bangkok   Bombay
Calcutta   Cape Town   Dar es Salaam   Delhi
Florence   Hong Kong   Istanbul   Karachi
Kuala Lumpur   Madras   Madrid   Melbourne
Mexico City   Nairobi   Paris   Singapore
Taipei   Tokyo   Toronto

and associated companies in
Berlin   Ibadan

Copyright © 1996 by Oxford University Press, Inc.

Published by Oxford University Press, Inc.
198 Madison Avenue, New York, New York 10016

Oxford is a registered trademark of Oxford University Press

Library of Congress Cataloging-in-Publication Data
Haliczer, Stephen, 1942–
Sexuality in the confessional : a sacrament profaned /
Stephen Haliczer.
p.   cm.   Includes bibliographical references and index.
ISBN 0-19-509656-8
1. Confession—Catholic Church—History—16th century.
2. Confession—Catholic Church—History—17th century.   3. Catholic
Church—Spain—Clergy—Sexual behavior—History—17th century.
4. Catholic Church—Spain—Clergy—Sexual behavior—History—17th
century.   5. Spain—Church history—16th century.   6. Spain—Church
history—17th century.   7. Inquisition—Spain.   I. Title.
BX2263.S7H35   1996
264'.020862'094609031—dc20   94-47094

1 3 5 7 9 8 6 4 2

Printed in the United States of America
on acid-free paper

Sexuality in the Confessional

FURTHER VOLUMES ARE IN PREPARATION

ACKNOWLEDGMENTS

This book could not have been written without the aid of archivists and librarians in Spain. I would especially like to mention the staff of the Archivo Histórico Nacional, particularly the archivists of the Sección de Inquisición, where the trial records of solicitantes are preserved. I would also like to express my gratitude to the staff of the Biblioteca Nacional in Madrid, where I discovered the many confessors' manuals and other printed sources that helped me to better understand what contemporaries expected of confession and confessors.

I would also like to thank a few individuals, especially Jaime Contreras, Virgilio Pinto Crespo, Jean-Pierre Dedieu, Richard L. Kagan, and Jack Weiner, who have offered advice at various moments. I am especially grateful to my colleague Stephen Kern, who showed me how some of Freud's ideas could be used in this study. I am also grateful to my colleague Catherine Jagoe for a stimulating conversation about Galdos and the Spanish naturalist movement. Karen Blaser of NIU manuscript services has been patient with my errors and done her usual excellent job. Deborah Haliczer has freely and unstintingly offered her excellent advice throughout the project, and without her sharp critical mind it would have been a far less readable book.

This project would never have been completed without the funding that has permitted my research in Spain. I am grateful to the U.S.-Spanish Joint Committee for Cultural and Educational Cooperation for a grant that enabled me to be in Spain for an extended period. I am grateful for the helpful advice offered by Nancy Lane of Oxford University Press and Catherine Clements for her excellent editorial work on this book.

DeKalb, Illinois   S. H.
March 1995

CONTENTS

Sexuality in the Confessional

INTRODUCTION

In spite of the reforms introduced during the reign of Ferdinand and Isabella that made Spain largely immune to the Lutheran threat, the Spanish Catholic Church remained a deeply troubled institution on the eve of the Reformation. Nowhere were these problems more evident than in the contemporary Spaniard's attitudes toward the sacrament of penance. Since the Fourth Lateran Council (1215), Catholics had been required to confess their sins annually to a legally qualified priest, but the evidence suggests that few did so.

There were a number of reasons for this mass abstention from the sacrament of penance. One obvious explanation was ignorance of the precept that mandated yearly confession. When the Spanish Inquisition turned its attention to religious offenses committed by the popular masses, such as blasphemy, bigamy, or superstition, officials were alarmed at what they discovered. Across large parts of Spain, especially in the more backward and inaccessible regions, peasants and artisans were largely ignorant of the basic tenets of the Catholic faith. Moreover, widespread absenteeism among both priests and bishops often left the laity without leadership or basic instruction.

Apart from ignorance, the most important reason given for abstention from the sacrament, revealed in the inquisitorial trials of the early sixteenth century, was distrust of the clergy, specifically in sexual matters. Members of the tight-knit village communities that made up most of Spain were well aware that many, if not most, priests lived in sin, routinely violating the rule of celibacy. Medieval Spanish literature as well as popular songs and refrains are full of references to the sexual activity of priests, friars, and nuns. In light of the well-known moral deficiencies of the clerical caste, it was difficult, if not impossible, for ordinary penitents to feel comfortable confessing sins to a priest who was just as much a sinner. The problem was especially acute in the case of sexual sins, which were beginning to be emphasized in late medieval confessors' manuals.

Since the shortcomings of the clergy were well-known to the delegates who attended the Council of Trent (1545–1563), it is not surprising that the Council legislated extensively on reform. But other councils, notably the Fifth Lateran Council (1512–1517), had passed similar legislation to no avail. What was new about the post-Tridentine period was the repressive machinery the Church hierarchy was now willing to deploy to enforce the legislation passed at Trent. This repressive machinery, which included greatly increased powers for episcopal courts, frequent visitations by bishops or their representatives to the clergy of their diocese, and systematic censorship of thought and expression through the indexes of prohibited books, also involved the great inquisitorial tribunals of mediterranean Europe.

The present study deals with sexual solicitation in the confessional, one of several spheres of activity where the Spanish Inquisition sought to enforce the new post-Tridentine moral order on the clergy. It begins by examining the transformation of the popular practice of confession and the emergence of a new, broader role for the confessor as a "doctor of souls," a genuine spiritual advisor who could offer consolation to ailing consciences. With the increasing popularity of confession among the laity, especially among women, the problem of sexual solicitation became acute and the Church hierarchy asked the Inquisition to assume responsibility in this area. In the chapters that follow, an analysis is made of the way in which the Holy Office carried out its responsibilities, the special trial procedures used with solicitantes, and the punishments they were forced to undergo. The devastating impact that punishment could have on the lives of those convicted is noted, as well as the difficulty of getting enough evidence to initiate prosecution and the long gap between accusation and trial. The final chapters are devoted to a discussion of the attitudes and sexual behavior of victims and soliciting confessors, and the way in which solicitation and confession became synonymous in the minds of nineteenth-century anticlericals.

The sources for this inquiry into confession and solicitation in early modern Spain are 223 complete solicitation cases from the tribunals of Toledo (79), Valencia (35), Córdoba (7), Cuenca (7), Madrid (2), Mallorca (37), and the Canaries (56), covering the period from 1530 to 1819. Although providing rich and valuable material on soliciting confessors and their victims, these sources have serious geographic limitations. Unfortunately, most of the actual case files have been lost, and historians have been dependent on the much less interesting and detailed case summaries, or relaciones de causas, to reconstruct the overall activity of the Holy Office.[1] The present study, therefore, has been forced to concentrate on the tribunals where complete case records are available, even though such case files represent only a fraction of the solicitation cases tried by the Spanish Inquisition. Furthermore, the archive of the Cuenca tribunal, the most complete and best preserved, was closed when the author was doing research for the project. The need to focus only on the available case records has made it very difficult to deal with the issue of the overall geographic incidence of solicitation, although the large number of cases from the Canaries and Mallorca may be a consequence of the late arrival of the closed confessional on the islands. The number of cases from Toledo not only represents the better state of preservation of the sources, but also the greater degree of activity of a prestigious tribunal located in Spain's largest archdiocese, itself a center of Counter-Reformation piety. Toledo's inquisitors could hardly have remained indifferent to an offense like solicitation that threatened to undermine so much of the Counter-Reformation program of catechizing, sacramentalism, and christianization.

This study also relies heavily on confessors' manuals and other works written by theologians for confessors and penitents. These little-used sources provide vital insight into the social role of confession, the standards of performance and morality demanded of confessors, and the numerous problems encountered by penitents in making their confessions.

Apart from a chapter in Henry Charles Lea's *History of Sacerdotal Celibacy in the Christian Church* and another chapter in volume four of his monumental *A History of the Spanish Inquisition*, historians have paid virtually no attention to the problem of solicitation in the confessional or the role of the Spanish Inquisition in attempting to repress it. We are somewhat better served when it comes to the history of confession yet serious lacunae still persist in our understanding of the shift to a confession of personal contrition and especially in analyzing how confession was actually practiced. Thomas Tentler's recent work, *Sin and Confession on the Eve of the Reformation*, is a valuable study, but stops with the early sixteenth century and leaves out the confessors' manuals of large parts of western Europe.[2] During the later sixteenth and seventeenth centuries, especially as confession began to be thought of as a medium of instruction, confessors' manuals proliferated. An entire ancillary literature aimed at instructing and informing confessors was created by the Catholic press. This literature, designed for the "confessors' market" of the better educated, more affluent Counter-Reformation priest, still awaits serious historical study.

The work of Jean Delumeau, especially *Le péché et la peur* (1983), is a treasure trove of information about the contents of sermons, confessors' manuals, and other publications for priests designed both to instruct and to suggest the best ways to convey their message to the laity. Unfortunately, the period that he has chosen to analyze stretches from the thirteenth to the eighteenth centuries and therefore blurs the very real changes in confessional doctrine and practice that took place after the Council of Trent. Moreover, his assertion that by the beginning of the sixteenth century the Church had fixed its teaching about sin in ways that remained unchanged through the nineteenth century appears to be directly contradicted in his later work, *L'aveu et le pardon*, with its extensive discussion of attrition, probabilism, laxism, and rigorism.[3]

The fundamental problem with all these works is that they deal with confession from the standpoint of theologians, who wrote to instruct confessors how to carry out their responsibilities. By the very nature of their sources the previously cited works can tell us little about confessional practice and still less about the relationship between individual confessors and their penitents.

Some understanding of the tensions and difficulties of this relationship can be gleaned from contemporary memoirs like those of Teresa de Jesús, but the experiences of a remarkable individual like St. Teresa are not typical of the ordinary confessor-penitent relationship. The present work does not and cannot fill the gap because it is concerned primarily with the sexual aspects of that relationship. What it can do, however, is to provide vital insight into the way in which the enforcement of clerical celibacy and the growing insistence on the disciplinary and consolatory function of the sacrament could generate an unprecedented level of sexual tension, anxiety, and guilt for both confessor and penitent. The clash between the private conception of confession and the new emphasis on celibacy cast a long shadow over the Church's efforts to rehabilitate the sacrament of penance. By the end of the old regime, compliance with the Church's precepts about confession was almost total in many regions, but new questions were being raised about the impact of the confessor-penitent relationship on women, the family, and society itself.

Chapter 1

Auricular Confession and the Crisis in the Church

Fundamental to the development of auricular confession and the inclusion of penance as one of the seven sacraments of the Roman Catholic Church is the Christian concept of sinful mankind. Sin, in the sense of the commission of willfully evil acts offensive to the divine order, did not exist for the ancients. For Plato, a moral error was a mere blunder on the part of an individual who thought he was in pursuit of the good. Such a well-meaning mistake could never be offensive to God.[1] Christianity, on the other hand, took over the notion of original sin from the Old Testament and made it into a deliberate contravention of God's will, an opposition that manifested itself not only by external acts, but by thoughts, beliefs, and intentions.

It is with St. Paul that the Christian notion of sin acquired its systematic character. After the fall of Adam, man was given over to the power of sin, capable of imagining and desiring the good, but incapable of achieving it. In several of his epistles St. Paul furnishes the first lists of sins, including apostasy, idolatry, lust, and greed. Christian thinkers of the second and third centuries continued to meditate on sin and reminded Christians that, as long as they lived in a mortal body, they were prone to fall into sin, even after baptism.[2]

Since the penalty for committing sins was partial or total removal from the Christian community, Christianity had to offer a way in which the individual could make amends.[3] In the primitive Church, this was an extremely difficult and painful process. Penitents would confess their sins to God, frequently in public, then undergo an extended and severe penance in order to expiate the sin before being readmitted into the community of the faithful. This

7

readmission, however, did not imply the recovery of God's grace, for only God himself could decide to offer forgiveness.[4]

During the twelfth and thirteenth centuries, the harsh penitential regime of an earlier period had been replaced by lighter penalties, frequently regulated by the priest who heard the confession. Instead of satisfaction, contrition—the sorrow felt by the sinner who realizes he has offended God—was seen to be the most important part of penance. But one of the chief virtues of the harsh old penitential exercises was the consolation they offered the sinner. It was easy to believe that one had been forgiven after undergoing the rigors prescribed in the penitentials, but impossible to know if one's contrition was perfect enough in the eyes of God.[5] Furthermore, if contrition was the key to regaining God's grace, what role did the priest play?

This dual problem was resolved by emphasizing the necessity of confession and placing the priest's absolution at the heart of the sacrament, regardless of the degree of contrition felt by the penitent. At the Fourth Lateran Council of 1215, confession was imposed on all Christians as a divinely ordained duty that each individual had to fulfill at Lent before the parish priest.[6] Subsequently, theologians like St. Thomas Aquinas and Duns Scotus stressed the centrality of the priest's role. For St. Thomas, contrition was the normal way to attain forgiveness for sin, but it was ineffective without the priest's absolution since grace was conveyed from the performance of the sacrament and not from the inclination or spiritual state of the recipient. For Duns Scotus, the priest's role was even clearer: the essence of the sacrament was not contrition or satisfaction nor even confession, but simply the utterance of the formula of forgiveness by a properly authorized priest.[7] Sacerdotalism could do no more; penitents, no matter what their state of contrition, were brought into absolute dependence on the priest for forgiveness and could only obtain the priest's absolution by going to confession.

The priest's power to grant or withhold absolution, to levy and control penance, and his superior education and social status made the confessional relationship inherently unequal. In effect, the priest was acting, directly or indirectly, to inculcate, maintain, and extend the system of values that supported constituted religious and political authority and the prevailing distribution of wealth and power.[8] The process by which the conscience of the individual was linked to the maintenance of prevailing social values through confession was greatly facilitated by the emergence of confessors' manuals from the end of the thirteenth century. These manuals, which were frequently written in the vernacular, like the *Specchio della confessione* and *Renovamini* of Antonio of Florence (d. 1459), had a dual purpose: to instruct the priest in how to administer and the penitent in how to receive the sacrament. At the heart of this process was the interrogatory, which was designed to provide a highly structured way of examining the conscience of the penitent and eliciting appropriate replies. According to the manuals, the penitent was to be questioned with reference to the seven deadly sins, the Ten Commandments, and the five senses. Certain manuals would broaden the questioning to include such matters as the four cardinal virtues or the eight Beatitudes.[9] By the late middle ages, the Ten Commandments had clearly superseded the seven deadly sins as the organizing principle laid down in most manuals.

The authoritarian and conservative tone of the typical interrogatory may be seen from an analysis of Martín de Azpilcueta Navarro's highly influential *Manual de confesores y penitentes*, which went through eighty-two editions in Spanish, Latin, Portuguese, French, and Italian between 1553 and 1620. Azpilcueta Navarro's strong support for the principle of hierarchy and subordination began with the family, where the wife was clearly seen as inferior to her husband and committing a mortal sin if she disobeyed him in any matter pertaining to the government of the household. He could chastise her physically in moderation, but she could not correct him or remonstrate with him since it was his place to correct her.[10]

In accordance with the dictates of the anti-Machiavellianism embraced by most Spanish political theorists, rulers were to obey the law, avoid excessive expenditure and taxation, and respect the liberties of their subjects. Judges and other officials were to exercise their offices with due respect for legal procedures and make sure that attorneys were provided even for those unable to pay. Officials committed a mortal sin if they accepted an office without being properly qualified or took money in return for favorable decisions.[11]

Moral constraints on the behavior of those of inferior social status were expressed in even more uncompromising terms. Subordinates had an absolute obligation to obey their superiors, defined as everyone from kings and other representatives of secular authority to parents, even if their superiors were evil. Any hatred or resentment of them was a mortal sin since it was defined as the most heinous form of unjustified anger. Under certain extraordinary circumstances, the social "superior" could even legitimately force a subordinate to commit a mortal sin.[12]

Obviously, the penitent was expected to accept all the tenets of Roman Catholicism since "those who believe consciously what is contrary to the Catholic faith are heretics and excommunicate." The penitent was expected to denounce instances of heresy to the proper authorities and reject as a mortal sin the belief that infidels can be saved if they live morally.[13] The reverence that the individual owed the Church went far beyond subscribing to its religious beliefs and was extended to the church hierarchy and members of the religious orders. Azpilcueta Navarro even taught that it was a mortal sin for heirs to unnecessarily delay payment for pious works stipulated by deceased relatives in their will. Those who refused payment of the ecclesiastical tithe not only fell into mortal sin, but could not receive absolution unless the debt was forgiven.[14] That this was no idle threat can be confirmed from the experience of Blas Hernández, an ironmonger from the village of Cienpozuelos. Testifying before the Holy Office in Toledo on January 25, 1531, Hernández stated that some years before he had heard acting curate Antonio de Pareja declare from the pulpit that anyone who had failed to pay the tithe and had the money to pay it would be refused absolution.[15]

Nevertheless, in spite of the growing popularity of confessors' manuals and a variety of other works on sin and penance that appeared in the vernacular during the fifteenth century, the average Spanish Catholic hardly confessed at all, even neglecting the annual confession that had been made obligatory at the Fourth Lateran Council. The diocesan synods that were held in León and Seville in 1512 lamented the fact that so many failed to observe the precept. Parish priests were told to divide each parish into districts, assigning to each a day on which those who lived there would come to confession. Lists of those refusing to confess were to be furnished to episcopal officials who were to take action against them, even if it meant having recourse to the secular authorities.[16] In spite of these and other measures taken at synods, little was accomplished and the laity continued to ignore their Lenten obligation. The situation in Cienpozuelos was so bad in the 1520s that the vicar-general of the Archdiocese of Toledo sent an official to the village every year in order to levy fines and imprison those who had failed to fulfill the precept.[17]

Apart from their ignorance, the most obvious reason for the distinct lack of public participation in auricular confession in the Spain of the early sixteenth century was the failure of Ferdinand and Isabella's ecclesiastical reform program to really alter the dissolute and corrupt lives of many clergy, both secular and regular. In 1528, Alfonso de Valdés, Latin secretary to Charles V, bitterly denounced the Spanish clergy for its greed and immorality.[18] The following year it was the turn of his brother Juan in his *Diálogo de doctrina cristiana*, where he allows the archbishop of Granada, the character who best represents Valdés's own opinions, to question the continued payment of the tithe to a clergy that has so shamefully failed to serve and instruct the faithful. The archbishop then goes on to criticize the carelessness and "ignorance" of many confessors, who by their injudicious questioning teach their penitents more about sin than they ever knew before they came to confession. Under these circumstances, the archbishop concluded that it would be better if the Christian never had the need to go to confession at all.[19]

But it was on the village level, and not at the imperial court that the struggle for the hearts and minds of most Christian Spaniards was to be won or lost, and by the end of the fifteenth century, the Spanish parochial system was considerably weaker than it had been one hundred years earlier. A century of population growth had left many new villages virtually without ecclesiastical services of any kind, so that it some places mass was said no more than once every fifteen days. Absenteeism was rife and the custom of allowing a single individual to hold two or more benefices simultaneously meant that the faithful were frequently served by an illiterate, half-starved clerk in minor orders instead of the incumbent. Moreover, on seignorial lands it was not at all unusual for the lay-patron to collect the tithe and other ecclesiastical revenues without even providing someone to minister to the needs of his vassals.[20]

To compound the gross inadequacies of the parochial structure, late fifteenth- and early sixteenth-century bishops were admitting large numbers of unqualified individuals to the ranks of the clergy. In 1519, for example, the Royal Council discovered a widespread pattern of ordinations of unqualified persons by the bishop of Guadix, and in 1529 the Empress Isabella had to write to all Spanish bishops to remind them that they should not ordain anyone who was illiterate, did not have the requisite age, or refused to obligate himself to follow an ecclesiastical career after being tonsured.[21]

The moral failings of the parish clergy were even more glaring than their educational deficiencies. Repeated prohibitions had entirely failed to prevent concubinage. A visitation to the cathedral chapter of Palencia in 1481 found that one-third of the benefice holders were openly living in sin.[22] Little wonder then that a poorly educated and morally deficient clergy were not only alienating the laity, but bringing sacraments like penance into disrepute. In 1530, for example, Alonso de Valdelomar, the curate of Almodóvar del Campo, was brought before the ecclesiastical court in Alcalá de Henares accused of a variety of offenses including attempted rape, blasphemy, consorting with prostitutes, gambling, and carrying prohibited weapons. Valdelomar also had a penchant for using his position as confessor to squeeze money out of his penitents. He would routinely demand a fee before granting absolution and would refuse to grant it if he was not satisfied. He also forced his penitents to purchase indulgences that were no longer valid. It is easy to imagine the frustration of the villagers who had brought the complaint against him when they learned he had only been sentenced to thirty days confinement in the parish church, where he had his lodgings, and four reales in fines.[23]

Pluralism, along with simony, nepotism, and absenteeism, were among the most serious problems to affect the Church during the period leading up to the Reformation.[24] On a parish level, pluralism would frequently leave the care of the faithful in the hands of a substitute priest whose income was so low that he had to resort to a variety of fiscal abuses in order to survive. We are fairly well informed about the activities of one such priest, who in 1530 was forced to defend himself against a charge of solicitation brought before the tribunal of Toledo. Sometime in the mid-1520s, Antonio de Pareja was appointed lieutenant curate in Cienpozuelos by Pedro Bermudez, canon of Toledo's cathedral, who owned the benefice. At his trial in 1530 to 1532, a parade of witnesses denounced Pareja for a series of abuses stemming from his role as confessor. Pareja routinely solicited his female penitents for sexual favors and had even lived openly with one of them in his quarters behind the church. After the girl, Catalina Roldana, became pregnant, she was turned out of her parents' home but received no help from the priest, and she and her son wandered the village barefoot and in rags.[25] Witnesses also told how Pareja had forced his penitents to give him wheat and wine, which he later sold, and attempted to coerce one of his penitents into paying him to say a number of masses for the soul of a departed relative.

Pareja's record of service to his flock was hardly inspiring, and the villagers had a correspondingly poor opinion of him. One witness, Juan Jiménez, called him "an evil and unscrupulous person," while another denounced him as a hypocrite. As a direct result of Pareja's example, the villagers were far from assiduous in carrying out their Christian duties. Juan Jiménez said that because he felt that Pareja was a "bad Christian," he avoided attending mass, while the villagers refused to confess with him because he revealed the things they told him there.[26]

If the popular masses were indifferent or hostile to confession because of the greed, ignorance, immorality, and corruption of the priests who administered it, radical intellectuals linked with illuminist and Erasmian circles rejected it because it seemed superfluous to their view of the relationship between God and man. In 1478, for example, Pedro de Osma, one of the most influential Spanish theologians of the late fifteenth century, was brought before a special commission established by the archbishop of Toledo because he had asserted that sacramental confession was not of divine origin and that mortal sins could be atoned for without it.[27]

Both illuminists and Erasmians shared a profound aversion to all kinds of religious formalism, and they felt that confession should form part of the direct and intimate relationship between God and man that they sought so fervently. For Juan de Valdés, confession really had no efficacy without contrition and should be resorted to as little as possible. Valdés believed that those who repeat the same sins over and over again, or confess frequently in the belief that there was something sanctifying about performing the act of confession were guilty of transforming the sacrament into just another observance, like saying the rosary, and therefore were perverting its real significance.[28] As far as the necessity of confession before communion was concerned, Valdés supported the idea that the only persons who should confess before communion were those who had some compelling need to do so.[29]

Erasmus himself expressed his views about confession in his *Pietas puerilis*, which was translated into Spanish in 1529 as *Amor de niños en Dios*. *Pietas puerilis* takes the form of a dialogue between Gaspar, a pious young scholar, and his friend, Erasmillo. Through Gaspar, Erasmus asserts his opinion of auricular confession as a formality that is done only because the Church demands it. Real confession consists of the individual confessing directly to Christ in a state of contrition. It is only through this private, intensely personal form of confession, during which Gaspar laments his sins, sheds a river of tears, and begs for mercy, that he achieves a feeling of justification.[30]

The trial of Diego de Uceda, a Córdoban in the service of D. Fernando de Córdoba, the key-bearer of the military order of Calatrava, for having declared that contrition rather than absolution was the essential part of confession, indicates the impact that Erasmian thought was having in Spain. After admitting under torture that he denied the validity of auricular confession and then retracting, he was forced to abjure de vehementi at the auto de fe of July 22, 1529.[31]

The greatest challenge to auricular confession as practiced by the Roman Catholic Church came not from illuminists, evangelicals, or Erasmians, however, but from Martin Luther and his followers. The theological basis for confession as practiced before 1517 was a belief in contrition as man's contribution to obtaining forgiveness and a belief that priests had the power to transmit grace through the words of absolution. However much Erasmus and his followers might have caviled at the latter doctrine and railed at the priesthood as corrupt and unworthy, they did accept the necessity of contrition and the yearly confession mandated by the Church.

Luther's theology, as expressed in his great treatises of 1520, amounts to a radical attack on both of these fundamental elements. The doctrine of the priesthood of all believers expressed in his *Address to the Christian Nobility of the German Nation Concerning the Reform of the Christian Estate* effectively placed all Christians on a equal level and eliminated the special spiritual status claimed by the clergy. As a consequence, the confessor's authority was removed and he could no longer dispense forgiveness by absolving the penitent. In the *Babylonian Captivity of the Church*, Luther reduced the number of sacraments to two: baptism and communion. His *On the Liberty of the Christian Man* advances the famous doctrine of justification by faith, which made salvation entirely dependent on the faith of the individual regardless of any observances or good works that one may have performed.[32]

What this new theology meant for auricular confession can be seen from a teaching sermon that was published in mid October 1519. In this sermon, Luther makes it very clear that God's forgiveness does not depend on the degree of human contrition, but on the degree of man's faith in God: "The forgiveness of guilt is granted to no one on account of the worthiness of his contrition over his sins, nor on account of his works of satisfaction, but only on account of his faith in the promise of God." God's forgiveness is objectively certain and unconditional; it no longer depends on the availability of a properly ordained priest: "For Christ did not intend to base our comfort, our salvation, our confidence on human words or deeds." Instead, the promise of justification attached to Christ's sacrifice is sufficient: "Then the word will sustain you, and so your sins will have to be forgiven."[33] Since baptism incorporated within it the promise of forgiveness of sins and combined it with water—a visible sign—it was no longer necessary to consider penance as a sacrament in its own right.[34]

In spite of the fact that numerous copies of Luther's works arrived in Spain, it took more than a generation for Luther's ideas to take root. Largely because the Inquisition had so thoroughly repressed the native illuminists and Erasmians, the nascent Protestant movement was denied the support that it needed to get started. Sometime in the late 1540s, however, two important groups of proto-Protestants had developed. The larger, numbering some 120 persons, was in Seville and included the prior and friars of the Jeronimite convent. Some of those who were able to flee Spain before the Inquisition caught up with them, including Cipriano de Valera, Casiodoro de Reina, and Antonio de Carro, played leading roles in the European Reformation. The religious views of both Cipriano de Valera and Casiodoro de Reina are well known from their writings. Both align themselves with the major tenets of Lutheran thought on confession. In his *Confesión de fe cristiana*, for example, Casiodoro de Reina accepts penance as a holy rite, but rejects its sacramental character.[35]

Another, smaller circle of Protestant sympathizers and Erasmians formed around the same time in the northern Castilian city of Valladolid. The most distinguished member of this group was Dr. Agustín Cazalla, chaplain to Charles V. Cazalla came from a family long identified with Spanish religious radicalism. Both his father, Pedro de Cazalla, a high treasury official, and his mother, Leonor de Vivero, had been closely associated with the Illuminist movement during the 1530s. His uncle, Fray Juan de Cazalla, bishop of Verisa, died in 1530 just before the Inquisition was about to put him on trial for heresy.[36]

Until now, historians have had little direct knowledge of Agustín Cazalla's religious views. Certainly his immediate associates, Carlos de Seso, the former civil governor of Toro, and Fray Domingo de Rojas, who was the son of the marquis of Poza, can be placed firmly in the Protestant camp.[37] Fortunately for historians, in 1580 a former servant of the family, who had entered a convent under the name of María de San Gerónimo, chose to unburden herself to the Inquisition. According to María de San Gerónimo, Cazalla lived a kind of double life. When preaching before the court or in public, he was always very careful to stay within the bounds of orthodoxy, but at home when preaching before a select group of friends and family, he showed his true colors. During one of these sermons, he rejected clerical celibacy and declared that priests and nuns should marry. Shortly afterward, wearing full vestments, Cazalla presided over the marriage of his sister, Beatriz de Vivero and Fray Domingo de Rojas. Cazalla also aligned himself with Lutheranism by rejecting transubstantiation, arguing that the priest had no power to consecrate the elements of the mass. María de San Gerónimo also told the Holy Office that she herself had often avoided confession because Cazalla had frequently told her that priests had no power to absolve sins.[38]

Confronted with a real Protestant threat after decades of false alarms, the Spanish authorities lost no time in unleashing a ferocious wave of repression. A series of great autos de fe held between May 1559 (when Cazalla was executed) and October 1562 succeeded in eliminating Spanish Lutheranism as a religious force, but did little to remove the root causes of popular dissatisfaction with the clergy and the way in which they were administering the sacraments.[39]

Disillusionment with the clergy helped make the late fifteenth and early sixteenth centuries the golden age of the devout laity all over Catholic Europe. The age of the indulgence, pilgrimage, mental prayer, confession directly to God, oratories, and intensified confraternity activity meant that the role of the priest was minimized. The admission of a critical need for reform by the papacy at the Fifth Lateran Council of 1512 to 1517 did little more than increase the level of dissatisfaction since it was clear that the reforms were very far from being put into effect.[40] As late as 1538, the special commission of cardinals appointed by Paul III to consider the best way to stem the tide of heresy was forced to admit most of the criticisms made by the reformers and even went so far as to propose the abolition of the religious orders.[41]

The Church might have gone on for a long time ignoring the growing demands for reform and the increasing indifference of the laity if it were not for the Reformation. Even so, it took unremitting pressure from the Emperor Charles V and the failure of his own efforts to bring about a reconciliation with the Lutherans during the colloquia he sponsored at Hagenau, Worms, and Regensburg to clear the way for the opening of the Council of Trent on December 13, 1545.[42]

According to the Bull of Convocation, the Council had two principal objectives: to formulate the fundamental dogmas of the Catholic faith and to set the framework for the reform of the Church.[43] That both of these issues were of critical and equal importance to the survival of the Church was recognized by the delegates to the Council, who decided to discuss dogma and reform simultaneously in spite of papal objections.[44] The key Lutheran doctrines of justification by faith and the priesthood of all believers had served to undermine the need for all kinds of devotions, especially the sacramental system, while denying the clergy any special role in mediating God's grace to mankind. Popular Donatism and anticlericalism and the growth of lay devotions, along with the manifest inadequacy of the priesthood were making the clergy irrelevant to many of the strongest and most vital tendencies of Renaissance piety. If the Council were to do its job effectively, it would not merely have to restate orthodox positions, but project a vision of a new kind of specifically Catholic spirituality in which faith and devotions were meaningfully linked to the ministrations of a reformed and disciplined priesthood.

Critical to this effort was the development of a comprehensive Catholic response to Lutheran teaching on grace and justification. If Luther's view of justification as a purely gratuitous act by an all-powerful Deity were to prevail, then works, observances, and sacraments were all equally useless, apart from the sacrament of baptism itself. On the other hand, if human endeavor was to be seen as essential to grace and justification, then observances and especially sacraments become necessary as the covenanted channels through which man seeks grace and God responds.

In spite of the fact that justification was one of the most hotly debated topics in pre-Reformation theology, the overwhelming majority of the theologians who considered the issue at Trent had little difficulty in agreeing that man must cooperate with the act of justification and willingly accept the grace of God.[45] In the Tridentine formula, faith, which was so strongly stressed by Luther, becomes a necessary but not sufficient condition for justification. Since it is impossible to know by faith alone that he enjoys God's grace, man is compelled to persevere in order to gain a second justification beyond the first justification gained through baptism. This second justification depends on the use that man can make of God's grace and on his efforts to increase it through participation in the sacraments, which effectively "contain the grace which they signify" and "confer that grace on those who place no obstacles in its way."[46]

The position taken by the Council on justification, therefore, meant that the sacraments recovered their central position in the Christian scheme of things. All seven sacraments were declared to be valid and instituted by Christ; not merely a means of "fostering" faith (Luther) but "necessary for salvation."[47]

The sacrament of penance was particularly important because it was so closely related to man's ongoing struggle for justification. Regardless of faith, man can never be certain of his salvation because of his propensity to sin, and mortal sins wipe out justifying grace. It is only through the sacrament of penance that man can hope to regain the grace of God.[48]

But if a revived sacramental system was to be the Church's answer to Protestantism, then the reform of the clergy who administered the sacraments had become even more imperative. The Tridentine fathers were well aware of the fact that, as Cardinal Pole declared at the Second Session of January 7, 1546, "we ourselves are largely responsible for the misfortune that has occurred—because we have failed to cultivate the field that was entrusted to us."[49] It was in order to remold the parish clergy as the fundamental building block of the post-Tridentine Church that the Council sharply limited absenteeism to a maximum of two months except under unusual circumstances and only if a replacement vicar could be found. Complaining of the widespread use of secular garb among the clergy, the Council demanded that all ecclesiastics wear proper clerical dress under pain of suspension from their benefice.

The profile of a new kind of cleric whose comportment would mark him as morally distinct from and superior to secular society was drawn by the fathers of the Council when they insisted that no ecclesiastic should by his "dress, attitude, speech, or behavior" give evidence of anything that was not "modest, sedate, and full of religion." In general the clergy were to inspire an attitude of veneration in the laity by avoiding any transgressions because even the smallest offense committed by an ecclesiastic was a grave error. The Council was particularly harsh with concubinary priests. To the behavioral constraints of outward modesty and conformity, it sought to add a sexual straightjacket in order to reinforce the institution of clerical celibacy that had been rejected by the Protestants. Denouncing concubinage as the "supreme disgrace on the clerical order" and speaking of the shamefulness of clerics who "live in the filth of impurity and unclean habitation," the fathers of the Council ordered priests to avoid contact with any suspicious women and threatened the contumacious with excommunication and loss of benefices.[50] The Council also sought to confront the grave problem of vagabond clerics who had no visible means of support. Henceforth no one could be admitted to clerical orders without being able to demonstrate that he was in legal possession of a benefice with sufficient income to provide for him.[51]

The Council was also concerned about the qualifications of those who were approved to enter the ranks of the lower clergy. Bishops were enjoined not to accept bribes or gifts in exchange for ordination, and a knowledge of Latin was made necessary for admission to minor orders. Minimum age levels were specified for deacons and subdeacons, and it was provided that at least one year had to pass before one could be promoted from deacon to priest. The prospective priest had to submit himself to a rigorous examination regarding his moral character as well as his knowledge of religion.

Forcing priests to attain a higher level of personal morality was insufficient by itself to transform the parish clergy into the real religious leaders of their congregation that the Council desired. In order to accomplish this goal, it was necessary to greatly improve the educational level of the average priest. At the famous twenty-third session, the Council did this by deciding on the creation of seminaries in each diocese.[52]

The Council's extreme sensitivity to the proper administration of the sacrament of penance is demonstrated by the fact that henceforth no one who wished to become a confessor could do so unless he held a parochial benefice or applied to the local bishop for a license. Such licenses were generally granted for only one year and frequently only after a rigorous qualifying examination.[53]

We can find out how the licensing system worked in Spain by referring to the actual license of a confessor: Fray Gaspar de Nájera, a Franciscan living in the Canary islands during the early eighteenth century. After passing his qualifying examination, Fray Gaspar was granted his first license to hear confessions by Bishop Juan Ruiz Simón on December 29, 1710. Excluded from this license, however, were two sensitive groups: women under forty years of age and nuns belonging to the Franciscan order. Later these restrictions were lifted, and on September 5, 1711, he was appointed confessor to the Franciscan convent of Buena Vista. On November 11, 1713, the license was extended for another two years, Fray Gaspar having undergone and passed a second examination.[54] Records of the licenses and the restrictions placed on individual confessors were recorded in a special series of books maintained at the bishop's palace.[55]

There can be little doubt that by the eighteenth century at least, possession of a valid license had become accepted among the clergy as the way of defining who could and who could not hear confessions. This is demonstrated by the curious case of Fray Juan Ascanio, another Franciscan who continued hearing the confessions of his paramour, Blasina Domínguez, and other women for nine or ten months after his license ran out. He then voluntarily stopped hearing confessions "because of the burden placed on his conscience by the improper administration of the Holy Sacrament."[56]

A wholesale remodeling of the parish clergy would make it possible for the Church to reverse the dangerous tendency toward lay devotions that was so characteristic of the pre-Reformation. Instead, religious worship for the laity was to be focused, to a degree never before seen, on the parish church, the sacraments, and the priest who administered them. Parish priests, who were now to be better prepared intellectually by the new seminaries, were to take on regular preaching responsibilities on Sundays and holy days and during Lent and Advent.[57]

The parish priest was also to make himself responsible for catechizing his flock in the vernacular, making use of the new Catholic catechisms that were produced after the Council. Catechisms published by the Jesuits Peter Canisius (1555) and Robert Bellarmine (1597) were frequently reprinted and translated into many languages and dialects.[58] Peter Canisius's *Summa doctrinae christianae* went through more than seventy German editions before 1800.[59] In Spain, interest in producing vernacular catechisms predated the Council of Trent and was inspired by efforts to convert the Jews and Moors. During the Council itself, Juan de Avila published a catechism designed for the instruction of children (1554), and later in the sixteenth century, popular catechisms were written by Jerónimo de Ripalda (1591) and Gaspar Astete (1599), among others.[60]

The new prominence given to the parish priest was also made evident by his expanded role in administering the sacrament of matrimony. Sweeping aside generations of tradition and the canon law doctrine that a valid sacramental marriage could be constituted by an exchange of consent between any two qualified individuals, the fathers at Trent insisted that all marriages would now have to be done before the parish priest and two or three witnesses after the publication of three banns. After the couple were properly joined together, the priest would make a record of the event in the parish register including the names of the newly married persons, witnesses, and the date and place where the marriage had been contracted. The Roman Ritual of 1612, which brought the ceremony from the church door to the altar, merely confirmed the transformation of marriage from a social process that the Church affirmed as sacramentally valid ex post facto to an ecclesiastical process through which grace was conferred on the betrothed parties by the parish priest.[61]

Baptism was another sacrament that was brought increasingly into the orbit of the parish priest. In addition to administering the sacrament, the priest was responsible for recording the event, including the names of the child's sponsors, in the parish register. This not only gave the child a legal existence in both civil and canon law, but asserted Church control over relationships of godparenthood and copaternity, which were to be extremely important to the child throughout his or her life.[62]

The Counter-Reformation also strove to make the church the sole or principal place of worship. This was accomplished by the reservation of the Host on the altar, whereby the parish church became the sole legitimate repository of the consecrated host and therefore the only place in the community where God was physically present. The new post-Tridentine devotions, especially the cult of the rosary, which proved to be so popular, also found a home in the parish church. By the late sixteenth century, even rural parishes in the mountains of Catalonia were equipped with altars dedicated to Our Lady of the Rosary.[63]

The Church's effort to refocus Catholic life on the sacramental system and the parish left little room for the continued independence of the lay confraternities that had become so important in many urban areas during the late middle ages. The fathers of the Council strongly asserted the supremacy of parochial mass on Sundays and holidays as opposed to the devotions of the confraternities.[64] The fear that the confraternities could become involved in superstitious practices or even be a source of heresy made the Church eager to curb their independence. Certain confraternities were dissolved, while others were placed directly under the control of the parish priest. Still others, like the French brotherhood of the Blessed Sacrament or Seville's Brotherhood of Holy Charity were encouraged because they were under firm episcopal control and dedicated themselves to devotions or activities that the Church found desirable.[65]

Given the generally poor quality of the parish clergy during the mid-sixteenth century, however, the Council's efforts to reform them would have been nullified unless episcopal authority could be strengthened. By the end of the middle ages, there were three major problems that had made it virtually impossible for bishops to fulfill their primary responsibility to oversee the cure of souls within the boundaries of their diocese: absenteeism, accumulation of benefices, and the weakness of episcopal control over the parish priests and other benefice holders in the diocese.

Absenteeism and pluralism were intimately connected because a bishop who held two or more episcopal sees could hardly be expected to be present in both of them, especially if they were widely separated geographically. Even though the cumulation of benefices was prohibited in canon law, the papacy easily found ways around the prohibition, freely awarding cardinals and members of the Curia episcopal sees that they were never expected to serve in personally or even visit. Cardinal Ippolito d'Este, for example, never personally visited Milan, of which he was archbishop from 1520 to 1550.[66] In Spain the policy of limiting appointments to natives was only partially successful, and during the reigns of Ferdinand and Isabella and Charles V, some forty-two episcopal sees were granted to cardinals or members of the Curia.[67] It was also quite common for Spanish monarchs to appoint bishops to the presidencies of the Audiencias of Valladolid or Granada or one or another of the royal councils. Such men were not only absentee bishops, but their influence at court gave them the opportunity to accumulate large numbers of other benefices, which they could retain or pass on to one of their relatives while reserving to themselves part or all of the revenues. Fernando de Valdés (1483–1568), bishop of Elna and archbishop of Seville, who was appointed president of the Audiencia of Valladolid in 1535 and Inquisitor-General in 1547, was probably the most successful collector of ecclesiastical benefices in the sixteenth century.[68]

From the discussions at the Council, however, it is evident that the desire to accumulate benefices or the use of bishops in bureaucratic positions were not the only reasons for absenteeism. Many bishops preferred staying away from their diocese because their power and authority was virtually nonexistent as a result of external hindrances or impedimenta coming principally from the Curia. We know the situation in Spain from the memorial that was presented to the Council of Trent by the bishop of Calahorra, Juan Bernal Díaz de Luco, who had also served as vicar-general of Salamanca and as an official in the administration of the archdiocese of Toledo. Echoing other memorials from Italian and French prelates, the bishop pointed out that the rights granted to chapters sede vacante, titular bishops, and nuncios to confer Holy Orders without consulting the ordinary made nonsense of any attempt by bishops to improve the quality of the pastoral clergy. At the same time, exemptions granted to important benefice holders in the diocese, such as archpriests, archdeacons, and cathedral chapters, allowed them "to scorn bishops and to live licentiously to the scandal of the people."[69] The exemptions granted to archpriests and archdeacons were particularly injurious because they were responsible for exercising ecclesiastical jurisdiction throughout the diocese.[70]

In many areas, bishops also had to confront powerful secular lords, who controlled presentation of benefices and collected the tithe that should have gone to the clergy. The bishop of Mallorca reported that only forty out of the six hundred benefices in the diocese corresponded to the ordinary, with the rest in the hands of the founders or other powerful laymen.[71] The authority of the bishops was also diminished by the rights of patronage exercised by monastic institutions and religious orders. In 1575 the wealthy monastery of Roncesvalles in Navarre enjoyed right of patronage to forty-five churches.[72]

In February 1547, even before the conclusion of the Council of Trent, Paul III took a major step in the direction of reform by prohibiting cardinals from holding more than one episcopal see at any one time.[73] The Council itself then proceeded to ban anyone from holding more than one benefice of whatever type except in certain special instances, while obliging those presently in possession of several benefices to choose one and resign the rest.[74] Having sharply curbed the problem of accumulation of benefices, the Council then turned its attention to absenteeism, issuing three decrees on the bishop's obligation to reside in his diocese and heightening the penalties for not doing so in the session of July 15, 1563.[75]

In order to avoid a potential conflict over papal authority, bishops were given sweeping new power to control diocesan life by virtue of their role as apostolic delegates.[76] Under this rubric, bishops recovered their jurisdiction over formerly exempt cathedral and collegiate chapters, as well as over archpriests and archdeacons.[77] Bishops also gained new authority over ordination and appointment to benefices with cure of souls, even those controlled by private patrons. Regardless of how or by whom he was nominated, the candidate would have to pass a qualifying examination given by a committee of examiners appointed by the bishop before he could take possession of his benefice.[78]

The Council also gave bishops extensive responsibility for supervising the religious activity of the clergy active within the diocese. As noted above, bishops licensed all confessors, even those from the mendicant orders. In addition, bishops controlled preaching throughout the diocese. They themselves were to be active preachers and see to it that preaching was carried on effectively on Sundays and Holy Days, appointing substitutes whenever necessary for parish priests who were incapable of preaching themselves.[79]

In order to enforce the decrees of the Council and improve the governance of their diocese, bishops were empowered to carry out annual or semiannual visitations of their entire diocese, including institutions or individuals previously exempt.[80] They were also mandated to attend provincial synods every three years and hold diocesan synods every year at which all those who had charge of parochial or other churches were obliged to attend.[81]

By the end of the Council of Trent on December 4, 1563, the Church had succeeded in setting the basis for the reorientation and renewal of Roman Catholicism. The new Counter-Reformation piety would stress individual rather than corporate expressions. It would be driven by the development of new forms of mental prayer and an urge toward good works as a way of attaining grace. Above all, the Counter-Reformation placed renewed stress on the sacramental system, which had been seriously undermined by the doctrines of justification by faith alone and the priesthood of all believers. During the sixteenth and seventeenth centuries, mass was said more frequently, the new form of marriage came to be more and more widely accepted, and frequent or even daily communion was advocated for the laity.[82]

Within the context of this new sacramentalism, it would be difficult to exaggerate the importance of the role given to sacramental confession. The more the old order was threatened by Protestants, the more the Church appreciated the importance of confession, which stood ready to uphold it in the forum of conscience.[83] With a revived and better-educated clergy, both secular and regular, ready to administer the sacrament and with a restored episcopacy now able to impose discipline, it had become possible to make the confessional the first line of defense against religious doubt, immorality, and disrespect for the sacred. The way was clear for an unprecedented social experiment: the widespread use of confession to induce a virtual "pathology of scruples," an anxious and even morbid examination of conscience in the interests of maintaining and enhancing the Church's hold over the individual.[84] Furthermore, the result of the Tridentine decrees regarding the sacrament of penance was to change significantly the relationship between priest and penitent. In demanding that penitents render an exact and minute accounting of their sins and the circumstances under which they were committed, the post-Tridentine Church also required the confessor to carry out a more searching interrogation and to be able to judge the relative gravity of the sins.[85] This more searching inquiry necesarily created an intense and potentially more intimate relationship between priest and penitent, with some manuals even encouraging priests to "confess" their own sins to the penitent in order to encourage him to be more forthcoming.

Priests, friars, missionaries, and the members of the new congregations of clerics (e.g., Jesuits) were all thrown into a massive effort to breathe new life into the sacrament of penance, which was fraught with opportunity and danger. The heavy demands made by the post-Tridentine sacrament of penance could result in alienating or confusing many penitents. The exalted new role of the confessors could and did lead to vast abuses; at the very same time, they and they alone were in a position to provide what every religious system claims that it can offer most effectively: consolation.[86] It was on the ability to offer consolation while inculcating post-Tridentine religious and moral ideals through sacramental penance that the future of the Roman Catholic Church came to rest in the critical period that followed the Council of Trent.

Chapter 2

*Confession and Confessors
in Transition*

One of the most striking characteristics of post-Tridentine Catholicism was the way in which sacramental penance emerged as a defining element of the new religious order.[1] In a very real sense, Catholic Europe became a confessionally oriented society with a heightened awareness of sin, increased frequency of confession, and a greatly enhanced role for the priest/confessor as the "doctor of souls."

The transition from a moral order based on the seven deadly sins, with its vaguely communitarian ethic, to one based on the Decalogue, which spelled out man's specific obligations to God, had already laid the groundwork for a new kind of confession stressing individual responsibility and the role of the confessor as spiritual guide.[2] This tendency, already quite marked before 1600, was consistent with other key elements in Counter-Revolution spirituality and struck a responsive chord among the laity, resulting in a dramatic upsurge in confessional frequency.

Interestingly enough, the Council of Trent, which had so strongly asserted the divine origins and sacramental character of confession, had little to say about frequency apart from endorsing the decision of the 1215 Lateran Council to require confession once a year.[3] Indeed, writing at around the mid point of the Council, Martín de Azpilcueta Navarro declared that annual—or semi-annual—confession before taking communion "seemed reasonable."[4]

The growing sentiment for frequent confession among Spanish theologians emerged from the debate over frequent or daily communion and was driven by the need for the communicant to be prepared in spirit to take the Host. The irony of this debate was that the idea of frequent communion came originally from religious radicals, some of whom expressed disdain for confession. When María de San Gerónimo lived with the Cazalla family, she would make the rounds of local churches with Beatriz and Leonor Cazalla and their friends, taking communion several times a day, but never going to confession, a sacrament that Agustín Cazalla and his circle openly rejected.[5] Another early supporter of daily communion was Francisco de Osuna, who, while not rejecting confession, certainly favored an interiorized form of Christianity and was sharply critical of the pope and the Church hierarchy.[6] Even though Osuna was eager to differentiate his beliefs from those of the suspect illuminists, they were still dangerous enough for his works to appear on the index of prohibited books in 1559 and 1612.[7]

Even after the doctrine of frequent communion had picked up significant support among theologians, it was still controversial in some quarters. As late as 1590, the Córdoba tribunal of the Spanish Inquisition convicted Fray Gaspar Lucas, prior of a local convent, for his "arrogant assertion of the dogmas of the illuminist sect" and noted that "he had many beatas under his spiritual direction and had ordered them to confess frequently and take communion every day."[8]

By the mid sixteenth century, in spite of the ferocious opposition of the Jesuits led by the redoubtable Luis de la Puente, the idea of frequent or even daily communion was moving into the mainstream. Among the Benedictines, Fray Alonso de Burgos wrote a brief tract supporting frequent communion in 1562, and in 1610 Fray Mauro de Valderas publicly defended the proposition that anyone who was not in a state of mortal sin could take communion on a daily basis. In the seventeenth century, frequent and daily communion was defended by Pedro de Marcilla, a professor at the University of Salamanca, who even went so far as to encourage individuals wishing to take communion to disregard their confessors if they prevented them from doing so without a good reason.[9] This was a radical stance indeed and, as we shall see, not shared by the majority of writers on this subject. By the mid seventeenth century, the chorus of supporters had grown so numerous that Juan Daza y Berrio, who opposed frequent communion, was forced to acknowledge "the large number of treatises in favor of daily communion that have recently appeared."[10]

A good idea of the arguments employed by those who favored frequent or daily communion can be gleaned from the *Enseñanzas espirituales*, which was published in Madrid in 1663. Written by Manuel Calisbeta, who was chaplain to Luisa de Sandoval y Rojas, the duchess of Medina Sidonia, the book opens with a dedication to the duchess, lauding her devotion to the sacrament, which she took every morning.[11] Calisbeta was openly critical of those who simply fulfilled the Church's rule mandating communion at Easter. Such individuals not only seemed to lack any genuine ambition for spiritual improvement, but by only seeking to fulfill the minimum requirement, they appeared to demonstrate a certain disdain for the sacrament itself.[12] Good Christians, he asserted, should take communion as frequently as possible, even daily if they could as a way of glorifying God and, by their example, moving others to greater piety. Moreover, by taking communion frequently, the Christian could build up a greater fund of grace since "the grace received today would augment the grace received yesterday and the day before, while the more grace that fills the soul the more it can receive at the next communion."[13]

What really linked the drive for frequent communion to increasing use of confession, however, was that one could not take communion in a state of mortal sin. Obviously this requirement was a powerful incentive to those who wished to take the sacrament frequently to live perfect Christian lives, but those who fell into sin could still take the sacrament if they first went to confession and received absolution.[14] According to St. Simón de Rojas, who was confessor to Queen Isabel de Bourbon and one of the most influential religious figures of the mid seventeenth century, those who failed to do this and dared to take communion were committing a sin worse than cold-blooded murder in a church or the assassination of "a priest, a king, or the pope himself."[15] Confession, therefore, was indispensable before communion and the more frequently one took communion, the more frequently one would have to confess because this was the only way of being sure that communion was being taken without sin.[16] As early as 1589, a strong link between frequent communion and an increase in the number of confessions was noted by Diego Pérez de Valdivia, one of Juan de Avila's most important disciples, when he wrote that "the devout take communion frequently and normally confess each time they do so."[17]

Confession also loomed large in the minds of those who favored frequent communion because most agreed that access to communion should be strictly controlled by the confessor. Speaking before the nuns at Madrid's aristocratic Descalzas Reales, St. Simón de Rojas praised frequent communion, but admonished the nuns not to take it without the explicit permission of their confessors.[18] Bernardino de Villegas, writing in 1635, went even further, warning any who dared to take communion without permission that the sacrament automatically lost its efficacy as soon as the confessor refused to sanction it.[19]

The impact that the absolute control that confessors exercised over access to communion had on the minds of certain individuals can be illustrated by the peculiar case of Gerónima de la Cruz. Gerónima was a pious lady and a beata who enjoyed her confessor's permission to take communion on a daily basis. In 1635, her attempts to do so, however, were thwarted because she believed the devil had begun to intervene to prevent her from arriving at the communion rail. Her problems started as soon as she tried to leave the house for church. The devil would prevent her from moving and whisper in her ear, insinuating that since she had offended God she was going to be damned whether she took communion or not. If she was able to free herself from his embrace and struggle to the church door, the devil would then prevent her from moving inside until her confessor came out and specifically told her that she could proceed. But the poor lady's torments did not end here because when she approached the communion rail and knelt down to take the sacrament, the devil took her by the throat, choking her so hard she thought that she was drowning. Once again, it took the direct intervention of her confessor, who had to come out and tell her that she could now proceed before she was actually able to get up and take the sacrament.[20] Apparently, in the minds of such anxiety-prone individuals as Gerónima de la Cruz, even the confessor's blanket permission was insufficient for them to feel totally secure about taking communion without his direct intervention and approval in specific instances.

Indications that ordinary people were taking communion more frequently come from accounts written by contemporary theologians and confessors as well as inquisitorial documents. In 1589, Diego Pérez de Valdivia commented approvingly about the way in which frequency of communion had increased over the forty years in which he had been active as a confessor.[21] Frequent communion was given strong support by reformers like Thomás Carbonel, bishop of Sigüenza, who urged his parish priests in pastoral letters and during his 1678 visitation to promote frequent resort to the sacrament by every means at their disposal. According to his biographer, Thomás Reluz, his efforts produced a substantial increase in confession and communion in the diocese.[22]

Many confessors also encouraged their penitents to take communion frequently. During the 1670s and 1680s, when the Augustinian friar Pedro Benimelis was an active confessor in Mallorca, five of his penitents took communion on a daily basis with his encouragement. One of these women, Isabel Riera, an illiterate beltmaker with a reputation as a visionary, even insisted on only taking communion from Benimelis himself.[23]

There is also evidence to suggest that nuns and beatas were taking communion more frequently during the seventeenth century. The 1638 rule of the convent of San Illdefonso of Las Palmas (Mallorca) allowed the nuns to take communion on Sundays and Thursdays and on the festivals of the Virgin Mary, Saint Joseph, Saint John the Evangelist and Saint John the Baptist, Saint Benedict, Saint Bernard, the founders' days of the religious orders, and the festivals of the four doctors of the church. As if this were not enough, the prioress could also grant the nuns permission to take communion on other days if necessary.[24] As early as 1575, a report from the inquisitors of Seville accused the city's beatas of daring "to take communion daily, and sometimes with insufficient reverence"[25]

Theologians who wrote in favor of frequent confession tended to follow the same lines of argument as those who supported frequent or daily communion. Like Manuel Calisbeta, Fray Cristóbal Delgadillo sought to justify resort to frequent confession on the grounds that the grace received by the soul would increase and its sojourn in purgatory would be shortened each time the individual resorted to the sacrament. Delgadillo was such a strong proponent of confession that he even encouraged penitents to come before their confessors with the same sins that they had confessed and received absolution for on previous occasions. Such a confession of the same sins would be valid, he argued, because the penitent would still experience the same feelings of contrition as had been felt previously.[26] For Francisco Farfan, frequent confession was beneficial even if the penitent felt no contrition before arriving at the feet of the confessor because "it often happens that the powerful influence of this great sacrament is sufficient to turn a heart of stone into a heart of flesh and blood."[27] Diego Pérez de Valdivia saw frequent confession as a kind of spiritual panacea capable of resolving doubt, giving strength to the weak in spirit, and giving and increasing grace; the soul that benefits from frequenting this sacrament "avoids sin and increases in piety."[28]

Some of those who wrote in support of frequent confession even felt that the sacrament could be the solution to moral and social problems. Francisco Farfan prescribed frequent confession as a remedy against the temptations of the flesh.[29] Francisco de Luque Fajardo, writing at the beginning of the seventeenth century, thought that the sacrament might even help to cure inveterate gamblers. In 1603, he published *Fiel desengaño contra la ociosidad y los juegos*, a unique work specifically utilizing gambler's argot so that confessors would be better prepared to deal with this particular type of penitent and more effectively bring them to repentance.[30]

It has long been asserted among scholars of the Counter-Reformation that confession became far more popular among lay people than ever before in the history of the Church.[31] The validity of this assertion for Spain is borne out by both literary evidence drawn from works published by confessors or other contemporary observers and Inquisition cases as they relate to confession. Pedro Galindo, who published a popular confessor's manual in 1680 when he had served as confessor for thirty-five years, complained about penitents who would preface their confessions with long preambles and disclaimers and thereby waste the time of "confessors who are already extremely busy." Other penitents confessed every eight days or even more often and at such length that just one of their confessions would be sufficient "to relate all the sins of a hardened criminal."[32] The anonymous author of a work published in 1845, when church attendance was already declining, called confession the "first and most important duty of the priest" and related a conversation among several priests in which they commented that they could frequently remain in the confessional "the entire day and yet still not hear the confessions of the huge number of penitents that present themselves."[33] That confessors did see large numbers of penitents even in rural areas far from the centers from which the new Counter-Reformation piety was being disseminated is demonstrated by the experience of Salvador del Castillo. Castillo, who was curate in the village of Ariço in the Canaries, testified in 1731 that in his thirty-four years as a confessor he had acted as spiritual advisor to some 7,000 individuals.[34]

Another good indicator of increased demand for confession even in relatively remote areas is the way in which members of the mendicant orders who had confessors' licenses were called upon to assist parish priests because the latter simply had too many penitents. The experience of Fray Antonio de Arevalo must have been typical. Shortly after he received his confessor's license from the bishop of the Canaries, Arevalo began touring rural areas preaching in local churches. His success as a preacher first led to an invitation to hear confessions in a sparsely populated rural area with about 180 families and then in several villages. He moved on to the village of Texira, where he was invited to assist with the large numbers who had arrived for a local feast day, and then to the village of Sauzel, where he assisted the local curate during Holy Week. Finally, after he preached with considerable success in the city of La Laguna, several local curates invited him to hear the confessions of the members of their congregations.[35]

A distinctly unflattering portrait of an active confessor comes to us from a letter written to the Suprema by the inquisitors of the Canary islands in 1787. The individual in question was Fray Nicolás Cabrera, a seventy-four-year old Augustinian who was accused of acts of solicitation with twenty-six of his female penitents. According to the inquisitors, Cabrera "performed many confessions with dispatch" and made sure to collect whatever little gifts his penitents could offer. He heard the confessions of many peasants, who would bring him eggs, milk, cheese, and fruit from their farms, and fisherman and sailors who kept him well supplied with fresh fish. Little wonder that this confessor was described as a "gay and mirthful" figure who always had plenty of company, especially of the female variety and could be seen every afternoon strolling about the village wearing his hat and carrying a cane, "amusing himself and conversing with all kinds of people."[36]

By the last quarter of the sixteenth century, the evidence suggests that the campaign to increase popular participation in the sacrament of penance was having dramatic success. As early as the period 1564 to 1580, 75 percent of defendants coming before the Inquisition of Cuenca claimed that they had confessed at Easter. By 1581 to 1600, after a campaign of indoctrination carried on by episcopal officials and the Inquisition, 85 percent were fulfilling the minimum requirement and a high percentage of the Old Christian social elite were going to confession even more frequently.[37]

Evidence drawn from an analysis of witnesses' testimony in solicitation cases also appears to bear out our thesis of more frequent confession among lay persons. Of the 137 witnesses whose confessional practices are mentioned in their testimony, only 5 limited themselves to fulfilling the Lenten precept. Far more common, comprising 10.9 percent of the sample were those who confessed each day, while 28.4 percent confessed one or more times per week. Overall some 60.5 percent of the witnesses in the sample confessed at least once a month. Among the laity, those taking frequent confession were drawn from every class, ranging from Queen Isabel de Bourbon, who confessed with St. Simón de Rojas three times a week, to the illiterate seamstress Teresa de Jesús from La Laguna in the Canaries, who confessed each Wednesday, Friday, and Sunday with Domingo Tomás Matos, an Augustinian friar.[38]

The case of Doña Isabel López Gascón, from the village of Herencia near Toledo illustrates the way in which changing personal circumstances could lead to the intensification of confessional practices. Immediately after the death of her husband, Doña Isabel took Antonio Ramón de Santa Olalla, who was acting as lieutenant curate in the village, as her confessor. Soon she placed herself entirely under his spiritual direction, paying him to say masses for her husband's soul and confessing with him twice a week over a period of two years.[39] In difficult times, confession could even be used as a way of avoiding harsh reality. During the terrible famine that affected Madrid in 1809 to 1811, Doña Bernarda Lanz was observed confessing two or three times a day in different churches, with each confession lasting several hours, while her daughters earned their living by prostitution.[40]

The life of St. Teresa de Jesús gives us an unusual instance of the saint herself encouraging her half-sister María to confess more frequently. Apparently María's husband had died suddenly without having the opportunity to make a last confession. This distressed Teresa very much and when it was revealed to her in a vision that her sister would also die suddenly, she wanted to be sure that the same thing would not happen again. After repeated requests, Teresa's confessor gave her permission to visit her sister, who lived in the village of Castellanos de la Cañada, about forty miles from Avila. Once there, she told her sister nothing about her premonition, but convinced her to "go to confession very frequently" for the sake of her soul. In this situation, frequent confession would at least guarantee that her sister would have confessed recently, even if she should be unable to do so at the time of her death. Some four or five years later, María died in circumstances very much like those of her husband, but because she ordinarily confessed once every eight days, her last confession had been just a few days before her death and her stay in purgatory would therefore be mercifully short. Less than a week later, just after the saint had taken communion, she was granted a vision of her sister being taken up to heaven.[41]

As early as the last quarter of the sixteenth century, frequent confession had become so widely accepted among ordinary Catholics that they tended to view anyone who questioned it with suspicion. After Francisco de Espinosa, a chaplain of the collegiate church in Huesca, made some cutting remarks to two local beatas about the frequency with which they went to confession and took communion, they denounced him during the visita that Granada's Inquisitor Dr. Diego Mesa de la Sarte made to the city in 1573.[42]

One obvious reason for the sharp rise in the number of confessions was that the sacrament was being so strongly promoted by the institutional Church and its representatives. In the diocesan synods that were held so much more frequently after Trent, bishops insisted over and over again that each parish priest should maintain a register listing the names of all those in the parish who were obliged to confess. The names of those who failed to do so were to be sent to the episcopal vicar, who was ordered to "prosecute them to the fullest extent of the law."[43]

Frequent resort to confession was championed by leading members of the clergy and humble parish priests alike. As Bishop of Sigüenza, Thomás Carbonel wrote numerous pastoral letters to his parish clergy exhorting them to induce their congregations to take confession more frequently. When he visited the diocese in 1687, he instructed his curates to arrive at their confessionals very early in the morning, especially on feast days, so that penitents could never excuse themselves from making their confession by saying that they could not find a priest.[44] Figure 2.1 presents an ascetic-looking Bishop

Figure 2.1. *Fray Thomás Carbonel, Bishop of Cuenca* [Bishop of Sigüenza, and Member of the Suprema] (Biblioteca Nacional, Laboratorio Fotográfico)

Carbonel with the symbols of his office and emphasizes his fervent devotion to Christ.

Reforming bishops also used synods as an opportunity to push for increased confessional activity. At the synod of 1592, called by Segorbe's Bishop Juan Bautista Pérez y Rubert, it was decreed that physicians should deny services to gravely ill patients who refused to confess, on pain of excommunication. In 1668, the synod called by Bishop Anastasio Vives de Sotomayor passed several decrees regulating confessional practices in the diocese and ordered the parish clergy to "strongly encourage their parishioners to confess more frequently."[45]

Individual parish priests also took a hand in encouraging more frequent confession without prompting from their superiors. Fray Mateo González, who acted as lieutenant curate of the village of Guía in the Canaries in the 1690s, built such an excellent reputation as a spiritual advisor that he was able to induce his parishioners to confess with him more frequently and in greater numbers. He was so proud of his role in encouraging confession that he used it as part of his defense when he was charged with solicitation in 1699.[46]

Penitential themes also became popular in the art of the Counter-Reformation. El Greco painted no fewer than five versions of St. Peter repenting his denial of Christ. For Catholics, the saint's contrition became a powerful symbol of the sacrament of penance and the ability of even the worst sinner to earn forgiveness. The penitent Magdalen was another favorite theme of this quintessential Counter-Reformation artist. El Greco painted five versions of *Mary Magdalen in Penitence*, the first of which, completed around 1577, was inspired by a picture by Titian that the young artist probably saw during his stay in Venice.[47]

Naturally, not all efforts at promoting confession were undertaken for purely altruistic reasons. When St. Simón de Rojas arrived to take over the Trinitarian house in Ciudad Rodrigo, it was small and poor, but within a few months, by making himself and his friars more available for confession and giving good spiritual counsel, he was able to build up a solid clientele of penitents from among the wealthiest citizens of the town, who made "significant offerings" to the convent. Shrewdly, instead of wasting this money on the poor, Rojas used it to embellish the chapel, purchase new ornaments, a larger bell, and even an organ. By upgrading the chapel, he was able to retain and even increase the convent's wealthy clientele and maintain the flow of contributions.[48]

Evidently the Theatines of Madrid made quite a business out of confession during the late sixteenth century. According to Fray Juan Campana, who testified before the Holy Office in 1594, members of that order would force their penitents to pay fees ranging from 15 reales to 3 ducats when they came for their monthly confessions. If a penitent should miss one of his regular sessions, one of the clerics would go to his home and denounce him right in front of his family for having gravely offended God. Use of such coercive techniques seems to have paid off since the Theatines were said to be making 8,000 ducats annually from confessional fees.[49]

But more than anything else, it was the new popular devotions that were so much a part of Counter-Reformation piety that drew unprecedented numbers of people into the churches and created an increasing demand for confession and confessors. These forms of devotion included the strong reassertion of saint cults like that of the cult of St. Joseph as patron of the Church or the cult of St. Charles Borromeo, one of the new Counter-Reformation saints.[50] The most obvious link between confession and the new devotions was the spread in Habsburg lands of the cult of the confessor St. Jan of Nepomuk (Juan de Nepomuceno), who died at the hands of a fourteenth-century Bohemian ruler because he refused to reveal the contents of the queen's confession.[51]

Undoubtedly the most important of the new devotions took shape around the image of the Virgin Mary. Marian observances were extremely important all over Catholic Europe, but nowhere more so than in Spain, where the mystery of the Immaculate Conception of the Virgin had strong royal support.[52] The result of all this was an extremely large number of religious festivals. By the beginning of the eighteenth century, there were more than ninety festivals at which attendance at mass was obligatory, including five festivals of the Virgin.

The larger the number of holy days that resulted from these devotions, the greater the tendency to take communion; the more people wanted to take communion, the more they needed to come to confession to make sure they were prepared spiritually. By the same token, the increased number of devotions induced a kind of penitential ethos into the culture in which people were moved to meditate on their sins and promise not to offend God any further. As the Jesuit José Fabiani observed in 1763:

> These pious and virtuous emotions have the effect that all, or almost all of the inhabitants of this populous city [Alicante], resort especially to the Holy Tribunal of the Sacrament of Penance, with everyone hating and detesting their sins, which are nothing more than further examples of the ingratitude shown to our beloved Redeemer.[53]

No one saw the relationship between devotions and confession more clearly than St. Simón de Rojas, whose rise to prominence in the Trinitarian order was closely related to his successful management of a series of floundering monastic enterprises. A strong supporter of the immaculist position, who would routinely greet people by saying, "Ave Maria," Rojas introduced Marian devotions with sermons, music, and flowers into the chapel of the order's house in Ciudad Rodrigo. He had his friars make themselves more available to hear the increasing number of confessions that he was sure would follow and did the same thing when he was sent to the convents of Alcira and Talavera. He also threw himself into the campaign for the canonization of the so-called Holy Child of La Guardia. The blood libel of the alleged crucifixion of the child Christobalico by Jews and conversos in the village of La Guardia in 1491, just before the expulsion, was especially taken up by the Trinitarians, who founded a small house in La Guardia in the sixteenth century. The devotion remained confined to the region, however, and it was in hopes of extending it that Rojas visited La Guardia, founded a confraternity dedicated to the Virgin, and put pressure on the officials of the archdiocese of Toledo to support canonization.[54] Later in his career, when he was a royal confessor, Rojas founded the aristocratic Congregación de Esclavos del Dulce Nombre de María.[55] The frontispiece of Francisco de Arcos's biography of Rojas shows his devotion to the Passion of Christ and the Virgin and his exemplary performance as confessor and preacher (Fig. 2.2).

Evidence taken from the testimony of witnesses before the various tribunals of the Holy Office bears out the relationship between confession and Counter-Reformation devotions. Isabel de Cristo and her sister Philipa, two pious sisters living in Buena Vista in the Canaries, were drawn to the parish church after Fray Diego Sánchez de Cubas introduced the devotion of the stations of the cross, which he was said to have celebrated with great fervor, ringing the church bells to announce it to the villagers. The new Marian de-

Figure 2.2. *Fray Simón de Rojas*. [Trinitarian,] *Confessor to Queen Isabel de Borbón* [and Founder of the Confraternity of the Slaves of María] (Biblioteca Nacional, Laboratorio Fotográfico)

votions also were a powerful lure, attracting people to the confessional. Both Gregoria González and her sister Ana would make a special point of confessing on the festival of Our Lady of Conception.[56] In a similar vein, Gregoria de Medrano, the wife of an impoverished silk worker from Toledo, first confessed with Fray Patricio Cerero on the occasion of one of the Marian festivals when a special indulgence was being offered.[57]

Recent historiography of the Counter-Reformation has accepted the idea that it led to a certain feminization of Roman Catholicism. In Spain, the continued importance of inner spiritual experience in the writings of religious leaders like Fray Luis de León tended to place everyone—priest and laity, educated or unlettered, man or woman—on the same spiritual plane. This allowed women to assert themselves spiritually, communicating with heaven directly without the need for male clerics.[58]

The larger number of devotions also allowed women greater participation since these did not require educational qualifications that were denied to them, but depended only on spiritual and emotional commitment. One of the most popular of the Marian devotions, for example, was that of saying the rosary in public processions. In Seville, processions of this kind began in 1690 and were wholly male, but by 1758 there were 128 such processions annually, of which 47 were exclusively feminine.[59] Women also were given a prominant role in other processions. In 1771 the diocesan visitor to the Catalan village of Olesa de Montserrat was shocked to find that four women were carrying candles before the priest and attendants of the Tabernacle or Bed of Our Lady in the Assumption procession.[60]

Some contemporary authors even said that women were more suited than men for frequent communion and other devotions. Diego Pérez de Valdivia felt that this was because women were more pious, lived more quietly, and had less occasion for sin.[61] Writing in the mid-1630s not long after the canonization of Teresa de Jesús, whom he greatly admired, Bernardino de Villegas went even further. For Villegas, women were at least the equals and even the superiors of men in their desire for spiritual growth. The evidence for this was everywhere, he stated, "since we can see how rare it is for men, even well educated ones, to frequent the sacraments or use the techniques of mental prayer, mortification, and penance." In return for this devotion, God has showered spiritual benefits on women like St. Teresa, "abandoning the men who have abandoned and forgotten him in favor of the women who adore him and serve him with greater fervor and devotion."[62] The example of Gabriela Suñer, an illiterate serving maid from Mallorca, would seem to indicate that by the eighteenth century the desire for spiritual perfection had filtered down to even the lowest classes of women. Again and again in her testimony before the Mallorca tribunal, Gabriela spoke of her "ardent desire to do whatever she could in order to excel in the love of Jesus Christ." Her efforts included such things as frequent communion, confession at least twice a week, and the wearing of a penitential bracelet around her thigh (silicio) that hurt her every time she moved.[63] So popular had confession become among women that conversations about confession and confessors were common whenever groups of women had a chance to be together. Testimony in the case of Fray Francisco Pons revealed three such conversations among the residents of the village of Manacor. In one instance, Margarita Feber y Fiol and two of her friends had gone to hear a sermon preached by some missionaries at a nearby parish and then decided to spend the night there, as they all wanted to make their confessions the following day. As they prepared for bed, the conversation turned to confessors, with the women trading experiences and giving each other tidbits of local gossip about the behavior of several local priests.[64]

Confession also offered women some unique opportunities for self-expression and spiritual growth. While subordinating her to a male priest, it did provide her with an opportunity to give voice to thoughts and feelings she probably could not express to anyone else, least of all her husband and family. Confessional interaction, while inherently unequal, entailed an obligation on the part of the priest to listen to his female penitent, treat her with respect, and provide her with spiritual guidance. It even could involve a certain personalizing of the confessor/penitent relationship, as such authorities as St. Francis Xavier advised the confessor to "make a frank admission of his own sins" to the penitent in order to induce a more complete confession.[65]

The feminization of confession during this period appears to be borne out by the fact that many of the confessors' manuals of the sixteenth and seventeenth centuries seem to be written about female penitents. When the veteran confessor Pedro Galindo addressed himself to the problems of anxiety-prone penitents or penitents who take an excessively long time to complete their confessions, he specifically refers to "simple women."[66] Other works, like Bernardino de Villegas's *La esposa de Christo instruida* or Diego Pérez de Valdivia's *Aviso de gente recogida*, were written specifically for the instruction of certain classes of female penitents.

Evidence for the feminization of confession also comes from the testimony of witnesses in solicitation cases. In 1699, when nineteen-year-old Michaela Francisca came to the Franciscan convent of Realejo to confess with Fray Gaspar Palenzuela, he summoned her to come forward ahead of "many other women who were waiting." On two other occasions, in 1703 and 1704, other women who were victims of Fray Gaspar's advances also commented on the fact that they were called up to confess ahead of numerous other women because they were young and pretty.[67] When Madalena Joffre went to the Trinitarian house of St. Eulalia on Mallorca to confess with Fray Antonio Ballester during the first week of Lent in 1688, she commented twice on the "numerous women that were waiting to confess."[68] Sometimes several women would make a group excursion to make their confessions at a nearby friary. In 1758, for example, sixteen-year-old María Alonso and five other friends left their village of Hoyo de Pinares near Avila in order to confess at the Franciscan house at Cebreros, a few hours away.[69]

An urge to participate in the new Counter-Reformation spirituality, along with the depletion of the male population due to military enlistment, emigration, and declining economic opportunities, all combined to produce the large number of beatas that were so much a feature of early modern Spanish society.[70] Beatas were generally widows or spinsters who had taken an oath of chastity and dedicated themselves to the service of God, but had not joined one of the religious orders.[71] Some beatas lived in their own homes while others grouped themselves together in a beaterio, but regardless of their living conditions, they all tended to place themselves under a male spiritual director. One group of six beatas in the village of Urda in the province of Toledo was actually formed by a Franciscan, who had first come to the village as a missioner and then received permission to act as vicar of the parish. He was their spiritual director, hearing all of their frequent confessions, and was fiercely jealous if they dared to go to any other confessor.[72]

Certain beatas, like certain female religious, found the confessional relationship liberating and fulfilling, especially when their confessors were tolerant and accommodating. Isabel Riera, who confessed and took communion every day with Fray Pedro Benimelis, was encouraged by him to write down her visions and prophesies, she even managed to gain a certain amount of ascendancy over him and form a small group of disciples who were so devoted to her that they burned incense in front of her picture.[73]

By the seventeenth century, the sacrament of penance had become a part of popular culture in a way that would have been impossible before the Reformation, and women especially heeded the call for more frequent confession. At the same time, the emphasis on confession led to heavy demands being placed on the confessors themselves to conform to an ideal of conduct that was described in confessors' manuals and held up for emulation in the lives of exemplary religious figures of the period. In the preamble to Jayme de Corella's *Práctica del confesionario*, the longtime confessor and missionary described the ideal confessor as sitting in place of God and exercising His authority in the confessional. He was to act as both a teacher, instructing the penitent in how to live a better life, and a doctor, administering suitable spiritual medicine that would inoculate against future sinfulness.[74] He should attempt by every means to move the penitent to heartfelt repentance and contrition by telling him that "you are in the prison of your own sins" and stress that sinning was "yet another crucifixion of the Son of God."[75] At the same time, the confessor was made responsible for testing the religious knowledge of his penitents and instructing them in the areas where they were deficient.[76]

In his admonition to a Dominican who was accused of solicitation and had therefore failed in his role as confessor, the prosecuting attorney of the Mallorca tribunal waxed even more eloquent. The ideal confessor, he declared, must be a "shining example of Christian virtue" and a "brilliant sun whose mere appearance puts error to flight and reveals truth."[77] That this was a difficult standard for most confessors to measure up to was beyond doubt, so Martín de Azpilcueta Navarro included a prayer for confessors in his *Manual*:

> purify my heart and place in the inmost recesses of my soul an upright spirit and honest intention so that I shall not be moved by glory, money or a desire to please and always have as my principal goal your glory and the well being of the soul that appeals to me for assistance.[78]

The same message was conveyed in the idealized portraits of noted religious figures whose role as confessors was stressed as proof of their spiritual attainments. Francisco de Arcos' biography of the Trinitarian St. Simón de Rojas stresses his enormous success as confessor and spiritual advisor from his first appointment as vicar of the convent of Villoruela.[79] When Rojas came to Madrid, Arcos tells us that he soon was deluged with requests for confession and those who confessed with him could attest to "the excellent doctrine with which he guided them."[80]

In his biography of the Jesuit Baltasar Alvarez, who spent nine years (1558–1567) as a confessor in Avila, Luis de Puente speaks glowingly of him as a man who maintained such high spiritual standards that some penitents avoided him rather than hear their faults criticized. He acted as spiritual advisor to people of all social classes and sharply criticized confessors who only sought their clients among the wealthy.[81]

If anyone in seventeenth-century Spain could be said to embody the ideal Counter-Reformation bishop it was Thomás Carbonel, who was named to the see of Sigüenza after acting as confessor to Philip III. In his biography of Carbonel, Thomás Reluz makes a point of how he "applied himself to the confessional with special care" after he came to Madrid in 1670. In addition to acquiring a clientele that included a number of influential persons, Carbonel demonstrated his exemplary virtue by hearing the confessions of the poor and seriously ill. These persons, he would declare, did not have ready access to a confessor, so he would act as their "spiritual almsgiver." So great was his reputation as a confessor that a nobleman who was gravely ill and on the point of death asked Carbonel to hear his confession. After Carbonel finished, the gentleman was "so well instructed and consoled and reconciled to the will of God that he needed no further instructions or consolation but only to remember what the venerable master had told him on that occasion." But the story even has a happy ending because the thaumaturgic power of the sacrament, augmented by the fact that it was administered by such a saintly figure as Thomás Carbonel, operated to effect a cure. Some time later the nobleman, now restored to health, chanced to see Carbonel on the street as he was passing in his coach. Remarking to his companions that "it is certain that there are still saints on this earth and within this Church militant because there goes one now," he alighted from the coach and knelt to kiss the feet of his former confessor.[82]

Hagiographies that were published in Spain placed special emphasis on a saint's success as a confessor. For example, in Fray Antonio de Lorea's account of the life of Pope Pius V, it almost seems as though this saint's rise to prominence in the Dominican order and eventual appointment as cardinal depended on his exceptional virtues as a confessor, which brought him such penitents as D. Alonso Davalos y Aquino, marquis of Basto and governor of Milan.[83]

Historians of early modern Spain have long been aware of the enormous influence exercised by the clergy over royal administration. Unlike France, where clerics were rarely chosen as councilors of state or presidents of the parlements, Spain routinely used them to preside over the Audiencias and act as presidents or members of the royal councils.[84] But nowhere was clerical influence exerted more strongly than in the post of royal confessor. As described in a memorial written in 1718, the royal confessor advised the king on every matter of state with any kind of moral or religious overtones and virtually controlled ecclesiastical appointments made by the crown.[85] Certainly the record seems to indicate that, with one or two exceptions, the royal confessors were so highly regarded for their virtue and orthodoxy that they could expect to be given important positions in the central administration. Of the twenty-nine royal confessors who served from the beginning of the reign of Ferdinand and Isabella to the end of the reign of Charles V, five were named Inquisitor-General, while others served on the Council of State or as Crusade commissioners. Royal confessors during this period included such distinguished figures as Tomás de Torquemada, the first Inquisitor-General (1483–1498), whose influence over Isabella was decisive in matters such as the expulsion of the Jews.[86] During the reign of Charles V, both Domingo and Pedro de Soto were royal confessors, and while the former was frequently at odds with his royal master, the latter influenced virtually every aspect of royal policy as confessor and member of the Council of State, helping to forge the alliance between pope and emperor against the Protestants, negotiate the Peace of Crépy, and guide the Council of Trent.[87]

That Spaniards in general endorsed the idea that the qualities of morality, orthodoxy, and discretion that suited a man to be royal confessor also made him fit for other high office is demonstrated by a poetry competition that was held in Saragossa to celebrate the appointment of a native son, Luis de Aliaga, as Inquisitor-General in 1619. The poets all seemed to agree that, as Diego Gerónimo de Aux put it, Aliaga, like his illustrious predecessors in the office of royal confessor, had already justified his elevation to head the Suprema since he had already been granted "the greatest confidence that a King can donate/to his heart and soul the key and the gate."[88]

On a less exalted level, among humble parish priests and friars who heard confessions in their convents or acted as assistants in towns and villages, we can observe the way in which the post-Tridentine ideal had been assimilated. A portrait of the Franciscan friar Diego Sánchez de Cubas by his superior, Fray Luis de Soto, reveals him as carrying out fully all the manifold responsibilities of the confessor and spiritual advisor. Shortly after arriving at the convent of Buenavista in the Canaries, Sánchez de Cubas threw himself into pastoral work with the villagers. He rapidly gained such an excellent reputation as a confessor that he could hardly keep up with the demand for his services. He was especially diligent in carrying out the catechizing function that was demanded of the Counter-Reformation confessor by instructing everyone in the village, young and old, in the tenets of the Church and bringing religious books to the chapel on Sundays and holy days for the edification of the faithful.[89]

When Jacinto de Belvis, in his capacity as prior and superior of the Dominican convent of Yepes near Toledo, carried out a series of visitations to monitor the activities of Fray Gerónimo de los Herreros, who was acting as assistant curate in Villaseca, the villagers begged that he be allowed to remain in his post because "the moral regeneration of many in the village depended on his example." The villagers testimony revealed that Gerónimo de los Herreros had compiled an enviable record of service to the community. He had greatly intensified celebration of Holy Days and introduced public rosary devotions while doing his utmost to teach the catechism and the rudiments of the faith to the villagers. He had also taught reading and writing to the children of the village and grammar to the adults. He had been known to rise from his sickbed to say mass and hear confession, and his success as a confessor and spiritual advisor was such that the villagers came to consult him at any hour of the day or night. Given this record, it is not too surprising that all of the friars in his convent agreed that his "exemplary life" made it far more beneficial for him to continue his pastoral work in the village than return to his convent.[90]

Sometimes a confessor's zeal could get him into trouble. During his pastoral work in the Canaries, the Franciscan Pedro Sobreras acquired such a formidable reputation as a confessor that all the most important people of the island wanted to have him as their spiritual advisor. When he served as assistant prelate in the village of Arucas, however, he made enemies because of his outspoken denunciations of moral laxity in the village. During his trial for solicitation in 1582, he was able to demonstrate that four out of the six witnesses against him were enemies that he had made while in the village. Unfortunately for the punctilious prelate, the two remaining witnesses were sufficient for the Holy Office to condemn him.[91]

The greater measure of trust that ordinary people reposed in their confessors and the increasing importance of confessors in their lives is demonstrated by the way in which people began coming to them for a whole variety of personal and family problems. Sometimes confessors were called upon to help a family through economic difficulties. Antonia Grande y Mirona, whose husband Antelmo owned a small cargo vessel, came to confess with Fray Gerónimo Vicente Mayano because she hoped the influential Dominican would be able to help her husband out of some business problems.[92] Francisca Jiménez, an impoverished sixty-year-old widow living in Toledo, entered the confessional in the Augustinian convent there simply in order to beg alms from Fray Fernando de la Rosa.[93]

Young women would also sometimes consult their confessors about their marital prospects. Juana Pita spent most of her time in the confessional discussing her relationship with a shoemaker who had expressed a desire to marry her. Her confessor, Fray Miguel Miguel, offered to meet with the young man in his cell and advised her not to accept a ring or presents from him until her father approved the match.[94] Some confessors were even willing to act as matchmakers. Ana de Artiega, a forty-eight-year-old widow living in Madrid, brought her twenty-four-year-old daughter Manuela to Atilano Ortiz, who was acting as assistant curate in the parish of San Gines in order to ask him to find her a suitable husband. Neither mother nor daughter had any intention of actually confessing when they entered the confessional with Ortiz, and they were both extremely grateful when he said that he had a prospective husband in mind for the girl.[95]

Individuals also came to their confessors for advice and assistance on other family matters. In 1680, for example, Isabel Bennassar went to consult with Juan Llobera, the prior of the Mercederian convent in Las Palmas, about her husband's nephew. It seems that the young man, who was a friar, frequently left his convent and consorted with secular persons, so she hoped that Llobera would use his authority as prior and prestige as ecclesiastical representative to the Cortes of Catalonia to restrain and discipline him.[96] Andrés Coll, the parish priest of Manacor on Mallorca went further than most curates would have done in protecting the family of one of his petitioners. When María Fernández entered his confessional to inquire about the fate of her brother who was wanted on charges of murder and robbery, he told her to keep quiet and come to his house later for information. Some hours later when she and her mother arrived, Coll allowed her to visit her brother, whom he had been concealing in a back room.[97]

Naturally, the enormous power and prestige enjoyed by confessors during the Counter-Reformation contained a tremendous potential for abuse. Some confessors used their position in an effort to encourage other clerical business. In 1778, the Inquisition's commissioner in Santa Cruz de Tenerife reported that a Franciscan, Guillermo de Cames y Home, normally visited the town at Lent and stayed until the end of May or the beginning of June. While in Santa Cruz, he seized every opportunity to hear confessions, largely, it was said, in order to make contacts that would increase his earnings from fee-paying sermons and funerary masses.[98]

Other confessors systematically abused their considerable authority by acting capriciously and without regard for the reputations of their penitents. In 1747 Bartolomé Bello, the chaplain of the hospital in Guía in the Canaries, wrote the tribunal there to inform the inquisitors about the activities of Ignacio Mederos, who was acting as assistant in the village. María Medina had informed Bello that Mederos frequently refused to hear her confession, or if he did hear it, he would interrupt her and force her to leave the church without giving her absolution, right in front of other villagers who were waiting to make their confessions. Even worse was the fact that Mederos failed to respect the secrecy of the confessional and would talk openly about what his penitents had told him, even if he exposed them to embarrassment or humiliation. In one instance, he blithely announced to a whole group of villagers that he had heard the confession of a man who admitted that he was having an incestuous relationship with his mother. Apparently Mederos gave enough of a hint as to the identity of the individual that several men in the group were able to find out who he was, and he was harassed and humiliated as a consequence. He also told two sisters about María Josepha's sexual relationship with a man, deeply embarrassing her and compromising her reputation in the village.[99]

Encouraged by the idea that humility and submissiveness were positive religious virtues, some confessors, acting in their role as spiritual directors, tended to behave with great callousness and insensitivity toward their female penitents. Even though Teresa de Jesús believed in the need for absolute

submission to a male confessor, she refers again and again to their ill treatment of her and their lack of understanding of her spiritual concerns. Even Father Baltasar Álvarez, who was one of her best confessors, forced her to give up certain of her friends even though her relationship with them was entirely harmless, cast doubt on her visions, and refused her plans to found the St. Joseph's convent.[100] In fact, it was precisely during the times when the saint most needed solace and understanding, when she felt her faith weakening and her soul "inwardly burning," that her confessors were of least use to her. On these occasions, "they would say such things to me, and reprove me with such asperity that, when I spoke to them about it later they were astonished at themselves." Their harsh language, which may have been meant to mortify her and which at other times she could have borne with good grace, was "pure torture" during these times of special spiritual stress.[101] Teresa's problems with her own confessors were probably the reason for her giving the prioresses of her convents the authority to freely select extraordinary confessors for their nuns without having to ask permission from the male superiors of the Carmelite order. This provision, and especially the clause that allowed the prioress to choose friars from any religious order and not just from among the Carmelites, led to friction with the Carmelite friars. With the election of Fray Nicolás de Jesús María Oria as superior of the order in 1588, this tension came to a head, and the friars moved to strip the nuns of their privilege. This proved no easy task, however, because of the firm opposition of Ana de Jesús, one of Teresa's most important collaborators, then prioress of the Discalced Carmelite convent in Madrid. Ana and a group of other prioresses sought and obtained a brief from Pope Sixtus V confirming Teresa's original constitution and were only defeated when Nicolás de Jesús María removed them from their offices, confined Ana de Jesús to her cell, and obtained another papal document that sharply restricted the nuns' privileges.[102] Ana de Jesús is shown receiving mystical communion in the frontispiece to Fray Angel Manrique's biography. This mystical communion, which she experienced during her confinement, was achieved without the intercession of male priests (Fig. 2.3).

From the end of the Council of Trent to the beginning of the eighteenth century, the role of the sacrament of penance in Catholicism had been profoundly transformed. No longer a yearly obligation that people fulfilled reluctantly if at all, it became an essential part of the new Counter-Reformation spirituality and one of the keys to Catholic revival. At the same time, the role of the confessor was greatly enhanced. Confessors, whether secular or regular, moved to the center of the Church's efforts to catechize the laity, purify the practice of religion, and stem the spread of heterodox ideas. But in order to validate the new importance of confessors and confession, the Church had to be able to confront the inevitable abuses among a clergy that was only slowly gaining the education and discipline required by its new role. Confessors who revealed the secrets of confession in violation of all the strictures of canon law or who abused and humiliated their penitents posed a threat to the Church's entire program. Perhaps the most serious threat was posed by the problem

Figure 2.3. *Ana de Jesús, One of Saint Teresa's Most Important Followers and Founder of Convents in France and Flanders* (Biblioteca Nacional, Laboratorio Fotográfico)

of sexual solicitation during confession. If this abuse were allowed to go unchecked, the popular masses might become alienated from the sacrament and the Protestant attack on it would gain credibility. It was because of the critical need to deal swiftly and effectively with solicitation in a time of crisis that the Church turned to the Spanish Inquisition as its most effective instrument of repression.

Chapter 3

The Spanish Inquisition and Its Jurisdiction Over Solicitation

Writing 131 years after Pius IV had granted the Spanish Inquisition exclusive jurisdiction over solicitation, the anonymous author of an admonition to a recently convicted curate declared that older works of canon law failed to mention penalties for solicitation because "lawmakers could not even imagine the existence of such depraved clerics and confessors."[1] Of course, solicitation was hardly new when Pius issued his bull of April 14, 1561. In fact, the Toledo tribunal of the Spanish Inquisition had tried a solicitation case as early as 1530.[2] What was new was the perception on the part of Church authorities that solicitation posed a serious threat to the entire Tridentine program of revitalizing sacramentalism and expanding the authority of priests and confessors. As early as 1543, Calahorra's reforming bishop, Juan Bernal de Luco, who was a leading member of the Spanish delegation to the Council of Trent, suggested that illicit relations between confessor and penitent should be severely punished if they became known publicly because of the danger that the sacrament itself would lose credibility.[3] It was another prominent Spanish delegate to Trent, Pedro Guerrero, archbishop of Granada, whose 1559 memorial to Paul IV first raised the alarm about the frequency of solicitation and led directly to the bull of 1561.[4]

Everyone from theologians and canonists to the penitents themselves were agreed on one thing: the serious nature of the offense and the need to repress it as rapidly and effectively as possible. One sure indication of the criminalization of solicitation is the increased attention given to it by writers on law and morality during the late sixteenth and seventeenth centuries. While the offense is not even discussed in the most popular mid sixteenth century

confessors' manual, Azpilcueta Navarro's *Manual de confesores y penitentes*, it is mentioned prominently in a number of important and widely circulated manuals published later, including works by Antonio de Escobar y Mendoza and Juan Machado de Chaves. The latter devoted a number of pages in the second volume of his 1641 *Perfecto confesor y cura de almas* to an extended discussion of the offense, including all the relevant papal legislation, and justified the attention that he paid to it by commenting that "no one doubts the gravity and atrocious nature of the crime committed by a priest who becomes lewd and impudent during confession," since in so doing he "sins against both charity and the virtue and power derived from the sacrament."[5] Leading Spanish and Portuguese canonists, like Rodrigo à Cunha and Juan de Azevedo, also turned their attention to the offense and published four works dedicated exclusively to solicitation between 1620 and 1726 (Fig. 3.1).[6]

Perhaps the best way of understanding the genuine repugnance solicitation inspired is to analyze the text of a series of late seventeenth-century admonitions that were copied into the books meant to provide models for judicial procedure in provincial tribunals. In inquisitorial law, the admoni-

Figure 3.1. Frontispiece to Rodrigo à Cunha, *Tractatus de confessariis solicitantibus* 1620 (Biblioteca Nacional, Laboratorio Fotográfico)

tion was a reprimand attached to the sentence, which was meant to make the accused think about the consequences of his criminal behavior and to exhort the accused to maintain better conduct in the future. A careful look at these mini-sermons reveals four major elements that marked the special heinousness of solicitation. In the first place, solicitation involved a radical reversal of the proper function of the sacrament. According to the 1687 admonition, Christ had established confession so that souls stained with sin could cleanse themselves, but the soliciting confessor, by "injecting his filth and obscenity" into the sacrament, had transformed it into an "open field for wickedness and a tempest for the repentant soul."[7] Secondly, the soliciting confessor was guilty of misusing his office, so that the "chair of the confessor from which only the soundest doctrine should be taught becomes the seat of lewdness and dishonor and the lambs who should have been put out to pasture are instead thrown to the wolves to be devoured."[8] A third aggravating factor was that it involved the misappropriation of sacred space, converting "the temples that are the armories of heaven and a bulwark against evil into cesspools of lust and obscenity."[9] Finally, and this must have seemed especially important in the face of a constant barrage of criticism aimed at confession by Protestants, the soliciting confessor gave comfort to the enemy "who rejoice to see how Catholics profane the sacrament that they have already rejected."[10]

While containing many similar themes and repeated phrases, the admonitions were tailored to the specific religious vocation of the individual offender. In the case of a Dominican, for example, the admonition made much of the fact that the order had a long and glorious tradition of upholding religious orthodoxy. Given that tradition and the excellent religious training he must have received, it was all the more astonishing that a representative of the order could be responsible for profaning the sacrament of penance.[11]

The Order of the Holy Trinity dedicated itself to the redemption of captives in North Africa during the early modern period, and when a friar of that order was convicted of solicitation, the admonition did not fail to point out that the same man who had rescued bodies after enduring the dangers and hardships of a redemptionist mission in Algiers had himself become a pirate in the comfort and safety of his own convent, "capturing souls in order to make them slaves of evil."[12] In a similar vein, a member of the Society of Jesus was reminded that his order had always dedicated itself to preaching and missionary work and was considered by heretics to be their most dangerous opponent. As a consequence, the crimes committed by a Jesuit father would inevitably give comfort to the heretics, who would be able to hold the entire order up to ridicule.[13]

When the admonitions turn to the parish clergy, they reflect the special bitterness of disappointment in the behavior of the men who were expected to take the lead in the entire effort to reform popular culture and catechize the masses. Evidently, according to an admonition addressed to a Valencian curate in 1692, he had been unprepared for the responsibilities of such an important office, so that instead of offering his congregation an example of virtue that would validate his religious and moral teaching, he rendered it ineffective. Moreover, having been entrusted with the care of souls who depended on him as their "good shepherd," he had betrayed their trust and turned himself into the instrument of their perdition.[14]

At the fourteenth session of the Council of Trent, the Church fathers made it very clear that the moral state of the priest who uttered the formula of absolution was irrelevant to the efficacy of the sacrament in conveying forgiveness and grace.[15] Several of the admonitions, however, seem to be almost asserting the opposite, implying that the sacrament would be ineffective without a moral priesthood to administer it. This becomes very explicit in a June 5, 1687, admonition, which declared that the hand that administers the formula of absolution has to be "clean and pure," while the hand of the soliciting priest is just the opposite, having been sullied by the filth of lust. Such a hand, the document concluded, can never become the instrument of spiritual cleansing.[16] The same view is at least implicit in a February 26, 1684, admonition to a Dominican, where it is noted that if the laity were to derive full benefit from the industry of priests both as administrators of the sacraments and preachers of sound Christian doctrine, priests had to maintain themselves in purity "without even an atom of corruption."[17]

In summary, what seems to be at stake with solicitation is nothing less than the credibility of the sacrament of penance itself and the ability of the priest to effectively administer it. Indeed, several of the admonitions warn that fathers and husbands would no longer send their daughters and wives to confession if lewd confessors remained unpunished.[18] Faced with this danger, and determined to make confession the centerpiece of its new sacramentalism, the Church needed to find a remedy for this problem that would remove soliciting priests from confessional activity, but also preserve the reputation of the clergy.

Clearly, the episcopal courts, which had jurisdiction over offenses committed by the secular clergy in the diocese, were not the appropriate institution to handle a matter of such importance and urgency. Juan Maldonado's description of the bishop's court in Burgos, published in 1541, gives us a depressing picture of a judicial system run more in the interests of the court officials than out of a concern for the correction of the vices of the parish clergy.[19] The situation in other parts of Spain was very similiar. Throughout the sixteenth century, the diocesan court in Catalonia remained largely ineffective and passive in the face of the moral offenses of the clergy. In any case, nearly three-fourths of the cases coming before this court involved financial matters.[20]

Another critical limitation of the diocesan courts was their dependence on fines and fees. Clerical offenders who were dealt with too harshly might flee the diocese, depriving the bishop's court of its means of subsistence. Consequently, serious moral offenses like drunkenness, gambling, and concubinage were punished with a modest fine, and the curate was allowed to return to home—and, presumably, family—and take up where he had left off until it came time to return to the ecclesiastical court to start the process all over again. This revolving door was hardly likely to improve the moral tone of the parish clergy and very likely to convince the laity that the justice dispensed by ecclesiastical courts was little more than a charade.[21]

That the corruption and excessive leniency of the episcopal courts remained a problem long after Trent had strengthened the judicial authority of bishops is demonstrated by the case of Juan de Villacastín, curate of San Benito. Villacastín, who was accused of a variety of offenses including improper dress, gambling, carrying a loaded pistol, failing to properly celebrate mass, and solicitation, was tried in Ciudad Real before Dr. Luis de Gamir, the vicar-general of the archdiocese of Toledo in 1585. Most of the sentence consisted of severe warnings not to engage in improper behavior like gambling and to carry out his clerical responsibilities properly. He was also told to maintain better relations with the members of the congregation. Spiritual penalties consisted of having to pray and recite the psalms in church on seven successive Fridays and to say four masses for the souls in purgatory without collecting the customary fees. He was also forced to pay a fine and court costs and told to buy a pound of wax for the parish church. On the specific charge of solicitation, he was admonished not to use smutty or suggestive language in the confessional and suspended from hearing confessions for two months under pain of a fine of 10,000 maravedís.[22] Since the ecclesiastical court lacked any system of monitoring compliance with its sentences, it is probably safe to assume that Villacastín ignored everything but his fine and, once he returned to his home village, resumed all his old habits.

Another major problem with the episcopal court system—and one that made it impossible to function effectively to repress an offense like solicitation—was that the bishop's jurisdiction was not recognized everywhere in his own diocese. In large parts of New Castile, for example, the bishop's officials found themselves in conflict with the Royal Council of the Military Orders, which claimed jurisdiction because the orders were also ecclesiastical foundations.[23] In many dioceses, moreover, the jurisdiction of the bishop's tribunal was limited by the rival authority of the archpriests, which continued even after Trent had removed their judicial powers.[24] In the diocese of Avila, the absentee bishops had largely abrogated control of the diocese to the powerful cathedral chapter, whose four archdeacons exercised jurisdiction over the parish clergy. When Bishop Pedro Fernández Tremiño attempted to extend his jurisdiction to the cathedral clergy in 1581 to 1590, the canons and prebendaries insisted that they and they alone had the right to punish their colleagues. After years of wrangling, the bishop lost the dispute when the papal nuncio ruled against him.[25]

Jurisdiction over the regular clergy was exercised by the superiors of the individual orders. By its very nature, this system was even less effective than the episcopal courts since it depended on the willingness of individual abbots or officials to enforce regulations that they might or might not think were important, while a desire to avoid scandal for the community could easily lead them to overlook an offense like solicitation. The only real check on offenses committed by the regular clergy were the visitations carried out by officials of the order, but these occurred irregularly and at long intervals and could hardly be viewed as an effective means of repression.[26]

There was, however, one Spanish judicial institution that did enjoy a high degree of popularity and respect and had the scope, organization, and infrastructure that would be required to deal with solicitation effectively. This, of course, was the Inquisition, which was first authorized by Sixtus IV's bull of November 1, 1478, and became fully operational in the early 1480s. In spite of the fact that the traditional historiography has made much of the opposition to the Holy Office in Spain, that opposition, where it existed, was mainly confined to the crown of Aragon and was based more on a desire to preserve local privileges from the encroachment of what was seen as a Castilian institution. Among the popular masses and most of Spain's political elite, especially in Castile, the Inquisition was popular for its repression of heretics, respected for its probity, and feared for the harsh punishment it could hand out. Even in Aragon, where resistance to the Holy Office had been a problem in the early sixteenth century, it had become so widely accepted that when a son of Saragossa, Luis de Aliaga, was elevated to the rank of Inquisitor-General in 1619, there was an outpouring of sentiment supporting the Inquisition and celebrating Aliaga's promotion. One of the poems in Luys Diez de Aux's compendium that was published on this occasion probably sums up what many felt about an institution that they had come to feel was uniquely Spanish:

> O Holy Inquisition, Glory of Spain/
> Which bathes souls in heavenly water/
> And doth the Christian faith sustain/
> Whose name alone sets trembling/
> So powerful is our saintly tribunal/
> Scoundrels vile and dissembling.[27]

The almost unquestioning acceptance of the Holy Office in Spain can perhaps be best summed up by the famous proverb "Con el Rey y con la Santa Inquisición, chitón! (Regarding the King and the Holy Inquisition, not a word!)." The proverb, of course refers to the respect felt toward the two most widely accepted institutions in early modern Spain: the monarchy and the Inquisition, although support for the latter was probably stronger as indicated by the fact that during the Comunero Revolution of 1520 to 1521, the revolt of Catalonia in 1640, and the unrest that followed the occupation of Aragon by allied troops during the War of Spanish Succession, mobs hostile to the monarchy refrained from attacking the Holy Office.[28] In addition to respect, of course, the Inquisition inspired a certain amount of fear. When Miguel Mir returned to Manacor after having gone to testify before the Mallorca tribunal, he commented to a friend who asked him how he had been treated that he had been shaking the entire time. In Mir's case, the fear inspired by the Holy Office had a positive effect since it brought him to finally admit that he had lied in earlier testimony that he had given against Dr. Andrés Coll.[29]

The Spanish Inquisition was founded initially to deal with the problem of religious backsliding among the converted Jews, and it continued to be concerned with the suppression of religious heresy throughout its existence as an institution. But during the mid sixteenth century, and especially after Philip II made the decrees of the Council of Trent a part of Spanish law on July 12, 1564, the Inquisition was enrolled in the gigantic effort to re-Christianize society and eliminate those elements of popular culture that smacked of blasphemy, superstition, or disrespect for the sacred. In fact, between 1540 and 1700 the so-called minor offenses committed mainly by Old Christians made up 57.8 percent of the 44,674 cases tried.[30] Consistent with the concerns raised at Trent about the poor educational preparation and low moral standards of the clergy, moreover, the Inquisition's authority was extended to cover certain offenses frequently committed by priests, especially heretical propositions, which were statements made in sermons, conversation, or in the heat of academic debates that appeared to vary significantly from orthodox opinion. In the kingdom of Valencia, for example, 30 percent of the cases of propositions tried by the Holy Office involved members of the priesthood.[31] The Inquisition's jurisdiction over solicitation, therefore, should be placed within the context of the acceptance by Church authorities of the need to greatly improve clerical education and morality through increased training and supervision.

Apart from the fact that the Inquisition was an ecclesiastical court using canon law procedure and therefore perfectly acceptable to the ecclesiastical hierarchy, its organization and structure made it ideal for the repression of solicitation. In the first place, the Inquisition was Spain's only national judicial institution, with thirteen tribunals in Castile and Aragon by 1561 and a further one established in Madrid in 1638. Offshore, the secretariat of Aragon controlled three other European tribunals in Mallorca, Sardinia, and Sicily. All of these tribunals, as well as the ones established in Spain's American possessions, were under the control of the Suprema in Madrid, which was composed of experienced inquisitors who had distinguished themselves on the provincial tribunals. The Suprema, in turn, operated under the general direction of the Inquisitor-General, normally a distinguished prelate who had served the crown on one or more of the royal councils and was therefore well acquainted with royal policy.

As a national institution, the Inquisition could operate with a consistency and efficiency that would have been impossible using the ecclesiastical courts, with their fragmented and frequently overlapping jurisdiction. Central direction also insured that judicial procedures would be uniform across the entire geography of the Spanish monarchy, while checking unusual or aberrant behavior on the part of individual inquisitors.

Furthermore, because it had several tribunals that covered the entire monarchy, the Inquisition was in an excellent position to track the movements of individuals accused of solicitation through the exchange of information among tribunals. This was particularly useful in dealing with the friars of the mendicant orders, who were frequently moved from convent to convent by their superiors. From the early seventeenth century, it became customary for provincial tribunals to circulate the names of persons who had been charged with solicitation by one witness in hopes of finding that somewhere else another charge had been made. Sometimes all the tribunals were circularized and sometimes only those in the immediate area. In 1685, for example, the Mallorca tribunal sent out a request for information about Fray Pedro Joseph Pons only to the tribunals of Barcelona, Valencia, and Saragossa.[32] By the mid eighteenth century, tribunals were even sending along detailed physical descriptions of suspects in order to help with identification.[33] In this way, the requisite two witnesses could be accumulated and prosecution could begin.

Pooling of resources by provincial tribunals also could prove highly useful in trapping suspects like Fray Guillermo de Cames y Home, in whose case a key witness had changed domicile. Cames y Home had been born in La Orotava on the island of Tenerife and, except for brief periods of residence in La Laguna to receive instruction in scholastic philosophy, had remained at the Augustinian house located just outside the village. In 1765 the tribunal had received evidence against him from Antonia Bautista, but was unable to take any action without a second witness. In 1784, however, the tribunal got a break with the receipt of a letter from its counterpart in Seville, requesting information about one Fray Guillermo, against whom testimony had been received from Juana Díaz Sol, formerly resident in La Orotava and presently living in Cádiz, which was in the Seville district. Apparently, Juana Díaz Sol had recently made a general confession with a Capuchin on mission in Cádiz, and when he asked her if she had ever had sexual relations with a person who had sworn a vow of chastity, she blurted out a story about an incident of solicitation involving Cames y Home that had occurred six years earlier when she was still living in the Canaries. The Capuchin promptly advised her to come to the Seville tribunal and make a deposition, and after it was received, Seville's inquisitors wrote to the tribunal in the Canaries to request information. Seville's detailed portrait of the accused as tall and corpulent with a pale skin, a round, pockmarked face; protruding eyes; and a large, flat nose was sufficient for the Canaries tribunal to clear up the confusion and identify him as the person against whom testimony had been received back in 1765. Since Cames y Home was still living in La Orotava, the tribunal wrote to Seville requesting a transcript of Juana Díaz Sol's testimony, which it received on May 11, 1784.[34]

Another successful instance of cooperation between tribunals involved the case of the Capuchin friar Isidro de Arganda. In May 1753 Arganda was living in the order's El Pardo house and acting as vicar in the village when the Toledo tribunal, in whose district El Pardo was situated, received its first testimony against him. After sending his description to other Castilian tribunals, Toledo received a letter from the Cuenca tribunal indicating that Arganda had been denounced by a woman from the village of Jadrique in the northern part of the district. Since Arganda had spent several years at the Capuchin house in that village and had been an active confessor while he lived there, the Toledo tribunal requested that Cuenca follow up on this deposition by reinterviewing its witness. The Cuenca tribunal responded by appointing Francisco de Isla, the parish priest of Jadrique, as special commissioner. Following his instructions, Isla interviewed Angela Pérez and from her testimony was able to call no fewer than eight other women who testified to similar experiences. All this evidence was then sent on to the Toledo tribunal, which ordered Arganda's arrest.[35]

Central direction also resulted in greater organizational efficiency. In order to direct the activities of the provincial tribunals, the Suprema issued a series of administrative minutes called cartas acordadas, which were copied into special record books and kept in the archive of each tribunal. In an indication of just how important the repression of solicitation had become, the carta acordada of August 15, 1601, ordered all provincial tribunals to keep special record books of those against whom evidence of solicitation had been received. These books were to be made available to the other tribunals, which would periodically request copies of them in order to update their own files. On February 16, 1644, for example, the tribunal of Murcia forwarded to the Toledo tribunal, at its request, a copy of its record book for the years 1602 to 1643 and asked Toledo to reciprocate.[36]

What a distinguished Inquisition scholar has recently described as "a network of agents unique in western Europe" was another organizational element that placed the Inquisition ahead of its secular or ecclesiastical rivals.[37] Each tribunal had a body of unpaid lay and clerical assistants—familiares, comisarios, and notarios—scattered through its district upon which it could call for such services as arresting and escorting prisoners and interviewing witnesses. These officials also served as the eyes and ears of the tribunal in the district, frequently receiving information that they would pass on to the tribunal for further action. Although the present state of research does not permit us to arrive at any final figure for the total number of such unsalaried officials, we can say that at least some tribunals had substantial numbers throughout most of our period. In the Valencia district, for example, a visitation carried out by a member of the Suprema in 1567 revealed 1,638 familiares in the district, with 183 in the city of Valencia itself. While total numbers serving at any one time probably declined in the seventeenth century, some 1,797 individuals can be identified as having served. Even in the eighteenth century, in spite of the decline in the general importance and overall popularity of the Holy Office, the Valencia tribunal was able to maintain respectable numbers until at least 1748, with some 356 familiares serving in that year.[38] Figures for other tribunals are spotty or nonexistent in part because of the provincial tribunal's remarkable unwillingness to furnish the Suprema with information about numbers, but we know that the Toledo tribunal had 99 familiares serving in its district as late as the mid eighteenth century, probably more than enough to handle its modest level of activity.[39] In the Galicia district, which was considerably poorer than the other two, the network of familiares was quite a bit smaller, reaching a maximum of 497 at the end of the sixteenth century.[40]

In spite of the fact that familiares rarely acted as the spies or agents of the Holy Office in the sense of actively gathering information as an older historiography would have us believe, they could and did serve as conduits of information to the tribunal.[41] Usually chosen from among men of some substance and local prominence, their relationship to the Holy Office was always well-known and individuals occasionally came to them to make depositions or seek advice regarding solicitation cases.

Even more important to maintaining the activity of the Holy Office in the interior of the district were the commissioners and notaries. A commissioner had the authority to receive information and transmit it to the tribunal and then carry out formal interrogations of witnesses. He could not actually carry out an arrest unless he felt a suspect was likely to escape, but could call upon secular authorities to hold an individual at the disposition of the Holy Office.[42] Commissioners were generally drawn from among benefice holders, such as canons of cathedrals or collegiate churches, rather than from among parish priests and were normally situated in the principal towns of the district. In the Valencia district, fourteen major towns were listed as authorized to have commissioners during the eighteenth century, but there were only eleven serving in 1784. The Valencia tribunal supplemented its network of commissioners with notaries, who carried out similar functions although they did not have the power to order anyone arrested. There were some fifty notaries in the middle of the eighteenth century, all drawn from the ranks of parish priests.[43]

In the Toledo district, on the other hand, the number of commissioners seems to have been much larger, with eighty-two as late as 1707. In this district, the role of the notary appears to have been limited to recording the testimony of witnesses interviewed by the commissioners.[44]

Galicia also had a substantial complement of commissioners, but here they were mainly parish priests, with only five canons out of the thirty-six listed in the archdiocese of Santiago in 1611.[45] By the end of the sixteenth century, there were more than forty serving commissioners in the district.[46]

As a prominent cleric and important official of the Holy Office, the commissioner would obviously be in a position to receive denunciations of solicitation. In 1695, for example, Luisa Borges finally worked up enough courage to come before Dr. Pedro de Guisla, commissioner in La Palma, and testify about several incidents of solicitation that had occurred over the last six years involving Fray Cipriano de Armas.[47]

It was more frequent that the commissioner would receive his information not from the victim herself, but from another person in whom she had confided. In 1576, Ana Carreras y Gamila, a resident of Mahon on Menorca, told Antonio Caules about an experience that she had had a year earlier with her confessor, Fray Jaime Barcelo. Evidently mindful of everyone's obligation to denounce all incidents of solicitation of which they had any knowledge, Caules went immediately to commissioner Simón Carreras, and four days later Carreras took a detailed deposition from Carreras y Gamila, which he then sent to the inquisitors of the Mallorca tribunal.[48] Commissioners, because of their influence and knowledge of local people, were also in a position to inform the tribunal about the reputation and potential veracity of witnesses. In the case of Luisa Borges, commissioner Guisla was able to assure the tribunal that he knew her to be a person whose life was above reproach and, therefore, could be trusted to tell the truth.[49]

Relying exclusively on the network of familiares, commissioners, and notaries, however, would have imposed significant limitations on the effectiveness of the Holy Office. For one thing, these networks never really covered the territory of the sprawling inquisitorial districts. In Galicia, for example, only 226 of the district's 3,511 population centers had familiares, and both familiares and commissioners were heavily concentrated along the coast, leaving vast areas of the interior virtually untouched.[50] There was also a general tendency for the absolute numbers of unpaid officials to decline. In the case of Galicia, the 497 familiares listed at the end of the sixteenth century had declined to 118 by 1663.[51] In the district of Catalonia, after 1585, when an agreement was made that prohibited public officials from becoming familiares, the office lost considerable prestige, and by 1632 the tribunal had only 5 familiares left in the city of Barcelona.[52]

In order to make itself heard everywhere in the district, the Inquisition turned early to the forum of conscience, making use of confessors and confession as a way of forcing individuals to come forward to denounce the heresies of which they had knowledge. So for the Inquisition, as for the Church in general, confession took on a regulative and prescriptive role that it had never had before, making it all the more essential for the Inquisition to throw itself into the fight against anything that tended to undermine public confidence in the sacrament.

As early as 1500, inquisitors carrying out their yearly visitations to the district were instructed to open with a public declaration ordering all those with knowledge of heresy to come forward to reveal it.[53] Eventually this became known as the Edict of Faith, and it was published annually on the second Sunday in Lent in the town that was the seat of the inquisitorial district, and elsewhere when inquisitors went out on their periodic visitations. Printed copies of the Edict were also sent to commissioners for distribution to parish churches, convents, and monasteries all over the district.[54]

Definitive inclusion of solicitation in the Edict after 1576 under the heading of "diverse heresies" gave the Inquisition a powerful new weapon. Individuals were told to denounce any confessor, whether secular or regular, who had attempted, by word or deed, to induce his penitent to commit any lascivious or immodest action either during or in close proximity to confession. Denunciations were expected within six days under pain of excommunication.[55] This was a threat not to be lightly disregarded, as Catherina Puig, the eighteen-year-old daughter of a master weaver from Palma, found out when she came before the Mallorca tribunal to give evidence against Pedro Onofre Martín, a benefice holder in the cathedral. After admitting that she had heard the Edict of Faith but failed to come forward out of fear of her parents, the Inquisitor informed her that she was excommunicate and that she would have to go to her confessor to receive absolution.[56] Powerfully reinforcing the Edict was the fact that confessors were instructed to withhold absolution to penitents who had knowledge of solicitation until they denounced it to the Holy Office.[57] Confessors who for any reason granted absolution to such a penitent would themselves incur excommunication.[58] It was the Holy Office itself, moreover, that had the authority to issue licenses to confessors to absolve their penitents after their evidence had been received.[59]

For a few individuals, amounting to no more than 15 out of the 560 witnesses in my records, the Edict of Faith and the Anathema that followed it were impressive enough to cause them to search their consciences and come voluntarily to the tribunal or to one of its local representatives. Lucía Hernández, a young woman from Piedrablanca in the Toledo district went to a nearby commissioner in order to denounce Gabriel de Osca, her local parish priest, after hearing the Edict read out because she realized that what had happened between them in the confessional was "contrary to our faith."[60] In some cases, hearing the Edict was sufficient to remind an individual of something that they may have long repressed. Francisca de Melo, a thirty-nine-year-old prostitute from San Sebastián de la Gomera in the Canaries went to see her confessor shortly after she heard the Edict being read out in the parish church, and when he asked her if she knew of anything that fell under its provisions, she told him about an incident that had taken place ten years earlier with Fray Cipriano de Armas. Her confessor advised her of her obligation to inform the Holy Office, so the following day she appeared before commissioner Manuel de Milan.[61]

Much more frequently, however, it was the confessor who through persuasion, outright denial of absolution, or a combination of the two brought about the presentation of his penitent's evidence to the Holy Office. Out of 560 witnesses, 191, or 34 percent, were either persuaded, or more frequently, forced to make a deposition before the Inquisition. Typical of this latter group was Isabel Baxach, who presented herself before Mallorca's Inquisitor Baltasar de Prado at his morning session on March 27, 1670, to denounce Fray Antonio Planes after having been denied absolution by her confessor unless she did so.[62] Some confessors, spurred by the traditions of their order and encouraged by confessors' manuals like the *Examen y práctica de confesores y penitentes* by the Jesuit Antonio de Escobar y Mendoza, were zealous in insisting on denunciations from their penitents.[63] Angela Mulet and Catalina Flexas y Proassi, two of the three witnesses against Gabriel Canevas, a benefice holder in the parish of Santa Cruz in Palma de Mallorca, were sent before the tribunal by the same confessor, the Jesuit Father Artalano.[64]

Sometimes, when a penitent seemed unwilling to make any move on her own, a confessor would use a combination of persuasion and coercion. In June 1741 twenty-year-old María Vásquez began confessing with an old friend of the family, Joseph Carrera, lieutenant curate of the village of Leganes. According to her own testimony, her "confessions" with Carrera turned into gossip sessions that became steadily more suggestive and indelicate until one day, when she went to kiss his hand after receiving absolution, he caressed

her face. Two months later, having gone to Madrid, she went to confession
with Father Joseph Beteta, who attempted to persuade her to go before the
Corte tribunal with her evidence, but she refused and he was forced to deny
her absolution. A few days later, conscience-stricken and frightened, she
returned and agreed to allow Beteta to send a written deposition to the
tribunal.[65]

A confessor's ability to act discreetly in order to relay information to the
Inquisition on someone's behalf could be of real benefit to a penitent who
found herself in an awkward situation that made it impossible for her to
approach the tribunal or even a commissioner directly. Francisca Calvo, a
young married woman, had an affair with Fray Jayme Barcelo for about six
years before she came to confess with another Franciscan, Mateo Ortila, who
happened to be the head of Barcelo's convent. Although she felt Barcelo no
longer loved her, she was afraid to denounce him because if her "husband
and relatives found out, they would murder her without pity." Therefore, she
was extremely grateful to Ortila when he suggested that he write to the tribunal on her behalf.[66]

Apart from those more or less forced to come to the Holy Office by their
confessors, many people, both clergy and laity, were eager to denounce solicitation. Its inclusion in the Edict of Faith made it synonymous with some of
the worst heresies known to Catholic Europe, heresies that the ordinary lay
person had been conditioned to abhor. The increasing importance of the
sacrament of penance and the enhanced social role of the confessor gave
priests and friars a powerful incentive to ensure the proper behavior of their
fellow clergy since the reputation of the clerical order itself was at stake.

One day in August 1688 Joseph Calafell presented himself before the
inquisitors of the Mallorca tribunal to denounce an incident that he had
observed while in the chapel of Palma's Trinitarian convent the previous year.
Having entered the chapel at nine one morning he saw Fray Antonio Ballester
hearing a woman's confession, and while Calafell watched, Ballester placed
his hand under the woman's shirt, touching her breasts. Calafell also informed
the tribunal that he had seen Ballester conversing with this same woman in
the church and that rumor had it that she was his mistress.[67]

The role of the confessor in the repression of solicitation was so important
to the curate and benefice holders in the village of Artá, a village on the east-
ern end of Mallorca, that they convened a conference to discuss it in 1687.
One of those present at this meeting, Mateo Rosa, the local vicar, denounced
Fray Jaime Barceló to the tribunal a few months later.[68]

Members of the regular clergy were also frequently eager to denounce their
fellow friars out of a sense of loyalty to their order. While carrying out a visitation to the Trinitarian convent in Palma, the order's commissioner, Fray
Pedro Amaros, received three denunciations from friars living there against
a fellow friar, Rafael Serre.[69] An even clearer example of how pride in the
order could generate denunciations to the Holy Office involved Juan de Robles and Diego de Vega, two Mercedarians from the convent in Toledo who

sent a memorial to the tribunal regarding the reputation of Fray Antonio del Viso on June 5, 1632. Later that day when Juan de Robles was called to the tribunal to explain the memorial, he explained that he and Vega had frequently spoken about del Viso's disgraceful behavior, which included leaving the convent at all hours, consorting with known prostitutes, and openly kissing and embracing a married woman in the chapel. Even though the bishop had ordered him scourged before the entire company, this had in no way reformed his behavior. Learning that del Viso had recently been arrested on charges of solicitation and alarmed at the "enormous scandal and damage to the reputation of the order" that his conduct was causing, the two friars had sent their memorial to inform the tribunal more fully, no doubt hoping that it would serve to strengthen the case against him.[70]

Missionaries also proved to be a fertile source of information for the Inquisition since they would habitually hear a great many confessions during the period of the mission. On May 21, 1759, Antonio Fernández Arcaya reported to his colleagues on the Mallorca tribunal that the previous morning he had been visited by the superior of the local Mercedarian mission, who had just received information from a missionary in Sineu that María Zabater wanted to make a deposition before the Holy Office. The tribunal promptly appointed special commissioners to hear her testimony, which resulted in the arrest and trial of Fray Pablo Ginard on a charge of solicitation.[71]

In fact, it was precisely this concern about the image and reputation of the clergy that provided yet another powerful argument for choosing the Inquisition to deal with the sensitive issue of solicitation rather than an ordinary ecclesiastical court. With greater status and increased responsibility had come greater scrutiny by the laity, so that, as a Franciscan observer remarked bitterly in 1675, "since the mob expects us to set an example of virtue, the sin of the one redounds upon us all and they regard us with spite and ill will for an offense committed by a single individual."[72] But the nightmare of respected members of the clergy being brought to trial for solicitation and publicly excoriated could be avoided by using the Inquisition because its proceedings were secret and even the sentencing and reconciliation of offenders could be carried on behind closed doors. As the inquisitors of Palermo commented in a letter sent to Inquisitor-General Andrés Pacheco in 1625 at a time when the episcopal court was attempting to take cognizance of a solicitation case, "if they were heard in the ordinary courts, such matters, and especially solicitation in the act of confession, would result in a horrible scandal and have a very bad effect, causing a loss of respect for confessors and for the sacrament of penance itself." Up to this point, however, the Sicilian inquisitors took pride in the fact that they had observed the utmost discretion in their proceedings, sentencing all of the cases that had come before them privately in the audience chamber, thereby avoiding "numerous embarrassments." Needless to say, Inquisitor-General Pacheco threw his full support behind the Palermo tribunal, which maintained undiminished its jurisdiction over solicitation.[73]

By the provisions of the bull of April 14, 1561, the actual range of activity included in the offense was sharply limited. Solicitation was restricted only to women and had to take place during the act of confession itself. In 1577 and later, the Suprema interpreted this to mean that if there was no actual confession, then there was no penalty for soliciting penitents in the place normally set aside for the sacrament. Theologians addressing themselves to the issue further explained that if the confessor made sexual overtures either before confession had actually begun or after absolution, no disrespect for the sacrament was to be imputed and, therefore, what had happened was outside the competence of the Holy Office. When theologians addressed the issue of what acts actually constituted solicitation, they introduced further restrictions. Many held that suggestive conversation such as praising the woman's beauty or seeking to find out her address for an assignation was perhaps imprudent but not necessarily a mortal sin or a temptation to evil. There was also controversy over whether a priest who attempted to set up an assignation for the benefit of another or who tried to convince a penitent to act as a procuress came under the definition of the offense.[74]

With such significant limitations, it was relatively easy for confessors to avoid solicitation while still making use of the confessional for illicit purposes. The curate of Santa Cruz on Mallorca, for example, was able to assure one of his penitents that they were free to say whatever they liked in the confessional so long as they had not crossed themselves preparatory to formally beginning confession.[75] Fray Juan de la Olmeda, a Franciscan who was acting as vicar of the convent of La Concepción in Oropesa, made a deliberate effort to avoid the provisions of the 1561 bull by stopping his penitents just before they began to confess or by containing himself until just after they finished.[76]

By the early seventeenth century, it had become obvious that the definition of the offense would have to be broadened if the effort to suppress it were to have a chance of success. On August 30, 1622, Pope Gregory XV issued *Universi Dominici Gregis*, which eliminated many of the weaknesses and ambiguities of the previous bull. Henceforward, solicitation was to include indecent and suggestive conversation and to cover events before and after confession. Feigned confession that took place where confession was usually heard and solicitation by the priest for someone else were also included. Both episcopal officials and inquisitors were to have jurisdiction over this offense, with the power to inflict punishment ranging from exile to galley service, or degradation and release to the secular arm for execution.[77] A copy of the bull was to be posted in the sacristy of each monastic house and to be read aloud to the entire community every year in the month of August.[78]

Eventually, after strong protests from Spain, the provisions of the bull allowing episcopal courts to share jurisdiction were suspended.[79] Special instructions were then sent out to the provincial tribunals incorporating the provisions of the bull and referring specifically to solicitation as covering any "obscene acts or indecent or provocative words" performed or uttered before, during, or after confession. Witnesses were to be examined in minute detail and were to specify the time, place, and circumstances of the offense.

They were asked to explicitly describe the conversation that had taken place, using the exact words as well as the details of any physical contact with the confessor.[80]

It seems clear from an analysis of these early cases, however, that the 1622 bull was, at least to some degree, meant to legitimize activities going on at Spain's provincial tribunals that had already moved beyond the limitations of the 1561 document.[81] Of the thirty-two cases recorded before 1622, fourteen involved events taking place only during confession itself, but sixteen included evidence of solicitation that occurred before confession had actually begun or after it had concluded. In 1586–1587, during the trial of Gabriel de Osca, two out of the nine witnesses for the prosecution testified that solicitation had taken place after they had concluded their confessions and received absolution.[82] In the case of the Jeronimite Fray Pedro de Villanueva, who acted as confessor at the convent of La Concepción outside of Toledo, one of the three nuns who testified against him had been solicited on twenty separate occasions, but always before she began her confession.[83]

Certain cases also exhibit a tendency to go beyond the limitations of the 1561 bull regarding the words or actions that were considered blameworthy. In nineteen cases the evidence was clear and unambiguous since the accused actually had physical contact with his penitent. But in nine of them there was no physical contact, so that the evidence consisted entirely of foul, smutty, or suggestive language frequently of a kind that many canonists felt really did not constitute solicitation. The evidence accumulated by the Toledo tribunal against Pedro de Ortega in 1588 consisted almost entirely of remarks made during confession that occupied a kind of gray area between the intrusive and excessively personal and the overtly suggestive. In only one instance, when he told Ana García that he would like to place a twig she was carrying between her breasts, did he cross that boundary. Otherwise, his confessional interrogations included such audacious but not necessarily culpable material as asking a penitent if she wanted to marry his brother, asking for her address, telling a penitent that she had beautiful eyes and hair, assuring her that it was perfectly acceptable for a young woman to use makeup and look at her face in the mirror, and warning another penitent that in confessing with him she was "confessing with the devil."[84]

Pre-1622 cases also included instances where a tribunal used evidence drawn from a feigned or pretended confession, something that was clearly not a part of the 1561 bull. In 1576, for example, Catalina Cernuscolo came to the Toledo tribunal to denounce Fray Luis de Valdivieso, an Augustinian from Madrid who had approached her while she was hearing mass in the chapel of his convent, asked to talk with her in the confessional, and then made a series of improper remarks to her without even starting the process of confession. Admittedly, Catalina Cernuscolo was only one of four witnesses against Fray Luis, so that he would have been convicted anyway, but the very fact that her evidence was being accepted and incorporated in the accusation indicates that the tribunal was struggling to break out of the boundaries set for it in 1561.[85] By the early seventeenth century, moreover, this effort was receiving powerful support from theologians like Fray Pedro de Ledesema who, in a book published in 1608, described solicitation as obscene language or comportment perpetrated either during or proximate to confession.[86] While greatly expanding the definition of the offense to incorporate a greater range of activity, the provisions of the 1622 bull were themselves open to interpretation and provided a fertile field for speculation and controversy both inside the Holy Office itself and within the wider community of scholastics and canonists. In spite of these disagreements, however, fairly well-defined parameters within which the Inquisition would exercise its newly expanded jurisdiction were worked out, enabling it to greatly increase its persecution of offenders. Judging by the kinds of evidence included in the arraignment of accused individuals and the comments of the Inquisition's own theologians (calificadores), there seemed to be general agreement that any kind of smutty or suggestive language uttered in proximity to or during the sacrament was sufficient for prosecution, in spite of the opinions of certain theologians and even of the Roman Inquisition that it was the intention and not the words themselves that counted.[87]

The issue of the length of time that had to ensue between an actual confession and sexual overtures on the part of the confessor was a much more difficult one that tended to divide opinion within the Holy Office itself. At one extreme were prosecuting attorneys like Luis Antonio Gomés Cabrero Colodrero of the Mallorca tribunal, who asserted that any sexual approach made by a confessor constituted solicitation provided he had an ongoing confessional relationship with his penitent regardless of the interval between confession and solicitation.[88] Generally, the theologians employed by the Inquisition rejected this position and argued for a relatively close connection between solicitation and confession, extending no further than the same day. Calificadores reviewing the evidence presented by the prosecuting attorney in the case of Fray Pablo Ginard, for example, threw out a charge that "some days" after confessing one of his penitents he had gone to her house for illicit purposes, while fully accepting another incident in which he had sexual relations with her that same afternoon. This incident, according to the theologians, constituted "the most obscene form of solicitation because it was immediately post confession."[89]

Moreover, unlike Cabrero Colodrero, whose charges included immoral behavior that had no direct connection with confession at all, theologians tended to stick to the idea of solicitation as manifest disrespect for the sacrament and, therefore, a mild form of heresy. In 1721, calificadores dismissed a charge against Fray Jaime Massanet because, although he had attempted to rape one of his penitents on the afternoon of the day she confessed with him, he had said nothing in confession about his intentions nor had he even commented when she told him about a lascivious dream that she had had the previous night. These same calificadores, however, rejected a particularly insidious notion held by some theologians and asserted by some accused confessors that if some new element, such as a change of location or a conversation about some other topic intervened between confession and solicitation, the provisions of the bull of 1622 would not apply.[90]

Equipped with a greatly expanded definition of the offense and with the structural and operational elements that made it an ideal instrument of repression, the Spanish Inquisition had little trouble gaining the acquiescence of episcopal authorities to the loss of what had once been a part of their jurisdiction. The Inquisition's success was acknowledged by Isidro de Aliaga, Archbishop of Valencia, in a letter he wrote to his brother, Inquisitor-General Luis de Aliaga (1619–1621). Replying to a demand from the Valencia tribunal that he relinquish control over a curate who had been arrested by his vicar-general on a charge of solicitation, Isidro de Aliaga defended the episcopal court's right to try the offense, claiming that the Inquisition had never been granted exclusive jurisdiction. But he ruefully admitted that, as a result of the inclusion of solicitation in the Edicts of Faith, with their insistence that confessors could not absolve their penitents unless they came before the Holy Office, "it is not surprising that since the Holy Office received its jurisdiction over solicitation many ordinary ecclesiastical courts have never handled a single case."[91]

In fact, by the later seventeenth century, recognition by bishops of the Inquisition's jurisdiction had become so complete that they were routinely passing evidence to the Holy Office whenever they came across it. In 1661, for example, the bishop of the Canaries referred to the Canaries tribunal evidence against Diego Clavijo Betancor that he had received during a recently concluded visitation to the island of Lanzerote.[92] That episcopal respect for the Inquisition's jurisdiction held firm even when it had become an almost moribund institution during the early nineteenth century is demonstrated by an incident that occurred in Valencia in 1814. In July of that year, María Masía sent a letter to Dr. Antonio Roca y Pertusa, vicar-general of the archdiocese, requesting permission to make a deposition before a notary of the ecclesiastical court regarding an important matter. The vicar-general promptly complied with this request, but when he realized that her deposition involved solicitation, he quickly sent it to the tribunal "so that your excellencies may continue to make use of your powers."[93]

Relations with the religious orders were considerably more difficult. The superiors of the orders jealously guarded their autonomy from outside interference and were extremely concerned about maintaining their orders' reputation, given the ferocious competition for penitents. The resulting campaign of obstructionism could be countered only by the most determined measures on the part of the Holy Office. In 1582, the Suprema ordered the Toledo tribunal to admonish Pedro de Avila, the guardian of the Franciscan convent of Guadalajara, for having proceeded against Fray Sebastián de Hontora on a charge of solicitation. Some days later, Pedro de Avila was summoned to the tribunal, where he was told in no uncertain terms that in future he was not to interfere in any matters that came under the jurisdiction of the Holy Office.[94]

The issue of the Inquisition's jurisdiction over regulars in matters of solicitation really was only decided with the resolution by Rome of a dispute involving two Jesuit fathers who were spirited out of Spain by their superiors after having been found guilty of the offense by the order. The Inquisition responded by prosecuting the Jesuit provincial of Castile and two of his assistants.[95] But the order intervened with Sixtus V, who invoked the case to himself and threatened Inquisitor-General Quiroga with the most dire penalties if he protested. The Jesuits then attempted to obtain a blanket exemption for all the religious orders from inquisitorial jurisdiction. In 1591, they succeeded in obtaining a papal brief that sharply curtailed the Inquisition's authority by ordering that no father could testify before any royal tribunal about matters concerning himself or any other member of the order, but instead had to go before the papal nuncio.[96] The Spanish Inquisition had friends in high places, however, and was able to put a great deal of pressure on the Vatican.[97] With the leadership of the Jesuits deeply divided and the Spanish viceroy in Sicily refusing to confirm its privileges, it was only a matter of time until the Inquisition prevailed.[98] On December 3, 1592, the Roman Congregation of the Inquisition, in the presence of Clement VIII, issued a decree declaring that the superiors of the regulars could not exercise jurisdiction over the members of their orders. This was further confirmed by Paul V in 1605 when he summarily revoked the jurisdiction of superiors in all matters relating to the Inquisition and again in the bull of 1622, which made inquisitors special judges over solicitation with jurisdiction over all the clergy both secular and regular.[99]

With the issue of jurisdiction resolved, the battle with the orders moved to disclosure since, for a variety of reasons, friars and their superiors frequently tried to prevent the Holy Office from gaining the evidence that it needed to undertake the prosecution of one of their number. Sometimes this obstructionism took the form of a friar simply trying to protect one of his monastic colleagues. When Mariana Gómez y Torana went to see Fray Juan Mora in Palma's Augustinian convent the day after another Augustinian had attempted to seduce her in the convent's confessional, he told her not to mention what had happened to anyone and specifically not to approach the Holy Office with the information.[100]

In other instances, it was the officials of the order who were responsible for obstructing the work of the Holy Office. When a conscience-stricken Fray Pedro Joseph Pons from the Augustinian house on Menorca wanted to come to the Holy Office to confess an instance of solicitation, his superiors refused to allow him to go in spite of his repeated requests.[101]

Sometimes intervention by superiors took an extreme and even violent form. When Fray Francisco de San Juan Bautista, who lived in the Augustinian house of Talavera de la Reina, denounced Fray Alonso de la Resurrección to the Toledo tribunal for solicitation, his superiors threw him into a cell and kept him chained there for forty days until he finally escaped. When the tribunal tried to get the Augustinian house in Toledo to accept him, its prior refused on the grounds that he was "indiscreet" and had disobeyed the rules of the order.[102]

Superiors also acted to prevent the possibility of inquisitorial activity by transferring friars who could provide evidence regarding solicitation. When Isabel de Tena's regular confessor, Fray Francisco de las Llagas was transferred out of the Franciscan house in Hinojosa, she began going to Martín Colero, another Franciscan who lived in the same house. When she told her new confessor that Francisco de las Llagas had made sexual overtures to her during confession, however, he declared that he would have to consult with his superior, warden Fray Pedro de las Missas, in order to find out if he could absolve her. When de las Missas heard about the situation, he became extremely alarmed and asked Isabel de Tena to come to the convent, where he interviewed her, told her that what had happened to her in the confessional was of no significance, and warned her not to say anything to anyone about it. A few days later, de las Missas went a step further and ordered Colero transferred to the Franciscan house in Puebla de Alcocer in order, as Colero explained to Isabel, "to prevent me from testifying about a certain matter that I discussed with the warden."[103]

Nevertheless, in spite of sporadic opposition from certain officials, the Inquisition was able to assert its jurisdiction effectively over the regular clergy. For one thing, after 1592, and certainly after 1622, the orders had no legal standing to prevent the Inquisition from investigating and punishing solicitation among their members. Apart from that, the Inquisition was quite sedulous in protecting its exclusivity by punishing or humiliating those officials who sought to obstruct its operations. Fray Pedro de las Missas paid for his temerity by being arrested and held for interrogation before the Toledo tribunal, while Fray Francisco de las Llagas, the friar whom he had tried to protect, was brought to trial and convicted despite his efforts.

But the thing that really placed limits on the effectiveness of obstructionism among the regulars was the attitude of both penitents and other monks. Penitents were always being exposed to the Edict of Faith, in which solicitation was described as a form of heresy, and they were told to denounce any priest, whether secular or regular, who was guilty of the offense. As a result, penitents were justifiably skeptical when any priest, even the superior of a convent, told them that sexually explicit behavior or smutty and suggestive language in the confessional were of no importance. Penitents like Isabel de Tena were also concerned about the validity of their confessions and the absolution that they received. This anxiety and insecurity drove them from confessor to confessor, and eventually they came across one who would refuse to absolve them unless they went to the Holy Office. Besides, as we have already seen, friars like Francisco de San Juan Bautista were zealous for the faith and eager to help the Inquisition, even at great risk to themselves. In the other instance, the decision to transfer Martín Colero undid the whole effort to prevent the Inquisition from prosecuting Francisco de las Llagas because with Colero gone, Isabel de Tena needed a new confessor, and it was this third confessor, Fray Juan de Savedra, another member of the Franciscan order living in the same convent, who refused to absolve her and sent her to the Holy Office instead.[104]

Making use of the greatly expanded powers granted to it in the bull of 1622 and able to count on the loyalty or acquiescence of most of the clergy, the Spanish Inquisition was ready to unleash a wave of persecution against soliciting confessors that would increase in intensity throughout the end of the seventeenth century and well into the eighteenth. But in bringing charges against members of the clergy for this offense, the Holy Office was going to have to confront some unique problems that would require novel solutions and challenge the evidentiary procedures commonly used by the entire Spanish criminal court system.

Chapter 4

Trial and Punishment

The trials of soliciting confessors, unlike the more serious offenses that came under the jurisdiction of the Holy Office in which partial proofs were acceptable, required a minimum of two eyewitnesses. Of course, the very nature of confession made it impossible for these witnesses to testify to the same occurrence, but under inquisition law it was perfectly acceptable if they testified to two distinct occurrences of the same offense. This rule was strictly observed by the Suprema in spite of the eagerness of certain overzealous prosecutors and provincial inquisitors who frequently urged arrests based on the testimony of a single witness of exceptional character. In May 1696, the Mallorca tribunal received an interesting deposition from Father Jorge Fortuny, a Jesuit who had recently administered the viaticum to a young married woman in her home. Gravely ill and on the point of death, the woman, twenty-nine-year-old Juana Anna Barbassa y Montagut, told Fortuny about her seven-year relationship with Sebastian Rigo, a Trinitarian who had formerly been her confessor. Since this relationship had included numerous instances of solicitation, it was obviously a matter for the Inquisition, and Father Fortuny refused to absolve the woman unless she made a deposition and allowed him to bring it to the tribunal. Experienced inquisitors and prosecuting attorneys were always happy to receive this kind of evidence because they knew that deathbed confessions were unusually reliable. Within ten days, the tribunal had Barbassa y Montagut interviewed, and armed with her detailed confession, prosecuting attorney Sebastian Ferragut wrote the Suprema requesting that Rigo be arrested and placed in the secret prison to await trial. The Suprema, however, refused this request, pointing out that the case could not commence without another witness.[1]

Rigid adherence to the two witness rule imposed a serious limitation on the effectiveness of the Holy Office in dealing with solicitation. Sufficient evidence for a trial would simply fail to accumulate against many individuals, who either had mended their ways or had victimized penitents who, for one reason or another, were reluctant to testify against them. In fact, Barbassa y Montagut was one of these, having assured Sebastian Rigo before he left Las Palmas that she would never betray him. At the very least, the rule meant that a long period could elapse between the time when a tribunal received its first piece of evidence against a confessor and the time of his arrest. In fact, it took the Spanish Inquisition an average of thirty-one and one-half months to actually bring an offender to trial after having received an initial denunciation, with the longest interval being the case of Salvador Quijada de Castillo, in 1732, where the delay reached twenty-nine years and two months.[2] Since it took the Suprema a full three years to even ratify the sentence, the cause of the delay in this case seems to have been the administrative lassitude that affected the Holy Office during certain periods.

The difficulty of obtaining the requisite number of witnesses, however, was still a major cause of delay in many cases. Evidence was first presented against the Mercedarian Fray Pedro Esteban in August 1606 when Juana Carriona asked her confessor to arrange an interview with a commissioner to tell him about an incident that had occurred two years before. But the Mallorca tribunal had to wait nineteen years, until April 5, 1625, before it got the crucial second witness and could proceed to arrest and prosecute Esteban.[3]

Frequently, even the arrival of a second witness was insufficient, either because that individual refused to cooperate with the Holy Office or because the testimony itself was inconclusive and, therefore, insufficient for an arrest. In the case of Dr. Jorge Rosselló, a benefice holder in the cathedral of Las Palmas, the Mallorca tribunal received its first solid piece of evidence in 1669 after Antonia March y Cifre, a forty-eight-year-old widow, came to the commissioner of Pollanca to testify about several instances of solicitation that had taken place one and one-half years earlier, when she had been staying in her brother's house in Las Palmas. Acting on this information, the tribunal ordered Rosselló to remain in Las Palmas, although he was permitted to serve his benefice as before.

On February 28, 1670, Rosselló came before the tribunal and stated that Feliciana Gari y Peris had invited him to visit her at home during her confession with him. Evidently suspicious of Rosselló's motives for coming before the tribunal, the inquisitors summoned Gari y Peris and questioned her very closely about her relationship with Rosselló, hoping to turn up evidence of actual solicitation. Gari y Peris, however, strenuously denied that she had ever made any suggestive remarks to Rosselló in the confessional and would not be budged even when Inquisitor Nicolás Fermosino solemnly warned her against obstructing the work of the Holy Office. The next act in this drama occurred in October 1672, when the tribunal received a second deposition against Rosselló. Unfortunately, the testimony of this second witness, which should have clinched the case, turned out to be inconclusive. According to this witness, Rosselló had asked her where she lived just after absolving her, but when he actually came to her house, he was unable to make advances because a number of her friends were present. Although he returned several days later and attempted to touch her breasts, this was so remote in time from the actual confession that it did not constitute solicitation according to the operational definition of the offense. It was not until February 1681 that the tribunal finally received the clear and unequivocal evidence that it needed to arrest Rosselló. On February 6, Francisca Marqués y Campins, the thirty-five-year-old widow of a weaver, testified that Rosselló had used indecent language while hearing her confession and had then gone to her house and attempted to have sexual relations. The tribunal arrested Rosselló and a few weeks later, on February 25, received even more conclusive evidence against him when Isabel Forteza, a slave, heard about his arrest and came to testify about her relationship with him on the advice of her confessor.[4]

Administrative lassitude, overcrowding of prison facilities, or the sheer poverty of certain tribunals could impose enormous delays in carrying out arrests, even after the requisite number of witnesses had been accumulated. The Canaries tribunal, which was one of the poorest and least active, took an almost unheard-of six years to carry out the arrest of Fray Gaspar de Palenzuela. It had the testimony of three valid witnesses as early as October 1700, but somehow only got around to voting for his arrest on July 12, 1703, repeated that vote on July 7, 1704, received the Suprema's permission to take action on September 8, 1705, but did not actually carry out the arrest until January 11, 1706.[5]

Unless witnesses presented themselves at the door of the tribunal to give their testimony, evidence usually arrived indirectly by way of a deposition brought by a confessor with the permission of his penitent, or was sent by a commissioner or notary, or forwarded by a familiar. When this occurred, the tribunal insisted on taking a direct statement from the witness, which might explore more fully matters that were perhaps only touched on in her deposition. For this, a variety of methods were employed, ranging from sending out a secretary from the tribunal to appointing a local priest, sometimes the very confessor who had sent the evidence in the first place, as special commissioner in places where the Holy Office did not have a representative.[6]

When the case was about to be brought to trial, all the witnesses' testimony was "ratified," confirmed by having it read to them by an official representative of the Holy Office in the presence of witnesses. In general, these ratifications provided few surprises, as witnesses either confirmed what they had said earlier or made minor modifications or additions. In a few cases, however, where witnesses revoked or denied making earlier statements, ratification could seriously undermine the case against an individual. When special commissioner Fray Juan Lezur visited María Jorge on January 19, 1692, to ratify testimony against Mateo Fernández Vello that she had first given in 1688, he stumbled into one of the most curious and tragic examples of the way in which family and social pressure could combine to destroy the credibility of a witness before the Holy Office. The first blow came when María

Jorge stoutly denied that she had ever made the statement attributed to her and confirmed that she was the only person in the village of Sauzel, where Vello acted as curate, who was named María Jorge.[7] The mystery was solved less than two months later when another young woman, María de la Encarnación, testified before a Holy Office commissioner that she was the original witness against Vello, but had simply assumed María Jorge's name in order to avoid complications with the Vello family. Two days later, on March 13, 1692, María de la Encarnación revoked her testimony, declaring it to have been a complete fabrication. For this she was arrested by the tribunal along with several others accused of perjury against Vello. But on February 10, 1693, she changed her testimony once again, declaring that her earlier deposition under the name of María Jorge had been the truth.

Evidently, María de la Encarnación had gotten herself into one of those complicated and difficult situations that could so easily arise in the narrow confines of village life, where family honor was held hostage to the sexual behavior of unmarried women while the choice of marriage partners was sharply limited. Several years earlier, María had had an illegitimate child by Vello's brother Miguel Fernández. Since the Vello family was one of the most important in the village and María's parents were modest labradores (peasants), Miguel Fernández refused to marry her, and she took him to court on a charge of breach of promise. In spite of his shabby treatment, she still hoped to marry him with or without a court order, so that after her present confessor Gaspar Pérez ordered her to make a deposition to the Holy Office regarding several attempts by Vello to solicit her in the confessional, she had decided to conceal her name when testifying against his brother. She had been forced to revoke her testimony when Miguel Fernández came to her house late on the night of March 10, 1692, and threatened to kill her and her parents. By this point, however, the tribunal, faced with these multiple contradictions and weighing defense evidence that María de la Encarnación had sworn revenge against Vello because he had opposed her marriage with his brother, decided to submit the case to the Suprema, which ordered it suspended on April 2, 1693.[8]

After sufficient evidence had been accumulated, the tribunal would sometimes convene a group of canonists, usually well-reputed members of the religious orders, to review it in order to make sure that it fell within the definition of the offense.[9] With the approval of the calificadores, or when there was little doubt about the evidence, the prosecuting attorney would formally arraign the accused before the inquisitors, bring information against him to their attention, and demand his arrest.[10] If the inquisitors agreed, a formal indictment would be drawn up. Since a cleric was involved, the tribunal would ask the Suprema for permission to arrest the suspect. After reviewing the evidence, the Suprema would either reject the request and order the case to be suspended or allow the tribunal to carry out the arrest. The tribunal would then draw up an arrest order, which also included a provision for the sequestration of the property of the accused.

We can trace the process by which a suspect was arrested and brought to the tribunal by following the case of Felipe de Medrano, a Jesuit who was tried by the Toledo tribunal in 1694. After receiving a letter from its commissioner in Alcalá de Henares stating that Medrano could be found in the Jesuit college there, the tribunal dispatched an arrest order to the commissioner, telling him to detain the suspect with the "greatest possible discretion." For his trip to prison, Medrano was to be allowed to take a bed on which to sleep as well as a supply of personal clothing and bedding. The remainder of his property was to be sequestered pending the outcome of his trial. He was also to be given fifty ducats by his superior in order to defray the cost of feeding him on the trip and later during his incarceration.[11]

At ten in the morning of August 23, commissioner Andrés Lorente, accompanied by a familiar who acted as notary, came to the Jesuit college of Alcalá to arrest Medrano. Encountering him as he returned from a walk with one of the college officials, the two men told him that they had something confidential to discuss with him and asked to be taken to his room. Once there they told him that they had come to arrest him by order of the inquisitors of Toledo. Shocked, but probably expecting something of the kind, Medrano submitted to the authority of the Holy Office with "the greatest humility" and declared that he now considered himself under arrest. The commissioner then drew up an inventory of Medrano's possessions for sequestration. Following his orders to maintain the utmost secrecy in the transportation of the prisoner, the commissioner entrusted him to a local familiar, who was instructed to leave for Toledo at nightfall. Finally, late the following evening, Medrano arrived at the tribunal and was turned over to the alcalde of the secret prison, who recorded in his admission book a minute description of the accused, along with the personal property he brought with him.[12]

Strenuous efforts to spare accused members of the clergy the shame of public exposure during their journey to the seat of the tribunal notwithstanding, trips from outlying villages in the sprawling inquisitorial jurisdictions inevitably required passing from one familiar to the next and could prove acutely embarrassing to the accused. The Toledo district, with its 47,770 square kilometers, occupying fully half of New Castile, was one of the largest. So when Fray Juan Girón, the warden of the Franciscan convent of Tamajón in the foothills of the Guadarrama was arrested by the commissioner of Torija, he faced several days of hard traveling and being transferred from one inquisitorial official to another before he could hope to arrive at the tribunal.[13] Obviously this long journey with its nights of lodging in the homes of familiares in several places could not be concealed, and this weighed on Girón's mind as he was turned over to the familiar of Casa de Uceda, who had journeyed up to Tamajón especially to receive him. After lodging overnight in Casa de Uceda, Girón continued his journey to Alcalá de Henares, where he was handed over to the familiar of Torres de Alameda. On his arrival, however, Girón fell ill and was forced to break his journey and remain at the familiar's house until he could walk. On September 8 he felt considerably

better, and the familiar told him that the following morning they would continue their journey to Toledo. That night something snapped in the mind of
Juan Girón. Tempted by the devil, as he later told the tribunal, and greatly
chagrined at the prospect of renewing his shameful journey in the company
of a familiar, he decided to escape. Clad only in a nightshirt and carrying his
breviary, he left the familiar's house after midnight and made his way first to
Alcalá, where he spent the night freezing in a grove of trees just outside the
city, and then to Madrid, where he got word to the provincial of his order to
send him a habit and other clothing so that he could pay him a visit. Throwing himself at the feet of his superior, Girón told him his story, punctuating
it with bursts of uncontrollable weeping, and then asked to be given an escort
to take him to Toledo. The provincial quickly agreed, and on September 13,
1676, six days after his escape from custody, Girón presented himself at the
door of the Toledo tribunal. Far from attempting to rebel against the jurisdiction of the Holy Office, Girón simply fled from the awful prospect of being
conducted as a criminal through towns and villages, wearing the habit of his
beloved Franciscan order. As his superior, provincial Fray Nicolás Lozano
explained in the letter he gave Girón to take with him to the tribunal, when
he left the familiar's house he was "almost out of his mind" and only came to
Madrid "to seek solace" from a person he obviously thought would be sym-
pathetic to his plight.[14] From Girón's subsequent conduct, his request to be
taken to the tribunal by a friar from his order (which would make anyone who
saw him pass think that he was on a perfectly ordinary journey), his obvious
aversion to being seen in the company of a familiar and his professed willingness to accept whatever punishment the tribunal sought to impose, there
seems little reason to doubt his claim that he was motivated solely by a desire
to "avoid the dishonor" of passing through populated areas as a prisoner. The
odyssey of this unfortunate individual illustrates very graphically the hold that
the Inquisition exercised over the minds of the Spanish clergy. Girón had
exploited a weak link in the chain of inquisitorial control and had gotten clean
away. He was even able to take refuge in the home of a peasant family during
his journey, but instead of continuing his flight, he turned himself in, happy
to have at least avoided the shame and disgrace of being publicly conducted
to the tribunal by a familiar.[15]

The absolute and complete obedience owed to the Inquisition, which was
seen by most Spaniards as the "impregnable stronghold of the Catholic faith,"
makes Girón's conduct comprehensible and allows us to accept an even more
curious phenomenon—the priests who, after having been notified of their
arrest by an official of the Holy Office, arrived at the seat of the tribunal
entirely on their own. On May 14, 1605, for example, the Canaries tribunal
had Fray Juan Felipe Cabeza brought up from his cell in the secret prison.
Fifteen days earlier, Cabeza had been informed of his arrest in the island of
Tenerife, where he resided in the Franciscan convent. In response to the
arrest order, Cabeza took the first available boat to Gran Canaria and then
presented himself at the tribunal for incarceration, all without escort of any
kind.[16] In another instance from the same tribunal, an order signed by a sec-

retary was dispatched to the convent of San Miguel de la Palma on the island of Garachico to notify the prior that he was responsible for seeing to it that Fray José de Acuña took the first available boat to Gran Canaria. On December 4, 1746, Acuña arrived at the tribunal unescorted and carrying the order, which he presented to the tribunal. He was promptly arrested and placed under detention in the local Dominican house, where he was told to remain in his cell except when he was summoned to appear before the Holy Office.[17]

Of course, some individuals were able to delay or even prevent arrest by making spontaneous confessions. If these confessions were made before any outside testimony was received, they were accepted as genuine and the individual was dealt with leniently. Fray Juan Llobera, a Mercedarian who had been warden of his convent in Palma de Mallorca on several occasions and had also represented the ecclesiastical estate at the Cortes of Catalonia, benefited from this leniency when he came to the Mallorca tribunal on April 18, 1689, to confess two instances of solicitation that had occurred some nineteen years earlier. Even though Llobera had probably been inspired to come in because three monks from his convent had recently been arrested on charges of solicitation, there was no evidence against him in the files of the tribunal and no suggestion that he knew that anyone planned to denounce him. Consequently, the prosecuting attorney Hidalgo asked that he be admonished, but released on the grounds that he had come forward solely because of the "prick of conscience and not out of fear that he was about to be denounced."[18]

On the other hand, most spontaneous confessions had little bearing on the way the accused was treated because the inquisitors had good reason to believe that they were motivated either by the knowledge that a complaint had already been lodged with the Holy Office or by a well-founded fear of denunciation in the near future. When Fray Bernardo del Castillo came to the Holy Office on May 26, 1698, the tribunal had already received three depositions against him. Under the circumstances his "spontaneous confession" meant little, especially as it failed to address any of the matters dealt with by the witnesses. Just five days later, the tribunal wrote the Suprema asking permission to arrest Castillo; this was granted on June 5, 1698.[19]

In 1787, when the Canaries tribunal received a spontaneous confession from Fray Nicolás Cabrera, it reacted with considerable suspicion. Not only did Cabrera already have three witnesses against him, but the present archbishop had publicly told the confessors of his diocese to urge penitents who had been the victims of solicitation and who intended to denounce it to the Holy Office to inform the priest who had solicited them so that he could confess "spontaneously" before evidence against him was received. Such confessions were bound to be insincere and motivated by a desire to benefit from the advantages of coming forward and confessing before being arrested by the Holy Office.[20]

All efforts at delay having failed and with the accused brought to the seat of the tribunal, he was usually placed in the secret prison that was meant to hold prisoners during their trials. Henry Charles Lea's famous dictum that "the secret prisons of the Inquisition were less intolerable places of abode than the episcopal and public gaols" can no longer be entirely accepted in the light of current research.[21] Some tribunals, especially the wealthier ones, had well-maintained prisons where the inmates enjoyed relative comfort. There are even instances like that of the priest confined to an episcopal prison in 1675 who made heretical statements so that he would be transferred to the prisons of the Holy Office.[22] On the other hand, the poorer tribunals never had enough money to keep their cells in proper repair, and prisoners' living conditions were frequently abominable. In 1672, for example, the inquisitors of the Mallorca tribunal described their secret prison as being almost uninhabitable, with the cells damp most of the time and the prisoners suffering unbearably.[23]

Conditions seemed to have changed little 116 years later when on April 5, 1788, Fray Nicolás Cabrera asked for an audience with the inquisitors. Cabrera, who had already been in prison for almost two months, complained of severe chest pains, chills, and a general feeling of exhaustion exacerbated by the extreme dampness of his cell caused by rain pouring through the holes in the roof of the building. After calling the tribunal physician to examine the prisoner, the inquisitors agreed with his request that he be returned to his convent in order to recuperate.[24]

In the Canaries tribunal, the ruinous condition of the prison itself was compounded by its lack of privacy. Prisoners were exposed to the public gaze from the flat roofs of houses surrounding the compound, so that the desired confidentiality in solicitation cases could not be guaranteed. Moreover, since the prison jailer's own house had fallen into ruins, he and his family were forced to live in the familiares' prison and, therefore, could not attend the needs of his prisoners. Even though the tribunal had written the Suprema about this disastrous situation eight times since May 1740, nothing had been done about it, so the tribunal was forced to place clerical prisoners in nearby convents.[25]

Apart from a lack of investment income, what plagued the Canaries tribunal, along with the rest of the Spanish Inquisition, was the cost of taking care of poor prisoners. In spite of the fact that some solicitantes did arrive with a certain amount of cash to be used to defray the cost of feeding them while they were in the secret prison, many were almost penniless, and if their home community could not contribute anything, the Holy Office was responsible for them. The account of Fray Pedro Barbero de Torres, who entered the secret prison of Toledo on September 19, 1690, and left on February 10, 1691, is fairly typical. The total cost of his stay came to 466 reales, of which he was able to contribute only 77, leaving the tribunal to pick up the remainder.[26] As the Canaries tribunal told the Suprema when it complained about the ruinous state of its secret prison, even those relatively small amounts were difficult to count on. The Inquisition regularly demanded a sum, usually between thirty and fifty ducats from the home convent of a regular accused of solicitation, but in the depressed economic conditions of the seventeenth century, some communities found it impossible to pay even these modest sums. When familiar Ginés de Prado was sent by the Toledo tribunal to collect thirty ducats from the Mercedarian convent of Ciudad Real in 1699, he found an impoverished community, which frequently "lacked bread" and had not served a drop of wine to its friars for three months. Appalled at the conditions, but determined to do his duty, he tried to find a ceremonial chalice or other valuable item to seize in compensation, but could find nothing. Prado found a way out of this embarrassing situation when he unexpectedly met his uncle, who promised to transfer the funds to the tribunal out of his own savings.[27]

Whatever the condition of the secret prison, however, merely entering it was bound to trigger off a deep psychological crisis. Inquisitorial prisons, after all, had been designed for heretics and enemies of the Catholic faith, so that any cleric, even if he was aware that his offense had little to do with heresy, could experience strong feelings of shame and self-hatred. Such feelings explain the attitude of Gabriel Canevas, who refused medical assistance, even though he had become seriously ill after several weeks in the infamous prison of the Mallorca tribunal, "because he was so ashamed at being imprisoned there that he did not want to be seen by anyone unless he was in great danger."[28]

With the accused's incarceration and his first audience before the tribunal, which normally came one or two days later, the trial phase began. Trials of accused solicitantes could be quite dilatory, with the longest, especially those where extensive interviewing of defense witnesses was required, taking as long as three years and five months. The average trial lasted around seven and one-half months, while 12 percent took longer than one year. A small percentage, usually trials where the accused confessed fully at an early audience or refused to offer any defense, lasted less than one month. Some prisoners complained bitterly about their long confinement and begged the inquisitors to conclude their case. In 1731, for example, Salvador Quijada y Castillo petitioned the Canaries tribunal for a speedy decision, reminding the inquisitors that he had already been imprisoned almost five months. During this period of useless incarceration, he pointed out sharply, the souls in purgatory were perishing without the benefit of the 144 masses that he would have said for them had he been free.[29]

During the first audience, which was one of the most important events of the entire proceeding, the accused gave his genealogy, with the names, ethnic origins, and sometimes the occupations of his parents, grandparents, uncles, cousins, and so forth. He also had to give the details of his education, demonstrate his level of religious culture, and furnish an extensive biography, including place and date of birth, age at which he first entered religious life, places he had been resident, and offices or benefices held up to the time of his arrest by the Holy Office. This interrogation not only gave the inquisitors a more detailed picture of the accused, but provided valuable insights into his activities and places of residence during the period when alleged instances of solicitation were supposed to have occurred.[30]

After the first audience and before the formal accusation, the accused was called before the tribunal for three more audiences and asked if he had anything to confess to the Holy Office. During this period, the trial generally moved forward quickly, with each of the audiences being held within one or two days of one another. Confession at this early stage of the proceedings might be of some help to the prisoner, but if it was incomplete and failed to include the names of witnesses from whom the tribunal had depositions, it did him little good. On the other hand, information supplied by the accused during these audiences could provide the tribunal with additional potential witnesses whom it could interview.

With the three audiences completed, the prosecuting attorney presented his formal accusation before the tribunal with the prisoner in attendance. This accusation normally incorporated any and all evidence, even hearsay evidence, that could be alleged against the prisoner, despite the fact that such material could not be used to convict. The prosecuting attorney would conclude with a general statement declaring that the prisoner, who was already guilty of a series of heinous crimes, was probably guilty of others as well, and he reserved the right to present other evidence in case it became necessary. In fact, the tribunal continued to interview potential prosecution witnesses throughout the trial, and their testimony could form the basis for a second accusation.

During the sixteenth and seventeenth centuries, the accusations tended to be extremely vague as to the time and circumstances of the alleged offense. The accusation that was drawn up against Fray Pedro Fiol by the Mallorca tribunal in 1619 spoke merely of an incident that had occurred in the confessional "several years ago" in "a certain place" in his convent.[31] During the eighteenth century, however, as the Inquisition faced a less favorable political climate and encountered a growing chorus of criticism from home and abroad about its procedures, it responded by modifying the accusation to make it far more specific as to date, time, and place. In 1722, before the very same tribunal, the accusation against Fray Jaime Massenet stated the year that the first offense had occurred and named the exact chapel in which it had taken place.[32]

The accused was forced to respond immediately to the accusation point by point. His lack of prior preparation might cause him to blurt out certain details that could aid the prosecution case or provide the Holy Office with additional witnesses against him. In spite of the tribunal's strenuous efforts to conceal the names of witnesses, the accusation necessarily provided certain details that might allow the accused to make an educated guess. In his reply to the accusation levied against him by the Canaries tribunal in 1686, for example, Fray Diego Sánchez de Cubas correctly identified both of the witnesses against him and denounced them as his mortal enemies.[33] The greater specificity of the charges against the accused in the eighteenth century, moreover, gave certain individuals an opening to throw doubt on the veracity of the prosecution case. Replying to the accusation against him before the Canaries tribunal in 1731, Salvador del Castillo pointed out that the first witness had allowed twenty-four years to elapse between the alleged incident of solicitation and her complaint to the Holy Office. Such a long delay, during which she would have had to ignore the demands of her confessors, repeated readings of the Edict of Faith, as well as numerous missions, appeared highly suspicious and might indicate that she had denounced him for reasons having nothing to do with any alleged act of solicitation.[34]

After the accusation, the accused was permitted to select a defense attorney. Choice was generally limited to the two or three local attorneys who were accredited to practice before the Inquisition.[35] These men had to be Old Christians and had been obliged to demonstrate that by submitting to a formal genealogical investigation. They were also officials of the court, with an obligation to promote its ultimate goal of obtaining the prisoner's confession, which by itself would constitute the most definitive of all proofs.[36] Consistent with their instructions, therefore, they would admonish the prisoner to tell the truth without concealing anything and without accusing himself of anything he had not done.[37] Furnished with a copy of the accusation, the defense attorney would then draw up a formal response, underscoring the matters of law that would make a sentence of absolution mandatory for his client. This document was usually brief and stereotyped. It generally did not reflect the attorney's opinion about the case against his client because the accusation revealed little about the evidence against him. Occasionally, however an accused might express dissatisfaction with his defense attorney even at this early stage of their relationship. In 1707, for example, Fray Juan de San Jacinto insisted on presenting his own defense statements, much to the dismay of the Toledo inquisitors, who warned him that so far he had said nothing that would even slightly mitigate the evidence against him and pleaded with him to use the services of the court-appointed defense attorney. For its part, the Suprema reluctantly agreed to his request for additional sheets of paper to present yet another statement, but showed its irritation with him by increasing the severity of his final sentence.[38]

At this point, the first phase of the trial may be said to have concluded. The accused had been detained by the Holy Office, had been urged repeatedly to confess, and had been finally presented with a formal accusation. The two sides ratified their previous actions and requested the disclosure of evidence for both the prosecution and defense. The prosecution proceeded to verify the testimony of its witnesses before a commissioner or other authorized individual in preparation for the formal presentation of their testimony during the second phase. The second part of the trial normally took considerably longer than the first half, especially if large numbers of defense witnesses had to be interviewed far from the seat of the tribunal. The first phase of the trial of Diego Sánchez de Cubas before the Canaries tribunal, from the day when he was admitted to the secret prison to the response to the formal accusation, took only twenty-four days. The second phase, from the publication of witnesses to the sentence handed down by the tribunal, lasted six months twenty-four days, largely as a result of extensive interviewing of defense witnesses in several locations.[39]

Phase two of the trial began with the "publishing" or disclosure of the testimony of prosecution witnesses. A detailed version of this testimony, omitting any material that would reveal the names of witnesses, was read out to the prisoner, who was again expected to respond to it immediately. The defense attorney was then given a copy of this document in order to allow him to formulate a detailed defense statement. He also had in his possession notes furnished to him by the accused regarding his reply to the points raised by the prosecution witnesses. It was at this juncture, with the outlines of the prosecution's case revealed and his client's response before him, that the defense attorney made a decision about whether it would be useful to his client to pursue the defense to the point of issuing a formal reply to the publication and actually calling defense witnesses. After evaluating this evidence, some defense attorneys simply washed their hands of the case and refused to offer any defense. Dr. Rafael Calafat, who was acting as defense attorney for Fray Jayme Barcelo in a case tried before the Mallorca tribunal in 1689, reviewed the text of the publication and his client's notes and simply informed him that his comments had no bearing on the evidence and that, therefore, he really had no defense. After his defense attorney reminded Barcelo that he had admonished him repeatedly to tell the truth, Barcelo agreed to accept the defense part of the case as concluded and threw himself on the mercy of the court.[40] Sometimes defense attorneys would even seek to help their clients by presenting a brief statement acknowledging that their client's guilt had been proven conclusively and asking the court to use him mercifully.[41]

Jayme Barcelo's experience with Dr. Calafat indicates the conditional nature of the role of the defense attorney in inquisitorial proceedings. In practice, while the accused was entitled to a defense attorney, he was not unconditionally entitled to present a defense. As an employee of the court, the defense attorney was almost duty bound to take a skeptical view of his client since even being summoned before the Inquisition was considered semiguilt. If the defense attorney, for whatever reason, refused to offer a defense, there was no way that the accused, who was frequently impecunious and whose property had been sequestered, could hire another one even if the Holy Office were willing to admit him. Moreover, an accused who was obdurate, who insisted on offering a defense even after his attorney had advised him against doing so, might incur the wrath of the inquisitors or even the Suprema itself. After the publication of witnesses in the case of the Augustinian Fray Juan Alcocer, his defense attorney Dr. Pedro Juan Canet informed him that "since he was already convicted by the testimony of two witnesses, he should stop telling fairy tales and admit the truth." When Alcocer persisted in his denials, Canet was reluctantly persuaded to draw up a defense statement replying to the publication of witnesses, but then refused to present it, grumbling that Alcocer "was already convicted and should give up his fantasies." Alcocer persisted and the defense statement was made a part of the record. But his lack of cooperation appeared to have angered the Suprema, which insisted on sentencing him to permanent deprivation of the right to hear confessions of both men and women instead of the temporary deprivation voted by the tribunal.[42]

It would be wrong, however, to assume from the above discussion that defense attorneys always took a negative view of the accused or that they were unwilling or incapable of carrying on an effective defense. Evaluating the evidence against the accused after the publication of witnesses was a genuine process and the same defense attorney who had declared one case hopeless could mount a stubborn defense if he felt the prosecution case was weak.

After reviewing the case against the Franciscan Fray Francisco Pons and finding that the prosecution had the testimony of seven strong eyewitnesses, Dr. Joaquín Foil, who was acting as defense attorney, advised his client that he had no recourse but to throw himself on the mercy of the court.[43] Several years later, when Dr. Foil found himself defending Fray Juan Llobera, he correctly perceived the prosecution case as weak and therefore was able to mount a strong defense. The prosecution did have the evidence of two witnesses, but the first one was of marginal value because, although the incident that she referred to in her testimony occurred in the place normally destined for confession, she had never confessed with him and had actually come to his convent to ask him in his capacity as warden to discipline her husband's nephew, who was a friar in the same house. The testimony of the second witness concerned incidents that may or may not have occurred in the place normally destined for confession, and Dr. Foil was quick to point out the witnesses' uncertainty about this point in his defense statement. Foil also struggled to save his client's status as a cooperative defendant, since he had made a spontaneous confession before any evidence against him had accumulated. Even though Llobera's spontaneous confession was incomplete, Foil stressed the fact that the tribunal had no indication that he feared denunciation before he made it and that he had voluntarily refrained from hearing confessions from women afterward. Evidently convinced by Foil's arguments, the tribunal only sentenced Llobera to be absolved de levi before the officials of the court instead of the usual audience, which included local curates and representatives of the religious orders, and simply asked him to continue to abstain from hearing women's confessions.[44]

In evaluating the defense, several themes designed to excuse or explain the conduct of the accused emerge, whether presented at the time of the publication of witnesses or by the defense attorney in a formal statement afterward. For one thing, confessors contended that it was precisely their zeal for the sacrament that got them into trouble. Arguing on behalf of Fray Miguel Miguel, who was accused of making smutty remarks to one of his penitents during confession, Dr. José Bassa acknowledged that Gregory XV's 1622 bull had incorporated such language into the definition of solicitation, but excused his client by saying that sometimes such language was "indispensable in order to understand the aggravating circumstances that could increase the perversity or change the nature of sins." While gentler language might be sufficient for a penitent who came from the middle or upper classes, questions addressed to someone who was crude and uncultivated had to be asked using "language appropriate to their estate."[45]

A variation on this theme was used by Dr. Joaquín Foil in order to explain sexually suggestive questioning by confessors. In the case of Fray Jaime Massanet, who was accused of asking a penitent if she had ever had an affair with a friar and trying to find out if she ever had lascivious thoughts, Foil argued that, far from indicating any evil intention on the part of Massanet, these questions were consistent with a confessor's duty to "delve into the consciences of his penitents." Claiming that Massanet was reputed to be a highly scrupulous confessor, Foil dismissed the witness's allegations as a "deliberate distortion undertaken for her own sinister purposes."[46]

Fray Francisco Pons sought to defend himself from allegations that he had asked suggestive questions during confession by stressing the responsibility of the confessor to ensure that the penitent made a full and complete confession, especially of sexual sins.[47] Although this was one of the most common requirements laid on confessors in such popular manuals as Jean Gerson's *On the Art of Hearing Confessions*, Gerson and most other authorities always cautioned the confessor not to be offensive and particularly to avoid inciting temptation.[48] It is highly doubtful that Gerson would have approved of Francisco Pons asking one of his female penitents if she was ever tempted by another man while her husband, a seaman, was away on a long trip or whether she ever masturbated when she thought about men. Certainly he failed to convince his defense attorney, who refused to defend him, or the Mallorca tribunal, which sentenced him to the maximum penalties for this offense.

Another defense typically made by those accused of touching penitents during confession was that they could not avoid doing so in the course of carrying out their duties. One of the more unusual instances of this defense was put forward by Dr. Joaquín Foil on behalf of Fray Jaime Massanet. One of the charges against Massanet was that he had put his finger through an opening in the screen that separated him from his penitent and touched her lips and face. Foil claimed, incredibly, that Massanet had only grabbed on to the hole in the screen to save himself from falling in the confessional, which was old and shaky, so that he had touched her face by accident.[49] Fray Francisco Pons, in his response to the publication of witnesses, replied to charges that he had rubbed his face against the cheeks of several penitents by claiming that he did this only to hear them better since the church was so crowded and noisy.[50]

After the publication of witnesses and the defense attorney's written reply, the defense was given the opportunity to draw up a list of defense witnesses and a series of questions that would be put to them by an official of the tribunal wherever they happened to be living. This questionnaire would typically have two objectives: first, to establish the reputation of the accused as an excellent priest and fine confessor who was extremely unlikely to have done what he was accused of, and second, to throw doubt on the prosecution's case by demonstrating that his witnesses were unreliable, either because they were the personal enemies of the accused or because they themselves had a doubtful reputation.

In drawing up his list of potential defense witnesses, the accused was forced to work within the constraints of rules that excluded anyone who might demonstrate undue bias in his favor, such as servants and relatives within the fourth degree.[51] Prosecuting attorneys were on the alert for any attempt to violate these rules, so that when it was discovered that two of the witnesses presented by Fray Gaspar de Nájera in his defense before the Canaries tribunal were relatives, their testimony was disallowed.[52] Fearful of possible criticism from the Suprema, Inquisitor Dr. Juan Eusebio Campomanes even went so far as to have his secretary certify that he had specifically informed Nájera and his attorney of the provisions of the 1561 instructions that governed the kinds of witnesses that could be presented by the defense.[53]

Of course, if the accused failed to identify all of the witnesses against him or was unable to demonstrate that the prosecution witnesses were unreliable, then his defense was unlikely to prosper. Juan de la Olmeda, a Franciscan who acted as vicar of the convent of La Concepción in Oropesa, was only able to identify two of the three nuns who testified against him, thereby leaving key prosecution testimony unchallenged. His efforts to undermine the credibility of prosecution witnesses by claiming that they were habitual liars were also directly contradicted by the commissioner of Oropesa, who had earlier reported that the nuns had an excellent reputation and came from good families, so that their depositions "should be accepted without question."[54] Olmeda's case was also not helped by the fact that he had made partial admissions in several of his audiences before the tribunal and in the defense statement itself. In reply to charges made by Bernarda de San Antonio, who had accused him of soliciting her both during and after confession, he at first admitted to having used suggestive language after confession and then, in his defense statement, made matters worse by claiming that the incident had occurred while they were using the confessional to gossip.[55]

Witnesses called by the defense could also prove to be unreliable, sometimes even giving testimony that directly contradicted defense allegations. The defense questionnaire drawn up for Fray Sebastián de Calçadilla asked witnesses to confirm that María Romera, one of his accusers, was a woman of "low condition and vile character," perfectly capable of lodging false charges against him since she was his mortal enemy. Unfortunately for Calçadilla, a parade of his own defense witnesses contradicted him. Mateo Rodríguez, the local schoolteacher, for example, expressed bewilderment over the defense question that dealt with María Romera's character since he had always known her to be widely regarded as "honest and retiring," while her parents were well-respected hardworking people who were very concerned to preserve their daughter's chastity. He also testified that he had never heard that María or her family were hostile to Calçadilla as alleged by the defense. To make matters worse for the defense, the schoolmaster even testified that he had heard a rumor that Calçadilla had used smutty language while hearing María's confession, thus practically transforming himself into a witness for the prosecution.[56]

Fray Bernardo del Castillo ran into a very similar problem with his defense witnesses when he tried to impugn the character of two women who had testified against him for soliciting them while he was on a mission in Orcajo. According to him, the women were little better than hussies who had denounced him because they were furious with him for admonishing them to change their evil ways. Testimony from three key defense witnesses, however, flatly contradicted defense allegations about the two women. Fray Alonso López, who had accompanied Bernardo del Castillo on his mission to Orcajo, testified that he had heard nothing but praise for the two women in the village, while Fray Miguel Duran, who had spent four months there as acting curate, described the women as "good and virtuous" and said that he had never heard anything to the contrary in all the time that he lived there.[57]

For an accused solicitante to be successful in having himself absolved or his case suspended was no easy task. Ideally, he would have to present a vigorous statement in reply to both the accusation and the publication of witnesses, correctly identify the witnesses against him, and establish a case for considering them as his mortal enemies and therefore unreliable. Examination of defense witnesses would have to strongly corroborate the allegations made in earlier defense statements, as well as demonstrate that the accused had a generally excellent reputation and would be unlikely to have committed the offense.

The case of Antonio de Contreras, a Jesuit from Cuenca, successfully brought together all of these elements. Accused of solicitation for the first time in 1691, the case against him was suspended since there was only one witness and a search of the registers failed to disclose any further evidence.[58]

The second proceeding against Contreras began with a denunciation by Juana de Salcedo, a nun in Cuenca's San Bernardo convent where Contreras served as confessor to many of the nuns, including the prioress. After making the decision to try him in Toledo instead of Cuenca, where there was only one inquisitor, he was arrested and confined in the secret prison. In his replies to the arraignment and the publication of witnesses, Contreras correctly identified Francisca de Cabreros and Juana de Salcedo as the key prosecution witnesses. Both of these women, he claimed, were his mortal and declared enemies. Francisca de Cabreros had threatened him because he had been instrumental in arranging a marriage between his nephew and her sister against the will of the entire family, which had wanted her to go into a convent. As for Juana de Salcedo, Contreras admitted that he had been her confessor for about a year, but claimed that she had made sexual advances toward him and that he had ceased serving as her confessor as a result. Moreover, he claimed that he had been ill during most of 1689 to 1690, exactly the period when he was alleged to have solicited Salcedo on forty-eight separate occasions.

Testimony of defense witnesses called in regard to Francisca de Cabreros was only partially successful in corroborating Contreras's allegations. Of the five witnesses called in Almagro, where the offense was alleged to have taken place, two said that they were unaware of any hostility over the marriage issue, with one pointing out that Contreras had left the village two years before it took place. The other three witnesses confirmed a certain amount of hostility over the marriage, but none had heard of any threats against Contreras.

If the defense testimony against Cabreros was ambiguous at best, testimony against Juana de Salcedo proved highly damaging. Credible witnesses like José

Núñez de Castilblanque, who was knight of the prestigious military order of Alcántara, declared that Salcedo was "unreliable, dangerous, and of easy virtue," while José Fernández, who knew Salcedo quite well, confirmed that she had threatened Contreras and, during a conversation that he had had with her, all but admitted that she had attempted unsuccessfully to seduce him. Dr. José Torralba, a familiar of the Holy Office in Cuenca and its official physician, described Salcedo as a dangerously unstable individual who had once attempted suicide. More importantly, both Torralba and the Cuenca tribunal's official surgeon, Gerónimo Andrés, confirmed that they had treated Contreras for a serious illness during 1689 and 1690 and that at that time he had been so incapacitated, he was unable to leave the confines of his convent. Salcedo's reputation for promiscuity and implacable hostility to Contreras was confirmed by the testimony of José Anezeto, who declared that he had denounced her to the prioress for having kept a man in her cell for a week. On that occasion, Salcedo and another nun who had also testified against Contreras were briefly imprisoned by the prioress. This testimony seemed all the more convincing because the tribunal had previously received three letters confirming the scandalous events in the convent involving the two nuns. With the prosecution's case heavily damaged by the testimony of defense witnesses, the vote on the consulta de fe was inconclusive. The case then went to the Suprema, which voted a second suspension on February 26, 1695.[59]

Of course, given the prosecutorial bias of the Inquisition in general, even the most successful defense might not have any impact on the final verdict. Defense witnesses called by Sebastián Menchero, the lieutenant curate of Daimiel in the Toledo district, succeeded in discrediting the prosecution's chief witness to such a degree that there was a rare split on the consulta de fe.[60] The three inquisitors voted that Menchero should be deprived of the right to hear confessions from women for eight years, while the consultor and the representative of the bishop declared themselves convinced of the overt bias of the second witness and, therefore, voted for suspension. When the case was referred to the Suprema, however, it chose to ignore the fact that even the inquisitors had voted for a lesser penalty than normal in these cases and sentenced Menchero to perpetual deprivation of the right to hear the confessions of both men and women and four years of exile.[61]

After the presentation of defense testimony, the case was ready for the final vote by the consulta de fe, consisting of the inquisitors, the bishop's representative, and several consultores chosen by the tribunal. One of the peculiarities of solicitation cases as opposed to other offenses coming under the jurisdiction of the Holy Office was that lay consultores were barred from sitting on the panel. The reason for this was stated clearly by the anonymous author of the "admonition to a Dominican" of 1667: fear of driving the laity away from the sacrament "if they should come to know of or hear about such evil confessors."[62] A typical consulta de fe, such as the one convened in 1589 to sentence the case of Fray Juan Colomer, consisted of the two inquisitors then serving on the Toledo tribunal; Alonso Serrano, the vicar-general of the archdiocese; and five consultores—Bautista Vélez, Mexía de Gomara, and

Pedro de Carvajal, canons of the cathedral; Dr. Salazar de Mendoza, administrator of the hospital of San Juan Bautista; and Fray Juan de Ovando, the
warden of the convent of San Juan.[63] Later in the history of the Holy Office,
as its political importance waned, consultores were drawn from a less distinguished group of clerics, while in some districts local bishops failed even to
send a representative, merely deputizing an inquisitor to act in his stead.[64]

Since solicitation cases involved clerics, the sentences arrived at by the
consulta de fe were carefully reviewed by the Suprema. In general, the
Suprema would confirm these sentences without change, only opting to alter
them in a little over 20 percent of the cases. Such alterations were almost
twice as likely to be in the direction of greater severity rather than greater
leniency. Sometimes changes were slight, such as the addition of spiritual
exercises to a sentence, but in other cases the Suprema significantly increased
the penalty.[65] In some instances, like that of Fray Diego Sánchez de Cubas,
where the Suprema moved to completely change the sentence passed by the
tribunal, it was indicating that it had no confidence in the deliberations of
the consulta de fe.[66]

Of the 223 cases in my data base, 36 percent were suspended mainly
because of lack of evidence, with suspensions during the eighteenth and early
nineteenth centuries running at a rate more than double that of the seventeenth century. Such a pattern is consistent with an institution in decline, an
institution that was increasingly unwilling to press home investigations at a
time when its very existence was in jeopardy.

Of the remaining cases, 68 percent abjured de levi, in other words, were
deemed to be lightly suspect of heresy. This was a serious but hardly a grave
designation and indicated the tenuous connection between an offense like
solicitation and major crimes like judaizing or Lutheranism, where true heresy was at issue and a threat to Roman Catholicism could be construed. Those
who abjured also were subjected to other disabilities that effectively destroyed
their careers.

Since solicitation was about the gross violation of the spirit and function of
the sacrament of penance, it should come as no surprise that 74 percent of
those convicted were deprived of the right to hear confessions. Even though
only a tiny minority of solicitation cases actually involved male victims, the
overwhelming majority of culprits were deprived of the right to serve as confessors to both sexes, with only a little more than 8 percent losing only the
right to hear the confessions of women.

Deprivation of the right to hear confession was incomparably the most
serious of all the penalties handed down for solicitation. It came closest to
the ideal of a punishment that would "strike such terror into the hearts of
other confessors that they would not dare to commit such a sacrilege," as stated
by the anonymous author of the "admonition to a Jesuit" of 1687.[67]

We can get a good idea of the fate of a friar who suffered this punishment
from a letter written by the inquisitors of the Canaries to the Suprema, begging for clemency for a Franciscan that they had just sentenced. Francisco
García Encinoso was sixty years old when his trial concluded, and the time

he had spent in the secret prison had ruined his health. The tribunal had only stripped him of the power to hear the confessions of women, but permitted him to resume hearing the confessions of men after a four-year suspension. In forwarding the case to the Suprema for review, the tribunal noted that if he were to completely lose his status as a confessor, he would be useless to any community he entered and would be exposed, therefore, to "the hunger, nakedness, and misery" that others from his order had experienced in similar circumstances.[68]

The profound personal humiliation experienced by the cleric who was deprived of the right to hear confessions is clearly indicated by a rather pathetic letter sent to the Toledo tribunal by Luis López de Quiros y Toledo in 1676. Quiros y Toledo, who came from a prominent hidalgo family in Alcázar de San Juan, had continued to live in his mother's house there and even held his benefice in the village, where he was curate of the parish of Santa Guitería. In 1664, with fifteen witnesses against him, he was convicted of solicitation, permanently deprived of the right to hear confessions and exiled from Alcázar de San Juan for ten years. Two years after his return from exile, he wrote reminding the tribunal of its sentence, which he had borne with resignation even though he felt constantly mortified. Now aged fifty-three, he begged for permission to hear confessions on holy days "so that by taking his seat with the other confessors he could begin to restore his reputation."[69]

Most sentences included a combination of penalties. The next most frequent penalty was exile (50 percent), which could range from six months to ten years or more. Normally a sentence of exile prevented the individual from residing in the place or places where the offense had been committed and usually barred him from staying in the city that served as the seat of the tribunal. Castilian tribunals like Toledo would frequently add a prohibition on residence in Madrid, presumably in an effort to collaborate with other royal courts in clearing the capital of undesirables. Exile was frequently accompanied by reclusion (43 percent), which for the secular clergy meant that they had to take up residence in a convent in a particular village or town where there was some official of the Holy Office to keep an eye on them. For the regulars, reclusion meant assignment to a convent of their own order, where they were deprived of voice or vote in community affairs and were to enter the choir and refectory last, except for novices and laymen. In a few particularly serious cases (7.7 percent) they were also required to fast on bread and water one day a week for a certain period, or were assigned spiritual exercises.

For both seculars and regulars, exile and confinement to a convent could prove to be a painful experience. The invidious position of a friar confined for solicitation could expose him to ridicule or abuse from fellow members of the order. In 1699, the Toledo tribunal had to intervene in order to protect the Carmelite Bernardo del Castillo from the prior of the convent to which he had been confined. The prior kept him chained up in his cell and half starved, even after his six-month period of solitary confinement had ended. After receiving information about the situation from its commissioner, the tribunal ordered Castillo set free and eventually transferred him to the Carmelite house in Toledo.[70]

On the other hand, even though he was a financial burden on his hosts, the confined regular was a member of the same order as the other friars and, therefore, had a natural claim on their sympathy. A demonstration of exemplary contrition and an exceptionally holy life on the part of an obviously repentant individual could guarantee good treatment and even intervention on his behalf with the Holy Office by his superiors. In 1591, for example, the newly appointed prior of the convent of San Augustín de Arenas wrote to the Toledo tribunal on behalf of Fray Luis de Valdivieso, who had been confined there after his conviction the year before. Valdivieso's humility and contrition had won over the entire community, so the prior wrote to ask that the terms of his confinement be altered to allow him to go a nearby farm where the friars were accustomed to take their exercise.[71]

Seculars would frequently arrive at their place of exile impoverished from the costs of their trial and the loss of the revenues of any benefices they might have held. In 1690, Sebastián Menchero, who had been sentenced to four years of exile, of which the first six months were to be served in a convent in Malagón, wrote the Toledo tribunal to complain that he had arrived in the village so ill that he could hardly walk. Trial expenses and the loss of his benefice had so impoverished him that he begged for permission to remain in the village after his period of reclusion where he could earn a living by teaching the local children.[72]

One of the most tragic cases of which we have a record is that of Gabriel de Osca, curate of Piedrabuena. Gabriel de Osca was one of those fortunate parish priests whose benefice was sufficient to afford him a comfortable lifestyle. By age sixty-three, when he was arrested by the Toledo tribunal, Osca had been able to accumulate considerable personal property, including religious paintings and figurines, a large amount of furniture, and an excellent library. He also had about twenty ducats in cash on hand, as well as some jewelry and a substantial amount of grain in his storehouse.[73] One year after his arrival at the convent of San Gerónimo de Guisando where he had been confined, however, he was described as so destitute that the community had to clothe and feed him out of its own slender resources. This was a direct result of the tribunal's refusal to allow him to return to Piedrabuena to sell his property, which eventually disappeared into the hands of those responsible for sequestering it.[74] Removed from San Gerónimo after its prior wrote the Suprema to complain that it was too poor to maintain him, Osca was transferred to the wealthier house of Valdeglesias, but here his situation was even worse because the valley where the convent was located was in the grip of an epidemic. Since Osca was very feeble, the abbot wrote the Suprema to ask that he be removed to a healthier location "since because of the plague even those who are young and strong can barely survive here."[75]

Sick and impoverished, shunted from place to place, the fate of Gabriel de Osca can hardly be regarded as unique. The poverty of many convents or their remote or unhealthy locations made it difficult for them to accommodate the "guests" that the Inquisition insisted on sending them. Confinement in a convent remained a serious, even life-threatening punishment for some people, especially the elderly, but it did succeed in removing the offender from public view and put an immediate stop to his illicit activities. The presence of disgraced friars or secular priests in a convent could also serve as a warning. These shadowy figures, existing on the margins of the life of the community, deprived of honor and position, gave chilling evidence of the power of the Holy Office that might have deterred younger friars or novices from committing similar offenses.

Another way that the Holy Office used to instill fear into the hearts of members of the regular orders was by ordering them to witness the reading of the accusation and sentence and then associating them with the punishment itself by forcing them to scourge the offender. Called "circular discipline," this particularly humiliating procedure was usually performed on the day after the sentence was read out in the chambers of the tribunal at a convent of the order to which the offender belonged. After being alerted by a secretary, the prior or warden convened all the friars except novices either in his own chambers or in the choir. The convicted individual was escorted into the chamber and the sentence was read in front of the assembled company. The offender then kneeled and bared his shoulders while each friar in order of seniority struck him with a switch.[76]

Appeals to the Suprema from sentences handed down by the consulta de fe were extremely rare and had to be couched in almost obsequious language in order to avoid offense since the Inquisition as a whole was notoriously thin-skinned about any criticism, however justified. These canons of behavior, which were probably well-known to Spanish clerics, were completely ignored by Jacome Campana, a Neapolitan Capuchin, when he decided to appeal a verdict handed down by the Toledo tribunal in 1594. Campana, who was seventy when he was arrested in Madrid and brought to the secret prison in Toledo, had been the general representative of the order in Italy and was a doctor of civil and canon law. While in Madrid, he acted as chaplain to the Prince of Salerno and said mass regularly in the house of the Venetian ambassador. In spite of these contacts, he seems to have been little more than another one of the pretentious and impecunious hangers-on who must have infested the palaces of the wealthy during the early modern period. Certainly when he was asked by the inquisitors if he had anyone who would help him meet the expenses of his imprisonment, he had to reply that he had "no lord or patron who could assist him."[77]

Having maintained throughout his trial that he was the victim of a conspiracy involving his political enemies, Campana was outraged when he was found guilty by the tribunal and insisted on appealing to the Suprema, even though his defense attorney strongly advised him against it. In his appeal, he claimed that the sentence was "extremely unjust" and based on insufficient evidence from female witnesses who had been willing participants in the offense and, therefore, were not credible. He also refused to abjure de levi because he claimed that he was innocent of any type of heresy, no matter how minor.

It is easy to see how the inquisitors of Toledo and the Suprema could have found his appeal offensive. Refusal to abjure de levi by itself was tantamount to calling into question the entire jurisdiction of the Holy Office, which was all the more dangerous because the connection between solicitation and formal heresy was extremely tenuous. In fact, far from admitting that a gross miscarriage of justice had occurred, which was very unlikely considering the evidence, the Suprema ordered the tribunal's prosecuting attorney to initiate a new proceeding against him because of the "many bold and impertinent statements" contained in his appeal. Brushing aside his objection that according to canon law he had a perfect right to appeal a verdict he considered unjust, the Suprema not only confirmed the original sentence, but increased the penalties contained in it. Finally, still protesting his innocence, Campana abjured de levi on July 7, 1595, and was sent off to a convent just outside Toledo to serve a six-year term of confinement. Under ordinary circumstances, advanced age and a distinguished record of service might have indicated clemency in this case, but Campana had so offended the Toledo inquisitors by appealing against their verdict that on two separate occasions they used their influence with the Suprema to block any reduction in his term of confinement.[78]

On rare occasions, the Suprema would reduce all or part of a sentence, usually when the accused was either a person of some political influence or had demonstrated exemplary contrition.[79] In 1637, for example, the Suprema removed four out of five years of exile from the sentence of Dr. Pedro Onofre Martín, a canon in Mallorca's cathedral. Onofre Martín was also permitted to become eligible for another ecclesiastical benefice to replace the income from the canonry that he had lost after his conviction. At the same time, however, the Suprema explicitly confirmed the permanent removal of his right to hear confessions.[80]

In an even more unusual action, the Suprema restored the power to hear confessions to Dr. Antonio Segui. In taking this decision, the Suprema must have been influenced by the fact that the consulta de fe was divided over his conviction. But what probably tipped the balance in his favor was the exemplary lifestyle that he led after his release from the secret prison. Exiled from the capital for four years, Segui took up residence in a hermitage near the village of La Pobla. There, according to the local commissioner, he had earned an enviable reputation among the local people for his saintliness. After an investigation by a commissioner confirmed this, the Suprema ordered his exile lifted and issued him a license to hear confessions.[81]

In spite of the obvious difficulties in getting enough evidence to bring a charge of solicitation before the Holy Office, there can be little doubt that trial and punishment were difficult, painful, and even tragic experiences for many accused clerics. Merely coming before the Inquisition, the very institution that had repelled the supposed threat to the faith represented by the hated judaizers and moriscos, was a profound shock to a devoutly Catholic priest who had probably never had an overtly heretical thought in his life. Moreover, sentences handed down in solicitation cases, while not involving execution or a spell of service in the feared galleys, were in keeping with an offense that was taken quite seriously by the authorities. Deprivation of the confessor's licence, which was a privilege eagerly sought by all clerics; loss of income from a benefice; long terms of confinement, sometimes under extremely uncomfortable conditions; periods of exile accompanied by virtual impoverishment were punishments whose severity was not to be underestimated. This is especially the case when we remember that they effectively destroyed the lives and aspirations of the clerical offenders, who could not hope to escape from their consequences by a timely career change. Unable to earn a living, afflicted by a disastrous loss of status, and regarded with suspicion and distaste by other clerics, the numerous convicted solicitantes dragging out a precarious existence in convents or villages must have provided a terrifying warning of the power of the Holy Office and an effective deterrent to prospective offenders.

Chapter 5

The Soliciting Confessor

Interestingly enough, analysis of the ecclesiastical status of offenders coming before the Inquisition demonstrates conclusively that the vast majority were drawn from the religious orders. Out of the 223 accused, only 59 (26 percent) belonged to the secular clergy. Among the seculars, the largest groups were composed of parish priests (13.9 percent) and lieutenant curates (4 percent), followed by much smaller numbers of canons and other benefice holders and a sprinkling of assistants and chaplains.

Among the regulars, members of the old-line mendicant orders predominated, with the Franciscans alone accounting for seventy-two cases, or 32 percent of the total. All in all, the mendicants, including Franciscans, Dominicans, Carmelites, Trinitarians, Augustinians, and Mercedarians, accounted for 96.9 percent of the cases of solicitation coming out of the religious orders, while only three cases involved members of the Society of Jesus. This is all the more remarkable considering the significant growth of the Jesuit order from 1,440 members around 1580 to 2,746 just before their expulsion in 1767.[1] Naturally, the monachal orders (Benedictine, Cistercian, Carthusian, and Jerónimite) accounted for very few cases because of their minimal involvement in matters outside of their monasteries. Registers of accusations kept for the period 1723 to 1820 bear out the impression of the preponderance of the old-line mendicant orders among those accused of solicitation. Of the 3,775 names recorded, only 981 were secular clergy, while 2,794 belonged to religious orders; of these, the various branches of the Franciscans furnished 1,297 (46 percent), while the Jesuits accounted for only 92 (3.2 percent).[2] One can only assume that the very low numbers of Jesuit solicitantes corresponded to the care with which its members were chosen and educated, their freedom from the boring and stultifying routines of convent life, and their emphasis on avoiding the kinds of activity leading to immorality and scandal.[3]

At first glance, the overwhelming preponderance of the mendicant orders among solicitantes may seem somewhat surprising, especially in light of the strong emphasis placed at the Council of Trent on the importance of the parish clergy in carrying out sacerdotal functions and the political stranglehold they had over many villages.[4] One fairly obvious explanation, of course, is mobility. Curates could not hear confessions outside their own parishes without special permission from episcopal officials, while members of the mendicant orders could range over entire dioceses hearing confessions wherever they went.[5] Friars who were charged with gathering alms for their orders also had many opportunities to hear confessions from women over a wide geographic area.[6] A more fundamental problem, however, was that the Spanish Church was never able to provide an effective network of curates capable of meeting the laity's increasing demand for confession and other sacerdotal services and, therefore, was forced to rely heavily on the friars of the mendicant orders to fill the gap.

In the first place, the number of curates was simply too small to serve the population, while most of the expansion that took place among the seculars was accounted for by benefice holders and chaplains, especially by clergy in minor orders, who could not hear confessions. In the diocese of Barcelona, between 1635 and 1717, only 622 diocesan priests were created out of the 2,667 who received the first grade of orders.[7] In the census of 1591, the Crown of Castile had 33,087 seculars, of whom only 13,000 were parish priests.[8] By 1768 the situation had worsened since, despite a population that had grown by at least one third over its late sixteenth-century peak, all of Spain could boast no more than 15,639 curates to serve 18,106 parishes, leaving 2,467 parishes entirely unprovided.[9]

In general, the large number of vacant parishes can be accounted for by another phenomenon typical of the Spanish Church during this period: the irrational distribution of financial resources. Although the tithe was initially designed to support the Church on a local level, most of it ended in the hands of bishops, cathedral chapters, or private individuals. Where curates were able to retain a significant portion of the tithe or had other types of revenue to sustain them, they could maintain themselves and there would be little difficulty in finding a successor. On the other hand, in cities like León, where parishes were too small or too poor, it was impossible to find a curate willing to take them and bishops were frequently forced to appoint a friar to act as parish priest.[10] The same was true in the Canaries, where in 1785 José Estrada, a Franciscan, was appointed as curate of Valle de Santiago in spite of his generally poor reputation because no one else would accept the position.[11] Inadequate income also prevented the parishes of Barlovento and Puntagorda from recruiting a secular curate, so they had to settle for the services of another Franciscan, Francisco del Castillo, who was arrested on charges of solicitation in August 1604.[12]

Apart from financial factors, the poor distribution of the Spanish secular clergy corresponded to certain historical realities closely related to the repopulation patterns that followed the Reconquest. For example, when the Duero region was repopulated during the Reconquest, there was a tendency to establish the new parish churches mainly in urban areas, so that Toro, which never had more than 10,000 people, could boast twenty-two parishes. The center and south, especially Andalusia (where resettlement tended to create large villages, many of which were provided with only one parish), became the major focus for the expansion of the mendicant orders. New foundations were especially frequent in the sixteenth and early seventeenth centuries until about 1650, when Spain had around 3,000 monastic establishments.[13] The inverse relationship between the number of parishes and the number of monastic establishments can be illustrated by comparing the northern city of Bilbao with the southern port of Málaga. In Bilbao the number of parishes and convents were almost equal, with four and five respectively, but in Málaga there were four parishes and twenty-two convents.[14] The insufficient number of parishes in Málaga makes it logical to assume that the regulars took on much of the responsibility for hearing confessions. But even in places where there seemed to have been an adequate number of parishes, friars were called upon to assist the curate. In the sprawling archdiocese of Toledo, with its 575 parishes, curates frequently needed the help of members of the mendicant orders. So it was that, in the late 1640s, Gerónimo de los Herreros, a Dominican, acted as assistant in the village of Villaseca de la Sagra, where he gained an excellent reputation among his parishioners, even though his presence was bitterly resented by local seculars. One of them explained to the Holy Office that although he had nothing against Herreros personally, he felt that regulars should remain behind the walls of their convents and "keep out of the villages where they compete with the secular clergy."[15] In fact, resentment and jealousy on the part of the secular clergy, who "become mortally offended at the slightest fault or deficiency among the regulars," was a major reason why the Inquisition sentenced solicitantes in camera.[16]

Even where parish priests were readily available, however, regulars were frequently the confessors of choice because they had certain advantages over the seculars. For one thing, the members of the mendicant orders had the power to absolve for most cases, even those normally reserved for the pope, something that ordinary parish priests could not do.[17] The regulars also had the advantage of sheer numbers. By 1768, the 15,639 parish priests were confronted by 55,453 regulars, many of whom had a license to hear confessions.[18] During important festival periods like Holy Week, when demand for confessional services sharply increased, even the most assiduous curate found himself forced to rely on help from the religious orders. Witnesses in the trial of Mateo Fernández Vello, lieutenant curate of Sauzel in the Canaries between 1684 and 1693, remembered that he had regularly called in Franciscans and Augustinians from two nearby convents to help him on those occasions.[19]

Apart from a few exceptional individuals like José de Barca y Zambrana, a secular from Málaga who eventually became bishop of Cádiz, regulars also dominated the missionary movement that became so important in the Spain of the late seventeenth and eighteenth centuries. The abysmal ignorance of so many parish priests, as well as lack of sufficient numbers, were the driving forces behind the missionary movement, as Inquisitor Alonso de Salazar Frías recognized when he called for the Jesuits and other orders to send missionaries to the region to confess and catechize the population in the wake of the witch craze in the Basque region.[20] Even in places where there was no special crisis, it was felt that the complicated moral climate of seventeenth-century Spain required missionaries because only their superior training and knowledge would be effective with certain sinners and certain types of sins.[21] Although almost all the religious orders participated to a greater or lesser degree in this activity, it was mainly dominated by the Jesuits and Capuchins (Franciscans), especially Diego de Cádiz (1743–1801), who became the most popular preacher of the last half of the eighteenth century.[22]

Generally traveling in pairs, the missionaries emphasized preaching and confession. When they turned up evidence of solicitation, they would routinely refuse to absolve their penitents unless they agreed to make a deposition before the Holy Office.

Finally, the preponderance of the regulars in overall confessional activity was assured by their complete domination of convent life and their role as spiritual directors and confessors of the growing number of beatas. A number of factors, including the rapidly increasing cost of dowries and the demographic imbalance between men and women that was accentuated by war and emigration, led to an increase in the number of female religious from approximately 25,000 in 1591 to 33,347 in 1747.[23] A decree of the Council of Trent required nuns to make confession at least once a month and obligated their convents to provide both an ordinary confessor and an extraordinary confessor in case the nuns wished to confess with greater frequency.[24]

Contemporary observers were well aware of the potential danger of having a male confessor in such intimate and frequent contact with women who were being more and more strictly enclosed behind the walls of their convents.[25] The pressure for strict enclosure meant that in many female houses the confessor was almost the only male figure with whom the nun could interact, apart from the occasional relative. The relationship between nun and confessor, moreover, was no ordinary one, as the nun revealed all her thoughts, feelings, and temptations to this man who, for his part, was presented as an exalted figure of learning and authority. Consequently, the Jesuit Bernardino de Villegas insisted that the confessor of nuns be a person of superior moral and intellectual attainments, with the patience and maturity to deal with all the special emotional problems commonly experienced by nuns.[26] Unfortunately, as Alonso de Andrade warned in a book he published in 1644, many nuns developed an excessive and unhealthy emotional dependence on their confessors, becoming "so obsessed by their regard for them that they neither thought nor spoke of anything else." Such nuns tended to idealize the learning and saintliness of their "spiritual fathers" and to seek any opportunity to confess with them at any hour of the day or night. This excessive familiarity, however, could transform the nature of the relationship from spiritual to sensual because "in the last analysis he is a man and you are a woman and both fragile creatures made of mortal flesh."[27]

Bearing in mind the many warnings of the dangers of the confessional relationship in the convent, the superiors of the male religious orders who had ultimate control over the convents were careful to appoint as confessors only those clerics who had gained good reputations in the order and had amply demonstrated their emotional maturity. Even so, the number of attractive young nuns in certain convents made it extremely difficult for some confessors to resist temptation.

The dangers and pitfalls that being a confessor of nuns could present even to the most dedicated cleric could not be better illustrated than by the case of the Jerónimite Pedro de Villanueva, who in 1601 was appointed confessor in the aristocratic convent of La Concepción in Madrid by his superiors. At forty-three, Villanueva had studied theology at Alcalá for five years and completed his education with nine years in the colleges that his order maintained in Sigüenza and Salamanca. After serving in several positions in the order, he was appointed prior of the important convent in Salamanca. With his hidalgo origins and distinguished career in the order, Villanueva would seem to have been an ideal candidate for the position of confessor to the nuns of La Concepción. Unfortunately for Villanueva, however, he had enemies within the order, and one of these spread the rumor among the nuns that he was frigid and impotent, so that soon after he arrived at the convent to take up his new post, some of the younger nuns began to tease and provoke him unmercifully, calling him a "saint or else hardly a man" behind his back and vying with each other to assure him of their affection for him and desire to please him. In spite of his earnest efforts to carry out his difficult task successfully and ignore all of this provocation, it did have an effect on him, as one of the older nuns in her testimony before the Holy Office recalled seeing him "going about the convent looking embarrassed and self-conscious because some of the nuns were calling him cold and impotent."[28]

Infuriated by these attacks on his manhood and determined to save his reputation, Villanueva eventually solicited three nuns who were among his worst tormentors, but who also confessed with him most frequently, as though compelled to show the very people who were attacking him how wrong they really were. According to Villanueva's testimony, the three cooperated willingly with his sexual demands, but when he began paying greater attention to a fourth nun, they became furious and denounced him to the Holy Office. As if to make some allowance for the extraordinary pressure under which he had been placed, the consulta de fe split on the final verdict, with two out of the three inquisitors voting only temporary deprivation of the right to hear the confessions of women. The Suprema, in a rare note of leniency, went along with this view, only sentencing Villanueva to a two-year suspension from serving as confessor to women and removal from anything to do with the convent.[29]

Sometimes a friar realized that he was incapable of withstanding the pressures and temptations of being a confessor in a convent and removed himself from the scene before he got into deep trouble. José de Jesús María was a Carmelite from Toledo who was very highly regarded by his order and, after serving in several responsible positions, was appointed confessor to the Carmelite convent in Malagón. Shortly after his arrival at the convent, he began to speak amorously to Sor María de Jesús and even contemplated removing her from the convent. Stricken by remorse, Fray José renounced his position as confessor and obtained a transfer to the desert convent of Bolanque, where he would be safe from temptation.[30]

During the late sixteenth and seventeenth centuries, fear of the devil and his activity in the world became an obsession shared by literati and popular masses alike throughout Europe. In this Spain was no exception, even though the Spanish Inquisition tended to take a rather moderate attitude toward witchcraft and was able to prevent the worst excesses of the witch craze from crossing the Pyrenees.[31] Spain, however, was fully exposed to the hysteria over demonic possession that gave rise to so many scandals. Between 1628 and 1631 Madrid's aristocratic San Plácido convent was the scene of frantic efforts to exorcise twenty-five of the nuns, including the prioress, who appeared to be possessed by the devil.[32] Later in the century, Royal Confessor Froilan Díaz used the words of the devil as spoken by the possessed nuns of a convent in Cangas (Oviedo) to prove that King Carlos II had been the victim of sorcery.[33] When nuns were possessed by demons, it was natural for their superiors to call in a male member of the order to drive them out through officially sanctioned forms of exorcism. Exorcism, however, could involve close physical contact with the possessed individual including touching, massaging, and anointing with holy oil, and in some cases, this led to significant abuses, including solicitation, especially when the exorcist doubled as confessor to the convent.

Exorcism was just one of the ways in which priests were brought into intimate physical and emotional contact with female penitents at a time when the sexual outlets that had served them so well in the past were being removed. It was just one more way for the confessor to assert his control over the inner lives of his penitents, but power and loneliness make a strange and volatile mixture that might explode inside the most virtuous cleric and lead him to the bar of the Holy Office.

The social origins of the priests who were brought to trial were mainly from the humbler strata, with only 20 percent of the seventy-two individuals whose father's occupation was mentioned claiming hidalgo origin and none coming from the ranks of the upper nobility. The forty-nine individuals who came from labrador, artisan, and merchant families (68 percent) clearly demonstrate that the Spanish Church remained a channel for social mobility at least at the lower level throughout the early modern period. Of course, among the twenty-one labradores there were several who came from wealthy families who even had enough influence in their home villages to make sure that their sons obtained local benefices. Salvador Quijada del Castillo was perhaps the wealthiest of those with peasant origins. He served as lieutenant curate in the village of Ariço, where his brother was alcalde and inherited wheatlands and vineyards from his parents.[34]

For the majority of those of labrador or artisan stock, however, the Church offered perhaps the only means of social mobility and the only chance of escaping a life of toil. In order to help his son enter the Church, Juan Alcocer's father, a carpenter, bought him a grammar book and helped him learn to read and write. After Alcocer entered the Augustinian order at age eighteen, he was able to complete his education at several of the order's colleges.[35] Other men of humble origins were able to attain positions of importance in the religious orders. Fray Pedro Estéban, whose family were labradores in the village of Realejo in the Canaries, attended grammar school in the village and then joined the Augustinians at age sixteen. After attending monastic colleges in La Laguna, Estéban served two terms as prior of the Vera Cruz convent.[36] Gregorio de Tapia's father took advantage of the abundant educational facilities in Alcalá de Henares, where he farmed, to send his son to grammar school. Tapia completed his education after he joined the Franciscans at age sixteen and went on to become warden of the Franciscan house in Toledo.[37]

The inventories taken of the accused's possessions at time of arrest, however, reveal that social origin was only one among several factors that determined an individual's relative level of material comfort in religious life twenty or more years after ordination. Among the poorest of the nineteen individuals whose property inventory was included in their case file were three alcoholics, one of whom came from a well-known family of hidalgos.[38] In other cases, impoverishment was the result of inadequately endowed benefices. Juan de Villacastín was a typical member of the ecclesiastical proletariat described by Juan Maldonado in his *Pastor bonus*.[39] One of the twenty-seven curates of Toledo, a city already beginning its long decline, he discharged his duties with indifference, gambled, and had been fined by the ecclesiastical court in Ciudad Real for various offenses. The inventory taken at the time of his arrest in June 1580 revealed a state of extreme poverty bordering on destitution as he only owned the clothes on his back, a rope bed, a table and two chairs, and a few books.[40] In contrast, when Dr. Diego Ordáz y Villalta, canon of the well-endowed collegiate church of Santos Justo y Pastor, entered the prison of the Toledo tribunal to await trial, he was able to deposit more than 1,400 reales to pay his expenses at a rate double that of the normal prisoner.[41]

Impoverishment could also be the result of burdensome and expensive responsibilities placed on a regular by his order. Domingo Tomás Matos, an Augustinian from a wealthy labrador family in La Laguna had the misfortune to have been elected prior of his convent at just about the time that Spain entered the coalition against Great Britain during the American Revolution. This led to a British naval blockade and sharp declines in trade with the Baleares, so that Tomás Matos was forced to borrow large sums of money in order to fulfill his obligations as prior. By the time his property was sequestered in the spring of 1782, he was 1,300 pesos in debt and his personal property had been reduced to his library and a few bits of furniture and worn clothing.[42]

Notwithstanding individual circumstances, social origins certainly played a major role in determining the situation that a cleric, secular or regular, would find himself in after twenty or thirty years of religious life. Not only could wealthier families leave houses and property to their children, but it is not hard to imagine them helping them out financially. This certainly must have happened to Patricio Cerero, a Trinitarian, who lived in the order's convent in Toledo, where he had been born the son of a wealthy merchant. Only financial help from his parents could explain his copious library of eighty books and his luxuriously furnished cell, complete with bed, several desks, bureaus, and numerous decorative items including religious paintings, crucifixes, and a silver reliquary.[43] Given Cerero's comfortable circumstances, it should not surprise us to learn that when Gregoria de Medrano, the wife of a silk worker, unburdened herself about her family's economic difficulties while confessing with him, Cerero could afford to offer her money in return for her sexual favors.[44]

Differences in the relative well-being of clerics can also be explained by the simple fact that some were considerably more enterprising than others about exploiting their financial opportunities. Luis López de Quiros, a curate in Alcázar de San Juan, who also offered several of his female penitents money while soliciting them, supplemented the income from his benefice by acting as collector for the revenues of the parish of Santa María.[45] Salvador Quijada del Castillo, lieutenant curate of Ariço in the Canaries, came of wealthy labrador stock and had inherited money and property from his parents. He was able to significantly increase his income by lending money to local farmers and by acting as the chaplain for a nearby convent at a fee of 200 reales. He became so successful that he was even able to embellish his parish church with several valuable items, including bells and a silver incense burner.[46] The considerable variation in the fortunes and relative well-being of the lower clergy that these inventories reveal should provide a warning against any attempt at easy generalizations. Much depended on the individual, and if some were affluent enough to try to buy the love of certain of their female penitents, others were so impoverished that they could barely maintain a semblance of respectability.

Analysis of the educational achievements of the 102 confessors whose educational background is listed in their case files supports the view that the seculars were lagging well behind the regulars. In spite of the decrees of the Council of Trent, the number of seminaries available to train parish priests remained woefully inadequate in Spain, with seventeen being founded in the second half of the sixteenth century and only nine during the seventeenth. The regulars were far better off, as they rapidly developed a system of colleges, some of which, like Santo Tomás of Seville, could almost be considered universities.[47]

Of the eighty-nine individuals receiving education beyond grammar school, only nineteen were seculars and of these only six had studied theology formally. In fact, some curates and lieutenant curates were among the worst educated of all the priests brought before the Holy Office. Gabriel de Osca, who was lieutenant curate in Piedra Buena, had attended grammar school in Alcañiz were he was born, but had not studied in any higher faculty.[48] In other cases, the education that a secular had received was irregular and spotty. Cristóbal Jacinto Mendez, curate in Santiago de Tenerife, had private tutors for both Latin grammar and moral theology. Since his father was only a silk worker and the tutors were all drawn from his home village, it is permissible to doubt the value of the education he had received.[49]

With the failure to fully establish the seminary system until late in the eighteenth century, seculars who wanted higher education and could not afford a university had to fall back on the ubiquitous colleges of the religious orders as a last resort. Antonio Segui served several years as assistant curate and afterward was named prior of the general hospital in Las Palmas. He began his education at eight years old with a private tutor, entered the Franciscan college of Sapiena, where he spent eight years studying arts and theology, and then took his doctorate at the university of Gandía.[50] Curates and other seculars who had a superior education were generally from better-off families that could afford tuition at first-rate grammar schools and universities. Juan Fernandéz de Villareal, who was curate of Villaseca de la Sagra and Mocedón, about thirty kilometers from Toledo, came of a hidalgo family connected to the Dukes of Albuquerque. At age fifteen, Fernández de Villareal left his home in Guadalajara as part of the retinue of the heir to the duchy and spent nine years in Salamanca studying Latin grammar and liberal arts, completing his education at the University of Sigüenza, where he took an advanced degree in theology.[51]

The regulars, with their dense network of colleges specifically designed for the training of the members of their orders, were considerably better off. Of those mentioning higher education in their testimony, 66 percent had studied theology for an average of four years. Monastic colleges were preferred for higher studies, with only about one quarter attending universities. Of course, education can be a dangerous thing, especially when it leads to the questioning of authority. It was the Naples-born Cistercian, Jacome Campana, who had studied theology in Siena and had taken a doctorate in canon law from Bologna, who gave the Toledo tribunal such a difficult time during his trial.[52]

The well-developed system of monastic colleges meant that ambitious and intelligent young men from poor families could find a place in the orders and obtain an education that, regardless of its limited scope, was far superior to what they could have gotten anywhere else. Juan de Monserate was born in Valencia to a French immigrant father and a Spanish mother who were willing to expend some effort on their son's education, as they taught him to read and write at home. Evidently, he acquired the rudiments of Latin on his own and then spent two years at Valencia university studying the liberal arts. Entering the Dominican order at the comparatively advanced age of twenty, he was sent to the Dominican college of Salamanca for two years to study theology and continued his education with stints at the monastic colleges in Valencia and Orihuela. After leaving Orihuela, he taught subjects ranging from theology to Latin grammar at several Dominican colleges and was eventually elected prior of the Dominican house on Ibiza.[53]

Apart from formal education, another way to assess the intellectual quality of the Spanish clergy is to know what books they had in their private libraries. Although such work has hardly begun in Spain, we are fortunate to have a few inventories of clerical libraries from inquisition sources since, at the time of arrest, officials appointed by the tribunal made a full inventory of all of the accused's possessions, including his books. In sixteen cases between 1576 and 1790, the Inquisition did sequester libraries with as many as 80 books. While some officials confined themselves to simply mentioning the number of books that an accused had in his possession, others listed the authors and titles. Of the 173 titles mentioned in the inventories, works of theology formed the largest single category, accounting for almost 17 percent. The next largest category, nearly 11 percent, were summas and confessors' manuals, one inventory containing 8 of them out of a total of 23 books. Breviaries appear to have been particularly prized since they are in all the collections, making up nearly 10 percent of the total. They were clearly the book of choice, sometimes the only book, that the accused would bring with them when they came to the Holy Office to stand trial.[54]

The two largest eighteenth-century libraries, one owned by the Augustinian Domingo Tomás Matos, the former prior of the convent in La Laguna, whose books were sequestered in 1782, and the other by Fray Guillermo de Cames y Home, who was arrested in 1790, were not only larger but more varied than libraries sequestered in the sixteenth and seventeenth centuries. Judging from the books they owned, both men had little interest in secular subjects, with only one nonreligious book out of ninety-nine in their libraries. On the other hand, their interest in religious subjects was fairly broad, with both libraries containing works on theology, ecclesiastical history, and hagiography. Particularly interesting is the presence of several multivolume editions of sermons by famous eighteenth-century preachers. These books of sermons, especially the 1776–1778 edition of the sermons of Nicolás Gallo owned by Cames y Home, indicate that both Augustinians were caught up in the movement to remodel and reform preaching that was such an exciting part of the eighteenth-century Spanish Church.[55] The fact that Gallo's sermons were being used as a model in the relatively remote Canary Islands demonstrates just how widespread the movement had become by the end of the century.[56] In general, the contents of the private libraries that have come down to us indicate that, within the context of a narrowly focused clerical education, at least some clergy were aware of the intellectual crosscurrents, doctrinal struggles, and reform movements that affected the Spanish Church, even if they resided in places located far from the Castilian heartland.

Held to a higher standard of morality themselves, the zealous parish priests produced by the monastic colleges and seminaries of the post-Tridentine period were far less tolerant than their predecessors of the casual immorality, superstition, and disrespect for the sacred that they found in many villages. Where once a curate might have accommodated himself to the moral indiscretions of his flock, the new generation of curates was far less willing to do so, but their efforts to impose higher standards frequently alienated the community in which they had to live.

When Mateo Fernández Vello returned to his native village of Sauzel on the island of Tenerife to take up a position as curate, he was an energetic 24-year-old with fourteen years of monastic college behind him and an advanced degree in theology. Soon after his arrival, he established a reputation for diligence in the fulfillment of his clerical duties, especially confession, which he "heard with great regularity."[57] At the same time, Vello refused to tolerate any immoral behavior among the members of his congregation. On one occasion, Vello publicly shamed Juan Baptista de Oliver for an adulterous relationship with Sebastiana de Heredia and denounced him to the ecclesiastical court, which imprisoned him for four months. Vello also denounced Salvador Díaz, a priest in minor orders, for having an illicit relationship with Francisca Riero, with whom he had five children. Responding to Vello's complaint, the ecclesiastical court fined and imprisoned Riero and expelled him from the village. These and similar actions served to alienate much of the village. Several of his enemies, including Salvador Díaz, tried to get him removed by accusing him of immorality before the ecclesiastical court. After an investigation of the charges by episcopal officials, Vello was released, but the strain caused by his imprisonment and his growing isolation in the village finally shattered his iron discipline and drove him to attempt to obtain the sexual favors of María de la Encarnación, a twenty-year-old woman who hoped to marry his brother Miguel, with whom she was having an affair.[58]

In addition to the strain of attempting to carry out the Tridentine program for the reform of popular culture against the sometimes tenacious opposition of their flock, the clergy faced a series of potential psychological problems caused by the very nature of ecclesiastical life itself. In all too many cases these problems, combined with the emotional and sexual frustration caused by the stricter enforcement of the celibacy rule, led to solicitation.

The post-Tridentine Church's insistence on improving the educational standards of the clergy meant that parents were forced to send their sons away from home at an early age so that they could obtain the proper schooling. Mateo Fernández Vello was only ten when his parents sent him to the Augustinian college in La Laguna, and he did not return for fourteen years.[59] Family circumstances or ambitions could also force a child from his home at a very early age. Diego Sánchez de Cubas was sent by his parents at age seven to live with his uncle, who was a priest, in the hope that he would give the boy an education.[60]

Even though all young men did not leave their parents so early, the average age for entry into the religious orders was seventeen, with many entering even younger, some as young as fourteen, or in one case at eleven years old.[61] Once in the order, the individual was subject to strict discipline and could be moved from place to place at the whim of his superiors.[62] By the time of their arrest, regulars had moved an average of six times, or approximately every four years eight months. Interestingly enough, especially considering the role of the order in filling the ranks of solicitantes, the Franciscans moved their friars much more frequently, averaging nine times, or once every three years two months.

The reasons for such frequent moves varied, ranging from the need to maximize the use of the order's educational facilities to a desire to use human resources to the best advantage. The Jesuit Felipe de Medrano, who was arrested by the Holy Office in 1694, joined the order at age fourteen and moved on the average of once every two years and four months. Born in Daimiel southeast of Toledo, Medrano received his early education from a local schoolmaster. After he joined the order, his education continued at various Jesuit colleges in widely dispersed locations from Madrid to Murcia on the Mediterranean coast, and then back to Huete in the province of Cuenca, where he took an examination. Transformed from student to teacher, Medrano then spent the rest of his time in the order at different locations in New Castile (Ocaña, Toledo) and Extremadura (Llerena) as reader of moral theology, preacher, and administrator, ending at the prestigious college in Alcalá, where he was arrested.[63]

Whether intended or unintended, the effect of such frequent moves was to make it extremely difficult for the individual friar or cleric to establish close and durable friendships among his fellows. The sense of isolation was further increased by extreme alienation from parents and siblings. Periodic demographic crises due to epidemics and harvest failure meant that by the time of their arrest, 71 percent of the priests in my sample had lost both parents.[64] Siblings also suffered high mortality rates due to the same causes, with 43 percent of brothers and 24 percent of the sisters listed by the accused having died by the time of arrest. In some instances, a priest's entire immediate family was deceased by the time he had reached his late forties. Mateo González, a Franciscan who was forty-seven by the time of his arrest on November 19, 1699, reported that both his parents were deceased, while his only brother had recently died while serving as a soldier in Flanders and his only sister, her husband, and both of their children had died in America. He had had several other siblings, but they had all died very young so that he did not remember their names.[65]

Long periods of absence from home also meant that even if a priest had surviving siblings, he frequently had scant contact with them and knew little about their lives. The Carmelite Diego de la Trinidad, who was forty-one when he appeared before the Toledo tribunal, was so out of touch with his family that he did not know if his elder brother was still alive, even though he lived in Soria where they had both grown up. He had no idea where his youngest brother was or what he did. He also could not remember his father's occupation or where he was born and did not know the names of his grandparents.[66] Isolation from siblings increased if they were also in religious life. Bernardo del Castillo, a Carmelite who was born in Toledo, had the good fortune to remain in his native city for virtually the entire twenty years that he had been a member of the order. But of his six brothers and sisters, two had died very young, another had joined the Franciscans and had died eight years earlier at twenty-four, and his only living brother was a Dominican in a convent "somewhere in Old Castile."[67]

Even living in the same village as members of the family, however, was no guarantee of closeness. Sebastián Menchero, who was lieutenant curate of a parish church in Daimiel southeast of Toledo, had lost both his parents, but still had six of his seven siblings. All six lived in Daimiel, but Menchero could not even remember the name of his eldest brother's wife or any of their children or the names of any of his youngest sister's four children.[68] Many factors, such as disagreements over inheritances, marriages, and dowries, could drive families apart and compound the priest's sense of alienation. Altogether, 36 percent of the accused did not know the names of their siblings' husbands or wives, while 31 percent could not remember the names of their nephews.

Given the fact that the average age of soliciting clerics whose age was listed when they appeared before the Holy Office was forty-six, with almost 64 percent of these 133 individuals falling between thirty-five and fifty, we can assume that many were experiencing a form of midlife crisis when they began soliciting their female penitents around age forty-one.[69] Psychologists are generally agreed that "midlife is a time of psychological, social and physiological vulnerability."[70] The emotional "stock taking" that accompanies middle age invariably switches attention to the individual's inner needs, and after spending about twenty-four years in religious life, the priest may have felt intensely frustrated as his needs for emotional closeness were not being met.[71] On the other hand, theorists have pointed out that the self-analysis that is inherent in "stock taking" may be especially stressful for men who have been taught to control any sign of weakness or emotional vulnerability, the very sort of training that seminarians and novices received during adolescence.[72] The result in many cases was increasing frustration with the constraints of religious life, a failure to perform their duties properly, and a frantic reaching out for emotional satisfaction otherwise unobtainable.

For many of the priests accused of solicitation, an appearance before the Holy Office was the culmination of a process of moral, emotional, and psychological decay that had begun some years before, signaling the onset of midlife crisis. At times their increasingly problematic behavior had already come to the notice of their superiors. In the case of the Dominican Francisco Carrascosa, it took the form of a struggle to escape from the constraints of monastic life. In 1743, when he was forty-six, he was assigned to be transferred from Oran to Granada, but instead he went to Portugal and served as chaplain on the island of Fuenteventura, all without the permission of his superiors. At the time of his trial before the Holy Office, it was learned that, several years earlier, he had been punished by his superiors on two occasions for having made suggestive remarks to a woman while he was her confessor.[73]

For José Estrada, the way to be free from the authority of his superiors was to secularize himself. After a turbulent career in a number of Franciscan houses including numerous transfers, he was made warden of the convent in Buena Vista, but removed when he struck another friar. Estrada then requested that his superiors allow him to become a curate. Permission was granted, but his conduct failed to improve, and his superiors had to remove him again, this time to the convent of La Orotava, where he was later arrested by the Holy Office.[74]

Another Franciscan, thirty-five-year-old José Nuela, recognized that he was simply unsuited to be a mendicant and begged the inquisitors at his trial to intercede for him so that he could leave the order. Nuela, too, had a very checkered career; just a few months before he was arrested by the Holy Office on charges of solicitation, he had been given six months of reclusion, and his superiors deprived him of the right to hear confessions after he had been caught masturbating in front of a young boy.[75]

For some, failure to advance their careers within the religious orders or just the sheer tedium of hearing endless confessions in one dreary village after another drove them to alcohol abuse. In his mid twenties, just a few years after he joined the Franciscans, Gaspar de Nájera seemed to have adjusted well to his life in the order. As described by Domingo Pinto, a young man who studied Latin grammar under his direction, Nájera had an excellent reputation and did nothing that could affront Christian morality. Some years later, when Nájera was thirty-three, Pinto met him again, this time in the remote village of Adzanete where Nájera admitted that his career in the order had not gone well. It was also about this time that other witnesses testified that they had found him drunk in the middle of the day. At one point, he even refused to give a sermon if they did not order him some wine. Two years later, at age thirty-five, he tried to force himself on a fifteen-year-old maid during confession, and when she refused, he followed her home, where her mistress found him in the kitchen drinking wine out of a copper bowl.[76] By the time he appeared before the Inquisition five years later, he had solicited nine female penitents and attempted to seduce a twelve-year-old boy.

One of the most interesting cases of alcoholism, and one that demonstrates that the stultifying nature of religious life could have a demoralizing effect on persons of imagination and sensitivity, concerns Antonio de Arvelo, a Franciscan who was detained by the Canaries tribunal in 1784. Obviously intelligent, Arvelo's career in the order had begun promisingly in his late twenties with teaching posts in the colleges in Izod and Santa Cruz, which he combined with hearing the confessions of the country people in the region. Sometime in his mid thirties, he appears to have become dissatisfied with life in the order and especially with the drudgery of confession and began to drink heavily. By age thirty-seven, he had been deprived of his academic posts and sent to the convent on Lanzerote, where he was ordered to assist the curate of the nearby village of Aria. Since hearing confessions was what he liked least about his work, he continued drinking at all hours in the company of the curate and sold his books in order to buy more spirits. He would hear confessions while inebriated and lying in bed in the curate's house, while a servant brought them both more liquor. In order to vary the routine of hearing the same dreary sins recited endlessly, Arvelo began telling his penitents their sins before they even began to confess, explaining to the inquisitors at his trial that it was very easy to guess what such simpletons would say.[77] Hearing women's confessions while drunk and in a state of undress could hardly be conducive to maintaining the necessary proprieties, and Arvelo was eventually denounced for soliciting several penitents. He was sentenced to be deprived of the right to hear the confessions of both men and women in spite of his claim to have been "demented" by his bouts of drinking at the time.[78]

Regardless of his religious status, the confessor's ability to solicit his female penitents was greatly enhanced by the Church's failure to fully impose the closed confessional until late in the eighteenth century. In the medieval summas and manuals, confessions were to be heard in a public place, and the evidence from the fifteenth and early sixteenth century suggests that penitents generally assumed a kneeling position close to the priest, who was seated on a chair or bench. Such forced intimacy afforded the confessor ample opportunity to abuse his penitents both verbally and physically. In order to reduce the danger to morality inherent in the old system, the post-Tridentine Church gradually introduced the confessional box with its partition separating priest and penitent.[79] Since the illicit activity of the soliciting confessor depends initially on his physical access to the penitent, the rapid deployment of a device capable of both concealing the identity of the penitent and protecting her from physical contact with the priest would have acted as a powerful deterrent.

Unfortunately, the Spanish Inquisition's trial records indicate that the closed or partitioned confessional diffused slowly and unevenly through the territory of the Spanish monarchy and that it provided indifferent protection at best against the efforts of a really determined solicitante. They also reveal a confusing and varied set of confessional practices in which the places where confession was actually heard depended more on tradition or expediency than the dictates of the post-Tridentine church.

Overall, the fully closed confessional box was used in only 41 percent of the solicitation cases I recorded. Close to 42 percent continued to use the traditional system with the priest sitting on a chair or bench and his penitent kneeling before him. Fully 68 percent of the places where the traditional system was still used were in the Canaries and Baleares, indicating a definite lag in these remote districts of the monarchy as compared to areas closer to the heart of the post-Tridentine reform, like the archdiocese of Toledo.

Regardless of where or when it was used, the traditional penitential posture offered alluring possibilities to a confessor bent on seducing his penitent. During the twenty years between 1667 and 1687, Pedro Pons, the prior of the Augustinian convent of Nuestra Señora del Toro on the island of Menorca, took advantage of his physical proximity to his female penitents to kiss them, grasp their breasts, and attempt to set up assignations with them. On one occasion, when a thirty-five-year-old widow with whom he had a longstanding relationship came to confess with him, they first excited each other with suggestive language and then engaged in mutual masturbation.[80]

Of course, confessing in a chapel or in the nave of the church itself exposed the soliciting confessor to considerable risks, especially if his activities were noticed by a nosy or vindictive colleague. On March 19, 1639, for example, Justo de Aguilera, a Trinitarian in the convent of the Santísima Trinidad of Toledo, denounced his colleague, Alonso Guerro, to the Holy Office because one day he noticed that while Guerro heard the confession of the wife of a local blacksmith, she had her hands under his habit. Since Guerro had been repeatedly punished by his superiors for living openly with a woman, he was already the object of suspicion and curiosity by his fellow friars, so it is not surprising that his reckless behavior in an open chapel led to his downfall.[81]

Adding to the Inquisition's problems in determining whether an offense had actually taken place was the fact that in many churches there was no fixed location for hearing confessions. Testimony in the case of the Carmelite Pedro Barbero de Torres indicated that in the parish church of Los Yébenes, a village southeast of Toledo where he was sent by his order to hear confessions, the priest simply moved his chair from place to place and heard confessions wherever he saw fit.[82]

In some places, the confessor did not even use a chair, but sat casually on a step or bench while his penitent kneeled before him. In 1674 the Franciscan Juan Girón sat on the steps of the high altar while hearing the confession of Francisca Gomez. In this posture, he made lewd and suggestive remarks to her on twelve separate occasions, and once when she tried to put a little more distance between them by kneeling further back, he grabbed her skirt and roughly hauled her closer.[83] The curate of the village of La Gomera on the island of La Laguna in the Canaries routinely heard confessions while seated on the steps of the baptistry. It was there that Francisca Paula, a twenty-one-year-old prostitute, found him one morning in 1710 when she came to confess. After hearing her confession and giving her absolution he asked if he could visit her house in order to sleep with her, but admonished her not to take other lovers "because the people in these parts tend to be jealous."[84]

In certain convents that might have been too poor to have confessional boxes, the porter's lodge was used when the nuns needed to confess. This was convenient and offered protection for the nun because the porter's lodge was normally the place where they talked with family members who came to visit them, so it was supposed to always have a screen. The porter's lodge was routinely used for confessions by the nuns of the Carmelite house in Guadalajara when Fray Francisco Corbera was assigned to hear the nuns' confessions in the 1670s. The screen did not prove to be much of an impediment to seeing or touching the nuns in this instance, however, because it was frequently missing.[85] On several occasions, one of the nuns, Sor Eugenia de Santa Teresa, even removed the screen herself and then raised her habit so that Corbera could see her thighs.[86]

Even more scope was given to the male vicars or confessors of female religious by the rule that allowed nuns to make their confession in the privacy of their cells when they were indisposed.[87] In 1705, Fray José Lozano, a Franciscan who was confessor of a convent in the village of Alcázar de San Juan, used the freedom this rule gave him to visit Sor Antonia de Santa Rosa Romani, a distant cousin who was one of the nuns and happened to be ill.

Just as she began her confession, Lozano told her that he was very attracted
to her. The astonished nun reproached him for his language "especially now
that I have started to make my confession." He shrugged this off, however,
remarking airily that the occasion itself was of no importance and proceeded
to try to insert his hand in her habit, while she squirmed away from him to
the other side of the bed. A tussle ensued with the nun trying to cover her
breasts with a mantilla and Lozano pulling it away. Things might have continued in this vein for some time had Sor Antonia not threatened to start
screaming and rouse the whole convent "so that they can all bear witness to
your lewdness."[88]

The parish clergy could also take advantage of the illness or indisposition
of female penitents to visit them at home in order to hear their confessions.
Once in the woman's bedroom, her state of dishabille and the lack of prying
eyes offered limitless possibilities. Of the nine witnesses testifying against
Gabriel de Osca, who acted as lieutenant curate of Piedrabuena in the late
1570s and 1580s, four had been solicited in their homes while they were ill.
In one case, Osca put his hands inside Lucía Hernández's shift under the pretext of soothing the place where she felt sick. When his hand wandered down
between her thighs, Lucía became alarmed and started to scream, forcing
Osca to remove it and assure her that he had not meant to offend her. Osca
even reversed this stratagem by inviting penitents to come to his lodgings when
he was ill so that he could hear their confessions. One of the women who fell
into this particular trap was Catalina Fernández, who was horrified when Osca
grabbed her and tried to kiss her as she knelt beside his bed.[89]

Where the confessional had been introduced, it was not always effective
in preventing intimacy between priest and penitent. For one thing, the confessionals had no fixed design, so that they could be made in such a way as
to afford scant protection. In 1684 the confessional that was used in the
Dominican convent of San Vicente Ferrer in Manacor (Mallorca) had a door
that was divided into two parts. When Antonia Fornes confessed with Fray
Antonio Gelabert, she found that she could place her hands on top of the
lower section of the door so that he could hold them during her confession.
In this particular house the confessional was not the only place where a friar
could hear confession. The confessional was situated in the San Román chapel,
but the friars also heard confessions in the Santa Rosa chapel, where penitents simply knelt before them. When Antonia returned to confess with
Gelabert later that same day he took her to the other chapel, where he touched
her face and breasts during confession.[90]

Even during the eighteenth century, when confessionals were becoming
much more common and use of a bench or chair by confessors had declined
by 52 percent from the level of the sixteenth and seventeenth century, many
of them were still rudimentary affairs. In 1722, the only "confessional" that
the Franciscan convent of Palma on Mallorca could boast consisted of a chair
with a table in front of it to which was attached a screen so full of holes that
Fray Miguel Miguel had no trouble touching the faces of his female penitents.[91] At around the same time, in the Carmelite convent the confessional

consisted of a partially enclosed structure. The confessor sat inside on a rickety chair, separated from his penitent by a flimsy blue curtain.[92]

Of course, even the strongest confessional box could do no more than prevent physical contact between priest and penitent. The confessor could not be stopped from making suggestive remarks through the screen. The screens themselves, even if they were not torn or missing, were often transparent, so that a confessor could easily identify a penitent and obtain an assignation with her outside the church, often with her cooperation. During several confessions in the spring of 1801, José Borges, a Mercedarian from Almusafes (Valencia) begged Mariana Mas, a young married woman, to have sexual relations with him. Mariana always indignantly refused, telling him that he should not speak to her that way in such a holy place. It was only after Borges was able to get permission from a widow who had a small house to use a bedroom to confess a penitent who was oversensitive and squeamish that she consented. From then on her refusals in the confessional always preceded another visit to the widow's house.[93]

Moreover, unlike the traditional confession in an open church or chapel, the closed confessional actually offered greater privacy to those who wished to discuss or plan an ongoing relationship. In 1781 María López Molina admitted on her deathbed that for two years she had carried on a relationship with Juan de la Visitación, the prior of the Carmelite convent in Ciudad Real who also served as her confessor. At their weekly or biweekly confessions, which stretched over a two-year period, he would tell her the exact time of their next assignation, which would frequently take place at a deserted sanctuary outside the walls, long after midnight when his duties in the convent were safely over.[94]

Like the seminary, the closed confessional did not become widespread until the mid eighteenth century and even then certain remote parts of the Spanish monarchy did not really see confessionals until the very end of the century.[95] But even the closed confessional was not proof against the determined efforts of priests who wished to use the sacrament as an opportunity to obtain sexual favors from their penitents. In an age when unprecedented numbers of women were attending church and coming to confession and more and more ecclesiastical manpower was being devoted to hearing confessions, solicitation would continue to pose a threat to the reputation of the clerical estate despite the Inquisition's attempt to stifle it.

In spite of improvements in education and training, the life of a cleric in the post-Tridentine Spanish Church was far from easy. The extraordinarily high social expectations placed on the clergy, the increasing demand for confession and other services, and the insistence on standards of morality that earlier generations of clerics were never expected to meet combined to create enormous tensions and anxieties that all priests must have felt to some extent. Additional pressure came from the loneliness and isolation that accompanied entry into religious orders and the problematic nature of the relationship between priest and laity on the parish level. Social stressors like the death of parents and siblings, constant movement from community to community, and demanding routine of religious orders affected individuals in different ways.[96] Many were able to adjust to these difficult circumstances, but others became demoralized, ceased to properly carry out their responsibilities, attempted to flee from their convents, or became alcoholics. Many others desperately sought affection from their female penitents in spite of the sinfulness and disrespect for the sacrament of penance implied by solicitation. But if auricular confession implied a relationship of inequality, it also placed the priest under a heavy moral and religious obligation that was generally well understood by his penitent. By making sexual overtures in the confessional, the priest divested himself of his moral authority in a particularly dramatic and unequivocal way and became a mere man whose future career, comfort, and freedom depended on the degree of his penitent's toleration, discretion, or affection.

Chapter 6

Victims and Unwilling Penitents

The victims of solicitation came from a broad cross section of Spanish society, ranging from slaves and prostitutes to the daughters of hidalgos. Entirely excluded were the women of the great nobility who, like the many aristocratic ladies who supported Teresa de Jesús, could have their pick of the finest confessors and whose social prestige would have protected them from any such indignity.[1] Among the fourteen nobles whom I have been able to identify, the majority were the wives or daughters of members of the lesser nobility, like María de Mora and Juana de Magan, two orphan cousins of a hidalgo family from Villaseca de la Sagra near Toledo. Both cousins were solicited by Gerónimo de los Herreros, a Dominican who assisted the local curate in carrying out his pastoral responsibilities in the village.[2] At the very bottom of the social pyramid were an almost equally small number of slaves (three) like Isabel Forteza from Oran, who turned Christian in Palma de Mallorca after being sold to a canon of the cathedral, and destitute individuals (six) like Gutierra González, who was a resident of the poorhouse in Ciudad Real when she made her deposition before commissioner Luis de Aguilera.[3] There were also six prostitutes whose status as "lost" women excited the erotic imagination of their confessors, even when they made an effort to rehabilitate themselves in a Magdalen house.[4]

The vast majority of victims (81.6 percent), however, came from the lower class and lower middle class. Particularly well represented in this stratum were the wives and daughters of artisans and textile workers (seventy), such as twenty-year-old Francisca Gómez, whose husband was a tailor. In April 1676 Francisca informed the Toledo tribunal's local commissioner that, two years earlier, her confessor, Juan Girón, the warden of the Franciscan house in Tamajón, had begun to importune her for permission to visit her at home whenever she was alone. Her refusal to listen to his entreaties only inflamed his passion and during one confession, while she knelt before him, he grabbed her vest and pulled her toward him, kissing her and thrusting his hand inside her shirt.[5] The large number of women from artisan families in these records is another indication of a mixed economy in Spain's small towns and villages, each of which had its own contingent of tailors, shoemakers, hatmakers, and the like.[6]

Another group that was strongly and probably disproportionately represented relative to its numbers in the population as a whole were servants, comprising some thirty-four individuals, or 6 percent of the victims.[7] Coming mainly from the lowest class of rural society and far from their families, many serving girls found themselves bound to harsh or intolerant masters. They could do little to resist exploitation, and for many, confession and other church devotions were their only source of relief from unremitting drudgery since their masters would find it difficult to refuse requests to fulfil religious duties. In 1702, for example, twenty-year-old Sebastiana Josepha, who was a maid in the home of the widow of a local notary, told her confessor that her mistress would not give her a day off and even forced her to work on important holy days, allowing her to leave the house only to confess in the parish church.[8] Sebastiana Josepha, who was an orphan from a tiny village near the country town of La Orotava in the Canaries, obviously had few resources and little recourse if she displeased her mistress and, therefore, had to put up with harsh treatment regardless of her feelings in the matter.

One of the most curious things about the social composition of the victims is that only thirty, or 5.3 percent, came from the agricultural sector, even though small proprietors, tenant farmers, and day laborers made up the overwhelming majority of the Spanish population. The overrepresentation of victims coming from cities and larger towns (31 percent), when the urban population of Spain probably did not reach 20 percent, is probably a function of the superabundance of clergy in urban areas. At the same time, we should bear in mind that employment patterns in the agricultural sector were extremely varied. Many agricultural workers and farmers formed a part of the urban population even in larger cities, while many peasants who did not have sufficient land eked out a living as artisans and textile workers.[9]

In general, victims of solicitation were fairly young, with an average age of twenty-seven when they made their depositions before the Holy Office. The impression of youth is confirmed by the fact that the first incident of solicitation occurred an average of six years earlier, with some victims delaying their testimony for as long as thirty years.[10] There were many reasons for this delay, from simply forgetting an incident that happened long ago and may not have made much of an impression to repression of something that was acutely painful. This was especially the case with the thirty-six victims who were age fifteen or younger when they experienced the first incident of solicitation. Such witnesses were frequently too upset to come forward or, because of their youth, unaware of their obligation to denounce the confessor. It was exactly this explanation that Jerónima Verd, a twenty-year-old inmate of the poorhouse in Palma de Mallorca offered when she was asked about the reasons for her five-year delay in reporting the Trinitarian Pedro Jorge Fiol.[11] Evidently, she had repressed the incident, which had deeply shocked her at the time, and it took a general confession before a Jesuit missionary to recall it. With Jerónima's permission, the missionary informed another Jesuit who happened to be a calificador of the Holy Office, who was then authorized to visit the poorhouse to take her deposition.

Very young witnesses presented special problems to inquisitorial officials in much the same way as their testimony in child abuse cases raises controversy in the law courts of today. D. Ambrosio Cayetano de Ayala Navarro, the commissioner who took a deposition from ten-year-old Catalina de la Cruz against Gaspar de Nájera, who served as preacher and confessor in rural Lanzarote, was extremely reluctant to take her testimony seriously even though he reported that Nájera had such a bad reputation that the children of Granadilla had made up a little ditty about him beginning with "boys and girls watch out for Father Nájera." When little Catalina presented herself, he warned her not to tell any lies "because liars go to hell," and after he finished taking her deposition, he expressed his doubts about accepting it as valid because she was so young and unsophisticated. But he was forced to admit that Nájera's reputation and the fact that his sexual molestation of the little girl had been witnessed by her grandfather and grandmother lent credence to her testimony.[12]

Although most of the Inquisition's activity dealt with men, one of the most interesting things about the victims of solicitation is that only four were men. This may be partially explained by the belated inclusion (1612) of male victims of solicitation under the jurisdiction of the Holy Office.[13] In the public mind, solicitation had become identified as an offense involving female victims, and men who had experienced it were less likely to be aware of their obligation to inform the Holy Office. As late as 1762 this was alluded to by Joseph de Ilisarri, who explained that his eight-year delay in coming before the Holy Office to report an incident of attempted sodomy involving his confessor was because, as a male, he was uncertain of his legal obligation.[14] Undeterred by the fact that few men actually experienced solicitation, nineteenth-century anticlericalism depicted the relationship between novices and their confessors as inherently suspicious (Fig. 6.1).

However, the real explanation for the small number of male victims is related to the extreme restrictions placed on the freedom of all kinds of women to move through the streets, visit their neighbors, admit strangers to the house, or even attend church. Such restrictions, of course, were derived from the ubiquitous fear of loss of family honor through a lack of sexual purity among women. Family honor would only be secure, therefore, if women refrained from engaging in conduct that might imply a lack of chastity, even if such behavior was perfectly innocent.[15] In order to prevent this, Pedro Galindo warned honorable young girls not to leave the "shadow of their parent's home"

Figure 6.1. A Young Novice Confesses to an Older Friar. *Two Friars Confessing,* by John Knight (Biblioteca Nacional, Laboratorio Fotográfico)

and put husbands on their guard against allowing fortune tellers or women selling cloth to enter the house because they could pose a threat to their wife's fidelity, presumably by bringing notes from potential lovers. As for widows, Galindo stated categorically that they could not even leave their homes without falling under suspicion.[16]

That such arbitrary restrictions on the movements and social interaction of Spanish women were not merely theoretical is amply demonstrated by a number of references drawn from testimony or descriptions by commissioners. Bernarda Suárez de Quintana, a thirty-one-year-old single woman, was so restricted by her parents that she had to wait for six years, until after both her parents had died, in order to go into the village of La Guía to make a deposition against her confessor.[17]

Pedro Galindo's warning to single girls that they would lose whatever innocent freedoms they possessed after they were married and that they would be tied down with "a thousand chains" appeared to have come true for Antonia Pennaroja y de Pedro, who was unable to denounce her confessor for soliciting her when she was still single because, according to the local commissioner, she was being watched all the time by her husband's family and was free only to go from her house to church and back.[18]

Such evidence reminds us very forcefully that the confessional was, in many respects, the most convenient and frequently the only way in which a priest could speak about his sexual desires to a woman. Women like Antonia Pennaroja y de Pedro were allowed to go to church but very little else, and visiting them in their homes was impossible. If they wanted to have an affair, as they did, Pennaroja y de Pedro and her confessor, Luis Climent, had to resort to the confessional. But such was not the case with the homosexual priest or friar, who had many outlets for his sexual needs. The greater personal freedom enjoyed by boys and men meant that there were always large numbers of vagabonds, foreigners, and itinerant laborers available for exploitation.[19] Furthermore, in many Spanish cities an organized homosexual subculture existed where a priest could satisfy his desires without incurring the risks of solicitation in the confessional.[20] The growth of monastic colleges, the increasing role of the priesthood in providing primary education for boys to which girls had no access, and the establishment of seminaries also provided homosexual priests with many opportunities. García Ferrer, a defrocked Augustinian who was sent to the galleys by order of the Suprema in 1617, was a schoolmaster in the village of Bétera and was convicted of sodomizing numerous students aged ten to twelve.[21] It is significant of the different way in which a seducer had to approach boys and girls that the bisexual Mercedarian Juan Nolasco was forced to use the confessional to try to obtain the sexual favors of nineteen-year-old Angela Regual, but was easily able to satisfy his homosexual proclivities by seducing the novices who studied under him in the monastic college.[22] Interestingly enough, Pedro Sánchez de San Basilio, one of our four male victims, was a fifteen-year-old seminary student in Getafe (Toledo) when Father Ildefonso Milla, reader in Arts at the seminary, attempted to seduce him. The scene was not the confessional, however, but Milla's cell, where the young seminarian had gone to make his confession on his saint's day. Instead of hearing his confession, Milla promised to hear him another time, thrust him on the bed, and began kissing and fondling him. Since confession had not really taken place, the case against Milla was suspended.[23]

Just over 50 percent of the female victims of solicitation were single, in contrast to the 35.5 percent who were married and 11.4 percent who were widows. It is probable that, in spite of the restrictions placed on the religious observances of many single women, especially from the upper and middle classes, married women and widows may have had greater difficulty in going to confession as often as they might have wished. In the latter case, social prejudice and poverty undoubtedly restricted their movements, while in the former, it was frequently a matter of being too busy at home. We can get a glimpse of the life of a busy married woman from the story of Ana María Ramírez, who asked her confessor for some exercises in mortification that she could do at home, as she found that with three young children it was impossible to pray or come to church for devotions as often as other women with fewer responsibilities.[24]

Of course, there was no shortage of moralists who insisted that the married woman's place was in the home and that, in the words of Luis de León, "as men were created for public life, so women were made for confinement." Although he insisted that a woman's chief virtue should be her fervent belief in God, he warned married women specifically against neglecting their homes for religious devotions.[25]

There is also no doubt that many husbands had no compunction about sharply restricting their wives' religious activity or preventing them from going to confession. A particularly glaring, but by no means unusual, instance of this surfaced in testimony taken in Granada in 1635. For three years, Gaspar de Espinosa's wife had witnessed him sexually abusing their daughter and eventually told her confessor about what was happening. Her confessor responded by refusing to absolve her unless she brought her husband in to confess and receive penance for committing such a grave sin. When she told her husband about this, however, he angrily demanded to know why she had confessed this at all and told her that her only obligation was to obey her husband in everything. He prohibited her from going to mass and confession, and she was so afraid that he would injure or even kill her that she had not confessed for a year.[26] That abuses of this nature were not uncommon is demonstrated by the fact that in his confessors' manual, the veteran confessor Pedro Galindo advised his colleagues to make married men aware that they were committing a mortal sin by preventing their wives from attending mass or other devotions.[27]

The victims of solicitation also included forty-six nuns, or 8.2 percent of the total. The relatively high percentage of victims relative to the number of female religious in the population as a whole indicates that, in spite of efforts to improve the quality of the confessors who were assigned to convents, a certain number were prepared to abuse their positions to satisfy their sexual needs.

A small number of beatas (fourteen) also experienced sexual solicitation. Ambivalent social attitudes toward beatas that might have led to solicitation are clearly revealed in Diego Pérez de Valdivia's *Aviso de gente recogida*, which was first published in 1585. Pérez de Valdivia, who held the chair of Holy Scripture at the University of Barcelona, wrote his book in an effort to help beatas behave in such a way as to counter their many detractors, who insisted that they had only become beatas to escape from male control and live as they pleased.[28]

In spite of his ostensibly favorable attitude toward beatas, however, Pérez de Valdivia was highly uncertain about how to deal with them. While admiring their austerity and religious fervor, he was deeply suspicious of any manifestations of spiritual power like the visions and ecstasies through which some beatas expressed their closeness to God. Such typically feminine forms of religious leadership could bring certain beatas, like Avila's Mari Díaz at the end of the sixteenth century, a position of considerable influence in the community.[29] But for Pérez de Valdivia, beatas like Mari Díaz were "secretly presumptuous" and have "much freedom and little modesty."[30] Modesty and discipline were indispensable if beatas were to be successful in fending off their critics, especially since for many "the devil, the world, and their own flesh" presented them with many temptations. The danger to chastity was so great that he advised beatas to avoid any contact with men, including their closest relatives. Even conversations about spiritual matters were inadvisable since "for every good one, I have seen 100,000 that were evil."[31] The only way to truly avoid the dangers and pitfalls that lay in wait for the beata was to find a good confessor and obey him without question since "it is nothing less than a temptation of the devil not to follow his orders."[32] As the most problematic of all the groups of women in early modern Spain and the one least compatible with traditional feminine social categories, the beata was in a particularly vulnerable position. By insisting on her vulnerability to the temptations of the flesh, Pérez de Valdivia ran the risk of enhancing the allure of the beata for certain confessors, who were encouraged to see her as a sexually desirable woman who merely used religious devotion as a smokescreen to hide her unbridled passions.

In a book published in 1529, royal chronicler and court preacher Antonio de Guevera bemoaned the lack of education among Spanish women of all classes. Guevera was one of those humanist intellectuals who, along with Erasmus and Luis Vives, strongly favored at least a minimum of education for women of the upper classes.[33] By the time large numbers of solicitation cases were being prosecuted by the Inquisition, the humanist dream was being realized; numerous upper-class women were receiving basic education and many were being brought into contact with higher learning through private tutors and convent schools. As early as 1572, Teresa de Jesús was requiring applicants to her convents to read Latin and her letters are full of glowing references to the learning and enthusiasm of her young novices, most of whom came from monied families.[34] It was from this base of educated upper class and upper middle-class women that there emerged such seventeenth-century literary figures as María de Carbajal y Saavedra and María de Zayas. Not unexpectedly, therefore, even though literacy rates for the female victims as a whole stood at 17.7 percent, the overwhelming majority of those who were literate (76.3 percent) came from the ranks of the lesser nobility and female religious.

At the same time, Spain's failure to establish teaching orders of women like the Daughters of Charity in France meant that lower-class women were largely denied basic instruction. The sharp class-based distinction between the educated few and the illiterate masses is illustrated by the fact that while there were no illiterate nuns and only two illiterate noblewomen, only three of the thirty-four servants could sign their depositions and, of these three, two had served for long periods of time in convents where they would have had access to educational opportunities.[35] Indeed, so unusual was it for a lower-class woman to have even a basic education, much less to have any higher educational ambitions, that when Isabel Riera wanted her confessor,

Pedro Benimelis, to teach her Latin, she had to tell him that she had been inspired by a divine revelation. Even though her confessor was one of her devotees, he greeted her request with the utmost skepticism since he felt that it demonstrated a "lack of proper humility." She had to repeat her tale of a vision on numerous occasions before he finally consented to teach her Latin, but only after consulting a senior colleague in order to find out if it was proper to do so "since he could not understand what use she would make of it."[36] It is easy to imagine what Father Benimelis's reaction would have been if such a request had come from a woman of the upper classes. In matters of learning, the woman of rank was accorded something of the social personality of men, and no one would question her right to education.

It was the cultural rather than the social superiority of the priesthood that tended to increase the social distance between priest and penitent. Literacy, travel, and access to the arcane world of Latin culture, which was directly connected to a knowledge of canon law, scripture, and ultimately divine revelation itself placed the confessor on an immeasurably higher level. The poor, illiterate penitent, with some interesting exceptions, could do little but accept his authority, while even relatively well-educated upper-class women fell easily under his spell because they remained critically dependent on his superior understanding of a male-dominated intellectual order.[37]

In drawing a profile of the typical victim of solicitation, personal characteristics that cannot be revealed by basic sociological data have to be considered. Although such information is notoriously difficult to tease out, one element that the sources do reveal is that many victims were frequent churchgoers interested in particular devotions, while many more practiced frequent confession and communion.[38] What this data suggests is that victims may have been more devout than the population as a whole, and therefore, by attending church more often and participating more actively, they would have had greater exposure to priests. For their part, the priests and friars with whom these women came into contact, seeing their heightened interest in religion, could easily have felt that they could urge their own case for emotional and sexual release on them with a greater chance of success than they could have had with someone less deeply religious.

Certainly, Rafael Serre's success in forming a group of seven women who could be induced to satisfy his sexual needs was directly related to the fact that all of them were not only extremely devout, but practiced frequent or even daily confession. In fact, it was one of these women who suggested the techniques of exorcism that Father Serre used as an excuse to become physically intimate with her and the other members of the group.[39] The potential danger to chastity of the excessive familiarity that might arise between confessor and penitent in the course of frequent confession was a cause of grave concern to Pérez de Valdivia, who warned that frequent confession inevitably brought the female penitent into contact with men and that the confessional does not change instinct since "confessors are men after all, however saintly they may be."[40]

A heightened religious sensibility could also cause certain women to go from confessor to confessor until they found one that could be a true spiritual advisor. Unfortunately, the emotional closeness that came with a more intense religious experience could easily lead to solicitation. In her testimony before the Mallorca tribunal, thirty-year-old Gabriela Suñer related that she came to confess with the Capuchin Father Pablo Ginard because she was dissatisfied with her former confessor. Not only had he ordered her not to confess more than twice a week, but he simply could not meet her need to "overcome all obstacles in order to excel in the love of Jesus Christ." In contrast, she was entirely satisfied with Ginard, who allowed her to confess on a daily basis and in whom she could confide her ardent religious feelings. Evidently, the fact that Ginard had proved to be an excellent spiritual director outweighed his use of filthy and suggestive language in the confessional and made it impossible for Suñer to testify against him even when she was brought before the bar of the Inquisition.[41]

Ingrained habits of religious devotion could also prove inconvenient and embarrassing when a female penitent wanted to break off a relationship with a confessor who had solicited her. One day, after Catalina Vives had confessed with the Franciscan Jayme Barcelo for a number of years, he asked if he could visit her home not to have intercourse, but merely to fondle her. She permitted him to do this, but then became overcome with guilt and decided to terminate the relationship. She stopped confessing with him, but continued visiting the chapel of his convent on holy days and because of certain special devotions. On one occasion during the feast of San Salvador, he approached her while she stood before the image and whispered that he would like to thrust his tongue into her mouth. A second incident occurred on Holy Thursday when he touched her back and sides with his foot as she knelt in prayer in one of the side chapels. Barcelo's unwanted attentions forced her to abandon her visits to the chapel, but her new confessor, who was the vicar of the parish church, insisted that she denounce Barcelo to the Holy Office.[42]

The anxiety that many female penitents felt about confession, which was intensified by fears of damnation and confusion over what constituted mortal and venial sins, could also give rise to difficult and embarrassing situations arising in the confessional. The problem of the "troubled soul" who approached the bar of the confessional with trepidation gave rise to an enormous but rather contradictory literature during the Counter-Reformation. On the one hand, penitents were enjoined to make full and complete confessions. In the second volume of his confessors' manual, Pedro Galindo emphasized this with the terrifying story of a penitent who had made a hasty and incomplete confession with no real intention of showing proper contrition. Just as his confessor was about to absolve him, Christ appeared in the air above their heads and solemnly condemned both of them. This incident, Galindo warned, was a visible and dramatic, but hardly unique, demonstration of God's displeasure with inadequate confessions because God was silently condemning many insincere penitents and lax confessors every day.[43]

But Galindo was even more concerned about the excessively "scrupulous" penitent, usually a woman, who had so many qualms about the validity and completeness of her confession that she could never feel any sense of confidence and had to constantly return to make additional confessions or confess things that were not really sins.[44] His advice to such anxiety-prone individuals was to put themselves completely under their confessor's control and follow his advice in a humble and obedient manner even if that advice was clearly in error.[45]

The combination of intense anxiety about the need to confess sins fully and the incessant demand for slavish obedience to the confessor created a situation in which penitents felt they could not refuse to discuss anything that a confessor saw fit to bring up, even if was overtly sexual. Confessors who crossed that thin line between prudent inquiry into sexual conduct and prurient interest designed to satisfy their own need for sexual excitement posed a serious dilemma for penitents. If they were devoted daughters of the Church and confessed frequently, as many of the victims of solicitation did, they were attuned to the idea of absolute obedience to their confessors, but when these same confessors began asking questions of an overtly sexual nature, their confusion and anxiety about making a complete confession made it impossible to resist, even though their replies spurred an even greater sexual ebullition in the mind of the confessor.

Practice of a variety of physical mortifications designed to tame the body had long been an integral part of Christian piety. Moreover, if the history of female saints may serve as a guide, it appears that spiritually ambitious women have always shown an affinity for penitential activities.[46] Even though medieval-style societies of flagellants had largely disappeared by the sixteenth century, physical penance remained an approved method of pursuing greater spirituality. While extreme forms of physical discipline were practiced by such prominent religious figures as St. Simón de Rojas, milder forms were warmly recommended for ordinary people by moralists and theologians. Pérez de Valdivia argued that beatas should undergo some form of physical penance at least two nights a week and demanded that they wear a penitential garment consisting of a belt or girdle with spikes (silicio) every day.[47] Among the victims of solicitation, forty can be identified as practicing some form of physical mortification, from flagellation to wearing the silicio on a regular basis. Normally a program of this kind was carried on under the supervision of a woman's spiritual advisor, but for certain confessors, such practices carried a powerful erotic thrust that led directly to solicitation.[48]

Even though a bare majority of the victims (50.7 percent) were either willing to accept their confessors' advances or were ambivalent about them to the extent of participating to at least some degree, the largest single group (228) rejected these overtures outright. The pattern of rejection, however, varied significantly from a high of 76.9 percent among those of aristocratic and bourgeois origin and a little better than 70 percent among artisans, labradores, and servants to a low of 58.6 percent among nuns. This extraordinarily low figure, would seem to lend credence to the many observers in the seventeenth century and later who bewailed forced religious vocations and warned of the dangers of excessive contact between confessors and female religious.

In analyzing the pattern of rejection, several distinct causes can be delineated. Clearly the negative reactions of some penitents reflected a heightened religious consciousness that demonstrated the success of the Counter-Reformation in creating greater religious sensitivity among the popular masses. For this sort of penitent, the confessor's behavior violated everything that they had been taught about his role as spiritual advisor and their violent reaction to his attempt to solicit their sexual favors reflected their bitter disappointment. When José Estrada, the warden of the Franciscan convent of Buena Vista in Realejo (Tenerife), attempted to seduce his penitent, Barbara Agustina Padrón, by telling her that her husband was unfaithful and that he alone would love her, she reminded him that "he was sitting in Jesus' place" and that everything that they did was being observed by an image of the Virgin of Sorrows that had been placed on the wall of the chapel. The idea of holy images watching over the confessional, which was so reminiscent of Pedro Galindo's tale of Christ observing and then punishing lazy confessors and sinful penitents, was repeated by another one of Estrada's penitents. On one of his trips to preach and beg for alms, Estrada had stayed in the home of María Barrosa and her husband, a well-to-do farmer. Barrosa asked him to hear her confession there, but was outraged when he tried to touch her breasts. Denouncing him bitterly for having betrayed her trust, she asked him what would happen to her if she should die suddenly without having made a proper confession. She then pointed angrily to images of Christ and the Virgin hanging on the wall and reminded him that the holy images were watching him. Shamed by this, and indebted to his hostess for her hospitality, Estrada promised to administer a proper confession and did so.[49]

Heightened respect for the sacred was also at the heart of Juana Díaz del Sol's rejection of the advances of her confessor, Guillermo de Cames y Home. In 1777, the twenty-three-year old widow encountered Cames y Home for the first time when she went to confess with him in the collegiate church of La Orotava. While hearing her confession, he asked her where she lived, and although she lied about her address, he was able to find her anyway. Juana was incautious enough to let him in, but as soon as she had done so, he said that he had come to have intercourse with her and proceeded to take off his habit. She fled the house, but a few days later, he sent her the key to a vacant house with a note suggesting that they could meet there to have sex. The following morning, Juana went to the church to return the key, only to have him suggest that they have intercourse there at night in one of the side chapels dedicated to the Virgin. Hearing this, Juana became infuriated and asked him "how he could be impious enough to sin like that in church and particularly in front of an image of the Virgin Mary."[50]

In spite of the poor morale in many convents and the large number of unwilling nuns who were socially and sexually frustrated and, therefore, vulnerable to the wiles of unscrupulous confessors, nuns were by no means an easy target. Many nuns had a genuine and profound religious vocation. In her *Letters*, Teresa de Jesús refers over and over again to the eagerness with which girls came to join the order. In a letter from Segovia written in September 1574, she speaks of a novice who was to arrive the following Saturday "whose fervor amazes everyone."[51] In January of that year, she discusses the case of aristocratic young Casilda de Padilla, who entered the discalced Carmelite house at Valladolid in the face of opposition from her parents and as a result brought no dowry with her.[52] That such enthusiasm was not confined to the daughters of the upper classes is demonstrated by the fact that around the same time she received a poor, illiterate girl who was extremely eager to enter the order.[53]

Some female religious communities also demonstrated a strong esprit de corps that enabled them to fight successfully against domination by the vicars appointed by the superiors of male religious orders. In many cases, the nuns gave as the reason for their struggle the sexual advances made by male religious.[54] In one instance, the nuns of the Bernardine convent in Alcalá de Henares were eventually able to force out their vicar, Dr. Diego Ordaz, because he had formed the habit of mumbling obscenities under his breath as he heard their confessions.[55]

Alongside the cautionary or obscene literature of the seventeenth and eighteenth century that made convents seem like houses of prostitution, there exists another literature that speaks eloquently of the frustrations of paying court to a nun. For Quevedo, loving a nun was like loving "a thrush in a cage," while an anonymous poet described the relations between nuns and their devotees as "impossible desires aborted" and "flames amidst cold iron."[56]

The social proscription against sexual misconduct by nuns was further reinforced by a whole series of horrific folk tales about the fate of those who violated it. If mortal husbands became incensed at their wife's infidelity, God's anger at the infidelity of any of his wives would be unimaginable. Alonso de Andrade picked up a whole series of these tales and retold them in his book of advice for nuns. Usually the story would involve the nun receiving her lover in her cell or meeting him in church, and just as they were about to embrace, the devil would appear to carry them off.[57]

But not all of those who rejected their confessor's sexual advances did so out of such high-minded motives. Lucía Vera, a nineteen-year-old from a prominent hidalgo family in La Laguna, simply could not take the advances of forty-four-year-old Juan Felipe Cabeza very seriously. After leaving the confessional without finishing her confession, she told her mother about the entire incident and the two women had a good laugh over it.[58]

Fear of the Inquisition was another reason why penitents might reject a sexual overture even though they may have been strongly tempted. Josepha María, a twenty-one-year-old single woman living in the village of Santa Cruz on the island of San Miguel in the Canaries was pleased when her confessor suggested that he might send a present to her at home. But a few days later, before anything had happened, she heard the Edict of Faith preached in the village church and turned her confessor in to the local commissioner.[59]

In certain cases, it was sheer prudery that led to rejection. The Augustinian friar Luis de Valdiviesa was courting disaster when he began telling Isabel Pérez de Salazar about his many affairs with women shortly after she finished her confession. Unbeknownst to him, Pérez de Salazar was official chaperone (duena) to the countess of Priego. She promptly reported him to the local commissioner, but was so disgusted by what he had said that she flatly refused to be specific about the terms he had used "because they were so lewd that modesty forbade her to utter them."[60]

For many penitents, loss of reputation and especially the potentially dire consequences of an illicit affair in a society where both law and custom sanctioned the murder of an adulteress by her husband prevented them from accepting their confessor's proposals.[61] Certainly the fear of the violence that she would have to face from her husband and in-laws was one of the things uppermost in the mind of Catalina Flexas y Proassi when she refused her confessor's repeated requests for an assignation outside of church. Throughout the six months that he heard her almost weekly confessions, she continually refused his demands, commenting that "he could not keep a secret," and warned him not to disturb the neighbors when he passed in front of her house. Her fear of her in-laws was so intense that she did not even dare to go to the Holy Office despite being ordered to do so by her new confessor because she was afraid that if they found out she had been solicited, they would murder her.[62]

The shock of discovering that a priest whom they had, in the words of one disillusioned penitent, "thought of as a saint" and in whom they had been told to have absolute trust was no more than a man caused some penitents to become extremely upset.[63] A few even sustained severe psychological damage whose scars they carried with them for some time thereafter. The most common reaction among the sixty-nine individuals who testified about having had extremely negative feelings about being solicited was to become highly agitated. Sometimes penitents tried to rise and leave the church without finishing their confession, but in more extreme cases, they would have physical symptoms. When Francisco Pons began asking twenty-five-year-old Catalina Real y Massanet about her sexual relations with her recently deceased husband, she broke out into a cold sweat and ran from the confessional.[64] For Madalena Joffre, a particularly devout young woman who normally confessed every day, the shock of her confessor's betrayal was even greater. After listening with increasing frustration and dismay as her confessor, Antonio Ballester, attempted repeatedly to get her to tell him the details of her sex life, she fainted and had to be carried home unconscious.[65]

Many penitents attempted to repress the feelings of anger and betrayal that they felt so strongly. When Antonia Pérez was solicited by her confessor, Pedro de Ortega, she became incensed and wanted to strike him. Instead, she did nothing and remained to complete her confession because there were many people in the church and she did not want to cause any comment.[66]

Repressed feelings of anger, shame, and disgust had tragic consequences for another devout young woman, Mariana Llorens, the daughter of a mas-

ter silk worker in Valencia. In 1764 she testified that, four years earlier, when
she was nineteen, she had gone to confess with José de San Miguel on the
feast day of the Virgin del Carmen. Although she was very devout, she had a
particularly good reason to come to confession that day since she had committed the sin of masturbation the night before. It is easy to imagine her horror
when, instead of assuaging what must have been a painful sense of guilt by
giving her penance, San Miguel blandly assured her that it was not at all sinful for a woman to touch herself with sensual intent. Obviously sensing an
opportunity, he then began asking her highly personal questions such as
whether she had grown any pubic hair and started menstruating. In her testimony before the inquisitorial official assigned to interview her, Llorens
graphically described how at that point she had felt "suffocated" and was
forced to flee the confessional. For the next four years, she was unable to
stop thinking about what had happened and felt extremely "depressed and
disconsolate," but was so ashamed and guilty that she was unable to talk about
her experience with anyone. Finally, one day when she was preparing to go
to church, she reached a kind of crisis during which the horror of what had
happened rose before her with extraordinary force while she also felt that
God himself was impelling her to relate her experience to her new confessor, in whom she had a great deal of confidence. Going to his convent, she
made a complete confession and felt an immediate sense of relief even though
he told her she had to make a deposition before the Holy Office.[67]

A woman who refused the advances of a particularly obdurate priest could
also find her personal life destroyed, especially if she could not find another
confessor who would support her in reporting the offense to the Holy Office.
Francisca de Jesús, a thirty-five-year-old single woman from La Orotava, had
the misfortune to encounter just such a situation when she went to confess
with Pedro de Castro in the absence of her ordinary confessor. Castro, who
was already having an affair with her sister and niece, immediately decided
that he wanted to add her to his conquests. After Castro held her hand in the
confessional and harassed her while she was in church for a vigil, her regular
confessor returned and she asked his advice about what to do. Instead of telling
her to go to the Holy Office, he absolved her and advised her to confront
Castro in the confessional and threaten to denounce him. This tactic was a
complete failure as Castro merely laughed off her threats and declared that
he was going to come to her house that night as he was madly in love with
her. Frightened of what might ensue, Francisca fled to a relative's house in
the village of Guía, where she remained for more than a month. But if she
hoped that in her absence Castro's passion for her would have cooled, she
was to be sorely disappointed since almost as soon as she returned, he forced
his way into her home and tried to rape her. Deprived of any support from
her regular confessor and with no husband or male relative to protect her,
she fell into a deep depression and was forced to remain in bed for several
weeks while doctors bled her. Hearing of her weakened condition, Castro
invaded her home on two separate occasions and assaulted her sexually.
Finally, after four years during which her confessor kept promising to com-

plain to the bishop on her behalf but did nothing, Francisca got up the courage to go to a Holy Office commissioner herself, and Castro was arrested and convicted on charges of solicitation.[68] For Francisca de Jesús and many other women who were vulnerable because they had no male protectors, the Inquisition offered them their only real opportunity to rid themselves of the unwanted attentions of an abusive confessor. Unfortunately, the Inquisition's jurisdiction over solicitation covered only a small percentage of the potential sexual harassment and abuse that priests could perpetrate. An exclusive concern with the misuse of the sacrament of penance meant that most women who were abused by priests were left to go it alone in a ecclesiastical court system that was frequently more concerned with avoiding scandal and protecting the reputation of the ecclesiastical estate than it was with providing relief for the victims of sexual crimes.

Of course, a clever woman could use solicitation to her advantage. When Juana Díaz went to confess with the Augustinian Ignacio Sauce for the first time, he hinted broadly of his desire to have sexual relations with her and then tried unsuccessfully to enter her house on several occasions. Díaz, the daughter of a wealthy labrador, was being courted by a mulatto, but the match was opposed by one of her relatives, Dr. Juan Díaz de Llanos, an influential local benefice holder. Seizing on her problems with Sauce as a way of removing Díaz de Llanos's objections to the match, Díaz went to confess with him and told him that she was beset by several aggressive suitors and had even been solicited in the confessional. This was the reason, she went on, why she "wanted to get married even if it were with a negro." This not so subtle appeal to male anxiety about the loss of family honor as a result of female promiscuity had an instantaneous effect. Díaz de Llanos removed his objections to the match, but insisted that Díaz denounce Sauce to the Holy Office.[69]

Solicitation also had a negative impact on the religious lives of its victims, increasing the anxiety that many of them felt in approaching the sacrament of penance and making it more difficult or even impossible for them to take communion. Some victims who realized they were not receiving a proper confession simply went to another confessor in order to receive what they thought was proper absolution. After Gaspar Palenzuela, a Franciscan from a convent in the village of Telde in the Canaries, had asked Barbara Rodríguez for intimate details about her sex life with her deceased husband, she knew she could not take communion and went immediately to the local curate to confess again.[70]

Things did not go as easily for Urusula Sardana, a thirty-two-year-old former prostitute living in the Magadalen house in Las Palmas. One day, purely by accident, she found herself confessing with Antonio Pastor, a Franciscan who happened to be one of her old lovers. He recalled their former relationship and began importuning her for sex. She became very upset, telling him that this could do her "great harm" because they were in the presence of the holy sacrament. Leaving the confessional, she felt an enormous wave of anxiety and fear and found herself unable to tell what had happened in her two subsequent confessions. This further complicated the problem, however, as she was aware that she had not made a full and complete confession on either of those two occasions and therefore felt she could not take communion. After two months, her failure to take communion came to the attention of the prioress, who questioned her about it, and Sardana was forced to discuss the details of the "impediment" that had kept her away from it. On the prioress's orders, she then confessed with the ordinary confessor assigned to the Magdalen house, who ordered her to denounce Pastor before the Inquisition.[71]

Interestingly enough, and in spite of the revulsion that many of them felt for the priest who had solicited sexual favors from them in the confessional, forty-nine victims returned to confess with the culprit one or more times after the first incident of solicitation. The uneven distribution of Spain's parish clergy meant that in some villages penitents faced the choice of not confessing or of confessing with the very same priest who had solicited them. This was exactly what happened in the tiny village of Piedrabuena (Toledo), where in the late 1570s there were only two confessors available, the lascivious Gabriel de Osca and Pedro del Pinar, who was old, sick, and partially deaf. As a result, when Lucía Hernández became furious with Gabriel de Osca after he had put his hands on her breasts while she confessed, she decided to drastically reduce the number of confessions that she made and just fulfil the yearly precept. On the other hand, María Díaz, another one of Osca's victims, did return to confess with him simply because no other appropriate confessor was available in the village.[72]

Traditional antifeminism and male anxiety about the possibe sexual misconduct of wives and lovers was also responsible for forcing many victims to continue seeing abusive confessors. María Quadrada tried to stop confessing with Pedro López after he solicited her in the confessional and then tried to rape her, but whenever she stopped, he would send her messages through her husband's servants asking her to come and speak with him and even threatened to come to her home in an obvious effort to use her fear of her husband to make her keep coming back.[73]

For single women living at home, the problem was a complete lack of personal autonomy. Bernarda Suárez de Quintana's confessor, Mateo González, was a friend of the family and frequent visitor to her home, so that when she tried to stop confessing with him, he went to her parents to complain that she had deserted him and was going to "strange confessors." Not only was she forced to return to his confessional, but when she became seriously ill, he was called in by her parents and raped her twice in her own bedroom.[74]

An even more terrible example of what could happen when children's needs were completely subordinated to the wishes of their parents and relatives is provided by the case of Paula Petronila de la Paz, the nineteen-year-old daughter of a labrador family from the village of Santa Cruz in the Canaries. Paula's confessor was her uncle, fifty-three-year-old Mathias de la Paz Carvello, a Franciscan and warden of the local convent, who began soliciting her during their second confession. The young girl was deeply offended by what had happened and made up her mind never to confess with him again, but when she tried to break off the relationship, Paz Carvello came to her home and convinced her parents that she needed to confess every week with him. These "confessions" took place in the wee hours of the morning at a time when Paz Carvello was sure no one would be in the chapel. Invariably he abused her sexually during these sessions, and when she protested, he mocked her and told her that she had no one to protect her at home. He also told her to forget her fiance because he wanted to reserve her for himself. After several months of this torture, Paula finally summoned up enough courage to go to her father and was able to convince him to put a stop to her uncle's abuses.[75]

Victims of solicitation and the priests who confessed them were both caught in the contradictions of the new sexual and moral ethic of the Counter-Reformation. Priests were expected to remain celibate as never before, while being taught that both married and unmarried people committed many unnatural sexual acts about which it was legitimate and necessary to inquire in the confessional. The laity were being taught to respect, even venerate, the priest in his role as confessor, while holding him to a standard of conduct unprecedented in the history of the Church. At the same time, women, who were increasingly restricted in their movements by social fears about promiscuity, were flocking to the churches attracted by the many new devotions and lured by the promise that a renovated sacrament of confession could offer them opportunities for self-expression unavailable with husbands and families. Sexual frustration, increasing devotion, and the need for self-expression could transform the confessional into a place of assignation. But those victims of sexual solicitation who resisted their confessor's advances could draw on the heightened awareness derived from Counter-Reformation religious education. They knew that indecent language, suggestive questioning, and outright sexual advances in the confessional were wrong and sinful. In spite of the pressure from families to continue confessing with abusive priests, which led to tragic consequences for certain individuals, the presence of the Inquisition gave victims an institutionalized means of retribution against a powerful priesthood that might otherwise have been immune from punishment.

Chapter 7

Submissive and Ambivalent Penitents

Although almost half of the penitents rejected their confessor's advances, sometimes with great indignation, fully 39 percent (220) greeted them warmly. In certain cases, defying the stereotype of female passivity that can be found in the contemporary literature, women even took an aggressive role and actively sought sexual favors from their confessor.

Among the laywomen who comprised the overwhelming majority of compliant penitents (84 percent), two characteristics are particularly worthy of note: such penitents were generally older than those who rejected solicitation, and married women were disproportionately represented relative to their number in the group of victims as a whole. The average age of the assenting penitents at the time of their testimony before the Holy Office was 36.8 years, considerably older than the average of 25.0 for those who rejected their confessor's advances. With an approximately six-year delay between solicitation and appearance before the Holy Office, that would make the average age of assenting individuals 30.8 years at the time when they were solicited. This impression of greater maturity is corroborated by marital status, with 39.6 percent of assenting penitents married, in contrast to 33 percent of those who refused solicitation. Widows also comprised a somewhat larger percentage of willing penitents, 14.0 percent more of the victims than of those who rebuffed their confessor.

What these figures suggest is that, in spite of efforts by the Church to ensure that young women could marry the person of their choice, marital problems were still extremely common and that the confessor provided one source, perhaps the only source, of emotional and sexual relief for many married women. In fact, some confessors were so accustomed to hearing marital complaints that they took them as a cue to make sexual overtures to their penitents. When recently married María Vélez told her parish priest Joseph Sánchez about the mistreatment she had suffered at the hands of her husband, he responded by telling her that "he could provide her with everything she needed and desired" and begged her not to leave the church before speaking with him further.[1]

The first obstacle to marital happiness was the choice of a mate by family agreement without consulting the individuals involved. Even though Church courts offered protection to young girls who eloped with their lovers against their parents' will, the Church was far from unanimous in supporting free choice. In the early sixteenth century, Juan Luis Vives expressed the prevailing orthodoxy when he declared that a young girl should have nothing to do with the choice of a mate, as her parents knew much more about the world and were, therefore, in a better position to judge what would make her happy. She could only watch the process, without making her desire for marriage too obvious, and pray that her parents would not choose someone who would impede her in the exercise of piety and Christian charity.[2] In 1642, the prominent Jesuit theologian and official censor for the Suprema, Alonso de Andrade, predicted disaster for those who married without their parents' consent. Their husbands would turn out to be "perverse and malicious" and would treat them badly, while those who accepted their parents' direction would enjoy all the felicity that a successful marriage could provide.[3] The widely used *Summa* of Manuel Rodríguez, first published in 1593, even went so far as to assert that children who married against their father's wishes were committing a mortal sin.[4] Certainly we can assume that in most instances, and especially in rural areas, girls did not expect to freely choose the person whom they would marry. When Pedro de Ortega, sacristan in the village of el Prado, asked nineteen-year-old María Izquierda if she would like to marry his brother, she replied that "that is something you will have to take up with my grandfather and not with me." Frustrated because he hoped to use the proposed marriage as a way of enjoying the girl's sexual favors with his brother's compliance, Ortega pressed her, declaring that it was her desire that he wished to learn, but she still refused to be drawn out even when he flattered her by telling her she was attractive and that it was no sin for a young girl to paint her face or admire herself in the mirror.[5]

In a remarkable work published in 1681, Pedro Galindo paints a doleful picture of marriage in contemporary Spanish society. Although Galindo represented the Catholic tradition of disparaging marriage in favor of celibacy, his long experience as a confessor who had interviewed thousands of women penitents makes his book an extremely useful guide to the problems of marriage in the seventeenth century. Galindo begins by bemoaning the frequency of arranged marriages with contracts signed long before the girl had reached the age of maturity. When these children grow older they usually go through with the match either because of their respect for parental authority or because of the "threats and ill treatment" that they had to suffer until they agreed.[6] The marriage itself often takes place with excessive haste, so that the couple have little time or opportunity to get to know one another. Once they are alone together, the naive young wife soon finds that her husband, who had been so gentle, polite, and generous when he was courting her, begins treating her harshly, forbidding her to visit her girlfriends and parents, insults, and even beats her. After the first blush of youth fades and the young woman becomes a mother, her husband loses interest in her almost entirely, begins to gamble away the family wealth and forces her to sell her belongings so that he can support a mistress. Later, after a visit from the tax collector, who confiscates virtually everything of value in the house including the shawl that she wrapped herself in to go to mass, she waits for her husband to return from his revels, afraid that if she does not open the door at his first knock, he will kick and beat her unmercifully. All this, of course, in marked contrast to the felicity and tranquility that she had enjoyed as a single girl in her parents' home.[7] To those who reply to this depressing story by averring that not all men are evil and that there are many who love their wives and carry out their family obligations faithfully, Galindo replied that they all make fair promises, but for many women things turn out very differently.

We can catch a glimpse of one of these brutal, abusive husbands through testimony received in an Inquisition case where the penitent had complained so often about her husband that her confessor came to believe that she would accept his advances. Vicenta Roig, who lived in Onteniente with her husband Antonio, a carpenter, confessed on a monthly basis with Vicente Yago, a Dominican from the convent of San Juan y San Vicente. Emboldened by her frequent complaints about her husband, Yago repeatedly suggested that they meet at the home of an "honorable" woman who would allow them to be alone together. Although she was so tempted that she went so far as to ask who would be her confessor if she accepted his proposal, in the end she did nothing because she was afraid of her husband, a man she described as having a "savage disposition," who would probably murder her if he found out.[8]

The enormous confusion, anxiety, and distress that a young wife could experience in the first few months of her marriage is clearly illustrated by the case of seventeen-year-old Esperanza Olivera, who came before the Mallorca tribunal in April 1636. Poor, illiterate, and frightened of her husband, who treated her so brutally that at one time he threatened to cut off her head if she refused to take off her shawl at a picnic, Olivera was also several months pregnant when she began confessing with Pedro Onofre Martín. Sensing that she was terrified of childbirth, Martín sought to win her over by offering her abortion tablets, which he claimed were safe since he had given them to some nuns. Although Olivera rejected her confessor's overtures and gave away the abortion tablets, she was sufficiently unhappy with her marriage to see a figure resembling Martín in a vision while she was in bed with her husband. In fact, not only could she see Martín, but he even spoke to her, confirming her fear that neither her husband nor her mother-in-law really loved her, and encouraged her to run away with him. Esperanza Olivera, like many other poor women, had little choice but to conceal her resentment and fear behind a mask of cheerful obedience. In the absence of divorce or legal separation on the grounds of mental or physical cruelty, fantasies about escape could do little to alter an unhappy situation.[9]

Galindo's pessimistic view of marriage was shared by many observers in the sixteenth and seventeenth centuries, including Fray Luis de León, who warned young women that "you lose your liberty on the day that you are joined in matrimony."[10] He, like Galindo, favored the life of the cloister, where women could express themselves more freely. Marriage was made to seem so unattractive that some women went to great extremes to avoid it. Isabel Riera, the spiritualist from Mallorca, spoke approvingly of a young woman who was pretending to be possessed by the devil in order to "avoid marriage and thereby serve God better."[11]

Apart from the fact that Galindo's ideas about marriage were based on the confessions of numerous women who had come to him with stories just as bad or worse than the one he told, what is interesting about his work is that he had a sense of some of the social constraints that made a happy marriage difficult, while his own conservatism made it impossible for him to suggest any real solutions. Galindo makes a special point of the extreme economic insecurity that many married women felt. They trembled whenever their husbands left the house even if it was only to go to the plaza, and if husbands left on a long trip, wives feared that they would be robbed or killed. If something were to happen to their husbands, they would be left destitute with children to care for and no marketable skills. At the same time, however, he describes the ideal wife as extremely timid and obedient to her husband, unused to social intercourse, and with limited educational qualifications, exactly the sort of person who would indeed be left destitute if her husband were to disappear from the scene.[12]

Galindo was also willing to admit that one of the worst problems connected with marriage was its indissolubility. Here, he uses one of his most colorful metaphors to compare an unhappy marriage to the way in which certain pagan tyrants martyred Christians by tying them to a dead man and leaving them there until horror and putrefying flesh brought about their own demise. In the same way, an unhappily married couple suffered their own calvary of suffering and spiritual death by being tied irrevocably to another person they abhorred.[13]

At times, solicitation itself could become caught up in the kind of violent mutual antagonism to which Galindo referred. Even though Barbara Agustina Padrón had repeatedly and indignantly rejected the advances of her confessor, Joseph Estrada, she continued confessing with him for more than a year after she had told her husband about the first incident in order to make him jealous.

This attempt to irritate her husband, however, nearly ended in tragedy. During a particularly violent quarrel over her relationship with Estrada, her mother entered their bedroom to find her son-in-law standing next to the bed with a cutlass and only just prevented him from killing her daughter by thrusting herself between them.[14]

Those women who realized, too late, that their husbands were neglectful, verbally abusive, or worse had little recourse. In some instances, ecclesiastical courts would order the removal of a woman from an abusive situation, but were generally reluctant to hand down a sentence of formal separation, which would publicize a failure of the marital bond. Of the 152 petitions for separation received by the ecclesiastical tribunal in the Barcelona diocese between 1565 and 1650, only 20 resulted in a sentence favorable to the petitioner.[15]

Violent quarrels were only the most spectacular manifestations of the deepseated problems that made marital happiness difficult to achieve in early modern Spain. Even though liberal theologians like Vicente de Mexía were willing to grant a wife a theoretical equality with her husband, most writers placed her in a distinctly inferior position. Wives were expected to tolerate their husband's behavior, whatever he was like because even if he was mean and disagreeable, a drunk, or a vagrant, he was still her husband "and no quality of his [could] remove her obligation."[16]

The double standard on adultery is perhaps the most conclusive demonstration of this inferiority since wives were enjoined to tolerate their husband's behavior "since he has more freedom to do as he wishes." The wife was to win over her husband with patience and forbearance. Juan Luis Vives even gives an example of a Flemish matron who invited her husband to bring his mistress home, gave up her own apartments, and treated the woman like a sister until the husband, recognizing his error, broke off the affair.[17]

On the other hand, since fidelity was the chief attribute of the good wife, sexual indiscretions were much more serious for wives than for husbands and an adulteress was little more than a "treacherous whore."[18] The virtual immunity from legal prosecution for adultery that the law granted to men stood in sharp contrast to the laws that called for the death sentence for women convicted of the same offense. Women's lack of legal channels to redress their grievances against an errant husband meant that her anger and jealousy was focused within the marriage itself. One of the main reasons for Barbara Agustina Padrón's reckless and provocative behavior was her husband's reputation as an adulterer.

High infant mortality, especially during the many epidemics that ravaged Spain during the early modern period, was another factor that tended to hollow out the emotional core of marriage and make women more vulnerable to the blandishments of male confessors. Frequent pregnancies exposed women to many tragic disappointments, as nearly two live births were necessary to produce one adult during the seventeenth century.[19] In order to minimize the effect of these shocks, women were advised to limit their emotional involvement with their children. According to Vives, the woman who could not conceive was "fortunate even blessed," as she would be spared the pains and dangers of pregnancy. Furthermore, he warned mothers against treating their children with excessive tenderness since they were all inclined to vice, especially the girls.[20]

Many married women were also exposed to the emotional and economic burden of husbands who were absent for long periods. Emotional deprivation and economic hardship, in turn, could make their confessors seem particularly attractive. Manuela Blesa, whose husband, an agricultural laborer, was frequently absent looking for work, was described by Father Felipe del Carmen as "running blindly after all her confessors" and becoming extremely angry if any of them refused her advances.[21] One of these confessors was Felix Petarch, the parish priest in Eslida in Valencia's remote Sierra de Espadán, with whom she had a three-year relationship that began in the confessional of the parish church.[22]

María Lorenzo's husband was serving as a sailor in the Indies squadron when she began her affair with Baltasar de Olivares, the acting prior of the Dominican convent in La Palma. In addition to kissing and caressing through the holes in the screen of his confessional in the chapel, they had frequent sexual relations in the home of one of her friends.[23]

One consequence of the economic difficulties and high unemployment that many parts of Spain experienced during the seventeenth and eighteenth centuries was that many men simply deserted their families. The refusal of the ecclesiastical courts to allow remarriage in spite of long desertion left the woman bereft not only of financial support, but of any legitimate outlets for her sexual and emotional needs, thus providing an opportunity for confessors bent on seducing their penitents. In his confession before the Mallorca tribunal, the Trinitarian Pedro Jorge Foil told of one penitent who responded to the standard confessor's question about whether she hated or wished the death of anyone by replying that she had frequently wished her husband dead as he had deserted her, leaving her destitute with three children.[24] Foil, who had solicited other married women, saw his opportunity and offered to aid her in return for sexual favors. In this case, the penitent refused, saying that she would rather remain destitute than offend God, but other confessors had more luck with the same situation. The Franciscan Juan Ascanio from the convent of San Miguel, for example, was able to have a four-year affair with Blasina Domínguez, whose husband had deserted her to go to the Indies some twenty years earlier.[25]

Even more fundamental to the failure of so many marriages were the feelings of sexual dissatisfaction and frustration that were an almost inevitable consequence of the traditional Catholic conception of nuptial relations. The earliest Church fathers were highly suspicious of sex, viewing it as a powerful impulse that could overcome human reason. Premarital sex was a mortal sin, but sexual relations in marriage were also suspect. For St. Augustine, any marital sex designed to avoid procreation was sinful and even married couples who behaved properly were enjoined to cease having sexual relations after having one or two children. St. Jerome took an even more negative view of sex in marriage, which he saw as having no value except as a way of avoiding illicit extramarital fornication. Consequently, he and other writers said that a man who had sex with his wife too frequently was an adulterer. Sex in marriage should be undertaken rarely and in a spirit of moderation instead of lust since "nothing is filthier than to have sex with your wife as you might do with another woman."[26] This famous phrase inspired much of the medieval thinking about the purpose of marital sex and gave rise to a number of opinions, some highly pessimistic and others more reasonable.[27] The fact that proper or licit marital sex was so hard to define created enormous confusion and insecurity and made each conjugal act a cause for anxiety. In spite of the fact that later theologians like the Spanish Jesuit Tomás Sánchez tried to moderate Church teaching on marital sex, the idea that there was something sinful about it had penetrated deeply into the popular imagination. Pedro Galindo alludes to this in his discussion of popular misconceptions about mortal and venial sins when he tells us that some individuals wrongly confess as a mortal sin sexual relations in marriage designed to secure or heighten arousal. Such popular misconceptions were reinforced by priests who continued in the old rigorist tradition. In a visitation carried out in 1585, Inquisitor Fernando Martínez received a deposition from a witness who declared that Dr. Francisco Bezerria, a canon in the collegiate church of Antequera, had declared in several sermons that "the sex act in marriage is always sinful" and that "Our Lord can no longer tolerate the sinfulness of coitus in marriage."[28]

Even though Tomás Sánchez and other post-Tridentine theologians took a somewhat more liberal attitude toward marital sex, they still left a cloud of suspicion over anything that did not lead to "natural" intercourse, which was carefully defined as coitus in the missionary position. Other positions were seen as making conception less likely and therefore subverting the proper goal of all sexual relations. Other sexual practices were permitted if they led to "natural" intercourse, but were venially sinful if they were done merely for pleasure. If orgasm resulted from foreplay, the sin was considered mortal.[29]

Apart from the strictures placed on foreplay, coital positions, and orgasm, moralists felt that women should play an entirely passive role in sexual relations. According to Juan Luis Vives, women should never be aggressive in seeking sex from their husbands. Instead, married women should follow the example of Zenobia, the ancient queen of Palmyra, who never allowed her husband to have sex with her unless she wished to become pregnant and "had no more sensitivity in her sexual parts than in her feet or hands."[30]

Confronted with a society that systematically ignored their sexual needs, condemned all forms of sexual experimentation, and sharply restricted the frequency of coitus, many women felt a profound sense of sexual dissatisfaction. These feelings were reflected in Pedro de Luxán's *Coloquios matrimoniales*, in which Eulalia, one of the women involved in the dialogue, declares that she would "sometimes rather sleep next to a pregnant pig" than share her husband's bed.[31] Sexual dissatisfaction was certainly one of the reasons for the remarkable string of successes that the Franciscan, Francisco de las Llagas, had with married women. His relationship with Victoria Casas began in the confessional when she complained about her sexual relationship with her husband. Carried away, as he later told Toledo's inquisitors, by "his desire" and "ensnared by the wiles of the devil," he asked her if she would like it better if he took her husband's place in bed. She agreed that she would and the next time she came to confess, told Llagas that she was feeling much better because every time she had sex with her husband she thought of him. As their relationship developed, it was marked by the breaking of numerous sexual taboos, including foreplay in the confessional box and mutual masturbation, which Victoria told him she enjoyed more than having intercourse with her husband.[32] Something very similar happened with twenty-five-year-old Isabel de Tena, who began her affair with Llagas by offering him flowers that she drew from between her breasts during confession. He responded by offering her almonds, which she took from his mouth through a hole in the confessional screen. She became obsessed with Llagas, thought about him every night, and had coitus with him in her home on more than twenty occasions. They also engaged in untraditional forms of sex, including oral stimulation and mutual masturbation in the confessional and in her home.[33]

At forty-three, when Francisco de las Llagas was brought before the Toledo tribunal, he had a long history of affairs, mainly with married women, that had been carried on both inside and outside the confessional. As an unusually sensitive and imaginative lover in an age of stultifying conformity, anxiety, and negativism about sex, he could offer the kind of sensual joy so often missing in the marriages of the period. For Isabel de Tena, who was described by inquisitorial notary Bartolomé Sánchez Plaza as "devout" and "extremely modest," his blend of gentle sensuality and daring sexual practices was simply overwhelming. She became so obsessed with him that she began confessing with him three times a week just to be near him.

But Llagas, too, was a victim of the Counter-Reformation's negative view of sex. He kept a scourge by his bedside and used it frequently on himself and was constantly feeling the shafts of God's anger entering his breast to alert him to change his life and resist temptation. Unfortunately for Llagas, but perhaps fortunately for some of his married penitents, he was unable to do this and therefore provided them with a degree of sensual pleasure sorely lacking at home.

If married women experienced frustrations and difficulties that made them willing participants in seduction by their confessors, widows also had special reasons for finding their confessors attractive. Theologians and moralists writing during the early modern period were agreed that loss of a husband was the worst calamity that could befall a woman, but were equally unwilling to support the most obvious solution: remarriage.[34] The traditional Catholic bias against remarriage was expressed by St. Augustine, who saw the death of a spouse as providing widows with an opportunity to gain spiritual merit by leading a life of continence. St. John Chrysostom, like Augustine, wrote in opposition to second marriages because they represented a concession to sensual desires. He advised widows to dedicate themselves to lives of religious observance and devotion after the death of a spouse.[35] Such attitudes continued to be repeated in confessors' manuals and other writings right through the end of the seventeenth century and beyond. In his *Excelencias de la castidad y virginidad*, published in 1681, Pedro Galindo follows this tradition by denouncing widows who remarry for "giving way to lust."[36] Law and custom also made it difficult for widows to remarry.[37]

The destitute state in which many widows were left, however, made it intolerable and unrealistic for them to follow the precepts laid down for them by the male Church fathers. They were desperate to remarry if at all possible, and that very desperation could drive them into the hands of a confessor who was determined to take advantage of their predicament to obtain sexual favors. A tragic portrait of one such widow, eager to remarry, but faced with intense opposition from her prospective husband's family, emerges from the case of the Augustinian Juan Alcocer, who was tried for solicitation in 1621.

Ana Conellas, who was left widowed and impoverished at age twenty-seven, succeeded in establishing a liaison with a young stonecutter who promised to marry her. His father was so strongly opposed to the match that he made his son enter a monastery in the far-off village of Mercadel as a border. This enforced separation drove Ana to despair, so that when Alcocer, her long-time confessor, promised to see her lover and encourage him to resist parental pressure while he visited Mercadel to give a sermon, she was intensely grateful.

On his return, however, he made it clear that he expected Ana to repay him by granting him sexual favors. Terrified at the thought that her lover would be unable to marry her and, as she described herself, "despondent and with no one to console her," she was willing to do virtually anything in order to assure herself of Alcocer's continued support. After he promised flatly that he would make sure that her marriage would take place, Ana allowed him to caress her body and sexual parts on six or seven occasions in the confessional, and then had intercourse with him in her house one day when she pretended she was very ill and needed a confessor. In the end, things ended happily for Ana Conellas since she did marry the young stonecutter after her future father-in-law relented. Her testimony clinched the Mallorca tribunal's case against Alcocer, who had already been denounced eleven years earlier. Her predicament illustrates the anxiety and insecurity that could make some widows easy prey to the wiles of an unscrupulous confessor.[38]

The motives that single women had for acceding to the blandishments of soliciting confessors were similar to those of widows, especially if they had passed their mid twenties or had little chance of marriage because of economic or personal circumstances. In an age when marriage was viewed as a business arrangement based on the ability of the wife to supply her husband through her dowry with some of the capital he needed to provide a living for her and their children, many women were obliged to remain single.[39] At the same time, their sexual conduct had to be above reproach since any misstep would be fatal to family honor. Like Antonia Sastre, whose brother forced her to end her affair with Father Jayme Massanet, single women were under close scrutiny and had little social or sexual freedom.[40]

In certain respects, the reformation of morals that was such an important part of the post-Tridentine period worsened the position of poor single women and made them even more desperately eager to get married. Concubinage, which was roundly condemned at the Council of Trent, became a less and less viable option for poor women who wished to establish a long-term affective relationship, but did not have the dowry necessary for marriage. The prohibition of concubinage meant that the old tolerance for unmarried mothers was replaced by hostility, and a woman who had an illegitimate child was often tempted to abandon or kill it.[41]

All of these trends came together in the tragic case of nineteen-year-old Antonia González, the daughter of a poor farmer in the village of Zujar in the Canaries, and provided her confessor Francisco Carrascosa with an opportunity for seduction. One day in the confessional Antonia told Carrascosa that she was pregnant by her fiance and that she would probably come to term shortly after they were scheduled to be married. Fearing that she would lose her honor and that her fiance's family would repudiate her, she begged Carrascosa to get her an abortion. He promised to procure a special potion that she could take, but told her that it would not work unless he had a piece of her pubic hair and allowed him have sexual relations with her. The desperate girl agreed, and they had intercourse in a disused room in her house, but she balked at taking the potion that Carrascosa had mixed up for her and ended by drowning the child.[42]

Some unscrupulous priests used a single woman's eagerness to get married at any cost to facilitate their sexual access to them by marrying them to a complaisant relative or friend. These quasi marriages may have been less than ideal for the couple, but they gave the priest a convenient means of continuing to enjoy the favors of the young woman in a way that did not compromise his role as confessor. One priest who used this device very successfully was José de Acuña, who served as prior of the Dominican convent on the island of San Miguel in the Canaries. Acuña, who admitted in his confession before the Inquisition in December 1746 to having had numerous affairs with women, was able to continue his relationship with Josepha Volcana by marrying her to her own first cousin in spite of canonical prohibitions. Volcana's new husband looked the other way as Acuña continued his affair with her and had intercourse with her in her own home on numerous occasions.[43] The complaisant husband eventually recovered the full sexual services of his wife when Acuña tired of her several years later.

Single women used a variety of ways of escaping from the scrutiny of parents and relatives in order to satisfy their sexual needs. Catalina Gascón, the thirty-year-old daughter of a silk worker from Carcagente in Valencia, was able to get her parents' permission to visit friends in Ayora where the family used to live. She went, accompanied by Estefana López, a trustworthy widow who was a friend of the family. But Estefana could do little to prevent Gascón from confessing at the local Franciscan convent, where she allowed her confessor to take sexual liberties in the confessional and in the porter's lodge. She was careful not to get pregnant, however, and confined herself to exchanging filthy language with him and permitting him to kiss her and touch and caress her breasts.[44]

Predictably, the result of the restrictions placed on single women was to increase their level of sexual frustration, especially if their marital prospects

were slim. At twenty-five, María de Rosario lived and worked in the convent
of San José in La Orotava. Since both her parents were deceased and she
was cut off from any normal social life by the walls of the convent, her prospects of meeting men, much less getting married, were almost nil. As a consequence, she was extremely receptive when the convent's ordinary confessor, Fernando Cabrera, told her he found her attractive and began leaving
love notes for her in the porter's lodge. She responded eagerly to his advances,
and they spent several delicious hours in the confessional, touching fingers,
and exchanging affectionate words. Shortly thereafter, Cabrera was transferred, but before he left, he wrote to her asking that she say nothing about
what had passed between them. Rosario burned his love notes and his letter
and kept silent, concealing the truth even from her confessors until one day
five years later when her sense of remorse overwhelmed her and she told the
story to her confessor, who forced her to make a deposition before the Holy
Office.[45] It was precisely this fear of exposure through confession of sexual
sins to another, less tolerant individual that formed the subject of a cartoon
in the anticlerical weekly *El Motín*. In this cartoon, a sleek, well-fed young
priest cautions a young woman, who is obviously his housekeeper and defacto
wife, not to speak of certain "sins" if she has to make her confession before
another priest (Fig. 7.1).

Sexual frustration and a lack of marital prospects also explains the conduct
of twenty-four-year-old Francisca Romero. Described by the Holy Office
commissioner in Almagro as coming from a very poor family, she was forced
to work at home under the harsh discipline of her mother. According to neighbors, Romero was already fighting with her parents when she began confessing with Narcisio Antonio Cabañas, a well-known preacher and librarian in
the local Franciscan house. During her third confession with Cabañas, she
seduced him openly by complaining that she had a pain in her breasts and
inviting him to examine them. Cabañas was eager to comply and, after feeling her breasts, invited her down to the porter's lodge where they proceeded
to have intercourse. In the end, it was a remorseful Cabañas who initiated
inquisitorial proceedings by denouncing himself to the Toledo tribunal. For
her part, Romero confirmed his testimony when interviewed about it by a
commissioner, but she did so only reluctantly and at one point even tried to
repudiate her statement and deny that she had had any contact with him.
Romero's extreme reluctance to testify against her lover and the anguish at
having harmed him reveals her relationship with Cabañas as having been a
brief shaft of light in an otherwise dreary existence. For a single woman like
Francisca Romero, whose poverty presented a serious obstacle to marriage,
a complaisant priest like Narcisio Antonio Cabañas, whose role as a confessor offered the possibility of discretion, was the best and perhaps the only
real source of sexual satisfaction outside of prostitution.

Sometimes extreme sexual frustration combined with guilt about sexual
longings could produce a psychosomatic response that would cause the individual to exhibit both physical symptoms and mental disorder. At thirty-one,
Francisca Noseras was well known in Las Palmas for hysterical fits, during

Figure 7.1. A Priest Cautions His Housekeeper/Wife Not To Confess Certain Sins. *El Motín*, 1885, num. 36 (Biblioteca Nacional, Laboratorio Fotográfico)

which she seemed like a "mujer loca" (madwoman) and complained about pains in her breasts, sides, and uterus.

At the same time, as she told Vicente Pellicer, one of her confessors, she experienced powerful sexual yearnings, which she had no chance of satisfying because she was very poor, single, and lived with her mother and sister. With local doctors having failed to help her, she turned to spiritual remedies and consulted several priests, who concluded that she was possessed and tried unsuccessfully to cure her by exorcism. It was at this point, when all available remedies seemed to have failed, that Catalina Roca, the widow of a doctor, recommended that she approach Rafael Serre, a Trinitarian who had been confessing and exorcising a number of women who had complained of similar disorders.

After agreeing to become her confessor, Serre commenced his "treatment" by assuring Francisca Noseras that he could solve her problem and then by making crosses with his hands over her breasts and sides. At the same time, he began questioning her very closely about sexual matters, and she was forced to admit that she was beginning to have strong sexual fantasies about him. Since, as he later admitted, he had used exorcism as a way of satisfying his own sexual needs, Noseras's confession allowed them both to give vent to their sexual desires, and they had a two-year affair during which sexual acts were performed in several confessionals in the chapel. The relationship with Serre, however, was to provide Francisca Noseras with only temporary relief. Her physical symptoms, which may well have been connected with menstruation, continued, and she experienced a profound sense of guilt that tormented her until she finally gained some relief by making a general confession with Vicente Pellicer. Ironically enough, it was this confession that gave the Mallorca tribunal the evidence it needed to convict her erstwhile lover of solicitation.[46]

Both single and married women as well as widows were vulnerable to extreme economic distress at some time in their lives. Such penury, temporary or permanent, played right into the hands of priests who, as we have seen, frequently had ready money on hand from benefices, inheritances, fees for saying mass, hearing confession, or giving sermons.[47] The Dominican Fray Juan de Monseratte had a long and distinguished career in the order, rising to become reader in theology and arts and finally prior of the Dominican convent on the island of Ibiza. As part of his duties, Monseratte was responsible for a charitable fund that had been established to provide dowries for the daughters of the soldiers in the garrison. Already in her mid forties, with little prospect of marriage without a substantial dowry, Francisca Salazara was willing to trade sex for his support in obtaining the funds she needed. By 1621, when Monseratte was arrested by the Mallorca tribunal for daring to assert publicly that the Dominican order had special powers to absolve for solicitation, Salazara was married and testified against her former lover and benefactor with considerable reluctance.[48]

Another Dominican, Baltasar de Olivares, subprior of the convent in Las Palmas, was able to take advantage of a single woman who had come down in the world after the sudden demise of her father. Catalina de Segredos was the daughter of a notary left virtually impoverished when her father died, so that when Olivares offered her money one day during confession, she thanked him profusely and allowed him to visit her at home. Over the next several months, Olivares gave presents and money to her and her sisters in return for sexual favors.[49]

Of course, sometimes a confessor who approached a woman with an offer of financial assistance could overplay his hand. This certainly happened to the Trinitarian Pedro Jorge Fiol, who told Inquisitor Juan de Godoy y San Clemente in 1619 that he had once solicited a young woman who asked him for money and new clothes after confessing certain sins of a sexual nature. Fiol, who was certainly no stranger to solicitation, saw his opportunity and presented the girl with a silver real and promised her a new shirt if she would rid herself of her lover. Evidently this was too much to ask, and Fiol ruefully admitted that he never saw the girl again.[50]

Frequently, a woman's willingness to become sexually involved with her confessor was not a snap decision based on extreme sexual frustration or the offer of money, but the result of a long and positive relationship with her or her family that produced feelings of trust or dependence. Father Antonio de Contreras, one of the few Jesuits convicted of solicitation, was able to take advantage of his relationship with the Cabreros family of Almagro to seduce young Francisca de Cabreros, with whom he had an affair that lasted for nine years. While Contreras's ability to enter the Cabreros home virtually at will was of critical importance in establishing this relationship, it also helped that the family lived right opposite the Jesuit College where he taught moral theology. Francisca de Cabreros also seemed to have had a marked partiality for members of the Society of Jesus. At one point in their affair, she was sharing her bed with another member of the College while continuing her relationship with Contreras.[51]

The increasing visibility and greater importance of priests in the lives of the popular masses of Catholic Europe was naturally conducive to the creation of a whole range of amicable relationships between laity and clergy. Most of these relationships were completely harmless, with priests able to maintain friendship without an excessive familiarity that could lead to compromising situations. In 1747, for example, the Carmelite José de Cristo was accused by some enemies in the order of having remained in the home of Ana Carrasco for a suspiciously long period of time while hearing her confession while she was ill. The case against Cristo was dismissed after a commissioner interviewed the lady, who insisted that they had merely remained talking about some mutual acquaintances, a wedding that she had helped to arrange, and religious topics like fasting and mortification.[52]

Even the most innocent of relationships between priests and their female penitents, however, had the potential to turn into solicitation. In 1607, when Juana Ana Piza began confessing with Father Pedro Estéban, the warden of the Mercedarian convent in Las Palmas, their relationship was close but perfectly innocent. During her weekly confession, Estéban gave her the best spiritual counsel that he could, urged her to "serve God with all her heart," and even read her the sermons he was going to deliver that Sunday. But, after a time, the relationship began to change. During one confession, Estéban remarked that if only he had her in his power, he would take her to bed and "offend God with her." In subsequent confessions, the two began kissing and using suggestive language, and shortly thereafter they formed the practice of having intercourse in her house before she came to confession.[53]

The increasing role of the clergy in education, either through private tutoring or in clerical or private schools, also opened up opportunities for them to establish amicable relationships that could later be turned into a pretext for solicitation.[54] A thirty-five-year-old widow, Mariana Mulet was extremely grateful to her confessor, Pedro José Pons, for undertaking to teach her son the rudiments of grammar. From then on, the friendship between confessor and penitent deepened. Gifts were exchanged, and Mulet began coming to his convent not simply to confess, but to converse about a variety of topics. It was on one of these occasions when she had come to ask him about her son's progress in school that she and Pons had their first conversation using overtly sexual language. During subsequent confessions, they engaged in touching, petting, and mutual masturbation. Before Pons left Las Palmas for Menorca in 1681, he swore Mulet to secrecy, asking that if she confessed what had happened, she should simply admit to a relationship with a person who had sworn a vow of chastity.[55]

Education also provided the basis for friendship between the Franciscan Manuel de Peraleja and fifteen-year-old Juan Antonio de Escobar. Although the relationship began when Peraleja was engaged to tutor Escobar in Latin grammar, it soon became much more than that, as Peraleja became his confessor and intellectual mentor while Escobar aided him in celebrating mass. The good treatment and excellent spiritual counsel that Escobar received from his teacher and confessor made it relatively easy for the bisexual Peraleja to seduce him. They had homosexual relations on numerous occasions in Peraleja's cell and other locations in the convent.[56]

The enhanced social status of the clergy in the post-Tridentine period, the growing importance of the confessor, and the impact that preaching had on Spanish life and culture combined to give some priests a star quality that inevitably increased the social distance between themselves and the laity. Contemporary accounts of preaching from the late sixteenth and seventeenth centuries frequently mention the crowds who waited to attend sermons given by popular preachers. Francisco Pacheco tells us that the popularity of the late sixteenth-century preacher Fray Luis de la Cruz was so enormous that, wherever he came to preach, so many people came to hear him that for morning sermons they would "line up at the door of the church before sunrise" and for afternoon ones they would "eat so early that they were already taking their places before eleven."[57] The same thing is reported about the famous Dominican preacher Augustín Salucio during the four Lenten cycles that he preached in Seville in the 1580s.[58]

In a society and culture very much attuned to preaching, a popular preacher could easily abuse his position in order to gain sexual favors from impressionable young women. When the Carmelite Fray Bernardo del Castillo was sent on mission to the remote Montes de Toledo district, the sermon that he preached in the tiny village of Hinojosa made such an impression on sixteen-year-old Ana Díaz and her friend, seventeen-year-old Josepha Ledesema, that they both came to confess with him the following morning. Although his attempt to seduce Ana Díaz came to nothing, Castillo was much more successful with Josepha Ledesema, who told him how much she liked the friars of his order, with whom she had had some earlier sexual experiences. After a preliminary sexual encounter in the confessional of the parish church, they had intercourse at her home that same afternoon. While in the confessional, it was Ledesema who initiated sexual contact by talking about her previous sexual experiences and taking his hand. Before they left the church, she even suggested that he give her absolution as a way of concealing what had really gone on during her confession.[59]

The Trinitarian Rafael Serre, who was a charismatic figure in more ways than one, was also a dynamic preacher. Engaged to preach a course of sermons at Lent in the Mallorcan village of Alaro, Serre impressed twenty-two-year-old Catalina Sastre so much with his "refined spirituality" that she went to confession with him every day during the final two weeks of the Lenten season. Within a few days, of course, Sastre began exhibiting the same signs of hysteria experienced by Serre's other penitents, and Serre lost no time in applying his spiritual remedies by ordering her to unbutton her blouse so that he could make the sign of the cross over her breasts. When she protested, he was easily able to convince her that this was all for her spiritual benefit and to rid her of evil spirits.[60]

As Freud was the first to acknowledge, power imbalance in a relationship can make for a potent aphrodisiac, and this was true of the confessional relationship even more than in the relationship between preacher and congregation. Kneeling before them during confession and revealing their deepest secrets, it became all too easy for penitents to idealize their confessors and for confessors to take advantage of their penitents' need for affection and approval.[61] This phenomenon, which is referred to in the psychiatric literature as transference, is a valid paradigm for the development of certain types of sexually exploitative relationships between confessor and penitent where emotional dependence and power imbalance can be as significant as they are in the psychoanalytic experience.[62] Just as in psychoanalysis, some penitents came to their confessors as individuals in need of help, thereby submitting themselves voluntarily to an unequal relationship in which the "doctor of souls" is conceded superior knowledge and authority. As a result, "transference feelings related to the universal childhood experience of dependence on a parent are inevitably aroused."[63]

In fact, some confessors even went out of their way to replicate the parent-child relationship with their penitents in order to increase their level of dependence and thereby make them more amenable to the priests' sexual demands. Juan Rosello's correspondence with Sor María Rafaela Alzamora combines obscene language with references to his desire to reduce the thirty-five-year-old novice to a childlike and dependent state. In one letter, he warns her to do nothing without his permission and even refers to himself as a "father who wants to bring you up like a little girl, small and humble because humility is satisfying to God and pleases your Juanito."[64]

The Trinitarian Fray Rafael Serre, whose fascinating case has been referred to above, developed a quasi-therapeutic relationship with his penitents that objectively was quite similar to the psychiatrist-patient interaction. Serre's penitents either came to him suffering from hysteria or exhibited symptoms of hysteria at some point after they began confessing with him. Since seven of the nine women he solicited spent almost every afternoon together sewing and talking, the similarity of the symptoms they exhibited can be plausibly attributed to the power of suggestion, especially since the women discussed their relationship to Serre among themselves. These hysterical fits included waves of intense anxiety and wild outbursts of uncontrolled excitement, as well as physical symptoms such as severe chest pains and shortness of breath, and pains in sides, arms, and shoulders. Transference feelings were aroused as penitents became dependent on Serre for a cure through exorcism and because they idealized him, in spite of the fact that he was using the exorcism process as a way of satisfying his own sexual needs.[65]

Moreover, like the repeat offenders in recent surveys of psychiatrists who had sexual contact with their patients, Serre was loath to acknowledge any wrongdoing.[66] When pressed by Francisca Noseras as to the reason why he insisted on placing his hands on her bare breasts, he assured her that his only intention "was to cure her in the places where she felt pain." He also attempted, without success, to rationalize his sexual contact as therapeutic intervention before the Holy Office by claiming that he had done nothing more than attempt to exorcise the women by blowing in their faces and making the sign of the cross over their bodies.[67]

The nineteen penitents who experienced transference as part of their relationship with their confessor are a clear indication of the dangers that such feelings represent to the viability of a close professional relationship based on extreme power imbalance. As a professional group that claimed special status and the ability to alleviate both spiritual ills and their physical symptoms, priests were under an extreme obligation to protect their female penitents from the consequences of such feelings. Perhaps that is one reason for the extreme modesty bordering on prudishness exhibited by some priests in the presence of women. Juan Machado de Chaves even advised confessors to hold their hands in front of their eyes when hearing women's confessions if they could not use a regular confessional in order not to "look them in the face."[68] Nevertheless, individuals like Juan Rosello or Rafael Serre consciously sought to encourage feelings of helplessness and dependence that would allow them to satisfy their own sexual needs. As recent studies of psychiatrists indicate, the priesthood is not the only professional group where feelings of transference have been manipulated by unscrupulous individuals to gratify their sexual desires.[69]

Of course, among the psychiatrists who have had sexual relations with their patients as well as the confessors who solicited their penitents, there were a certain number who were motivated by genuine affection. Unlike psychiatrists, who have the option of marrying patients who return their affection, love relationships between confessor and penitent were apt to end tragically, as marriage was impossible and the guilt and anxiety experienced by both parties would frequently lead to the termination of the relationship and denunciation to the Holy Office.[70]

One of these love relationships that ultimately had tragic consequences for both parties sprang up in 1705 between Margerita Baretta, a twenty-eight-year-old servant, and her confessor, Cristóbal Mendez, the curate of Santiago de Tenerife. The two fell in love a little more than two years after Baretta began confessing with him. At about that time, both Isabel de Sacarias, her mistress, and Teresa, a black slave who worked in the house, noticed that she was beginning to dress with care before going to confession. After several weeks of this, her mistress reproached her for such unseemly preparations and ordered her to change confessors, but Baretta refused, saying that she "was settled on her confessor and there could be no harm in going to confession." Of course, as Teresa was able to confirm when she hid by the door of the church and overheard the two making plans to meet later, Mendez and Baretta had been having an affair for some time. As their emotional involvement grew, the two lovers were frequently seen talking together both inside and outside the parish church. Baretta also began visiting Mendez at his house where they had intercourse on numerous occasions. In an unusual twist, and one that more than anything else demonstrated his affection for Baretta, Mendez began feeling remorse over the affair, telling her that she should stop seeing him and "find a husband worthy of her," but she replied that she loved him in spite of his clerical status. Eventually, Baretta became pregnant by her confessor and went to her home village to give birth. After the baby was born, she abandoned it at a foundling hospital and returned to her mistress, who denounced Mendez to the Holy Office. Armed with this testimony and that of Teresa, the local commissioner called Baretta before him, and she reluctantly admitted the facts about her relationship with Mendez. In 1712, after a second denunciation had been received, the Canaries tribunal tried and convicted Mendez on a charge of solicitation.[71]

A love relationship that followed the more typical pattern of guilt and remorse on the part of the female penitent rather than her male confessor developed between the Dominican Fray Francisco Marrero and Luisa Ramírez, who lived in the village of Garachico on Tenerife. Luisa, who was twenty-two when she began confessing with the Dominican in the chapel of his convent, fell in love with him when she was twenty-eight after he told her that he was "crazy about her." He began having intercourse with her when her mother was absent from the house and then made her confess what she had done, granted her absolution, and warned her not to go to any other confessor. Driven by anxiety about the validity of her confessions with him, which deepened when he refused to allow her to take communion on two occasions after he had fondled her in the confessional, she went to another confessor, emerged feeling guilty for what she had done, determined to avoid sin by terminating her relationship with Marrero. But when she returned to confess with him, he was able to persuade her to continue, and in this manner the cycle of sin, repentance, and renewed sin went on for another six years. The relationship came to an end only when Ramírez became gravely ill and finally found peace by calling in Garachico's commissioner, Gaspar de Montesdoca, to denounce her lover just after she had received the last rites of the Church.[72]

Love relationships proved to be a significant barrier to the exercise of the Inquisition's jurisdiction over solicitation since female penitents would often conceal what they had done in order to protect their clerical lovers in spite of their own feelings of anxiety. Madalena de Saavedra was on her deathbed when she finally confessed an affair that she had had with the Augustinian Diego Núñez some twenty years earlier.[73] Phelipa de Morales was forty and married before she finally came to a Holy Office commissioner to confess that she had had a relationship with Salvador Quijada del Castillo. In fact, Morales had confessed her sin previously with the parish priest of a nearby village, who told her that she was obliged to denounce Quijada del Castillo to the Inquisition, but instead of doing so, she went to Quijada del Castillo and told him what the priest had said. He begged her not to denounce him, so she kept their secret until a new parish priest arrived in Ariço and gave her the opportunity to unburden her conscience to him twenty-two years after Quijada del Castillo had first solicited her in the confessional of his convent.[74]

Some penitents were even prepared to perjure themselves before the Inquisition in spite of the risk of prosecution. On June 17, 1625, two days after he entered the secret prison of the Inquisition in Las Palmas, Fray Pedro Estéban confessed that he had solicited Juana Ana Piza. However, when she was called before the tribunal on July 7, she denied having ever been solicited and continued her denials even when the inquisitors questioned her using part of Estéban's testimony. Inquisitor Pedro Díaz de Cienfuegos was so incensed at her obduracy that he took the unusual step of calling a consulta de fe to consider charging Piza with perjury and obstruction of the Holy Office, but the consulta voted for suspension of these charges until Piza could be brought in for a second round of questioning. On August 9, Piza was again brought to the tribunal and again denied any knowledge of having been solicited by Estéban, but two days later her feelings of guilt and anxiety about deceiving the Holy Office finally overcame her and she came to confess. Even so, she still attempted to protect her former lover by implying that he had done nothing more than use suggestive language in the confessional and that when this happened, she had not really come to him with the intention of confessing. In early September, her testimony was directly contradicted when Onofre Llompaid, another cleric from the same Mercedarian house came to testify that one day, nine years earlier, when he was at work decorating an altar, he had noticed Juana Ana Piza kneeling in the confessional in front of Estéban with her hand under his habit.[75]

Francisca Noseras's attempt to free Fray Raphael Serre after his first arrest provides us with perhaps the most striking example of just how far some penitents would go to protect the confessor whom they loved from the toils of the Holy Office. On February 24, 1688, fearing trouble after the conclusion of a visitation to his convent, Serre told Noseras not to confess with him and instead go to his friend Dr. Nadal, the curate of the parish of Santa Eulalia. A few days later, she learned that Serre had been placed under strict reclusion and that he was probably going to be charged with soliciting her and several other women. Although Noseras had already promised Serre that she would deny any involvement with him if she were called before the Inquisition, she was very frightened that the inquisitors would guess that she was lying and decided to seek advice from Catalina Pont, another one of Serre's penitents. Several days later, she made her first visit to Catalina Pont's house and was introduced to several other members of the group. Although admitting that they had each been solicited by Serre, they agreed that if they were called up before the tribunal, they would say that he had done nothing more than touch their clothing during exorcism. Still unsure of herself and fearful of the Inquisition, Noseras then went one step further and decided to contact Serre directly to get his approval. Even though Serre was closely guarded, she managed to get a message to him through his brother-in-law and was rewarded a few days later when Catalina Pont showed her a note from Serre that had been smuggled out of the monastery in which he made known his approval of her plans.[76] Faced with the refusal of its key witnesses to testify against him, the tribunal had little choice but to temporarily accept Serre's mendacious "spontaneous confession" of March 15, 1688, which largely coincided with what he had told the women to say, and suspend the case pending the receipt of new evidence. Serre was set free as a result of what Francisca Noseras, Catalina Pont, and the other women of his cabal did for him in spite of their almost paralyzing fear of the Inquisition. It was not until March 9, 1691, almost three years after Serre's first brush with the Inquisition, that the Mallorca tribunal felt that it had sufficient additional evidence to indict him again. Unfortunately for Serre, by that time the guilt and anxiety that Francisca Noseras and the other women felt about deceiving the dreaded Holy Office had grown to the point that they all eventually admitted that they had had sexual relations with him during and after confession.

In other illicit relationships between priests and their female penitents, there was no question of mutual affection and every indication that the confessor was simply using her for his own sexual gratification. Juana Oliver's first encounter with the Trinitarian Fray Antonio Ballester occurred not in the confessional but in the home of Antonia Tomás, the wife of an oil merchant. Juana, an eighteen-year-old from a poor family who lived with her mother and sisters, instantly fell in love with the forty-six-year-old Ballester, who was not only the warden of his convent, but extremely popular with women who flocked to his confessional. Shortly afterward, Oliver began confessing with Ballester, however the two seemed to have mainly used the occasion to make assignations. They had intercourse on numerous occasions in the home of Antonia Tomás when she was ill and in Oliver's house when her mother and sisters were absent.

After about a year of this, however, Ballester began to tire of Oliver and decided to stop seeing her. Oliver became extremely upset at this, and with no other way of communicating with him, went to see him at the chapel. While pretending to confess, she reproached him bitterly for leaving her and tried everything that she could to entice him back. Finally succumbing to her blandishments, Ballester did return to her for about six months, and they had intercourse on several occasions in a disused house near the convent and even in his cell. But Ballester, who had other lovers, had really lost interest in the relationship and decided to end it definitively. In desperation, Oliver prevailed upon Antonia Tomás to go to his confessional and plead with him to return. Ballester remained unmoved, and when Tomás told him that Oliver cried every time she thought about him, he replied coldly that "she really should weep for her sins and entrust herself to God."[77]

Mysticism, just because it depended on direct and immediate feelings and was fundamentally irrational, stood outside of the formal structure of the Church from which women were barred. These same elements, however, offered women the opportunity to gain authority and respect among male clerics and in the male-dominated society at large just because, as the allegedly irrational sex, they were deemed to have a special aptitude for communicating with God using such means. The sixteenth and seventeenth centuries were replete with such "women of power," from Isabel de la Cruz and Francisca Hernández at the beginning of the sixteenth century to Sor María de Jesús de Agreda in the 1640s. Such "spiritual mothers" as they came to be known, were able to gather a coterie of male clerics and lay followers and sometimes exert an influence out of all proportion to their position in society.[78]

For the most part, such women led saintly lives and came to occupy a position of authority and respect because their supernatural powers were accepted as real by the public at large. But throughout the entire history of Spanish mysticism, there is a considerable amount of sexual tension. At times sexual interaction between the spiritual mother and her male disciples came as a result of a belief in the fundamental goodness of any impulse that came from God. The cult that formed around Gertrudis Tosca, a young Valencian woman in the mid 1660s, was typical of this belief in impeccability. Her male disciples, including three priests, believed that she was especially favored by God, and their devotions included frequent kissing on the hands, mouth, and neck. When the three priests became her lovers, they justified their conduct on the grounds that it had been ordained by God and was a way of advancing toward spiritual perfection.[79]

Clearly, in the case of Gertrudis Tosca and other spiritual mothers, sex was not only a way of achieving spiritual goals, but also served to cement the support of male disciples. Sometimes confession became the vehicle of such a woman's struggle to sexually manipulate a male priest in order to gain her ends.

In the mid 1680s, Isabel Riera had attracted a small group of disciples, including two important local prelates, archdeacon Gabriel Mesquida and canon Juan Martorell. She also advised wealthy and devout individuals on their spiritual lives and family problems and was even presented to the viceroy so that she could tell him about a vision in which she saw the solutions to many of the problems afflicting the region. Determined to add the influential Augustinian Fray Pedro Benimelis to her list of conquests, she selected him as her confessor. Since Benimelis was probably the most famous exorcist on the island, she began by telling him that she had been invaded by the devil and begging him to exorcise her. Benimelis willingly complied and began a regimen of exorcism that included making crosses over her breasts and forcing her mouth open with his hand after the devil had closed it. One day while she was making her confession, Isabel threw her arms around him and touched his face, shoulder, and habit, saying that God had ordained it. Far from being repelled by this aggressive behavior, Benimelis was delighted by it, especially as she assured him that her prayer—that he would always remain pure and chaste so long as he was her confessor—had been answered. In the ensuing months, Benimelis became Riera's most devoted disciple, burning incense in front of a portrait her followers had made of her and faithfully recording her visions and prophecies "because they will contribute to the greater glory of God." During this period, Benimelis gave Riera gifts of food and money, taught her special prayers, and even acceded to her request that he instruct her in Latin. He even began to credit her with the ability to exorcise demons, normally a prerogative jealously reserved for the male clergy.

The relationship continued for some period in this way, even though Benimelis later claimed that he was beginning to become disenchanted with Riera because some of her prophecies had proven false. But what kept him involved, as he later admitted in his testimony before the Holy Office, was the sexual thrill that he experienced whenever she embraced him or he put his hand on her arm during confession. It was the Inquisition that finally ended the affair when, on November 5, 1688, it ordered Benimelis to stop serving as her confessor and turn over all the books in which he had recorded her visions.[80] Pedro Benimelis may have learned a hard and valuable lesson, but the problem of how to deal with female mystics and visionaries who could use the confessional as a way of sexually manipulating male clerics continued to trouble the ecclesiastical authorities long after his case was concluded.

In addition to the two categories of penitents already discussed, there were a certain number whose reaction to their confessor's advances can best be described as ambivalent. Among these fifty-three individuals, ambivalence was evinced by a certain degree of attraction toward the confessor and a limited acquiescence in his sexual demands, but an unwillingness to permit a full-fledged sexual relationship from developing. Frequently, penitents in this category would find ways of rationalizing their behavior in order to continue it without experiencing the overwhelming feelings of guilt and sin that would have compelled them to denounce their confessor to the Holy Office. When thirty-three-year-old Francisca de Santa Ana came before the Canaries tribunal to denounce Francisco del Rosario for having caressed her face and tried to put his hands down her blouse, she claimed, rather disingenuously, that since she was able to prevent him from actually touching her breasts, she had felt that there was no need to denounce him. This explanation is even harder to accept in light of the fact that she admitted returning to confess with him several months later, claiming that she had forgotten the first incident. Of course, exactly the same thing happened, but Santa Ana continued to maintain her silence even after having a conversation with certain other women who related similar experiences with him.[81]

Francisca de Santa Ana's cousin, Barbara Osorio, was perhaps even more disingenuous when she explained that she had returned to confess with Rosario after he had thrust his hand down her shirt because she believed that this had been his way of encouraging her to confess her sins. Even though he held her hand during the entire confession, she failed to report him to the Holy Office until forced to do so by another confessor.[82] In both of these cases, similarities in the life situation of the two women make it easy to imagine why they might have tolerated a limited degree of sexual contact with their confessor. Both women were alone, with Santa Ana a recent widow and Osorio's shoemaker husband having deserted her, and neither could have had much licit contact with men. By allowing their confessor a certain amount of sexual contact and then rationalizing their behavior, they could find some temporary relief from loneliness and sexual frustration while limiting their involvement in order to avoid a more protracted affair that would have ruined their reputations.

In the minds of certain women, undoubted sexual attraction for their confessors struggled with prudishness and fear of sin to produce an uncomfortable off-again, on-again relationship that ended before the bar of the Holy Office. On February 6, 1681, Francisca Marquéz y Campins, a thirty-five-year-old widow of impeccable reputation, presented herself at the offices of the Mallorca tribunal to denounce her confessor, Dr. Jorge Roselló, one of the four curates attached to the cathedral of Las Palmas. Marquéz y Campins, who was on good terms with most of the benefice holders of the cathedral, had begun confessing with Roselló about eight months earlier and confessed with him on a weekly, sometimes daily basis during that period. Her first two sessions were perfectly normal, but at her third session, Roselló told her that he had seen her talking to Mateo Gari, another benefice holder, several days before she began confessing with him and that he had remarked on how lucky Mateo was to be talking to "such a delicious young woman." This obviously suggestive remark, made during confession, shocked Marquéz y Campins, but it did not prevent her from telling Roselló where she lived after he had asked for her address with the flimsy excuse that he would need to visit her if she became ill.

The following afternoon, Roselló came unannounced to visit Marquéz y Campins at her rooms while she was conversing with Pedro Gelabert, a priest who also lived in the house. Leaving Gelabert, she took Roselló on a tour of her rooms, but became very offended after he tried to put his arm around her and later in her bedroom looked at her in an extremely lascivious way. Angered by this, she cut short his visit and brusquely ordered him to leave the house.

Several days later, just after she had begun her confession, Roselló told her that he was so angry with her that he wanted to scratch her face with his nails. Alarmed at the prospect of losing the attentions of a man she found so attractive, Marquéz y Campins took a more conciliatory tone and the two conversed about a variety of topics, including certain women who wore perfume made from flower petals. Marquéz y Campins even remarked rather coyly that she was in the habit of bringing a fresh rose to church when they were in season. Encouraged by her more favorable attitude, Roselló invited her to his house to have dinner and meet his mother and nephew, assuring her that she need have no fear of any loss of reputation since he was visited by many persons. Marquéz y Campins accepted his invitation and, after eating, went down to Roselló's room, where he read aloud from Saint Teresa de Jesús while making her sit on a chair so close to his that their knees touched. Obviously pleased by her complaisance on this occasion, Roselló began asking her a series of deliberately provocative questions during a subsequent confession, eventually getting her to admit that she frequently thought about sex and masturbated thinking of her dead husband. Further emboldened by these revelations, Roselló invited her to his house again and after dinner she followed him down to his room, where he began kissing her and touching her breasts and ended by throwing her rather roughly on his bed. By now thoroughly alarmed, especially when she noticed his sexual excitement, Marquéz y Campins stopped things from going any further by announcing that they should both go to pray since if they persisted in what they were doing, "they would both end in hell." Guilt and fear had combined to cause revulsion in the mind of this exceptionally devout lady, who was a member of both the Dominican and Franciscan third orders. On the following day, she entered his confessional only to announce that his sexual overtures had had absolutely no effect on her, but that she dreaded the possibility that in the hour of her death the devil would resurrect these disgraceful scenes to torment her. Roselló, who was probably expecting her to revert to her earlier hostility, could do little more than beg her to spare his honor by not denouncing him to the Inquisition, but he did so in vain because she quickly went to consult with another one of the cathedral curates, who advised her to make a deposition.[83]

The problem with ambivalence is that it may be read as coquettishness or sexual teasing that could engender a violent response in the other person. Shortly after sixteen-year-old Inés González began confessing with the Franciscan Fray Pedro de Castro in 1600, he began telling her that he loved her and begged her repeatedly to go to the home of Mencia Rodríguez, a mutual friend, where they could have sex. As she admitted in her 1604 testimony before the Canaries tribunal, González was highly ambivalent about Castro's overtures, usually telling him that she would not and could not have sexual relations with him, but sometimes indicating that she might under the proper circumstances. Pedro de Castro, who was anything but a gentleman, interpreted this as a green light. One day when González was visiting the very house where he had suggested a rendezvous, Castro happened to be passing along the street. Spotting her through the window, he entered the house, dismissed Mencia Rodríguez's daughter Tomasina, who happened to be in the room, and forced González onto a nearby bed where he raped her. To compound her shame and humiliation, González was forced to return to Castro's confessional on several occasions in order to prevent her mother from suspecting that anything unusual had happened.[84]

The motives of the twenty nuns who accepted their confessor's advances are to be found primarily in the changing circumstances of convent life during the Counter-Reformation. These changes had the effect of isolating convents from secular life while at the same time it produced a wave of new recruits. While most of the women who flocked to the female houses during the sixteenth and seventeenth centuries either had a genuine religious vocation or saw the convent as a way of avoiding an unwanted marriage, many others were more or less forced into religious life or found that it was not to their liking after they had taken their vows.

Certainly the increase in the number of convents that were founded in the last half of the sixteenth century corresponded mainly to social factors that had little to do with the undoubted religious zeal of their founders. Throughout the sixteenth and seventeenth centuries, dowries increased so rapidly as to become one of the major causes for the heavy indebtedness of noble families.[85] As a result, many families preferred to send their daughters into the convents, where dowries were lower. Many of these girls became nuns as adolescents, sometimes after spending a considerable period as boarders in the same convent.[86] The rules of some convents, in fact, specifically permitted girls to take their vows before age eighteen, which was the minimum decreed by the Council of Trent.[87] Frequently, violations of the Tridentine decree by Spain's impecunious female orders were caused by financial considerations. In one of her letters, Teresa de Jesús advised the prioress of the convent of Seville to accept fourteen-year-old Elvira de San Angelo as a novice in spite of her age because the relatively high dowry that her parents were willing to pay would help the convent meet its expenses.[88]

High dowry payments were only one of the problems that elite families sought to avoid by sending their marriageable daughters into convents. After taking their vows, monks and nuns became nonpersons as far as civil society was concerned and were unable to claim worldly rights or property. This state of civil death assured families that their daughters' claims would not complicate inheritance and lead to further division of family property or further indebtedness.

The financial appeal of an arrangement that would allow families to keep heritable property intact and save on expensive dowries meant that in all too many cases vocations were made under extreme familial pressure leading to emotional turmoil and sexual frustration for the young woman. In her testimony before the Toledo tribunal, María Magdalena de San Antonio, the daughter of D. Fernando Moscoso, a member of the Council of Castile, recalled how shortly after she took a vow of chastity and entered the Carmelite house in Guadalajara, she fell in love with a young man and was sorely tempted to leave the order. Miserably unhappy, torn between her desire for marriage and her duty to her parents, she made the mistake of confiding in her confessor, Fray Francisco Corbera. Corbera, who had already tried to embrace and kiss her in the confessional, now advised her to leave the convent and marry because then "no one could prevent him from coming to her house and doing what he wanted with her." In the end, she was able to obtain emotional support from the other nuns and remained in the order in spite of the fact that Corbera, who obviously knew the young man quite well, kept bringing him up every time he had a chance to talk with her.[89]

In other cases, women who were forced into convent life displayed signs of emotional instability, hysteria, and maladjustment that created serious problems for the community. The reformed Carmelite convent that Teresa de Jesús founded in Seville was almost destroyed when one of the nuns accused the others of immorality and heresy.[90] The following year, the same convent was rocked by the sudden departure of a novice who declared that the prioress had flogged the nuns and left them tied up by their feet. A nun who failed to come to terms with convent life could become a long-term problem for the entire community. María del Sacramento, a nun in the Bernardine convent of La Concepción, had entered as a lay boarder at age eleven, but was so difficult and quarrelsome during her novitiate that when it came time for her profession, the mistress of novices had to go from cell to cell begging the nuns to vote for her. Evidently kept in the convent by intense family pressure, María made the other nuns miserable by constantly fighting with them and the female servants. She was particularly prone to jealousy over her confessors, and at one time even physically attacked a servant who was a penitent of Fray Pedro del Cristo, whom she later accused of soliciting her. María del Sacramento's poor reputation in the convent and the negative report on her character filed by commissioner Joseph Antonio de Medina y Beltrán was enough for the Suprema to order the case against Fray Pedro suspended.[91]

The presence of such maladjusted individuals in so many convents may be one explanation for the waves of demonic possession that swept over the female religious houses during the seventeenth century. A good example of the impact that such a person could have on a community is provided by Catalina Maura, who entered a convent in Las Palmas as a way of avoiding an unwanted marriage, but never was able to adjust to monastic life. From her very first month in the convent, she fought constantly with the prioress, refusing to study, coming late to choir, and leaving the chapel before the nuns had finished their prayers. Within six months, Catalina was already showing signs of being possessed, so that the prioress had to call in the Augustinian Fray Pedro Benimelis to exorcise her. When Benimelis arrived at the convent, however, he was dismayed to find that the other nuns had begun to gather around Catalina whenever she was possessed and were conversing with her evil spirit. Fearing an outbreak of possession among the other nuns and shocked by the foul language that Catalina used when she was raving, Fray Pedro immediately began his course of exorcism, which seemed to have a calming effect on the community if not on Catalina Maura herself.[92]

Families who had placed their daughters in convents wanted to be sure that they were effectively "dead to the world."[93] They feared that without a strict and binding rule that would effectively isolate them from worldly concerns, daughters might one day claim a share of the family estate. It was, at least in part, to respond to the concerns of secular society that the Church fathers at Trent imposed strict claustration on women religious.[94] Even though strict claustration was not imposed everywhere and exceptions were made for some of the religious orders created after the Council of Trent, there can be little doubt that it had the effect of greatly increasing the sexual frustrations of the nuns who experienced it. Inevitably claustration focused their sexual desires on their confessor, the only man with whom they were permitted any kind of regular contact.[95] For three young nuns, sixteen-year-old Eustacia del Sacramento, sixteen-year-old Inés de San Francisco, and seventeen-year-old Jerónima Evangelista, life in Madrid's aristocratic convent of Nuestra Señora de los Angeles must have seemed particularly grim. The rule was one of absolute silence except during confession, and the nuns were so strictly enclosed that even relatives were forbidden to visit unless there was some family emergency. This situation was ready-made for a lascivious friar like fifty-two-year-old Sebastián de Hontora, a Franciscan who had been appointed vicar of the convent in 1577. Hontora was determined to seduce all three girls, and he began by telling each one of them that he had fallen in love with them and that he wanted to see their breasts and "enjoy them." Bored, frustrated, and restless in the confines of an excessively strict monastic rule, the girls cooperated eagerly. Eustacia del Sacramento told Hontora about an erotic dream during one of her confessions and allowed him to kiss and embrace her. One night he was able to persuade Jerónima Evangelista to masturbate him through the communion window, and on another occasion he kissed and fondled both Jerónima Evangelista and Eustacia del Sacramento at the communion altar. By now the girls were ready for anything, so Hontora persuaded them to sneak out of the convent and meet him in the chapel where they could have group sex. One night, Sister Inés managed to obtain a key to the side door of the convent and descended to the chapel to meet her lover. After having intercourse with him there, she summoned the other girls, who entered the chapel where Hontora kissed, embraced, and fondled all three. Unfortunately for Hontora, his relationship with the girls had not gone unnoticed, and it eventually reached the ears of the prioress, who informed the provincial. Hontora was immediately suspended and punished by the order's commissioner, Fray Pedro de Alva. Meanwhile, the Toledo tribunal was made aware of the situation by Hontora himself, who made a spontaneous confession claiming that he had been unaware that what he had done might fall under the purview of the Holy Office until he had heard a recent Edict of Faith. After Inquisitor Juan de Llano de Vargas interviewed the nuns, the tribunal censored Commissioner Alva for interfering in a case that he should have reported to the Inquisition and ordered Hontora's arrest. Armed with the somewhat reluctant testimony of the three nuns, the tribunal convicted Hontora of solicitation, although its sentence followed closely the one handed down by the order.[96]

Women in early modern Spain, except for those whose social status gave them privileges normally associated with men, were confronted with a similar set of harsh realities. In an age of sexual imbalance, economic decline, and political instability, marriage was difficult for many and impossible for some. Restrictions on freedom of individual choice imposed by families for economic or status reasons had the effect of forcing some women to marry men they did not really love and forcing others into a religious life for which they had no real vocation. Many women were, therefore, left in a state of sexual frustration and emotional dissatisfaction that made their confessors appear attractive and desirable. Society's failure to provide women with alternatives to marriage, male chauvinism, and general insensitivity to women's needs created a situation in which many women became receptive to the sexual advances of their confessors in spite of the social ostracism or even physical danger that such a relationship might entail.

Chapter 8

Carnal Behavior and Sexual Disorders

Everywhere in Catholic Europe, the Counter-Reformation brought a new and more repressive attitude toward sexual expression. In the arts, the repaintings of the nudes in Michelangelo's Last Judgement demonstrate the Church's more restrictive attitude about depicting the human body. Francisco Pacheco, Spain's preeminent art theorist, reflected the new prudery in his famous work, *A los profesores del arte de la pintura* (1622), where he stressed decorum in religious paintings and criticized painters who depicted mythological themes with excessive sensuality.[1] In sixteenth-century France, official toleration for collective rapes and the "joyous confraternities" of young men who perpetrated them slowly gave way to prohibition.[2] The municipal houses of prostitution, which had provided a much-needed outlet for the sexual frustrations of young males in a society characterized by late marriage, were first banished to the outskirts of towns and then closed between 1520 and 1570.[3]

In Spain, fear of syphilis and increasing concerns about the sins caused by prostitution led the government of Philip II to issue new ordinances in 1570 that compelled prostitutes to reside in a regulated municipal brothel,where they would have to undergo regular medical inspections.[4] But regulation was not enough for the coterie of pious laymen, clergy, and members of the Jesuit order, who became increasingly influential in Seville during the first decades of the seventeenth century. Critics such as Juan de Mariana and Pedro de León deplored the harm that legal prostitution was doing to the city's young men and undertook an increasingly vociferous campaign against the brothel. Bowing to this pressure, the city government closed it in 1620, only to reopen

149

it the following year in the face of complaints from brothel padres and the institutions that received a portion of their income from the brothel. In spite of the new and even more restrictive regulations that they placed on the brothel, however, Seville's municipal authorities could not prevail against a powerful wave of revulsion against legalized prostitution, and Philip IV decreed the closure of all of Spain's legal houses of prostitution in 1623.[5]

The closing decades of the sixteenth century also saw the beginning of a concerted campaign carried out by Spain's inquisitorial tribunals to stamp out the widespread popular belief that coitus with an unmarried consenting female did not constitute a mortal sin. This campaign against "simple fornication" was clearly designed to discredit easy acceptance of premarital sex and prostitution as tolerated forms of sexual commerce, thereby bringing popular culture more into line with the views of leading theologians. In November 1573, the Suprema circulated a letter to the regional tribunals announcing that, henceforth, the belief that simple fornication was not sinful would be treated as heretical, even though it conceded that the heresy was not intentional but the product of ignorance.[6] Between 1575 and 1590, "simple fornication" accounted for more than one-third of the activity of the Toledo tribunal. The Inquisition reinforced its judicial campaign against "fornicarios" with a program of education. Preachers and confessors were requested to denounce the belief and officals were to post special edicts on the subject. By the early seventeenth century, evidence from case files suggests that the Inquisition had been quite successful in convincing even rustics that consorting with prostitutes or other women of easy virtue was a sinful act.[7]

At the same time, the post-Tridentine Church made a strenuous effort to define a new, more restrictive sexual morality. By separating betrothal and marriage and insisting that betrothed couples abstain from sexual intercourse until they had celebrated ecclesiastical marriage, the Church virtually declared war against traditional customs allowing various forms of premarital sex.[8] Variously called "albergement" in Savoy, the "escraignes" in Champagne, or "truwen" in East Friesland, these were the ways rural communities had of channeling the sexual drives of young people who would frequently have to wait until their mid twenties to actually get married. Beginning in the early seventeenth century, bishops in France and the Catholic states of Germany began condemning these practices and forbidding them under pain of excommunication.[9]

The shifting attitude in Spain toward traditional forms of premarital sexual relations may be seen by comparing the views of two important theologians. Martín de Azpilcueta Navarro, whose popular confessors' manual was first published in 1553, specifically approved of premarital foreplay among persons engaged to be married as a legitimate way of "enjoying the beginnings of matrimonial bliss."[10] In 1612, however, the Dominican Bartholomé de Medina, who occupied the prestigious chair of theology at the University of Salamanca, condemned all forms of premarital sex among engaged persons, including touching, embracing, kissing, or even exchanging letters as a mortal sin.[11] In Catalonia, the Church undertook a long campaign to eradicate secular marriage, and bishops and synods reiterated prohibitions against couples who began living together before celebrating church marriage. In May 1620, the vicar-general of the diocese of Barcelona prohibited diocesan priests from carrying out the marriage ceremony for men who had begun living with their betrothed on pain of a fine of ten ducats.[12]

The overall impact of this campaign of moral policing on sexual behavior is a little difficult to assess. The Inquisition's offensive against simple fornication had been an obvious success, but the closure of municipal brothels simply drove prostitution into the streets and alleys. On the other hand, unremitting pressure from bishops managed to eliminate certain traditional customs that sanctioned premarital sexual relations. In Savoy, for example, the custom of albergement, prohibited under pain of excommunication in 1609, had virtually disappeared by 1820. The Jesuits were also quite active against secular marriage and claimed to have stamped it out in the marquisate of Cenete by 1591.[13] Municipalities all over Europe also passed severe laws against adultery. In sixteenth-century Valencia, the Justicia intervened to punish adultery with fines and periods of exile of up to three years for repeat offenders.[14]

Even though the actual incidence of illicit sexual activity may not have fallen, there is growing evidence to suggest that the increasingly repressive attitude of both secular and ecclesiastical authorities had a profound effect on sexual attitudes. Disputes among the casuists about such critical issues as whether it was proper for the husband to demand the conjugal debt during menses, or for the couple to have sex before communion, as well as the increasing scope of questioning about sexuality in the confessional, left many married persons with a pervasive sense of uneasiness and guilt about their sexual relations.[15]

These reactions, in turn, may well have been responsible for the increasing number of cases brought before the courts demanding dissolution of marriage because of impotence.[16] Given the prevailing atmosphere of anxiety, guilt, and fear, it would be hardly surprising to find that impotence was becoming a serious problem for certain individuals who might not have suffered from it otherwise. In 1738 Fray Francisco Carrasco told the Canaries tribunal that in spite of having masturbated frequently as a child and adult and engaging in such foreplay as caressing, kissing, and touching of genitalia, he had never been able to have intercourse and had frequently been mocked by women who called him impotent because he was unable to have an erection.[17]

For the unmarried, opportunities for socially tolerated sexual activity were either being closed off or made significantly more difficult. Closing the official brothels made prostitution less socially acceptable and therefore less accessible to the respectable, the devout, or the timid, who not only had to risk the unsupervised private brothel or independent practitioner, but could not pretend to be unaware of the sinful nature of their conduct.

Even though many engaged couples continued to cohabit in violation of the Church's ban, their sexual activity had also entered a twilight zone. By the early seventeenth century, marriage contracts even in rural Catalonia reflected the new morality. Before Trent, contractants were called "husband" and "wife," but later contracts termed the couple "husband" and "wife" "to be."[18] Betrothed couples, therefore, could not help feeling that cohabitation for long periods was no longer socially acceptable and tended to celebrate the nuptial mass within months instead of years of drawing up the initial contract, thereby legitimizing their sexual union.[19]

In fact, even before the Council of Trent, moral behavior and especially the sexual comportment of boys and young men had come under increasing scrutiny and regulation. The many secondary schools that were founded under humanist influence all over Catholic Europe subjected adolescents to strict discipline.[20] After Trent, the increasing role of religious orders like the Jesuits and Oratorians in lay education and the establishment of boarding schools and seminaries intensified the atmosphere of repression.[21] Moral discipline was emphasized as a major goal of Jesuit education in a memorandum to Duke Cosimo I of Florence, written in 1551 to elicit his support for a projected Jesuit college by Diego Lainez, founder Ignatius Loyola's close associate and the future general of the order. Lainez wrote that such a school would force local youths to abandon their "rowdiness, blasphemies and dishonesties" and make them "temperate, devout and obedient to their parents." In the numerous schools that the Jesuits founded throughout Catholic Europe, they applied a strict moral discipline to their students. The Jesuits who ran the school in Novara west of Milan, for example, segregated students from the life of the city, forbidding them to visit shops and associate with "bad women."[22]

The education of girls during the Counter-Reformation was also marked by an extreme degree of sexual repression. The Ursulines, one of the major teaching orders in seventeenth-century Catholic Europe, drew up a catechism that was specifically designed to avoid, as much as possible, references to the sixth commandment. Some of the feminine teaching congregations were so reticent about sexual matters that they refused to use the word marriage. This prudishness led the teaching congregations to impose strict morality on their students, forbidding them to go to dances, sing worldly songs, wear provocative clothing, or consort with young men.[23]

As far as the clergy were concerned, the manifest need to counter Protestant rejection of clerical celibacy forced the Council of Trent to issue a strong condemnation of concubinary priests and to reaffirm all the old canons penalizing them and their illegitimate children.[24] There was nothing particularly new in all of this, but the success of the post-Tridentine Church in getting most, if not all, priests to accept celibacy was due not to new fulminations against clerical offenders, but rather to giving bishops and their vicars increased power over the diocesan clergy and altering the nature of clerical education.

During the debates on the obligation of residence that were held at Trent in May and June 1546, many bishops pointed out that one of the major reasons for nonresidence was that the bishop had lost authority over the priests in his diocese because of the intervention of curial offices and tribunals. The archbishop of Sassari declared that more than half of the clerics in his diocese were exempt from his jurisdiction. How could the prohibitions against concubinary priests be made effective under these circumstances? Refractory priests could and did defy episcopal authority, and the celibacy rule was routinely ignored. In his *Constituciones Synodales,* issued in 1531, Cuenca's reforming Bishop Diego Ramírez de Villaescusa sharply criticized the negligence of his mostly absentee predecessors for not punishing violations of celibacy and denounced the fact that many priests in the diocese were so blatant about ignoring the celibacy rule that they openly celebrated mass with their "family" in church and even attended their children's weddings.[25] During the discussions at Trent, the bishop of Lanciano reported that in his diocese a concubinary had secured exemption by getting himself appointed an apostolic protonotary, thereby avoiding punishment.[26] The extent of the problem was made painfully obvious by the duke of Bavaria's representative, who noted gloomily that a recent visitation had demonstrated that ninety-six Bavarian priests out of one hundred kept mistresses or had clandestine wives.[27]

Given the seriousness of the celibacy issue, the Council made sure to specifically place concubinary priests firmly under episcopal jurisdiction so that "the ministers of the Church may be brought back to that continency and purity of life which is proper to them."[28] Post-Tridentine bishops like Juan de Ribera in Valencia or Charles Borromeo in Milan were scrupulous in enforcing stringent discipline on their diocesan clergy, although Borromeo found that some of his priests were able to flee to neighboring Como, where ecclesiastical discipline was less strict.[29]

The dramatic change in the degree to which diocesan clergy and laity were exposed to pressure from the hierarchy can be illustrated by visitation records. In the diocese of Pamplona, most of the bishops of the late fifteenth and early sixteenth centuries never even came to the diocese. Many were foreign, such as Antoniotti Pallavicino (1492) or Alejandro Cesarini (1520), while others, such as Cardinal Labrit, were figures of great political importance who had little time or inclination to deal with the mundane business of their diocese.[30]

Pamplona's pre-Tridentine reform began in 1540 with the appointment of the Castilian Pedro Pacheco as bishop, and it was he who initiated the first episcopal visitation that had ever been carried out in the diocese. Pacheco, who was elevated to the rank of cardinal in 1545, was followed by a series of resident bishops who were zealous reformers and, in some instances, distinguished prelates who had served as delegates to the Council of Trent. Alvaro de Moscoso, who was appointed bishop in 1550, had taught at the Sorbonne, served as rector of the University of Paris, and had accompanied Charles V to the Diets of Worms and Ratisbon. In 1551 Moscoso went to the Council of Trent at the express invitation of the emperor, where he served until the spring of 1552.[31] The impact of these bishops on the spiritual and moral life of the diocese can be seen in the *Libro de Mandatos de visita* of the parish of San Vicente in San Sebastián, which records thirty-two visitations by bishops or their officials between 1540 and 1670.[32] Legislation after 1564, when pastoral visitation applied the canons of the Council of Trent to the diocese, included ordinances on regular instruction of the catechism, licensing of preachers and confessors, clerical dress and morality, clandestine marriages, and the maintenance of a register of confession and communion. Failure to observe these mandates would be punished by fines as high as fifty ducats, suspension from benefices, or excommunication.[33]

No less important to the success of the Church in imposing clerical celibacy was the establishment of seminaries for the training of priests following the decree "Pro Seminariis," issued by the Council of Trent on June 15, 1563. In spite of considerable opposition coming from cathedral chapters, twenty-eight seminaries were founded in Spain between 1565 and 1670, with another eighteen between 1700 and 1797.[34] By grouping aspirants for the priesthood in boarding schools during their formative years between ages twelve and twenty, the Church not only provided more uniform and systematic intellectual preparation, but instilled a stern moral code as well. Discipline was strict, with each little fault carefully noted by student "acusadores" appointed weekly by the rector. Punishment was frequent and harsh, including stocks, fasting on bread and water for extended periods, and imprisonment. The seminarians were to be totally cut off from secular society and all forms of diversion. They were not allowed to participate in any unseemly games, have musical instruments, or invite any friends or relatives into the seminary. Naturally, any and all dealings with women, however innocent, were prohibited. They were trained in mental prayer, went to Mass, said the rosary and the Angelus every day, and confessed and took communion each week.[35]

Without a doubt, the harsh disciplinary regime imposed by Spanish seminaries was deliberately designed to inoculate aspirants for the priesthood against the allures of secular society and powerfully reinforce the practice of celibacy by training them to sublimate sexual temptations through immersion in the routines of religious ritual and devotions. Instead of emphasizing the intellectual development of older students, the seminary of San Julián, which was established in Cuenca in 1584, deliberately recruited boys between the ages of twelve and eighteen when they were most malleable in order to better inculcate the ideals of the post-Tridentine clergy. The boys' every waking moment was controlled by the rector; they were only allowed to leave the seminary in pairs and for specific purposes, and they were not even permitted to take vacations or receive visits by relatives.[36]

Prudery was also the order of the day in the growing number of religious colleges where young friars received their training. In the institutions run by Jesuits and Trinitarians, novices were prohibited from taking baths except for medical reasons and were never permitted to bathe or swim in rivers for fear of exposing their nude bodies to one another.[37] A document containing rules to be applied to Trinitarian novices in Spanish convents calls for them not to undress in front of one another if they share a cell and to always sleep wearing their scapularies with their hands folded over their chests.[38] The religious orders, especially the Jesuits, were also extremely concerned about the sexual conduct of their members. A system of regular visitation served to prevent the worst abuses, and visitors would punish sexual misconduct with reclusion, transfer, and deprivation of the right to hear confessions.[39]

The potent combination of increased episcopal authority and education in seminaries and religious colleges succeeded in producing a change of attitude among the clergy themselves toward violations of sexual celibacy. Like legal prostitution or socially sanctioned premarital sex, clerical concubinage moved from the category of an openly tolerated quasi-legitimate sexual outlet to an unacceptable and sinful activity that reflected badly on the clerical estate. This attitudinal transformation among the clergy is well illustrated by a request from the benefice holders of Alcaraz to their Bishop García de Loaysa before the Synod of 1596 to crack down on those diocesan priests who supported illegitimate children or maintained "suspicious women" in their houses.[40]

Concubinary priests or friars were also less likely to gain preferment or coveted positions. In 1718 the Valencia tribunal received an application from a Dominican, Fray Pedro Soler, a popular preacher and professor of theology at the university, for the coveted post of calificador. In spite of Soler's superior educational attainments, the tribunal rejected him as unsuitable on moral grounds. Several years earlier, a woman with whom Soler was having sexual relations had been forcibly deported from the city by the alcalde de crimen. More recently, Soler had been observed entering the homes of several women of ill repute, and this had caused such a public scandal that the tribunal secretary commented that it would be "unprecedented" for it to appoint such an individual. It was also feared that other members of his community would denounce him to the provincial of the order, who was about to carry out a visitation. Since transfer was the way in which the orders dealt with friars who engaged in illicit sexual activity, Soler would probably be removed from Valencia, and the tribunal decided that his "excesses" would make it impossible for it to defend him.[41]

At the same time, however, a large number of clerics found it impossible to maintain celibacy. With the relatively open sexual activity of the past now forbidden, such clerics were forced to make use of the secrecy of the confessional as their only or chief outlet. The sharp upsurge in the number of solicitation cases coming before the tribunals of the Spanish Inquisition in the 1600s and especially after 1650 indicates the increasing desperation of a clergy exposed as never before to enforcement of the celibacy rule. The admittedly incomplete records of the seven tribunals covered in this study reveal only twenty-nine cases for 1535 to 1599, increasing to forty-seven between 1600 and 1650 and eighty-one between 1651 and 1699.

For these priests, the confessional offered perhaps their only real opportunity to talk alone to women and to broach sexual topics under the rubric of asking about sins committed under the sixth commandment. It also afforded a measure of privacy either because it was closed or because confession took place in deserted churches or unfrequented side chapels where observation would be difficult or impossible. As we have seen, confession sometimes also took place in irregular locations like the homes or cells of penitents who were too ill to come to church. Analysis of the sexual behavior of priests and penitents during confession or as a consequence of arrangements made while confessing reveals a wide range of sexual activity and interaction constrained by the location and particular circumstances under which it had to be carried out. This analysis also indicates a pattern of sexual disorders that demonstrates the way in which emotionally disturbed individuals reacted to one of the most extensive experiments in sexual repression in human history.

Taking into account the physical constraints imposed by the confessional itself and the risk that the priest would be observed if he attempted to make an overtly physical approach to a female penitent, it is to be expected that the largest single category of offense was verbal. Altogether, victims of solicitation experienced 405 separate incidents of verbal abuse, of which 335 involved some form of provocative language, 35 involved sexual fantasies or sexual dreams experienced by the confessor and related to the penitent, and the remaining 35 stemmed from curiosity on the part of the confessor about some aspect of the penitent's sexual life.

Provocative language frequently involved assertions of love or affection on the part of the confessor, whether or not these were reciprocated by the penitent. In 1699, when twenty-five-year-old María Sarmiento went to confess with Salvador Quijada del Castillo for the first time, he abruptly told her that he "loved her and esteemed her highly." Sarmiento was so shocked that she said nothing, and Quijada del Castillo must have interpreted her lack of response as a negative because when she returned to confess with him two months later, he said nothing inappropriate and comported himself properly.[42]

Sometimes expressions of affection would be accompanied by more direct indications of the confessor's desire for an overtly sexual relationship. While hearing the confession of Sebastiana Josepha, a sixteen-year-old orphan from Ariço on the island of Tenerife, Quijada del Castillo first told her how attractive she was, then asked where she lived, and when he found out that she worked as a servant, asked if her mistress ever let her out of the house so that she could meet him.[43] After Dr. Diego Ordáz y Villalta, who was capellán mayor of the Bernardine convent in Alcalá de Henares, told Sor Manuela González that he found her very attractive and remarked, "I am just like the Turks; I can enjoy many women," he asked her if they could find a way to "copulate together."[44]

Confessors would sometimes make a suggestive remark with the clear intent of provoking lascivious thoughts or actions in a penitent who had never considered her confessor as a sexual partner. On two occasions, after he had finished hearing the confession of Sor Bernarda de San Antonio, Fray Juan de la Olmeda told her of his desire to kiss and fondle her and suggested that she think of him when she urinated.[45]

Suggestive or provocative language could also form an exciting part of an ongoing relationship that included sexual foreplay during confession and other sexual activity outside the confessional. Isabel de Tena was fifteen when she began confessing with Francisco de las Llagas, a Franciscan, who resided in the convent in Hinojosa de San Vicente northwest of Toledo. Llagas began using suggestive language almost from the beginning of the twelve years during which she was his penitent. At first, he simply told her that he loved her, but later, as their relationship intensified, he would say that he could not live without her and could not put her out of his mind awake or asleep. On the twenty or thirty occasions when this would occur, he would then ask her to kiss him and put his tongue through a hole in the confessional screen so that she could take it in her mouth. Isabel willingly complied, even though she made a pretence of reluctance by asking coyly, "But Father Llagas how could you do this . . . and in such a holy place?" After the excitement of the confessional, Llagas and Isabel de Tena went on to have coitus and engage in mutual masturbation in the home of a widow who made extra money by making it available for assignations.[46]

It is in chronicling the sexual fantasies of soliciting confessors that we can perhaps best illustrate the psychological impact of sexual repression on the clergy during the Counter-Reformation. Bizarre sexual fantasies haunted the imaginations of even the most devout, reflecting the extreme sexual frustration and repressed longings of the age. Even the saintly Diego Pérez de Valdivia, whose *Aviso de gente recogida* presented beatas with an extreme model of asceticism in the tradition of the contemptus mundi, was not immune from such fantasies. In the *Aviso*, Pérez de Valdivia revealed his own sadistic obsessions and fascination with rape by relating the visions of female saints that were filled with images of "lewd men" who abused them sexually and the dreams of pious men who imagined raping or otherwise defiling holy women. In order to demonstrate the classical idea that God will always give strength to a virtuous woman in order to avoid being raped, Pérez de Valdivia inadvertently revealed his own erotic dreams by telling the story of a beautiful virgin who had been captured by corsairs and brought before the Moorish chieftains in Algiers naked to the waist. Before she could be abused, she was able to mutilate the very breasts that they found so attractive and was soon released from captivity. At the end of this curious little homily, Pérez de Valdivia remarked ruefully, "Today we are far from such heroic times as women sell their virginity so easily and cheaply."[47]

On a more prosaic level, divorced from the guilty longings of the spiritual elite, the fantasies of ordinary confessors were directly related to the frustrations that they experienced as celibate individuals in frequent contact with women but unable to satisfy their sexual needs. Sometimes, confessors simply dreamed about having an ordinary married life and enjoying the benefits of wife and children. Diego de Rocha, a Franciscan residing in the convent of Santa Cruz on Tenerife, had established friendly relations with the Puizada family and visited their home frequently. He also began hearing the confessions of their youngest daughter, Beatriz, with whom he soon fell in love. One day, after she finished confessing, he asked if she would remain in the church as he wanted to speak with her. She agreed, and when they were alone he told her that he loved her and that if she would return his affections, he would escape from the order and take her to the mainland or even to America where they could get married.[48]

Gabriel Canevas, who was a benefice holder in Las Palmas, wanted to experience becoming a father without losing the benefits of his position. While her husband was absent on a commercial voyage, Catalina Flexas y Proassi was repeatedly propositioned by Canevas, who begged her to have his child, which he averred modestly would turn out to be as handsome as himself. He assured her that her reputation would not suffer as everyone would attribute the child to her husband. Of course, at an earlier time, Canevas would have been able to have a child by his mistress or "housekeeper" and not only bring it up openly, but pass his benefice on to him. After the Council of Trent, with its violent attack on concubinage and legislation against the illegitimate sons of priests, this had become far less possible, and Canevas was forced to resort to begging an unwilling woman to have a child that he would never be able to acknowledge or assist.[49]

In other cases, sexual fantasies were triggered off by the frustrations of a celibate existence. Manuel Ibáñez shocked María Antonia Miñana, a nineteen-year-old servant girl, during one of their weekly confessions when he told her that he had dreamed of having had intercourse with her the previous night. Apparently, the origin of this erotic fantasy was not Miñana herself, but the sight of another girl who was wearing a low-cut dress.[50]

Sexual frustration was also directly responsible for the erotic fantasies experienced by Pedro Sobreras, a sixty-year-old Franciscan. After spending months trying vainly to seduce one of his young penitents, he told her that he had dreamed that he had coitus with her the previous night while hugging his pillow.[51]

While the sexual fantasies of someone like Pedro Sobreras appear rather unremarkable, in certain individuals, such fantasies become so powerful that they intensified sexual arousal and made celibacy almost impossible to bear. At the beginning of a letter sent at the request of the Valencia tribunal in April 1819, Cristóbal Valles, the warden of the Mercedarian house in Valencia, admitted that Fray Juan Ibáñez became extremely jealous if any of his female penitents used another confessor and that he had a habit of staring longingly at any attractive woman who entered the chapel. So obvious and offensive had this habit become that the husband of one of his penitents told his wife that she was not to confess with him any further.[52]

Ibáñez was clearly chafing under the rule of celibacy and had already solicited one of his penitents without success when Sor Agustina del Corazón de Jesús selected him as her confessor. Within a few days he conceived a violent passion for her and told her that he thought about her by day and dreamed about her at night. He heard her confession in a closed confessional, and when he heard her enter the other side and say "Ave María," he would put his head down on the rail and dream that it was pillowed between her breasts. On one occasion, Sor Agustina was incautious enough to agree to put her finger through a small hole in the confessional screen only to have Ibáñez grab it so hard that he hurt her badly. He then became very agitated, muttering fiercely that he wished that he could enter her side of the confessional and be alone with her and banging on the rail "like a madman." After a few moments of this, he calmed down and bitterly remarked that "in the end I am a friar and you are a nun, and it is not proper for us to do anything because we have both taken a vow of chastity."

A desire to witness forbidden or sinful sexual acts also figured strongly in many sexual fantasies. Fray Juan Ibáñez repeatedly urged Sor Agustina to clean herself after menstruation by inserting her finger deep inside her vagina, but was also extremely excited by the idea of female homosexuality, and at one point expressed a desire to see Sor Augustina and another nun engage in sex play.[53]

Fantasies involving bizarre or unusual types of sexual behavior were also experienced by a few confessors. Fray Pablo Ginard expressed a desire to shave Juana Ana Tarrasa's pubic hair and wash her clitoris. He also betrayed his own fascination with bestiality by asking her if she had ever experienced any erotic sensations when watching dogs copulate.[54]

A variation on the theme of female masturbation appeared in testimony given to the Valencia tribunal about Vicente Ripoll by Sor Catalina Angelo, a nun living in the convent of the Holy Trinity. A few months after he had begun serving as her confessor, they were on such intimate terms that they would make extra appointments just to get each other excited by using smutty language. It was on one of those occasions that Ripoll begged her to insert her fingers inside her vagina and then put them through the holes in the confessional screen.[55]

Finally, cunnilingus, which was extremely rare among the priests and penitents in the Inquisition records and undoubtedly rare in the sexual practices of Spanish society as a whole, appeared in the perfervid sexual imaginings of Gabriel Canevas.[56] After trying and failing to get Catalina Flexas y Proassi to masturbate him, he offered to kiss her clitoris "many times" if she would allow him to do so.[57]

In a society that severely restricted sexual activity of all kinds, sexual fantasy could serve as an effective symbolic substitute or replacement for the physical gratification that had become difficult or impossible.[58] In the case of the priesthood, where the enforcement of celibacy raised significant barriers to physical sexual behavior, mental sexual activity was just one of a number of ways of sublimating sexual needs. Theologians even gave such erotic fantasies some legitimacy in their discussions about voluntary and involuntary masturbation. While willful masturbation was condemned as a mortal sin, most casuists were willing to exempt involuntary masturbation, specifically during erotic dreams.[59]

The Church had long had an horror of nudity. In the fifteenth century, St. Bernardino di Siena advised wives to die rather than allow their husbands to see them in the nude, and in later centuries, preachers inveighed against nudity and indecent fashions. In a work published in 1700, Jean Leduger advised young missioners to dress with the utmost circumspection in the mornings as God is watching them and to "never appear naked to anyone else, especially the opposite sex."[60]

Curiosity about the body is a natural instinct and a normal aspect of sexual maturation, however, so the extreme prudishness that characterized their training in seminaries, schools run by religious orders, and monastic colleges left many priests with a strong desire to find out more about the female body and its sexual functioning. Once, while hearing the confession of Antonia Grande y Mirona, Geronimo Vicente Maymo told her that his greatest happiness would be if she would disrobe and allow him to "see every part of her body."[61]

Priests were also extremely curious about sexual activity, especially among the married. The Augustinian friar, Joaquín Ubeda, asked María Teresa Cervera, a thirty-six-year old married woman about the positions she assumed when she had sex with her husband.[62] The Dominican Fray Andrés Frau was really fascinated by the sex life of his married penitents and constantly badgered them for details. While hearing the confession of twenty-eight-year-old Barbara Morney, Frau placed his hands on her breasts and asked her to tell him how many times she had had intercourse with her husband. Frau also interrogated Gerónima Obrador, the wife of a local physician, about her sex life and asked her if she had copulated with her husband the previous night and if she had enjoyed it.[63]

The attention that traditional cultures paid to the bride's chastity at time of marriage may account for Gaspar de Nájera's questions about the events of the first night.[64] When fifteen-year-old Lucía Rodríguez, who had recently married a labrador, came to him for confession, he demanded to know how big her husband's member was and if he had thrust all of it inside her on their first night together. He was also interested in finding out how much blood she had lost and where it fell. Nájera's own obsession with deflowering a virgin is clearly revealed by another incident that took place with fifteen-year-old Ana de Jesús. After asking her a few perfunctory questions about whether she was obedient to her father and mother, he announced that he was going to travel to her village in order to hear the confessions of the children of a local notable. While there he intended to visit her house one night and take her to bed, and then he promised, "you will shed three drops of blood and find out how it hurts the first time."[65]

Doubtless, the motives for at least some of this questioning went beyond mere curiosity. Francisco Pons, a Franciscan from La Palma, questioned his penitents about the details of their sex lives in order to find out if they were sexually frustrated. When he found out that Catalina Real y Massenet was a widow, he encouraged her to talk about her relationship with her husband and asked if she missed having him beside her when she went to bed at night. When she admitted that she did, he tried to provoke her further by asking her how many times they had had coitus in one night, while bringing his face close to hers. Pons did something very similar with Francisca Juan, a twenty-two-year old who was married to a tanner. After she told him that she was childless, he asked her if her husband embraced her in bed and if she enjoyed sexual relations with him, while offering to "serve her in anything that she might require."[66]

Many traditional cultures all over the world have interdicted sexual relations during a woman's menstrual flow, either because of fears and anxieties surrounding menstruation or because it was assumed that coital activity would cause the woman extreme physical distress.[67] Medieval and early modern Europe was no exception to this rule, and most theologians felt that it was sinful and dangerous to engage in sexual activity during menstruation, based on the Old Testament prohibition in Leviticus. Even the summas that tended to reduce coital relations during menstruation to a venial sin were still opposed to it because of a long-held view that offspring might turn out deformed.[68] Even Martín de Azpilcueta Navarro, who had a fairly liberal attitude on this issue since he believed that coitus during menstruation was not even a venial sin if it was done to avoid incontinency, nevertheless warns of the risk of "conceiving a monster" as a result.[69]

Curiosity about menstruation among confessors undoubtedly stemmed from its inexplicable nature and origin, while the traditional prohibitions against sexual relations during the menstrual period that were contained in every confessors' manual only served to heighten the mystery. When José de San Miguel served as confessor to Mariana Llorens during the summer of 1760, he pressed her again and again to show him where her menstrual fluid came from.[70] But it was Fray Juan Ibáñez who was really obsessed with menstruation. During the time that he acted as confessor to Sor Agustina del Corazón de Jesús, he was constantly asking her if she was having her period and would often walk around to her side of the confessional and open the door in order to see if she were pale or had a discolored complexion. He also repeatedly urged her to wipe herself and evidently thought of menstruation as some kind of illness since he expressed a desire to stay with her in her cell in order to "see that she was completely cured."[71]

The next most common form of sexually oriented behavior among offenders was what is commonly called "petting" in modern society. Among the 246 instances of petting are included a variety of activities like kissing, fondling, and caressing of the face and body that stops short of orgasm. For the solicitante, petting assumed two distinct functions. In the first place, petting, whether done very infrequently or at virtually any opportunity, provided a substitute for orgasm or coitus. In such cases, petting becomes a form of sexual compromise between the manifest needs of the individual for sexual gratification and the enormous weight of social discipline pressing down on his sexual life.[72]

The burden of social discipline, fear of punishment, and the extreme degree of sexual inhibition inculcated in seminary and religious college probably account for the fact that some of the confessors who engaged in petting did so with the utmost timidity and then were immediately overcome with fear and remorse. The single instance of physical contact that led to José Carrera's denunciation before the Corte tribunal in 1741 involved twenty-year-old María Vázquez, an unmarried girl from the village of Leganes where Carrera was lieutenant curate. In the two months prior to the incident, María had come to the confessional numerous times, but not always to confess. Frequently she and Carrera simply gossiped about village affairs. The young woman's complicity in feigning confession in order to talk with him must have convinced Carrera that she was attracted to him. All this came to a head one day when she had come to church and spent more than an hour gossiping with Carrera in the confessional about the women of the village. As she got up to leave after pretending to receive absolution, she took the priest's hand in order to kiss it, but Carerra ran his fingers lightly over her face and then begged her to say nothing to any other confessor about what had happened.[73]

Some confessors were able to engage in a consistent pattern of caressing or touching their penitents that was so carefully calculated that they were able to avoid punishment for years. The Dominican Francisco del Rosario enjoyed an excellent reputation both within his order and among the general public. In 1690, his community in the convent of San Pedro Martyr in the Canaries had named him to be their representative to the provincial synod held on the island of Tenerife and then elected him their prior. According to information received by the tribunal from its commissioner, there had never been a breath of scandal about Rosario before his arrest, and he was known as a "pious brother of excellent habits."[74]

But Francisco del Rosario's carefully constructed exterior was a fraud. Behind the facade, there was a deeply troubled and intensely lonely individual who, for at least the last seven years, had been seeking sexual gratification by touching and caressing his female penitents in such a subtle way that they were convinced that he was only doing it to encourage them to make a more complete confession. When called before the tribunal in July 1691, Gerónima Díaz, who began confessing with Rosario when she was only nineteen, admitted that he had always touched her face while hearing her confession, but affirmed that she always felt that he was doing it for her own good since as a young and timid girl she might have "omitted one of her sins."[75] Rosario was even more careful with Ana Joachim. Instead of touching her every time she confessed, he only risked it twice, once on her face and once on her throat, during the entire three-year period that she came to him for confession. Under the circumstances, it is hardly surprising that Joachim never came forward to denounce Rosario and that she was convinced that he had only touched her in order to make her feel more secure since, as she told the inquisitors, "sometimes people don't make a complete confession because the confessor is a little too severe."[76]

Even Rosario managed to convince himself that he was acting in the interests of his penitents. During his first two audiences before the tribunal, he admitted nothing, in his reply to the formal arraignment, he said only that he might have alarmed some of them by getting too close during confession, but that he never had any evil intentions. Finally, on July 3, 1691, eleven days after his arrest, he admitted that, "carried away by his own misery and by the sensual pleasure that he hoped to obtain," he had caressed his penitents.

Constrained by the position that he occupied in the order and desirous of maintaining his reputation in the community, Francisco del Rosario adopted his technique of petting as his chief or only form of sexual gratification when a life of total celibacy became unbearable. By carefully restraining himself from doing anything overt, by touching and caressing rather than fondling, and by studiously avoiding suggestive or obscene language, he was able to gain a small measure of sexual gratification. But not everyone was completely taken in. While some penitents were willing to accept Rosario's actions as a legitimate part of his role, others, more "scrupulous," more concerned with making a full and complete confession of all their sins, went to other confessors to assuage the guilt and uncertainty that confessing with Rosario had inspired in them. Still others, innocent of any suspicions about Rosario's conduct but simply talkative, horrified their friends by telling them how he had tried to "encourage" them to confess properly by touching them in a reassuring manner. Driven by increasingly urgent sexual needs, Rosario was unable to confine his attentions to one individual. With news of his activities traveling by word of mouth and with pressure building on some of his former penitents who were being denied absolution because of their failure to denounce him, his arrest by the Holy Office was inevitable.

Instead of becoming an end in itself, petting could also be a way of testing and nourishing the sexual desires of a female penitent, thereby providing an intermediate step that could lead on to more significant sexual interaction. Pascual de la Hoz, the curate of Benimodo in the Kingdom of Valencia, also acted as confessor in the local Franciscan convent, where he encountered twenty-nine-year-old Sor María de la Purificación. After the first few confessions, they began meeting in the confessional to gossip, and la Hoz kissed her several times through a hole in the screen. Having once crossed this threshold of intimacy, it was not too difficult for la Hoz to embrace and caress Sor María and then to convince the by now thoroughly aroused nun to expose herself to him, which she did on eight separate occasions.[77]

Petting to orgasm was followed by sexual intercourse in the relationship between the Dominican Juan de Monseratte and two of his penitents, Margarita Tura and Catalina Planellas. In both cases, sexual interaction began with Monseratte kissing and caressing the women, then fondling their breasts, and finally inducing them to masturbate him. In this case, as in many others, sexual interaction between priest and penitent was made extremely convenient because the convent chapel did not have a closed confessional, so that the women merely knelt before their confessor in a submissive posture. After both women had been thoroughly aroused during confession, Monseratte had intercourse with them in the home of a woman who made extra money by renting it out for use as a rendezvous for illicit sexual interaction.[78]

Disruption of long-accepted practices of sanctioned premarital sex, the elimination of official prostitution, and the substitution of disciplined, formal schooling for the informal apprenticeships and private masters of the medieval period meant that the opportunities for licit, socially tolerated sexual contact were being steadily reduced during the early modern period. Even among the married, anxiety about sexual relations made marital life increasingly difficult. In such an atmosphere, it is highly likely that solitary practices, particularly masturbation, not only flourished, but spread to social groups who may hardly have practiced it at all in earlier times.[79]

A small but nevertheless significant indication of the increasing frequency of masturbation in Spanish society comes from the fact that although the word "polución" is listed but not defined in the famous Covarrubias Orozco dictionary of 1610, it is fully defined in the 1726 dictionary of the Real Academia Española.[80] Considerably more important is the change in the treatment of masturbatory practices in confessors' manuals. For Azpilcueta Navarro, masturbation was not a cause for special concern. Of course, masturbation went against the natural order, but involuntary masturbation or even the desire for a "wet dream" was not especially serious. Amazingly, Azpilcueta Navarro even remarks that some physicians encouraged their patients to masturbate for reasons of health, something which he believed they could do without fear of sin.[81] By 1612, increasing preoccupation with the frequency of masturbation among the general public was reflected in Bartolome de Medina's warning to confessors about the need to exercise extreme caution when discussing the subject with their penitents. Masturbation was not only "so common that it was becoming a habit" among many individuals, but there was also a great deal of misunderstanding about the meaning of the sin involved and so much shame and guilt surrounding it that many were not willing to reveal what they had done. As a consequence, confessors would have to use subtle means to find out the truth and prescribe a whole series of remedies such as spiritual exercises, fasting, increased devotion to the Virgin Mary, and more frequent confession in order to help their penitents.[82] Later in the seventeenth century, growing concern among theologians, preachers, and missionaries over the increasing frequency of masturbation was reflected in the Jesuit *Christian Pedagogy* and by Lazarist preachers, who denounced it as a sin against nature while noting that "alas, this sin is only too common."[83]

By the early eighteenth century, penitents must have spoken about masturbation so often during confession that Jayme Corella was even able to present a realistic dialogue between a confessor and a penitent concerning it. This dialogue, which was undoubtedly drawn from Corella's long experience as a confessor and missionary, concerns a peasant who came to confess that he had begun masturbating two or more times per week when he was twelve and continued until he married at age twenty-four. In his comments, which are meant to advise confessors on the knotty problems that they will have to face, Corella reveals not only that masturbation was becoming widespread among the peasantry, but that they were using it as a substitute for the kind of premarital sex with single women or prostitutes that was being repressed under the rubric of "simple fornication." Warning confessors to inquire whether such penitents were aware of the sinful nature of masturbation, Corella says that this is necessary because such "rustics" frequently think that there is no sin in sexual matters if they do not lie with a woman, so that "I myself have found many who were blind to the fact that masturbation is a sin."[84]

Since priests were even more vulnerable to official discourses than laymen and suffered significantly more sexual repression in the period after Trent, it is to be expected that solitary practices would have increased among them as well and that the confessional, where contact with women was combined with a certain degree of privacy, would provide an ideal venue for masturbation.

This hypothesis is partially confirmed by the contrast between Azpilcueta Navarro's relative lack of concern about the potential for involuntary ejaculation during confession and Bartholomé de Medina, who depicts the confessional as a place where the priest could expect to experience erection and ejaculation while hearing the confessions of female penitents. Under these circumstances, ejaculation was seen as involuntary and, therefore, not sinful, but simply one of the moral risks that came with the job of the confessor.[85]

Of course, Bartholomé de Medina and every other casuist condemned voluntary masturbation as a mortal sin wherever it occurred. Voluntary masturbation in the confessional was viewed as especially serious since it combined elements of blasphemy and profanation. Official disgust with priests who violated this ban was articulated by the prosecuting attorney of the Mallorca tribunal, Luis Antonio Gómez Cabrero Colodrero, in his arraignment of Dr. Jorge Roselló in 1682. Cabrero Colodrero condemned Roselló for having committed the "most odious and detestable offense that it was possible to imagine against the performance of such a sacred ceremony and in such a holy place" by inducing Antonia March y Cifre to masturbate him in a chapel in the cathedral of Las Palmas.[86]

However, in spite of strong social proscription and the risk of punishment for solicitation, confessors engaged in voluntary masturbation with sixty-three penitents. Of these instances, the overwhelming majority (74.6 percent) involved only the priest himself, who either induced or forced his penitent to manipulate him or, more commonly, did so himself while hearing her confession. One woman that Córdoba's Inquisitor Miguel Ximénez Palomino encountered while carrying out a visitation to his district in 1607 had exceptionally bad luck with the friars of the Mercedarian house in Baeza. Shortly after she began her first confession with Fray Ginés de Carranza, she saw him throw himself down in his side of the confessional and begin "making disgusting movements as if he were a woman engaging in the sex act." After ejaculating, he regained his composure and without saying anything, helped her to complete her confession. Horrified by what had happened with Carranza, she decided never to confess with him again and turned instead to Antolín Cavallero, another friar in the same convent. Unfortunately, the result was the same, and she saw him masturbate through the confessional screen "with great filth and lewdness." After trying still another friar and finding that he kept rubbing his member during confession, she decided to abandon any attempt to find a confessor from among the Mercedarians and left angrily, declaring that "this convent is more like a house of prostitution than a house of worship."[87]

Automanipulation was not the only or preferred method of achieving ejaculation, as greater sexual gratification could be achieved with the cooperation of a female partner. Juan Llobera, another Mercedarian from Mallorca, had considerable success in inducing his female penitents to masturbate him by speaking to them affectionately and promising them, not always truthfully, that he would seek to have intercourse with them outside the confessional. In April 1689 he came to the bar of the tribunal to confess that nineteen years earlier he had induced a young serving girl to masturbate him in the confessional, but failed to make good on his promise to find a room where they could have coitus. Another woman who came to him originally for help in redeeming an article that she had pawned was induced to masturbate him as the price for his assistance. After Llobera's confession, Juana Mulet, a thirty-seven-year-old married woman came forward to testify that she had confessed with him for more than a year on the average of two or three times per month and that on each occasion she had manipulated his genitals. In this instance, Llobera had also promised that he would seek an opportunity to have intercourse with her, but only visited her house once and abandoned any further attempt when he found he could not get her alone. Juan Llobera is a good example of a priest who used masturbation as a form of sexual compromise. As warden of his convent and delegate for the ecclesiastical estate at the Cortes of Catalonia, he could not afford the scandal of an illicit sexual relationship. Instead, he used his charm or his financial resources to gain the extra sexual thrill of petting to climax by a person of the opposite sex until guilt or fear of exposure brought him to the Holy Office.[88]

Mutual masturbation occurred in sixteen cases and is an indication that women were also seeking release from the unresolved sexual tensions caused by a sexually repressive society. One of the most complete descriptions of mutual masturbation in the case records is contained in testimony taken from Eugenia Ordóñez concerning her affair with Alonso Guerrero, a Trinitarian friar. Testifying before the Toledo tribunal on June 19, 1639, Ordóñez described how on numerous occasions she had knelt before Guerrero, who was seated on a bench in a side chapel where the friars normally heard confession. After exchanging filthy and lascivious language with him, she would put her hand inside his habit and manipulate his genitals until he achieved orgasm. He would then lift her skirts and insert his fingers inside her, rubbing her until she, too, experienced orgasm. Immediately afterward, they would kiss passionately. For Eugenia Ordóñez and Alonso Guerrero, mutual masturbation was not merely a sexual compromise, but a part of a complex sexual interaction that included the use of provocative language and proceeded on to intercourse both in her home and beneath the church choir.[89]

Sexual compromise was, however, the role that mutual masturbation played in the relationship between the Trinitarian friar Patricio Cerero and María Barrientos, a nun in the convent of the Encarnación in Toledo. María Barrientos began confessing with Cerero sometime in her late teens while she was still in secular life. Early in their relationship, Cerero expressed strong affection for her, which she evidently returned, but she refused his sexual advances, limiting herself to kissing him once when he invited her to his mother's house for dinner. Telling him of her desire to enter religious life, she declared that she wanted him to be her confessor and that if they engaged in any kind of sexual relationship before she entered the order, she would lose respect for him and, therefore, could never see him again. Faced with the choice of abstaining from sex and never seeing María Barrientos again, Cerero agreed to these terms and began serving as her confessor in the convent when she entered at age twenty-one. However, María Barrientos's refusal to have coitus with Cerero meant that both were denied sexual relief, and during their confessions in the convent, he became increasingly restive, repeatedly telling her that he loved her and using suggestive language to indicate his desire for her. As his sexual frustration increased, he began showing her his genitals through the confessional screen. He also masturbated on at least six occasions, either in the confessional or in the porter's lodge where they sometimes went to talk. Greatly excited by this, Barrientos reciprocated by masturbating on her side of the confessional, telling Cerero exactly when she was doing it and how it felt even though she refused to show him her genitals. Finally, eight years after Cerero had been transferred to another convent, Barrientos denounced her former lover. In her letter to the tribunal, Barrientos claimed that she was unaware that they had done anything wrong, thereby bearing out the view expressed by Jayme Corella and other contemporary observers that there was a tendency among laymen to accept masturbation as a legitimate substitute for coital sex.[90]

Ultimately, in spite of the risk of discovery and prosecution and the growing social pressure against priests who broke their vows of celibacy, intimate relations between confessor and penitent in the confessional sometimes led to sexual intercourse. This occurred in seventy-eight cases, almost the same incidence as that of masturbation, but considerably less than verbal offenses or sexual foreplay. The relatively small number of incidents of coitus is an indication of just how difficult it was to arrange a secure and private location for it, as well as the enormous inhibitions that some priests had to overcome before they would engage in an activity that constituted a final violation of years of training in seminaries and colleges.

The extreme anxiety that was focused on intercourse but did not seem to be present with other forms of sexual activity can be illustrated by the case of the Carmelite friar Agustín de Cervera. So long as he confined himself to using suggestive language or touching or caressing his female penitents, he had no remorse, but in the two instances where his relationships came to the point where intercourse was involved, he became extremely anxious and overcome by an unbearable sense of sin. In his testimony before the tribunal, he recalled that before having coitus with Ana de Tovar he "trembled" with fear because he knew that he was offending God. He prayed afterward that God would send a bolt of lightning to destroy him before he could sin in such a way in the future. Interestingly enough, Cervera was affected by impotence on the second occasion. After Ana de Carvajal, another one of his penitents, brought him to her house so that they could have intercourse, he was unable to manage an erection in spite of his strong desire for her because he was so conscious of the "grave sin" they would be committing.[91]

When it occurred, coitus between confessor and penitent was most often the result of a previously established pattern of sexual interaction during confession, including caressing, kissing, or even masturbation, that went on over a fairly long period of time until the sexual compromise that sustained that level of activity no longer proved sufficiently satisfying. Jaime Massenet's relationship with Antonia Sastre began in the confessional at the end of 1713. During one of their early confessions, he began kissing her and using suggestive language. Then, for a period of almost a year, they petted and engaged in mutual masturbation in a poorly frequented chapel on almost a daily basis. They performed a variety of sexual acts in the chapel, but according to Sastre, Massenet refused to have intercourse there, preferring to ejaculate between her legs no doubt in an attempt to avoid adding the sin of coitus in a holy place to his other transgressions.[92] They actually consummated their relationship the in home of Margarita Canelles usually about two hours after they had finished confessing. In this case, intercourse appears to have entailed a financial obligation since Massenet admitted that he gave Sastre small amounts of chocolate or money after each incident.[93]

Sexual intercourse between Fray Raphael Serre and Francisca Noseras also did not begin until after a prolonged period during which they only engaged in foreplay. In this case, however, it was the difficulty of finding a secure location, rather than any sexual inhibitions, that prevented the couple from engaging in coitus. Since Noseras lived with her mother and sister and never had any privacy, it proved impossible for her to accede to Serre's repeated demands for greater sexual intimacy, but she assured him of her willingness to go wherever they could be alone. He finally was able to obtain a small room near one of the local convents, and in her testimony before the Mallorca tribunal, she described how she met him there one afternoon. After satisfying each other's anatomical curiosity by undressing completely and looking at and fondling each other's genitalia, they proceeded to have intercourse four times in succession.[94]

Violation of the injunction to procreate contained in traditional Christian ethics and the association of homosexual behavior with heresy meant that sodomy came to be considered the most serious of all sexual offenses by medieval canonists like Raymond of Peñafort.[95] After 1348, because of concern over the drastic decline in the population caused by the Black Death, sodomy came to be regarded as a serious threat to the survival of society itself and a whole series of new laws were created that laid down new and more gruesome punishments. Burning alive or beheading were commonly prescribed in municipal ordinances, and the town of Bergamo not only demanded a public burning, but obliged the culprit's family to be present as his body was consumed by the flames.[96] In the medieval Spanish Partidas (legal codes), sodomy was punishable by death, while in their edicts of August 22 and 27, 1497, Ferdinand and Isabella declared that those found guilty were to be burned alive in the place where the crime had been committed. The criminal code of Valencia also contained very severe penalties for sodomy, ranging from scourging and the galleys for minors to death by fire for those over twenty years of age.[97]

These draconian punishments and the popular abhorrence for homosexuality were probably responsible for the fact that only two of the ten homosexual or bisexual priests charged with solicitation would admit to anal penetration. The remaining offenders claimed merely to have engaged in mutual masturbation. Such behavior seemed to be the minimum expected from a homosexual encounter, so that when sixteen-year-old José Vernad refused to masturbate José Gracian, the Franciscan friar threw himself on top of the boy and rubbed his genitals against him until he was able to ejaculate.[98]

The fact that bisexuals outnumbered homosexuals six-to-four among solicitantes appears to bear out certain modern studies that have indicated that a significant number of males have had at least one homosexual experience during their lifetime.[99] Since none of the priests admitted to any more than one homosexual incident, but all of them had solicited several females, we can safely conclude that bisexuality was a strategy that they adopted when they were deprived for long periods of any sexual contact with women. In the eighteen years between 1608 and 1626, Pedro Estéban had attempted sexual solicitation of four women, one of whom had simply left the confessional in disgust when he began masturbating, while two others allowed him to caress them on one occasion. Estéban was only able to achieve coitus with one of his penitents with whom he had a relationship during 1608 and 1609. In order to make up for his sexual failures and the severe heterosexual deprivation that life as a Franciscan entailed, Estéban was able to fall back on what appears to have been a well-established homosexual subculture in his convent. As warden, Estéban could gain easy access to the coterie of homosexuals and force his attentions on those he desired.

On one occasion, he ordered Fray Onofre Llompaid, who was later expelled from the order for his rampant homosexuality, to come to his cell under the pretext of helping him clean his private parts where he claimed he had an infection. Fray Llompaid's assistance proved more sexual than hygienic since Estéban embraced and kissed him and then had anal intercourse with him three or four times. In the case of Pedro Estéban, a bisexual orientation may well have been facilitated by a certain degree of confusion about proper sexual role playing since he also confessed to an incestuous relationship with his sister before he entered the order.[100]

Societal rejection of homosexuality made it difficult for bisexual offenders to admit to a homosexual relationship even though they might be willing to admit to soliciting females. In audiences before the Mallorca tribunal held on May 15 and June 2, 1614, José Nuela admitted soliciting three of his female penitents, but indignantly rejected the charge that he had seduced Guilén Mas in his cell three years earlier. Nuela's vehemence in denying the charge of sodomy may well have stemmed from an uncomfortable awareness that his real sexual orientation was more homosexual than heterosexual. The only instance of intercourse in the record occurred during the incident with Mas, while his relationship to his female penitents was confined to timidly touching their faces while wishing them good fortune just before they left the confessional.[101]

Interestingly enough, none of the inquisitorial tribunals concerned in these cases made any effort to give especially harsh punishments to those accused of sodomy. Cases were either suspended for lack of evidence or offenders were punished for solicitation only. This pattern of leniency was entirely consistent with the moderate policies of the Supreme Council toward sodomites and stands in sharp contrast to the hysterical attitudes of secular tribunals in Spain and other parts of Europe toward similar offenses.[102]

From earliest times, Christian teaching about sexual matters has condemned any form of sexual experimentation on the grounds that it was unnatural to deviate from the normal mode of coition. What this meant in practice is what is now identified as the "missionary position." Variants from that position, especially anal intercourse, which tended to be regarded as a form of sodomy, or other deviations from sexual behavior regarded as normal, such as oral sex, constituted serious offenses and were roundly condemned.[103]

Nevertheless, in spite of these longstanding prohibitions, a few undoubtedly heterosexual confessors and penitents had the courage to engage in various forms of "unnatural" sex. In 1696 the Carmelite friar Alejandro Lloret came before the Valencia tribunal to confess that he had had anal intercourse with María García, the wife of a shoemaker in Játiva, on seven occasions. Apparently, the lady liked this form of lovemaking so much that when Lloret stopped seeing her, she threatened to "make him pay" for his neglect. It was probably a fear of denunciation, rather than any qualms of conscience, that brought Lloret before the bar of the Holy Office. Because of the fact that, as an Aragonese tribunal, Valencia had jurisdiction over sodomy, the prosecuting attorney in this case insisted that Lloret be placed in the secret prison and brought to trial after first consulting with the Suprema. The Suprema, however, gave little support to Valencia's overzealous prosecuting attorney and merely ordered the tribunal to formally admonish Lloret on the charge of sodomy and suspend the case.[104]

Oral sex, which was condemned by Theodore of Canterbury and other casuists as being worse than anal intercourse, was still relatively rare among couples in postwar America.[105] The Kinsey studies from the late 1940s indicated that only about 50 percent of women had any experience with fellatio and cunnilingus and less than 45 percent of males reported mouth contact with the female genitalia.[106] Considering the strength of traditional prohibitions against oral sex even in late twentieth-century America, it is hardly surprising to find that there were only three instances of oral sex among soliciting confessors. The only case of cunnilingus involved a friar who had a history of alcoholism and claimed to have been drunk when the incident occurred.[107] Evidently, in order to carry out an act that was subject to such strong social proscription, Fray Antonio Planes had to be at least partially inebriated so that his own inhibitions were lowered.

The two incidents of fellatio involved friars who were multiple offenders and had already demonstrated a certain tendency to experiment with daring modes of sexual expression. Religious enthusiasm, evidenced by vows of poverty, chastity, and obedience, provided the context in which twenty-two-year-old Magdalena Aldover consented to fellatio with her longtime confessor, Pablo Ginard. The relationship between Ginard and Aldover was compounded of the most fervent religious devotion and sadomasochistic practices rationalized as mortification of the flesh. It was precisely within this context of religiously inspired obedience and self-abasement that Ginard asked

Aldover to perform fellatio as "an act of humiliation." On this occasion, even the form that fellatio took was consistent with religious excitement since Ginard ordered her to trace a cross on his genitals before taking them in her mouth.[108]

The Aldover sisters, Magalena, Francisca, and Margarita, must have been unusual for their time, place, and social status as all three were prepared to engage in sexual experimentation. Francisca and Ginard engaged in mutual masturbation on numerous occasions, and she allowed him to caress her breasts in the porter's lodge of his convent. Emboldened by this, Ginard tried, unsuccessfully, to get her to perform fellatio. Her younger sister, Margarita, accepted a dildo from Ginard and kept it in her home for two weeks since, as she told the inquisitors, she saw nothing sinful in making use of such a device.[109]

Since traditional religious prohibitions against the use of cult objects for impious purposes were strongly reinforced during the Counter-Reformation by the renewed emphasis on respect for the sacred, some individuals felt an overwhelming temptation to break the taboo by employing them for sexual purposes.[110] As confessor in the Carmelite convent of Guadalajara, Francisco Corbera was called to exorcise María Leocadia de la Santísima Trinidad after she became hysterical and the doctors who examined her concluded that she was possessed. Part of Corbera's "treatment" was to apply a consecrated host to the affected areas. But, as, María Leocadia confessed in a letter to the Toledo tribunal, he had also used the host on her genitalia, rubbing them with it and inserting it inside her on several occasions.[111] Use of the host as a phallic object was not only sexually stimulating and emotionally exciting to some, but could easily be rationalized by both parties as part of the cure for demonic possession because it was widely believed to have important thaumaturgic powers.

The resacralization of the church as a vital place for sacramental observance, especially in the area of marriage, confession, and communion, and the increasingly obligatory nature of attendance at Mass also provided a powerful incentive for violation of the taboo against fornication in sacred space.[112] The human need to break social proscriptions may well have been largely responsible for the number of women who acceded to the sexual demands of their confessors inside churches or chapels. As Jaime Barcelo told the Inquisitors of the Mallorca tribunal, it was not unusual for him to deal with penitents who not only admitted to having lascivious thoughts, but who said that these thoughts became stronger when they entered a church.[113]

Consequently, apart from the sexual interaction that took place in the confessional, there were twelve incidents that involved additional sexual activity in some location within the body of the church. Cristóbal Jacinto Mendez, the parish priest of the village of San Sebastián on the island of La Gomera in the Canaries, would regularly hear the confession of Juana de Armas Cabeza while seated on the steps of the baptistry. During confession, he would tell her of his amorous feelings for her while she placed her hands on his genitals. On one occasion, in the middle of confession, he took her hand and led her to a place in the choir where they had intercourse.[114]

Sacred space outside of churches was also sought out as a venue for sexual interaction. In a confession made just before she died, María López Medina shocked the Carmelite friar Juan de San Ildefonso by telling him about a two-year affair that she had had with his superior, Fray Juan de la Visitación. During confession, he would indicate the place where they were to meet later to have coitus. These places were always within the precincts of local convents or at shrines outside the city walls. Once when they were making love in the wee hours of the morning inside the santuario de Cristo, they were seen by some passing vegetable farmers, who threw stones at them, and were forced to find another trysting place.[115]

A variation on the theme of the violation of the sacred that involved both sacred space and sacred objects is provided by the case of Dr. Juan Ibáñez, the parish priest of the village of Anna in the kingdom of Valencia. Ibáñez took thirty-three-year-old María Angela Polop to the sacristy and had intercourse with her on the ornate cushion that was placed under the effigy of Christ during Holy Week.[116]

Of course, sexual relations between priests and penitents were not confined to churches or other sacred space. The records indicate twelve instances of sexual intercourse that took place in the homes of the women themselves, sometimes with the acquiescence of their husbands. The Franciscan Antonio Refold freely admitted several incidents involving a married woman whose husband looked on while he had sexual relations with his wife.[117] Fray Francisco Deya was able to have coitus with his penitent, Juana Parello, because one of his closest friends in the convent was having an affair with Juana Masquida, a young married woman who was separated from her husband. Learning of his difficulties in finding an appropriate trysting place, his friend invited him to bring Parello to Masquida's home, where each friar had intercourse with his respective lover. Then, over the next eight months, the two friars alternated in using Masquida's home for sexual purposes, one in the morning and the other in the afternoon.[118]

Some female penitents who were unable to offer their own homes to their clerical lovers were able to make other arrangements. María Lorenzo, who was married to a seaman, was too afraid of her neighbors to invite Fray Baltasar de Olivares to her home, but was allowed to make use of the home of one of her friends on several occasions.[119]

It was also possible for clerics to make use of their own domicile or lodging as a place of assignation. Friars of the mendicant orders did a great deal of traveling, not only in order to obtain alms, but also to hear confessions in rural areas where the secular clergy were not present. This gave the Franciscan Marcos de la Tançon the opportunity to use his lodging in a private house in the village of Orche as a place where he tried to seduce or rape several young girls.[120] However, the fact that there were only twelve instances of priests successfully using their lodgings as venues for sexual activity indicates just how difficult it was for them to find enough privacy to carry on a sexual life.

Priests could occasionally make use of the services of women who supplemented their income by making their homes available for assignations. When

Vicente Yago was unable to persuade Vicenta Roig to allow him to come to her home, he managed to obtain the use of a room in the home of a silversmith whose wife evidently specialized in making these kinds of arrangements.[121] Sometimes these women would also agree to act as intermediaries, not only offering their homes for assignations, but agreeing to carry love notes or persuade a reluctant penitent to give in to the libidinous demands of her confessor. After María de Solis had rebuffed his offers of clothing and money in exchange for sexual favors, Francisco de los Cobos turned to Magdalena Hernández, a widow who made a living as a procuress. On several occasions, Magdalena brought María de Solis notes from los Cobos begging her to accept his presents and offering the widow's home as a place of assignation.[122]

The failure of most of these attempts to use intermediaries in order to gain the sexual favors of female penitents is a good indication of the difficulties that Counter-Reformation priests encountered when they tried to establish sexual relations with women outside the confessional. Vicenta Roig never contacted the silversmith's wife out of fear of her husband and in-laws, while María de Solis and her sisters had a violent quarrel with Magdalena Hernández over her role in helping Francisco de los Cobos. Regardless of how these women might have felt about illicit sexual relationships, consorting with a priest outside of church would have caused, as Vicenta Roig observed, "a great deal of comment" and would have undoubtedly led to a serious and perhaps fatal loss of reputation.

The broad range of sexual behaviors described so far were clearly deviant relative to the norms of post-Tridentine Catholic society. In a social context where celibacy was prescribed for the clergy and where confessors, in particular, were subjected to greater scrutiny and held to a high moral standard, the sexual activity that they carried on both inside and outside the confessional was not only blasphemous, but manifested a threatening degree of carnal excess. In forty-eight cases, however, confessors engaged in behavior that departed significantly from normative sexual arousal patterns. Although such behavior was not punished with any greater severity than ordinary solicitation, it illustrates the extreme reactions of certain individuals to the prevailing atmosphere of harsh sexual repression.

Scatologia, or the persistent need to hear obscene sexual language, accounts for over 40 percent of these incidents. Related to the socially deviant attempts by many soliciting confessors to seduce their penitents by the use of suggestive language, it differs in that the use of such filthy or indecent language appears intimately related to or essential to erotic arousal on the part of the male confessor. Of the twelve incidents of solicitation involving Fray Manuel de Peraleja, for example, eight involved his insistence on the penitent saying or repeating obscenities or naming sexual organs. Six of these incidents took place on the same day, when several young women made a pilgrimage to his convent in order to confess the sin of having used obscene language. In each case, Peraleja insisted that the penitent repeat the exact terms that she had used "as expressively as possible." After they had done so, he would either ask them to name the sexual organs or quiz them about their knowledge of "exactly what went on between a man and a woman" during coitus. In a separate incident, Peraleja interrupted the confession of a young single woman to tell her that when she got married she should never deny sex to her husband and always tell him that her "cunt" (coñito) was at his disposal. He then repeated the word "cunt" several times and tried to get her to say it after him.[123]

Although for Manuel de Peraleja the preference for verbal stimulus seemed to occur only episodically and not to interfere with normal sexual functioning, the case of Juan de San Jacinto, who assured the Toledo tribunal that "in matters of the sixth commandment, I am as pure as the day that I was born" indicates how sexual disorders are sometimes accompanied by impairment in the capacity for sexual activity.[124] By exhibiting both scatologia and sadism, San Jacinto's case also bears out modern clinical observations of such individuals that indicate they frequently have more than one sexual disorder.[125]

The San Jacinto case involved Rosa Díaz Moreno and Catalina de Jesús María. Both the women were widows and beatas living in the village of Herencia (Toledo), where San Jacinto was resident in the local Mercederian house. In 1703, Rosa Díaz Moreno asked San Jacinto to be her confessor because he enjoyed an excellent local reputation. Everything went well for several months, so she decided to make a general confession, but when she began discussing her married life, he insisted that she relate everything having to do with her sexual activity before and during marriage "clearly and unambiguously" including "words, actions, and thoughts." Although she was at first reluctant to do this, he convinced her by appealing to her desire for spiritual perfection, telling her that this would be a measure of her love for God and that she would be able to attain "many degrees of blessedness" by obeying him. Further linking his sexual urges with religious observance, San Jacinto made Díaz Moreno repeat what she had told him about her sex life during all of the major Catholic holy days.[126]

For the next two years, in all of the confessions that she made with him, Fray Juan insisted that she repeat the same sins "using the exact words that she and her husband had exchanged." During one confession, he even made her repeat the names of the male and female sexual organs fifty times and threatened to slap her if she refused to do so. Frequently, just before she was about to begin her recitation, he would experience an enormous rush of sexual excitement at the prospect of hearing dirty words and would urge her to "say them, say them you impudent whore." When she finished, he would inform her that she had behaved like a "filthy prostitute" with her husband. It is difficult to imagine, especially in light of the sadomasochistic episodes that punctuated their relationship, that on some level Díaz Moreno did not enjoy this verbal abuse and find it sexually stimulating. In order to increase her mortification, he also insisted that she look straight at him while she said dirty words as if she were looking into the eyes of God, whom he represented. Later in their relationship, sadomasochistic themes were carried further when he insisted that she repeat the same language before him in her own home and then forced her to partially disrobe so that he could scourge her shoulders.

San Jacinto's relationship with his other penitent, Catalina de Jesús María, was somewhat similar in that many of the same elements were present. Since she was also a widow, he insisted that she relate all of her sexual experiences, repeat the names of the sexual organs, and use filthy language. At one point, he even demanded that she repeat scatologia while she held a consecrated host in her mouth. He also frequently humiliated her by slapping her in the confessional and regularly beat her with a belt in her home while insisting that she repeat dirty language.[127] With both of these penitents, therefore, scatologia and sadomasochism formed a well-integrated pattern of sexual activity that, on some level, must have been satisfying to all parties. In neither case, as San Jacinto proudly informed the tribunal, did he attempt to seduce either of the women and that clearly indicates that these sexual disorders were his chief form of sexual gratification.

The proof that Juan de San Jacinto's sexual disorder formed a part of a wider pattern of mental and emotional instability is furnished by his delusional behavior after he was incarcerated in the Inquisition's secret prison during his trial in 1706–1707. About eight months after his arrest, he began hearing a voice that he identified with God. This voice directed his movements and instructed him as to how he was to behave before his judges while promising him that he would be exonerated. A little more than a month later, when he entered the audience chamber for an interview with Inquisitor Estéban Francisco de Espadaña, he insisted that the tribunal's secretary leave the chamber as he had important and confidential matters to relate to the inquisitor. When the inquisitor explained that his secretary had to remain in order to record testimony, Fray Juan suddenly pointed at the secretary and shouted "in the name of our Lord Jesus I order you to drop dead this instant." Upon being interrogated by Inquisitor Espadaña as to the reason for this outburst, San Jacinto told him about the voices and explained that they had ordered him to do it. Inquisitor Espadaña responded by admonishing San Jacinto to confess the truth about the charges against him and expressed skepticism about the meaning of his visions, telling him that they were probably little more than "delusions of the devil."[128]

As his mental disorder worsened, Jacinto continued to cause problems for the tribunal. About two months after the incident in the courtroom, he requested and received ten sheets of paper in order to write his defense but used only five. Upon being asked to return the unused sheets, he refused and, after several attempts to find the paper in his cell had failed, he was put in irons for four days. Instead of pacifying Jacinto, this harsh treatment had the effect of triggering off an even more violent emotional disturbance. Deeply angry at the tribunal and still imbued with the delusion of his own spiritual power, he began sending his chamber pot back empty. When the jailer asked him where he was eliminating his bodily wastes, he asserted that he had no need to do so since God had given him a special grace that allowed him to eat and drink without defecating. Unmoved by this remarkable declaration, the jailer and his assistant began searching and finally found several days' worth of feces mixed in with a pile of garbage in the corner of his cell. At this point, the tribunal called in its physician, Dr. Escudero, to do an analysis of San Jacinto's mental capacity. On July 21, 1707, Escudero entered the cell and examined San Jacinto, but declared that he found no signs of any mental disorder, so two days later the jailer began administering a course of enemas to "cure" San Jacinto's obduracy. Even though the enemas went on for four days, this still did not bring San Jacinto to his senses. Several days later, the jailers noticed a horrible odor being carried to them by the hot July breeze. Since Fray Juan had once again stopped handing in his chamber pot, it was not too difficult to imagine what had happened. This time, instead of trying to hide his feces in the garbage, San Jacinto had cleverly mixed them into the earthen floor of his cell. It took another round of four enemas administered over the next thirty-six hours before San Jacinto begged them to stop for the love of God and declared himself cured. Nevertheless, even though he became more manageable for the rest of the trial, he continued to bombard the tribunal with written statements, denouncing his accusers and declaring that the Holy Spirit would free him since he would not have been granted the extraordinary favor of God through such "prodigious" voices and revelations if he had been guilty.[129] Unimpressed by his "divine" revelations or his appeals, the tribunal sentenced him to several years of reclusion. From this he appeared to emerge chastened and sufficiently calm to be partially rehabilitated by being allowed to resume his functions as confessor, though restricted to men only.

From earliest times, the Christian ideal of the holy life included intense self denial, penance, and humility. The striving for humility had two aspects: obedience designed to tame the will and physical discipline to subdue the body. Medieval and early modern ascetics slept on the ground in the coldest weather and wore hair shirts or corselets fitted with iron studs that bit into their flesh.[130] Flagellation and other forms of physical mortification were also practiced by such prominent religious figures as St. Catherine of Siena in the fourteenth century and St. Louis of Gonzaga in the sixteenth. Flagellation became a part of popular culture in the period of the Black Death when it became one of the most important activities of the many lay confraternities. In the seventeenth century, Pérez de Valdivia recommended flagellation and other mortifications for all Christians.[131] The example set by extreme ascetics also exercised a powerful influence on those who wanted to lead a holy life, and saints or would-be saints frequently tortured themselves in order to emulate these "athletes of Christ."

For the saint, the physical manifestations of humility were designed to serve the faithful by gaining the extraordinary spiritual power they would need to act as intercessors before God. An account of the life of St. Rosa of Lima, who died in 1617, recounts that "whenever some calamity threatened the republic, it was Rosa who expiated it through bloody scourging."[132] By punishing her body, the saint took on herself the blame for God's wrath at sinful mankind, thereby hoping to evade the calamity that must surely follow. By sacrificing herself, the saint bestowed protection on others.

Although the altruistic motives of the saints are hardly open to question, the acceptance of extreme forms of mortification and physical abuse as a sig-

nificant, even indispensable, component of the ascetic life tended to legitimize the expression of the sadomasochistic urges that provide carnal gratification for certain individuals. These tendencies represent an exaggerated
element in the aggressive urges that form an important part of sexual life,
but were given unprecedented scope by the link between mortification and
holiness in Catholic Europe.[133]

For St. Simón de Rojas, the Trinitarian who became a royal confessor at
the court of Philip III, insistence on imposing a regimen of scourging in the
convents that he visited as a representative of his order was matched by his
own bloody mortifications. The underlying sexual motivations of this regimen
were unwittingly revealed by his admiring biographer, Francisco de Arcos,
when he related an incident that occurred during Rojas' sojourn as superior
of the Trinitarian house in Madrid.

Shortly after his arrival, a friar of particularly robust constitution came to
him asking if he would act as his confessor. After hearing the friar's confession, Rojas demanded that he take a belt and drag him around the floor of
the chapel "as if he were a filthy dog who had been unfaithful to God." The
young man agreed, and night after night, he pulled Rojas around the chapel,
halting at each station of the cross, where Rojas bared his shoulders to receive
a scourging. Between cutting his knees on the sharp stones that served to pave
the chapel floor and the effects of the flagellation, Rojas shed a great deal of
blood, which the friar cleaned up in the morning. When questioned about
these practices by some older friars who wondered if they were necessary for
salvation, Rojas insisted that he was merely following the example of the saints.
But unlike St. Louis of Gonzaga, whose physical penance was always solitary,
Rojas's behavior fits much better into a sadomasochistic pattern of dominance
and submission where violence and humiliation rather than sexual interaction
was the goal.[134] The "submissive" Rojas recognized and used the potential
for violence in Fray Bartolomé de la Cruz, who played the "dominant" role
in the little drama that was played out each night in the chapel. But Rojas, as
well as the solicitantes who engaged in sadomasochistic behavior, could always
justify themselves by claiming that they were striving for religious perfection.
The solicitantes, of course, made the mistake of using the confessional as a
venue for their activities and thereby ran afoul of the Inquisition, while Rojas
used the more accepted location of the friary of an order whose members
were proud of a long tradition of physical mortification. By using the appropriate social definitional context to give vent to his psychological need for
physical abuse, Rojas retained and even enhanced his reputation for sanc-
tity. By choosing an inappropriate context, the solicitante became a convicted
offender; lost reputation, honor, and position, and was forced into reclusion
in a convent where he was frequently despised and mistreated.

The relationship between St. Simón de Rojas and Bartolomé de la Cruz is
a good example of the way in which domination far outweighed sexual gratification as a motivating factor. In the same way, sex played only a peripheral
role in the relationship between María Mallon and Francisco Miralles. During the ten years that María lived with him as his putative housekeeper,

Miralles would frequently caress her and kiss her, but when she responded sexually he would admonish her and threaten to administer a severe beating if she ever sought sexual relations with him. Having induced strong feelings of guilt, Miralles continued the pattern of sexual manipulation and denial. Since Miralles was also her only confessor during this period, he could carry his emotional and psychological torture of his victim to a new level by failing to bring up any of the sins she had committed with him during confession. Mallon was extremely timid and could never bring herself to mention them either, but frequently failed to take communion afterward because she was afraid that such an incomplete confession did not give her the right to do so. Miralles, however, would always interrogate her about communion and, if she admitted that she had not taken it, would scourge her "for her disobedience."[135] In this relationship, therefore, sexual gratification was not an end in itself, but a key element in the pattern of domination and manipulation of a submissive individual.

For certain individuals, on the other hand, carnal excitement cannot be separated from the infliction of pain. As Antonio Nieto described his relationship with his penitent Feliciana Zeballos, it constantly passed from "tenderness to cruelty." Both within the confessional and outside of it, he would caress her and she would respond with extreme forms of submissiveness, embracing him and even washing his feet. At the same time, probably out of an unconscious desire to provoke him to violence, she would constantly break the instructions that he gave her concerning her spiritual welfare, and he would respond by scourging her.[136]

Sometimes the sexual fantasies of confessors who were aroused by the desire to hurt their penitents went considerably beyond what even the most submissive would tolerate. Fray Pablo Ginard insisted that Francisca Gilbert lie on the floor "as if she were dead and allow him to slap her face" in order to practice humility. She refused, but did allow him to scourge her on her naked back with his belt.[137]

As Freud himself noted in his study of sexual aberrations, one of the peculiarities of sadomasochism is that "its active and passive forms are regularly encountered together in the same person."[138] The notion that "a sadist is simultaneously a masochist" is borne out by two out of the ten cases of sadomasochism under review where both sadistic and masochistic tendencies were displayed by the same individual. Antonio Nieto recalled that he had allowed Feliciana Zeballos to bite his side and that when she cried out ecstatically that "blood or milk was coming out," he encouraged her to "catch it, drink it, suck it."

The dual aspect of this sexual disorder was especially evident in the case of Alonso Pérez de Bascones. Pérez de Bascones, who was parish priest in the village of Morata de Tajuna in the Toledo district, was fortunate in being able to find six women among his parishioners with whom he could indulge his proclivities. His behavior with each of them was remarkably similar. In each case, they had confessed with him for several years before he insisted that he come to their homes to administer a scourging. Several of the women, like the thirty-seven-year-old widow Mariana Serrano had already manifested masochistic tendencies by scourging themselves and, therefore, readily agreed. For those who were unwilling, like María Sánchez, Pérez de Bascones simply forced his way into her home and made her surrender the keys to the cabinet in which she kept her scourge. He would then make the women lie face down on a bed, raise their skirts to expose their buttocks, and spank or scourge them for about fifteen minutes. After he finished scourging them, he would always run his hands over their buttocks. These scourgings would occur several times a week, and in the case of Mariana Serrano, there were more than 100 separate incidents.[139] After several months of this, he would then insist that the women scourge him in the same place. In every case, he would demand that they maintain absolute secrecy about their relationship with him.

Whenever any of the women would express doubts or anxiety about the moral or religious value of what they were doing, he would reply indignantly that they were "gaining great merit in the hereafter" and that he had pre-scribed mortification not in order to "bring their souls to perdition," but to save them. After he was arrested, he continued to insist that whatever he had done was for the spiritual benefit of the women and that when he ran his hands over their buttocks after scourging them, it was only to ease the pain. Never-theless, the theologians that the Toledo tribunal consulted about the case entirely rejected his arguments, pointing out that in this case mortification of the flesh was just an excuse for the indulgence of sexual desire.[140]

The tribunal's prosecuting attorney was similarly unimpressed. In his sum-mation on September 2, 1674, he ridiculed Pérez de Bascones' religious pretensions by pointing out that he had always insisted that his penitents say nothing about what had happened to them, something that would have been unnecessary if he had really believed that he was bringing them spiritual benefit. In fact, according to the prosecuting attorney, mortification of the flesh had only been a pretext for "lascivious and obscene caresses."[141]

Finally, Pérez de Bascones caved in under this bombardment. In his reply to the prosecuting attorney, he confessed tearfully that he had always been aware of the sinful nature of what he had done and that he had been moti-vated entirely by carnal desire to "enjoy administering the scourgings with his own hands and seeing the naked flesh" of his penitents.[142]

If Alonso Pérez de Bascones had scourged himself or even required his penitents to mortify themselves in penance for their sins, he would have remained a respected member of the religious community. But even during a period when society accepted extreme forms of physical mortification as saintly, the theologians and judges who dealt with his case felt that there was something distinctly aberrant about his behavior. They recognized that Pérez de Bascones's urges were sexual, not religious, and prodded him into admit-ting that he enjoyed the physical suffering of his victims. However crude the terminology employed by the seventeenth-century jurists who tried the case, they understood that they were confronted with a sexual disorder that involved inflicting pain. This case, and others like it in the files of the Holy Office, should provide a useful corrective to the relativism that has become such a dominant feature of historical writing in recent years. In spite of the vagaries of collective interpretation and cultural significance over a five-hundred-year period, early modern and modern western society have shared certain common notions of sexual aberrance and have recognized and stigmatized certain kinds of behavior as inherently pathological.

Partialism, or the focus of sexual excitement on a particular part of the body, affected six confessors. This disorder took the form of an obsessive concern with pubic hair in the case of the Capuchin friar Isidro de Arganda. Arganda had spent some time as the spiritual advisor of María Morales, and her decision to become a nun in Guadalajara, thereby making it impossible for him to see her with any frequency, triggered off an intense emotional crisis. Shortly after she entered the convent, she wrote to him for advice on how to comport herself and how to confront any dangers or temptations that she might encounter. His reply began as the very model of what a spiritual advisor might say under such circumstances. He mentioned another nun whom he had known who entered that convent and how she had been able to overcome her spiritual problems, and he comforted María by telling her that her belief in God would fortify her against depression and despair. By the end of the letter, however, it was obvious that Arganda's fragile emotional equilibrium had begun to crack. He asked her to write him specifically about any "dreams or nocturnal pollutions" that she experienced. In a second letter, he insisted that she inform him fully about her menstrual pain and bleeding and demanded that she cut off all of her pubic hair "without leaving one single piece" and send it to him by the first available mail.[143]

From then on, Arganda became obsessed with obtaining pubic hair from his female penitents. Of the sixteen witnesses at his trial in 1753, fifteen testified that he had demanded that they cut their pubic hair and bring it to him. Sometimes he would pretend that he needed it to help "cure" vaginal infections, and on one occasion, he even pretended that he needed it to verify a penitent's story of being raped by her former lover while she was bewitched. However he received it, Arganda felt compelled to dispose of the pubic hair immediately and in as degrading a way as possible. Sometimes he had the women burn it in front of him, and on several occasions he threw it into a cesspool.[144]

Incest may well have been one of the elements involved in the sexual behavior of Fray Agustín de Cervera, who was obsessed with the breasts of his female penitents. In a space of less than fifteen months in 1572 to 1573, Fray Agustín solicited fifteen penitents. In fourteen of these cases, he touched or looked at the girls' breasts while asking them about their size and relative maturity. Interestingly enough, while caressing three of the girls, aged fourteen, fifteen, and sixteen, he made a point of telling them that he liked them because they looked like one of his sisters. The role that incest may have played in conditioning Cervera's sexual proclivities is further indicated by the fact that he began soliciting these girls shortly after he returned from an unauthorized visit to his home village, where two of his sisters still lived.[145]

Cervera also provides us with our only case of pedophilia. Although children were not his exclusive choice as sexual partners, fifteen of the seventeen penitents that he solicited were sixteen or under, while three were ten years old. His compulsive need to tell his teenage penitents that he found them attractive because they resembled his sister also seems to fit the pattern of those suffering from pedophilia, since incest or other forms of sexual abuse in childhood are frequently indicated in such cases.[146]

In a culture that invested objects connected with religion with such a high degree of significance, it is not difficult to imagine them being turned into fetishes by certain individuals.[147] Fray Francisco Corbera, a Franciscan who had had a distinguished career in his order, had been Eugenia María de Santa Teresa's confessor for more than seven years when one day, just before she began her confession in the porter's lodge of her convent, he noticed that she seemed to be experiencing some discomfort. When he asked her what was wrong, she told him that she had begun to wear a silicio on her thigh, consisting of an iron ring studded with barbs that hurt her every time she moved. Evidently, simply hearing that she wore such a device provided Corbera with a surge of sexual excitement, and he immediately insisted that she raise her habit to "show him the silicio and where it rested on her thigh." After she complied with his wishes the first time, he made the same demand on eleven other occasions. That Corbera was fully aware of the sexual stimulation he was deriving from the situation is demonstrated by the fact that when he perceived that Eugenia María had lost her initial reluctance to comply with his demands, he told her they would have to stop since "the devil could deceive us into some lewdness," as well as his later admission before the tribunal that he had been driven by "curiosity and lust."[148]

Of the two cases of fetishism in the records, the most curious involved Juan del Castillo, a Dominican, who was brought before the Cuenca tribunal in 1641. Juan del Castillo was particularly obsessed with ornamental cups and chalices used in church services. Castillo had invested glass or ceramic containers with special significance from childhood, when he made it a practice to steal them whenever he could so that he could smash them. Evidently the more they resembled the vessels that were used in church, the more he enjoyed destroying them. Later, after he joined the order, his obsession took on a more complex form. Instead of simply destroying vessels, he stole them, brought them to his cell, and filled them with some kind of liquid. He was once punished by the order for having taken the most beautiful chalice used in the chapel to his cell, making soup in it, and then cleansing it with his urine.

The offense that brought him to the attention of the Holy Office occurred after he was invited to preach the Corpus Christi sermon at a local convent. While preaching, he noticed a particularly beautiful silver chalice that had been used to say mass. After some persuasion, he was able to convince one of the nuns to bring it to him so that he could examine it more closely. That evening she handed it to him in the porter's lodge, but after commenting briefly on its beauty and workmanship he suddenly announced that it would be ideal "for an obscenity like the one that you would perform in a woman's hole," thrust it under his habit and masturbated into it. By this point, Fray Juan's delusional system had become so powerful that when the horrified nun asked him how he could possibly perform such an obscene act in such a sacred object, he expressed surprise that she had never heard of anyone doing this since "it is not only practicable but done frequently."[149]

Throughout the course of human history sexual behavior has responded to a variety of social values, norms, and sanctions. As special targets of the most comprehensive attempt to repress and regulate sexual behavior that western society has ever undertaken, the post-Tridentine clergy were forced to accept celibacy for the first time in the history of the Roman Church.

Many priests, successfully indoctrinated by seminary and college, were able to come to terms with celibacy and find ways of sublimating their sexual needs in work, prayer, meditation, or penance. But for others, such abstinence was difficult to maintain. Restricted in their movements, subjected to the scrutiny of their superiors, and newly vulnerable to the jurisdiction of the episcopal courts, some priests found that the confessional provided their only sexual outlet, the only place where they could be alone with a woman and where they could engage in some form of sexual activity unobserved. Sadly for them, the sexual activity that they could engage in was minimal. Most never got beyond using suggestive language or petting, few ever achieved coitus, while the incidence of masturbation merely reflects the heightened degree of sexual frustration that led to a greater incidence of solitary practices in the society as a whole.

As in all societies, the impact of social proscription fell most heavily on individuals who were already emotionally unstable. Such individuals found it impossible to achieve sexual satisfaction through normative patterns of sexual activity and were, therefore, subject to a variety of sexual disorders. While the typology of many of these disorders is remarkably similar to that found in modern clinical practice, the form that they took was profoundly affected by the societal context, while the frequency of certain disorders undoubtedly varied considerably from that of modern society.

Chapter 9

Solicitation and Confession in the Anticlerical Imagination

Although the Spanish Inquisition was not formally abolished until the decree of July 19, 1834, issued during the regency of María Cristina, it had really ceased to function by 1820, when it was suppressed by order of Ferdinand VII in the face of a resurgent liberalism. His refusal to reestablish the institution after the fall of the liberal regime was an indication that it had long since outlived its usefulness, even to a ruler whose government had been marked by intolerance, brutality, and obscurantism.[1]

With the demise of the Holy Office, organized prosecution of solicitantes came to an end in Spain. But well before 1820, solicitation had begun its evolution from a criminal offense whose punishment was designed to restore public confidence in auricular confession to the defining element in the reaction against confession that was beginning to sweep the Catholic world.

Already by the end of the old regime, theologians and experienced confessors like St. Alphonsus Liguori (1696–1787) were warning that the increasing rigorism of many confessors, who were routinely denying absolution to their penitents, was driving people away from the sacrament.[2] Even worse from the standpoint of the Church, anticlericals and liberal Catholics were openly questioning practices that encouraged an excessive emotional closeness between confessor and penitent.[3] The most extreme expression of this view was to make solicitation synonymous with confession either directly, through the fear of the physical seduction of penitents by confessors, or indirectly, through an insidious form of moral seduction by which "through the confessional the priest is much more the husband of the wife than the man to whom she was wedded at the foot of the altar."[4]

An early work that openly discusses sexual solicitation was written by Antonio Gavin, a renegade Spanish priest who fled to England shortly before the signing of the Treaty of Utrecht in April 1713.[5] As a secular priest and confessor for several years in Saragossa and as a member of the so-called moral academy, where local confessors would routinely discuss their most difficult cases with their colleagues, Gavin was in a good position to learn about instances of sexual solicitation.[6]

Within a few years of his arrival in England, Gavin had published *The Master Key to Popery,* in which he denounced questioning of penitents on sexual matters as a school for scandal by which "the penitents learn things of which they never had dreamed before."[7] *The Master Key to Popery* is filled with stories about the lewdness of priests, which were obviously well calculated to satisfy and titillate a Protestant audience already disposed to believe the worst about the papists. Although Gavin's book is marred by a fantastic tale about a seraglio maintained by the Saragossa Inquisition and an obvious degree of exaggeration, some of the solicitation cases he discusses have the ring of truth. In one instance, Gavin even formed one of the group of priests and friars who were traditionally brought to hear sentencing of a convicted *solicitante.*[8]

Gavin's discussion of solicitation begins with a story designed to illustrate not only the lewdness of priests, but the untoward influence that confessors gain over families. As we shall see, this latter point was to become considerably more important in later works attacking auricular confession. Brought before the moral academy of Saragossa because of the difficult theological problems that it presented, the case involved a young woman whose family had fallen under the influence of their confessor to such a degree that they made him her guardian and left him most of their money. After the girl's father died, he seduced her, then left her destitute. With no means of support, the young woman had little choice but to become the mistress of an army officer, who died while serving with his regiment in Catalonia. Shocked by her lover's demise, she determined to change her life. She went to another confessor, who promised to help her find a suitable husband if she would turn over all the jewels that the officer had given her. She did so, but on the following day her new confessor came to her and threatened to denounce her to the Inquisition if she refused to have intercourse with him.[9]

Another of Gavin's stories recalls the case of Isabel Riera and her confessor, Pedro Benimelis. Like Riera, María Guerrero was of humble origins, and she sought to achieve social prominence by distinguishing herself as a holy woman. She was able to convince her confessor, a highly regarded Dominican doctor of theology, of her extraordinary spiritual gifts, and soon a cult formed around her, while her confessor began writing the story of her life. Spiritual closeness between confessor and penitent soon gave way to physical intimacy, and by the time María Guerrero and her confessor were arrested by the Saragossa tribunal, it appeared that the "Blessed" Guerrero "was not overshadowed by the spirit but by her confessor; for she being at that time with child, and delivered in the Inquisition, one article was that he had his bed near her bed and that he was the father of the new child or monster on earth."[10]

Gavin also describes the way exorcism could provide sexual opportunities for confessors. Unlike the cases from the Inquisition trial records where the victims really seemed to believe that they were possessed, Gavin presents possession as little more than a plot concocted by sexually frustrated beatas and lascivious confessors to deceive jealous husbands. After describing in general terms the way women use the excuse of being possessed to have intimate relations with their exorcist, Gavin describes the case of sixteen-year-old Dorothea, who was married to a fifty-three-year-old man whom she hated. Since her husband was exceedingly jealous and would not let her go anywhere without him, she decided to pretend demonic possession in order to have intimate relations with her confessor, Fray Juan, a young man with whom she was passionately in love. Fray Juan having achieved some success against the demons, the husband rewarded him generously and called him whenever his wife showed any signs of a relapse. As this happened frequently, Dorothea began spending more and more time in Juan's company while her deceived husband slept "quiet and easy thinking that his wife, having the devil in her body was not able to be unfaithful to him." The illicit relationship between Dorothea and her confessor/exorcist went on for two years, at the end of which they were betrayed by some of Juan's enemies. As a result, his superiors transferred him to another convent.[11]

Regardless of the degree of exaggeration contained in Gavin's discussion of solicitation, *The Master Key to Popery* is important because the shameful secret of sexual solicitation by priests, which had been so carefully preserved by the Holy Office, was revealed to a popular audience and by no less a source than a former Spanish Catholic priest. Gavin's book, like other eighteenth-century works critical of the Roman Catholic Church, proved extremely popular in liberal and Protestant circles. It had three German editions (1717, 1735, and 1735), five British editions, including two in Dublin (1724 and 1727), and no less than fifteen in the United States between 1815 and 1860. The work was also translated into French in 1727 under the title *Le Passe-partout de l'Église romaine ou histoire des tromperies des prêtres et des moines en Espagne*. It was this edition that was prohibited by the Spanish Inquisition in 1747.[12]

Like so many other sacrilegious or anticlerical works that entered Spain during the eighteenth century, *Le Passe-partout* was allowed to circulate for a long period before it was prohibited by an Inquisition hamstrung by government interference and a lack of persons qualified to undertake censorship duties. The wide circulation of this work assured that its major themes, including the potential dangers of questioning women about violations of the sixth commandment, the undue influence of confessors on the family, the frequency of sexual solicitation and other violations of clerical celibacy, and the hypocrisy and greed of confessors who used their influence to obtain money for their religious orders would help to define the wave of anticonfessional sentiment as it developed during the nineteenth century.

Antonio Gavin was not the only eighteenth-century Spanish priest to voice grave doubts about auricular confession and link confession and solicitation.

José Blanco White was born in Seville of mixed Irish-Spanish parentage in 1775. He was ordained in 1799 and, after experiencing a religious crisis fed by his encounter with the ideas of the Enlightenment, fled to England in 1810. Throughout his adult life, he had a visceral hatred of confession that probably stemmed from certain childhood experiences described in his *Letters from Spain,* which was first published in English in 1822.[13]

Even though Blanco White wrote his books for an English audience and *Letters from Spain* was not translated into Spanish until 1972, there can be little doubt that he was a representative of a growing malaise among liberal clergy who were being increasingly exposed to the intellectual ferment of the Enlightenment. He himself alludes to this when he mentions the ease with which he was able to borrow prohibited books from other priests "profoundly versed in French philosophy."[14]

In this work, as well as the later *The Preservative Against Popery*, Blanco White warns against the pernicious effects of auricular confession on children and the family and the danger it poses to the female sex. Since the priest was obliged to probe sexual sins in order to carry out his duties as confessor, "filthy communication is inseparable from the confessional."[15] As a consequence, Blanco White declared that auricular confession could easily lead to "direct seduction" of female penitents. This danger was held in check so long as the Inquisition continued to function, but without that institution, "it would be simpleminded to believe that a discretionary power of this order, left in the hands of thousands of men—exposed to extraordinary temptations to abuse it—would always be used with due precaution."[16] Later in *Letters from Spain*, Blanco White relates a particularly grisly story about a Franciscan friar who fell madly in love with one of his female penitents and then stabbed her to death when he learned that she was about to be married.[17]

The Spanish Inquisition's jurisdiction over solicitation was also discussed in a sensational work about the Inquisition that was published in France in 1817 to 1818. Like José Blanco White, Juan Antonio Llorente went through a religious crisis and became converted to the principles of the Enlightenment. In 1785 he was made commissioner of the Logroño tribunal, and in 1789 he became first secretary of the Corte tribunal in Madrid. After the French invasion of 1808, Llorente joined the many enlightened Spaniards who supported the government of Napoleon's brother, Joseph, and was placed in charge of the archives of the Suprema.[18] Llorente's long experience as an inquisitorial official and his unprecedented access to the Inquisition archives gave him the material that he needed to write the first modern history of the Spanish Inquisition. This work appeared in Paris after Llorente had been forced to flee his native land by the defeat of French forces in the Peninsular War. Llorente died within a few days of his return to Madrid in 1823. His book proved to be extremely popular and was translated into English, German, and Italian. A Spanish edition appeared in 1822 during the period in which the Spanish liberals were able to force Ferdinand VII to reinstate the 1812 Constitution.[19]

Llorente provided his French readers with a full account of the Spanish Inquisition's jurisdiction over an offense that he described as inspiring a "legitimate revulsion" in all those who became aware of it.[20] He also discussed trial procedures and typical punishments and excited his reader's erotic imagination with the case of a Capuchin friar who had seduced thirteen beatas by convincing them that he had a divine vision in which he was ordered to satisfy their sexual appetites.[21]

In the nineteenth and twentieth centuries, the physical seduction of female penitents by their confessors became a perennial theme of anticlerical literature. In France, anticlericals like Michel Morphy and Leo Taxil would take excerpts from confessors' manuals and quote them out of context to convince their readers that husbands and parents would be ill-advised to send their wives and children to confession. Michel Morphy's *Les mystères de la pornographie cléricale* (1884) described Jean Baptiste Bouvier's classic *Manuel de confesseurs*, which was a standard text in the seminaries of the day, as a "course in vice without parallel." As a result of the instructions contained in the text about sodomy, cunnilingus, fellatio, and masturbation, Morphy asserted that seminarians were corrupted to the point that not one priest in a hundred could remain celibate, while as confessors they used this "pornographic code" as the basis of their work. Referring to Bouvier's discussion of the sexual potency of older men, Morphy commented wryly that it seems to have been designed to encourage "the young woman who wanted to amuse herself by having intercourse with her confessor."[22]

In his introduction to Gabriel Pages's *Les livres secrets des confesseurs dévoilés aux pères de famille*, Leo Taxil attacks the principle of taxpayer support for seminary education on the grounds that while the law prohibits instruction contrary to the public morality in secular schools, nothing is being done to reform the instruction given in seminaries "where lewdness is taught with the most degrading luxury of detail." If the public were ever to become aware of this situation, "what father would allow his children and what husband would permit his wife go to confession."[23]

The themes of clerical hypocrisy, the excessively frank questioning of female penitents, and sexual solicitation are also linked in a novel published in 1935 by Pierre Longin. At the beginning of *Une passion dans le confessionnal*, the bishop has sent one Vannier, a rigorist priest, to become the curé of a village in Burgundy that had refused to pay anything toward the upkeep of the church. The bishop sees Vannier's appointment as a way of punishing the village for its obduracy. Vannier proves himself to be as harsh as the bishop had wished, condemning any immodesty in dress or behavior "with demented fury" and refusing absolution to women who intend to go to a dance that is to be held next to the church.[24]

Like the confessors described by Antonio Gavin, Vannier's probing of sexual sins serves to instruct his penitents in sexual perversions that they would have never practiced on their own. After one of these sessions during which he asked her about fellatio and other sexual "tricks" that she might have used to avoid conception, a young married woman told her neighbor that "one would have to be as depraved as a curé in order to imagine such things."[25]

But beneath the soutane of this rigorist priest beat the heart of a man whose lusts were repressed but not destroyed by his oath of celibacy. One day while passing along a country road on his way to thank a local peasant for a gift of some fruit, he became excited by glimpsing a young servant girl's breasts as she was working in the fields. On another occasion, after seeing a farm girl in dishabille harvesting potatoes, he was so stirred up that he returned home immediately to masturbate. Driven nearly insane by his loneliness and sexual frustration, Vannier could no longer restrain himself, and on the day after he had declaimed a fiery sermon against dancing at weddings and declared that he would only give communion to women who were "pure," he shocked a respectable young married woman by touching her thighs while hearing her confession. After this incident of solicitation, he had little recourse but to leave the village "where men had already found a paradise on earth" for a parish in another village "sunk in poverty and superstition, in short everything that was required to justify the presence of a priest."[26]

In Spain, censorship and the political power of the Church made it impossible to publish works that openly attacked confessors' manuals, but sexual solicitation and illicit sexual activity during confession was a constant refrain in Spanish literature and the popular press. Critical discussion of clerical celibacy and the relationship between priest and penitent in the confessional was just one element in the broader debate over repression and liberation that preoccupied Spanish society from the mid nineteenth century to the beginning of the Spanish Civil War. Within that debate, especially from around 1890, there was an increasing willingness to explore the issue of sexuality in a variety of formats, from novels, short stories, and cartoons to the more than 250 scientific or quasi-scientific works published on sexual themes between 1900 and 1936.[27]

As part of this literature, the issue of clerical celibacy and the sexual abuse of the confessional by priests played a significant role. During the 1880s and 1890s, the satirical weekly *El Motín* mixed drawings of lewd priests and confessors with attacks on the Church and right-wing politicians. Between 1910 and 1936, the artists of the popular anticlerical magazine *La Traca* followed this tradition by drawing numerous cartoons featuring a grotesquely distorted priest touching or fondling a woman during confession or in close proximity to a confessional.[28]

Mercedes, an anonymous work with clear pornographic overtones published in 1890, concerns a young traveling salesman who becomes enamored of the daughter of his innkeeper while on one of his sales trips. He promptly forgets about his catalogues and samples and gives all his attention to finding a way to seduce the young girl. Thwarted by her father's vigilance and aware of her reputation for sensuality, he decided to send her a book with illustrations of sexual positions without identifying himself at first. If she was willing to accept the book and permit him to put into practice some of the things it contained, she was instructed to come out on her balcony wearing something in her hair.

Figure 9.1. A Lascivious Priest Reassures His Penitent While Holding Their Illegitimate Child. *El Motín*, 1885, num. 30 (Biblioteca Nacional, Laboratorio Fotográfico)

In order to justify sending this rather unusual present, he explained that it would be sure to give her hours of pleasure and instruction while providing fuel for her erotic imagination. At the same time, his availability as a lover would ensure that she would not become frustrated since she could easily find a remedy in his arms. This, he averred, was surely preferable to the situation in the confessional, where she could easily become aroused by the probing, even "insolent" questioning of the priest about sexual matters without any means of satisfying herself. On the contrary, the confessional relationship only provided sexual satisfaction for the priest since if she could peer into the other side of the confessional, she would see "his disordered garments, his hands hidden and his eyes glistening, and when he interrupted his questioning, it would only be because he had reached the climax of his lust."[29]

Eduardo López Bago's *El confesionario* is a more serious naturalistic work that explores some of the implications of clerical celibacy for the confessor-penitent relationship. Like Leopoldo Alas's (Clarín) *La Regenta*, López Bago presents us with a situation in which an intelligent, ambitious priest with an excellent reputation as a spiritual advisor takes a beautiful young woman as his penitent and seeks to mould her to his will. But Román Acebedo, the chief protagonist of two novels, *El cura* and *El confesionario*, is hiding a monstrous secret—his incestuous relationship with his own sister with whom he had intercourse when she was sixteen.[30] Early in *El confesionario*, López Bago makes it clear that this crime was not entirely Román's fault. Under normal circumstances, this handsome young man would have been able to find an appropriate outlet for his sexual needs, but as a priest he is forced to be celibate by the unnatural policy of the Roman Catholic Church, which "proclaims the eunuch as the height of human perfection."[31] This incestuous relationship explains much of what motivates Acebedo throughout the novel. His profound sense of guilt leads him to become an assiduous confessor as a way of expiating his sin by saving souls and also makes him sublimate his desire for Gertrudis, the marchioness of Florida, assuming his passion for her as a form of penance.[32]

Guilt as well as ambition also drives Román to see the marchioness's wealth as an instrument of his desire to bring himself to the notice of his superiors, even as far as Rome itself. By making her abhor material things and devote herself to religion, he hopes to make her give her fortune to the Church, and he dreams of presenting it personally to the pope as a contribution gained by his extraordinary skill in the confessional. This, in turn, would allow him to realize his ambitions to rise in the Church from simple presbyter to a cardinal's hat, even to wear the papal tiara itself. The marchioness of Florida was simply to be a means to an end, love was to be sacrificed on the altar of guilt and ambition.[33]

Nevertheless, in spite of his most fervent resolutions, Román is physically attracted to Gertrudis from the first moment that she entered his confessional.[34] After she invites him to visit her and pours out her heart to him about her problems with her syphilitic husband and her own adultery, this feeling only increases, so that the only way he can avoid giving in to the powerful emotions that threaten to overwhelm him is to go to a brothel conveniently situated close to his church. Once inside, Román assaults one of the women with such brutality that she flees screaming, and he is forced to beg the outraged prostitutes, who wanted to drive him into the street, to allow him to stay until nightfall in order to avoid running into any of his fellow benefice holders.[35] His life, as he admits ruefully to himself, has been a constant struggle against the temptations of the flesh, "which rebels each time with greater intensity."[36]

In spite of a physical attraction so strong that Román feels that he would even be capable of necrophilia if he were to be presented with Gertrudis's dead body, he is able to keep playing the role of the virtuous and stern confessor. Rejecting her advances as immoral, he insists that she give in to her husband's demands for sexual intercourse as her wifely duty, in spite of his illness. After his death, she finds that she, too, has become infected. For several months after this, the unhappy lovers carried out a "parody of the contemplative life," each trying to avoid confronting their desire for one another. The marchioness accedes to Román's demands for money for the Church and turns her boudoir into a chapel, while Román hears her confession at least once a week.[37] At the same time, in order to avoid giving in to the temptation to which he is subjected whenever he goes to the palace, Román continues his visits to the brothel. This fragile equilibrium is rudely shattered one evening when Gertrudis intimates that she has received a favorable prognosis from her physician. A mere hint of her sexual availability is enough for Román, who immediately throws himself upon her and rapes her before she can even explain that she is not completely cured and wants to wait until spring before having intercourse.[38] Nevertheless, having finally become Gertrudis's lover brings Román richer financial rewards than he had gained when he was only her confessor. Instead of the 400,000 reales that he had pried out of her by manipulating her newfound spiritual devotion, she now promises him a million reales since, as she explained, her most recent lover had cost her much more.[39]

In 1820, around the time of the liberal revolution against the repressive regime of Ferdinand VII, José Marchena published the first critical history of Spanish literature. Marchena, whose life and work have only recently become better known, was born in Utrera on November 18, 1768, and took minor orders in Seville. In spite of this, Marchena was a harsh critic of the Church and his first work was an attack on clerical celibacy. Marchena welcomed the arrival of the French Revolution with enormous enthusiasm, and after becoming involved in a plot to overthrow the Spanish monarchy, had little choice but to flee to France, where he became a French citizen and was awarded a position on General Moreau's staff with the army of the Rhine.[40] It was during this period that he wrote *Fragmentum Petronii*, a brilliant diatribe against sexual morality as taught by Catholic theologians and confessors, in which "sovereign virtue is made to consist of abstinence, and sensuality is placed on the same level as the most odious crimes."[41] In the introduction to *Lecciones de filosofía moral y elocuencia*, Marchena deplored the impact that this traditional teaching had had on the development of Spanish literature and the consequent lack of an "honest" eroticism, while denouncing the censorship and lack of freedom of expression that had always characterized Spanish society.[42]

It was only around 1900, however, that José Marchena's dream of a Spanish erotic literature began to be realized with the work of such authors as Felipe Trigo and Llanas Aguilaniedo.[43] Eroticism became popularized in the 1920s with the emergence of cheap editions like "La Novela Semanal," which was published by the Prensa Gráfica between 1921 and 1925, or "La Novela de Hoy," which published 525 numbers between 1922 and 1932.[44] The more open attitudes of the liberal governments of the early years of the reign of Alfonso XIII, the anticlericalism of the Liberal party, and the relaxation of the censorship laws also encouraged the emergence of a pornographic literature during the mid 1920s, which has yet to receive the attention it deserves from historians and literary critics.[45] Defying the increased repression of the

Primo de Rivera dictatorship, authors like Artemio Precioso and Fernando de la Milla published their works in series with suggestive names like "Colección Venus," "Colección Safo," or "Libro Galante."[46] In spite of Marchena's call for a Spanish eroticism free of a morbid preoccupation with the "sinful lusts" of the priesthood, however, this early Spanish pornography continued to be full of references to the clergy and especially the opportunities for seduction presented to them by their role as confessors.[47]

Francisco Bullon's *Colegiales Adorables* (1930) is an excellent example of the way in which the theme of sexual solicitation entered the mainstream of Spanish popular culture through the new medium of the pornographic novel. In *Colegiales Adorables*, the intensely erotic text, which features graphic descriptions of masturbation, anal sex, fellatio, and cunnilingus, as well as the use of contraceptives in order to facilitate intercourse, conceals a subtext containing many of the sexually charged preoccupations of the critics of auricular confession. The two levels of narrative are linked by the use of irony and plays on words, such as the term "blandón," which means a large church candlestick, to refer to the confessor's sexual organ.[48]

As the novel opens, we are introduced to father Canuto, who has just been appointed as the new private chaplain of a school for girls aged fourteen to eighteen run by the order of Hermanas de la Tentación. Here again, we can see the effects of irony and wordplay, since King Canute II (944–1035) of England and Denmark was fabled for his sexual prowess, while the sisters of temptation were quite obviously going to fail in their task of protecting the chastity of their charges. Bullon's description of the young priest would have delighted the readers of *El Motín* or *La Traca*, for whom all priests were actual or potential libertines. At the time of his arrival at the school, Canuto is described as a young man of almost feline sensuality, dressed in a soutane trimmed in silk which was so "molded to his body that the outline of his chest could be seen clearly." This garment was closely fitted at the waist, but flared out at the hips, giving him an almost "coquettish air." His outfit was completed with a pair of elegant, cork-soled shoes with shiny buckles. As the young girls passed in front of him, he "rubbed his slender, beautifully manicured hands together with the relish of a voluptuary."[49]

As mentioned above, one of the constant refrains of anticonfessional propaganda was to warn of the extreme danger that the priest's obligation to "listen to the most abominable descriptions of all manner of sins" posed to his own morality.[50] This theme is treated satirically in *Colegiales Adorables* when Father Canuto, determined to be on his best behavior because of the confidence that the bishop had placed in him, was confronted by Margot, one of his first penitents.

Unfortunately for Father Canuto, seventeen-year-old Margot was not only extremely pretty, but belonged to the so-called "Trio Fantástico," the three most daring and shameless young girls in the college. In spite of her youth, Margot is presented in the best style of traditional Catholic misogyny as an "agent of the devil," whose every glance spelled danger, and a hypocrite whose piety was belied by her seductive clothing.[51] Arriving at the sacristy, where instead of having a confessional, Father Canuto heard the girls' confessions as they knelt before him, Margot wore a semitransparent blouse and a skirt that was considerably shorter than that permitted by college regulations.

The "filthy communication" that Blanco White had warned against began almost as soon as Margot began her confession, when she informed Father Canuto that she had committed various sins of the flesh with one of the other members of the "Trio Fantástico." Even though poor Father Canuto's "hair stood on end" as he listened to Margot's halting account of her misadventures, he was caught in the kind of dreadful predicament that Blanco White must have had in mind when he described the recitation of sexual sins as a major cause of solicitation. On the one hand, if he allowed Margot and other penitents to fully describe their sexual sins, he would "suffer a torment whose refinement was unequaled even by the most zealous inquisitors of the realm, or by Torquemada himself in the time of the autos de fe." On the other, he feared that if he cut off his penitents too abruptly, they would no longer come to confession and end by being condemned to eternal damnation.[52]

Since the very thought of this horrified the good father, he made a superhuman effort, and piously commending himself to all the saints in the calendar, he continued to encourage Margot to confess her sins. That mischievous young lady, however, was not about to be cheated of her prize and redoubled her efforts at seduction. The parody of confession finally ended when Margot exposed her breasts and Father Canuto, realizing "that he was lost," commended himself to God and proceeded to have sexual relations with Margot and her two friends, Lolin and Inés, who were waiting outside the sacristy door for their turn to confess.[53]

It is only later in the novel that we learn that in spite of his youth, Father Canuto had had more than his share of sexual adventures, which began when he was put in charge of a class of small boys while still a novice at the seminary. Attracted by the relative safety of the practice, he began a little game that always ended when he "thrust his implacable battering ram into their round fleshy posteriors." Later, he satisfied his lusts with serving girls, but his favorite field of action was the confessional. After seducing his penitents during confession, he ordered them to place themselves near enough to the opening in the confessional box so that he could have anal intercourse with them. As he did this he would pretend that he was punishing them for their sins, while the girls would reply meekly, "Yes father, give me more penance" and beg him to thrust the penitential tool deeper inside them.[54]

In the remainder of the novel, the solicitation theme is relegated to a minor key since Father Canuto becomes so worn out by his sexual activity in the confessional that he decides to restrict confession to only one day a week. In spite of breaking with the solicitation theme in the middle of the novel, *Colegiales Adorables* presents a remarkably complete digest of its most important elements in a popular format. The dangers of excessively detailed discussion of sexual matters during confession, the lascivious priest who uses his position as confessor to seduce his female penitents, and the dangers posed by confession to the morality of impressionable young girls are all present, along with a rich mixture of other elements drawn from the Spanish sexual imagination.

During the nineteenth century, as more and more men began withdrawing from active participation in the Church, intense religiosity came to be viewed as the domain of women.[55] The widening gulf between male and female religious practice, which had really begun during the last half of the eighteenth century, led to increased concern with the way ecclesiastical power, especially asserted in the confessional with women, could reduce the authority of the husband in marriage. This invisible influence could not only undermine the principle of male dominance that was the basis of the bourgeois family, but could also serve to thwart liberal social and political goals.[56]

The most famous and influential work to sound the alarm about what might be called the moral solicitation of women in the confessional was published by the brilliant French historian Jules Michelet (1798–1874). Michelet's highly anticlerical *Le Prêtre, la femme et la famille* (1845) presents an almost tragic picture of the bourgeois husband who loses influence over his wife and children and eventually becomes a stranger in his own home through the actions of the confessor. Drawn more and more deeply into religious devotions by the overweening influence of the confessor/spiritual advisor, the wife "has become another person; she is present physically but her spirit is elsewhere."[57] The waning influence of the husband is paralleled by the growing influence of the priest, until the husband is forced to accept a humiliating bargain: a division of his wife's affections. He was still to control his wife's body and have exclusive access to her sexually, while the priest, master of her secrets, which he has learned in the confessional, and master of her thoughts, was to have her soul. But since the mind is dominant in the human personality, the priest has the better part of the bargain, in reality, everything of real importance. In effect, what rights the husband still enjoys he has on sufferance from the priest and these could be denied him at any time.[58] In this way, clerical influence on women asserted through the confessional becomes the key to the Church's continued influence on society as a whole. By controlling women, especially married women, the Church influences education and is able to thwart plans for liberal reforms. In Michelet's formulation, therefore, confession represents the chief obstacle to the creation of a liberal and republican social order.[59] The fear that reactionary priests would use confession to destroy the families of men with liberal or anticlerical opinions is reflected in this cartoon from *El Motín*. Here, a confessor advises a woman to leave her husband if he continues to espouse liberal views and attack the members of a religious confraternity (Fig. 9.2).

Jules Michelet's *Le Prêtre, la femme et la famille* proved to be one of the most influential anticlerical works of the nineteenth century. Eighteen editions were published between 1845 and 1918 in France, Spain, Great Britain, Belgium, the United States, and Hungary. [60] Furthermore, Michelet's warnings about the dangers of confession struck a responsive chord in writers as far away as the French-speaking regions of Canada, who began alerting their readers about the moral seduction of women in the confessional. In 1885

—Es preciso, hermana, que dejes á tu marido, si se empeña en ser liberal y en querer apalear á los del Rosario de la Aurora.
—¿Y cómo quiere V. que me arregle sin marido?
—No tengas miedo, que no te faltará nada de todo lo que él pueda darte. Yo te protegeré contra tu herege marido. Vente; á casa y serás mi ama.

Figure 9.2. A Priest Urges a Penitent To Leave Her Husband Because of His Liberal and Anticlerical Tendencies. *El Motín*, 1885, num. 36 (Biblioteca Nacional, Laboratorio Fotográfico)

Charles Chiniquy, a follower of Michelet's, published a book based loosely on *Le Prêtre, la femme et la famille*, significantly entitled *The Priest, the Woman and the Confessional*. In 1908 it was translated into Spanish and published in Barcelona by the anticlerical Centro Editoria Presa with the title *El cura, la mujer y el confesionario*. In this work, Chiniquy blames the French defeat in the Franco-Prussian War on the "degradation" of women and the destruction of the family through confessional practices.[61]

According to Chiniquy, the destruction and moral degradation of women is an inevitable product of the "unmentionable questions" that the Catholic confessor is forced to put to his female penitents.[62] Such questioning not only leads many women into sin by teaching them about illicit sexual practices, but condemns others to a permanent state of anxiety because of their inability to overcome their natural modesty and refer to sexual matters during confession.[63]

In assessing the impact of confession on the family, Chiniquy follows Michelet in denouncing the "unfathomable abyss that has been dug by the Church of Rome between the heart of the wife and the heart of the husband."[64] In the conflict between husband and confessor, the priest will always triumph not only because he knows her innermost secrets, but because he promises her eternal salvation. The wife's relationship with her confessor destroys the mutual sharing that should form the basis of any sound marriage, so that in Catholic countries like France men have little incentive to marry and the population declines relative to the powerful Protestant countries that surround them. France's defeat at the hands of Prussia was, therefore, inevitable since the French woman had "surrendered the citadel of her heart, intelligence and self-respect into the hands of her confessor long before her sons surrendered their swords to the Germans at Sedan and Paris." "The first unconditional surrender had brought the second."[65]

Growing popular anticlericalism and the sharp conflict between liberalism and the clerical right made it almost inevitable that Michelet's book should have had its greatest influence in Spain. Two of Spain's greatest modern novelists, Benito Pérez Galdos (1843–1920) and Vicente Blasco Ibáñez (1867–1928), were fascinated by Michelet's theme of the moral seduction of women in the confessional and the impact that it could have on the family and society. Each wrote novels that drew extensively on Michelet's ideas. The theme was also taken up by one of Blasco Ibáñez's contemporaries, Segismundo Pey Ordeix, whose novel *Sor Sicalipsis* (1924, republished 1931) fell victim to official censorship during the dictatorship of Primo de Rivera, when 3,000 copies were destroyed by order of the government censor.

In *La familia de León Roch* (1878), the last of four novels dealing with the impact of religion on the family that Benito Pérez Galdos wrote between 1876 and 1878, themes and even characters are modeled on Michelet.[66] As the novel opens, we are introduced to León Roch, the brilliant son of a wealthy industrialist, who is the very epitome of modern rational man. León is engaged to the beautiful María Egipciaca, a passionate young woman whose thin veneer of education acquired at the feet of her maternal grandmother and later at a girls school had left her largely ignorant of the world.[67] Following Spanish Krausist thinking and drawing on the traditional model of female mental and emotional inferiority, Galdos's León states bluntly his intention to mold María's as yet unformed personality.[68] Léon is disconcerted to find, however, that instead of being tractable, María is determined to resist his efforts.

The power struggle at the heart of the novel begins with an incident that occurs within one year of their marriage when María tells León that, in spite of being a "weak woman inferior to you in many things and chiefly in knowledge and experience," she dreams of winning a victory that he will never be able to achieve over her. Instead of permitting him to change her character, she intends to "make him over into her own image" and seizing the book that he is reading, she thrusts it into the fireplace where it "burns with a bright flame." This shocking incident, with its specific evocation of the flames of the Inquisition as León reaches desperately into the fire to "save the poor heretic," indicates the gulf that divides the couple.[69] Like her namesake, Mary of Egypt, who evolved from prostitute in Alexandria to hermit in the desert of Palestine, María Egipciaca will ultimately reject the life León offers her and withdraw into a rigid and fanatical religiosity.

María Egipciaca has demonstrated a disturbing tendency to appropriate the traditional male role of domination and control, but as a "weak woman," she needs an ally in her struggle for power. She finds this ally in her confessor, Paoletti, who strengthens her in her determination to fight off her husband's influence and gives her the arguments and the vocabulary to sustain her in her domestic warfare.[70] Unable to accept his wife's assertion of independence, León bitterly accuses Paoletti of molding her and becoming "the governor of my house, the owner of my wife's conscience and the arbiter of my marriage."[71] Resistant to her husband's attempts to shape her personality, María is all too vulnerable to those of her confessor. At the end of the novel, León encounters Paoletti praying before his wife's sepulchre, and he could not help "admiring the fidelity of the spiritual friend who was her owner in life and wanted to be her guardian in death." Paoletti's victory was complete. As the Italian noticed León's presence, he looked up sharply and then glanced down at his prayer book "and that delicate movement of the eyes contained the most supreme contempt that could ever be imagined."[72]

In *Sor Sicalipsis*, Segismundo Pey Ordeix also took up Michelet's theme of the pernicious influence that confessors could have on young women. *Sor Sicalipsis* tells the story of an adolescent girl who becomes enamored of her confessor, Father Sical. Insinuating himself into the household, Sical carries out a "spiritual kidnapping," robbing her parents of all real authority over the girl and subtly turning her toward the cloister where he can dominate her completely.[73] The pernicious role that a confessor could play in turning a young girl away from marriage was a major theme of nineteenth-century anticlericalism. It is reflected in this cartoon from *El Motín*, in which a priest tells his penitent that she must enter a religious order if she is to save her soul and promises to help her escape from her parents. The cartoon implies that a sexual price will have to be paid for his protection (Fig. 9.3).

After seducing Sicalipsis on a trip to the Holy Land, Father Sical is forced to abandon his relationship with her as the time has come for her to actually join the order. Neither can forget the other, however, and the novel ends tragically, with the two lovers seeking martyrdom as missionaries "since death is the only wedding for the religious."[74]

In the introduction to the third edition of his book, Michelet underscored the fact that it had stirred up so much hostility in clerical circles precisely because it had touched on the "vital part of ecclesiastical power"—their influence over women. Through the confessional, the clergy could not only undermine the bourgeois husband, normally considered more liberal and progressive than his wife, but could also ensure that the children were educated in church schools since the confessor would instruct the women of the family to oppose any other arrangement. In this way, clerical influence could be perpetuated and extended throughout society by the younger generation.[75]

—Hija, si quieres salvar tu alma, es preciso que entres al servicio de Dios.
—¡Pero si mi padre dice que primero me matará que dejarme ser monja!......
—Déjale decir, Dios es primero. Esta noche, cuando todos duerman, te escapas de casa. Yo te esperaré en la calle; vendrás conmigo, harás el papel de sobrina, y lo demas ya lo hás viendo.

Figure 9.3. A Priest Tells His Penitent To Enter a Religious Order. *El Motín*,
1885, num. 36 (Biblioteca Nacional, Laboratorio Fotográfico)

Vicente Blasco Ibáñez, who provided the first Spanish translation of
Michelet's *Histoire de la révolution française* in 1898–1900, takes up the
theme of the pernicious social impact of the confessor's influence on women
in his novel *El Intruso* (1904), but places it in a somewhat different context.
Instead of clerical influence over education, the evil extension of Church
authority through the moral seduction of women is seen in politics and the
economy. *El Intruso* locates the epicenter of this thesis in the relationship
between José Sánchez Morueta, a wealthy Basque industrialist, and his first
cousin, Dr. Luís Aresti. At the beginning of the novel, Sánchez Morueta is
presented as hostile or indifferent to religion and extremely close to the free-
thinking Aresti.[76] Like León Roch, Dr. Aresti is presented as a man of sci-
ence whose marriage to a devout young society woman has been a failure
because of his inability to wean her away from her religious devotions. Blasco
Ibáñez introduces the image of the statue used frequently by Galdos to describe Aresti's wife as she became cold and indifferent to her husband and
repelled his sexual advances.[77] Aresti finally concluded that his wife was no

longer fully his own and that he had been forced to share her with her spiritual advisors. After two years of marriage, during which his wife and mother-in-law became increasingly critical of his progressive views and hostility to religion, Aresti packed his few belongings and went to practice medicine in a remote mining region.[78]

Although spared open hostility by his enormous wealth, Sánchez Morueta finds himself in a very similar position. As she approaches middle age, his wife Cristina becomes more devout and falls under the influence of her Jesuit confessor, Father Paulí. Under Paulí's direction, Cristina's religious devotions intensify. She begins sleeping on the floor, wearing a penitential garment, and mortifying herself on a regular basis. At the same time, she becomes a strong supporter of right-wing political activities led by the militant Father Paulí. There is a growing void at the center of this marriage, and Sánchez Morueta, like Michelet's bourgeois husband, feels unwelcome in his own home, "what they call my palace is just like a boarding-house for me."[79]

Alienated by Cristina's religious devotions and indifferent to her fervent partisanship of the religious right, Sánchez Morueta seeks to recapture his youth in the arms of Judith, a young Frenchwoman. When Cristina tells Father Paulí about the affair, he orders her to recapture her husband's affections at any cost since he hopes to win over the industrialist and use his money and influence to support the clerical cause. As an obedient tool of her confessor, Cristina agrees to do this in spite of her repugnance.[80]

When Judith leaves Sánchez Morueta for a younger man, he falls into a deep depression and becomes seriously ill. As a result, Cristina's influence over him increases and, through her, so does the influence of Father Paulí. The once proud and independent industrialist becomes a mere automaton, putty in the hands of Cristina and Fermín Urquiola, a distant relative by marriage who acts as a proxy for Father Paulí. Sánchez Morueta largely abdicates control over his enterprises to Urquiola, who proceeds to replace workers and managers who show insufficient respect for religion with staunch Catholics, regardless of their experience or ability. Gradually, Sánchez Morueta himself is drawn into Father Paulí's orbit, attending a religious retreat, making a general confession of all his sins, and accepting Urquiola as his son-in-law.[81]

In the climactic scene of the novel, Aresti has a final encounter with Sánchez Morueta during a religious procession organized by the Jesuits in honor of the Virgin of Begoña. Caught in the middle of a riot that breaks out between workers and the faithful led by the odious Urquiola, Aresti encounters Sánchez Morueta, who is lashing out at the workers with his enormous fists, and spits in his face as a final expression of the hatred that Aresti feels for what the industrialist has become.

Deeply shocked at being treated this way by the cousin who had once been his closest friend and confidant, Sánchez Morueta is just about to speak when he is pulled away by "a black phantom." It is Father Paulí, who shouts, "On to Begoña, Don José, on to Begoña," and leads the poor befuddled millionaire off in the direction of the shrine. Later, musing on the tragic end of his friendship with his cousin, Aresti blames Father Paulí, "the intruder, the damned intruder, how he had interfered between them, killing all affection and wiping out a past of fraternal love with a cold deathly hand."[82]

It is significant of the rising level of concern about confession in the nineteenth century that the finest and most sensitive treatment of solicitation, physical and moral, in modern literature is to be found in *La Regenta* (1884), the masterpiece of Leopoldo Alas (1852–1901), who wrote under the pseudonym Clarín. On one level, *La Regenta* is the story of the relationship between two individuals who are driven together by their loneliness and intense need for emotional and physical gratification. On a deeper level, the novel presents us with an ironic meditation on the sacrament of penance and the role of the confessor. It is *La Regenta*, rather than any scholarly work written to date on the topic of confession, that provides us with the deepest insights into the moral dilemmas and sexual frustrations faced by confessors in the Counter-Reformation Church.

During the course of the novel, we are presented with three confessors: Fermín de Pas, the brilliant young magistral of the cathedral in the provincial city of Vetusta; Alvaro Mesía, a libertine who seduces Ana de Ozores, the principal female character; and Dr. Benítez, who comes to take care of her after she suffers a nervous collapse. Of the three, only Dr. Benítez exemplifies the virtues of the ideal confessor, demonstrating the understanding and disinterested compassion for his patient of the true doctor of souls.[83]

In the beginning of the novel, we are introduced to twenty-seven-year-old Ana de Ozores, the wife of the former presiding officer, or regent, of one of Spain's provincial law courts. Like so many women in this study, Ana is vulnerable to solicitation because she is sexually and emotionally frustrated. Her husband, Victor Quintanar, described as a man of almost fifty who looks close to sixty, loves her platonically, but is absorbed in his own activities and has little sensitivity to her needs. "Her husband was a botanist, ornithologist, hunter, drama critic, actor, everything but a husband."[84] Childless at twenty-seven, Ana feels that her youth is escaping her and that she will die without knowing the transports of romantic love.[85]

Fermín de Pas is also an intensely frustrated individual. Brought up by a domineering mother who sacrificed everything to give him an education and still treats him like a child, Fermín feels stifled by the provincial society in which he lives and by his complete lack of a satisfying emotional life.[86] Although he has attained a measure of success and is the envy of his colleagues, he realizes that he will probably never achieve his youthful ambitions to rise to a more important position in the hierarchy and is filled with bitter regret over his "sterile life." Although he owes everything to his mother, he recognizes that her love alone is not sufficient and that he needs a "home of his own" and a relationship that is "milder, more intimate" with someone closer to his own age and interests.[87]

Ana is delighted by her very first confession with the magistral. Adopting a warm and familiar tone different from the one he uses in his sermons, he creates vivid images to illustrate his points and reassures her about the value of her early mystical experiences. Articulating the highest ideals of the Catholic confessor, he encourages her to think of him as a spiritual father with whom "pains are alleviated, hopes are confirmed, anxieties are communicated, and doubts are made to disappear."[88]

But in a moment of reflection, Fermín himself is forced to admit that he is unworthy of the faith that he has encouraged Ana to repose in him. In reality he is what his many enemies in Vetusta say about him: "I am ambitious, miserly, I have kept ill-gotten gains, I am a tyrant instead of a good shepherd, I traffic in the religion of the one who drove the money changers out of the temple."[89] Nevertheless, in spite of his self-loathing and strong feelings of guilt, the magistral cannot bear to lose his new spiritual friend. Instead, in a reversal of the normal confessor/penitent relationship, he hopes for redemption at her hands: "If one day his friendship with Ana Ozores reached the point at which he could also confess before her, he was sure that she would absolve him of the sins he had committed." In this way, while he was saving her, she would save him as well.[90] Emotionally, psychologically, spiritually, Fermín had a great deal at stake in his relationship with Ana. Only a noble and disinterested passion based on spiritual communion could save him from the sterility of his existence in Vetusta, so that in spite of feeling physically attracted to Ana, he is determined to avoid the "temptation to convert this wonderful new friendship into a vulgar story of base passion."[91]

For her part, Ana also looks to the magistral for salvation and not only from the tedium of her passionless marriage and boring existence in Vetusta. Finding herself strongly attracted to handsome, vain, and materialistic Alvaro de Mesía, she hopes that Fermín will be able to guide her to a life of mystical exaltation that would protect her from Alvaro's "frankly criminal intent." Mixing the sacred and the erotic, she expresses this alternative by using "entregar," the word for sexual surrender. She will "abandon herself" to Don Fermín, confident that he will save her from committing adultery with Alvaro.[92]

If the magistral violates the true meaning of the sacrament of penance by seeking an intense and intimate relationship with his penitent that borders on the erotic, Alvaro is the confessor who seeks only sensual gratification. In his relationship with his many mistresses, Alvaro constantly mixes confession with eroticism. He forces then to "strip naked their souls in his presence" and, "like a bad priest who abuses the confessional," confess to him in the transports of passion, revealing their most intimate and most shameful sexual sins.[93] Through the sexual charge that he derives from this blasphemous parody of confession, Alvaro hopes to enjoy new forms of erotic satisfaction. The connection between seduction and confession is made explicit again later in the novel when Alvaro presides over a dinner of twelve anticlericals and "in a soft, slow, gentle tone beg[ins] to confess" his sexual adventures, not to receive absolution for his sins, but to garner admiration for his daring from his fellow libertines.[94]

Since Alvaro's "religion" was materialism, he quickly identified the magistral as his rival for Ana in spite of the fact that their relationship appeared purely platonic. Cynically convinced that "no one can resist natural impulses," he fears and resents the sexual power of the priest in the confessional over the woman who tells him her sins.[95]

Even though actual physical contact between Ana and the magistral is confined to him taking her hand on one occasion, Alvaro's "straightforward realism" is fundamentally sound. In their effort to disengage themselves from the physical world and live purely on the spiritual plane, Ana and Fermín are the victims of a dangerous illusion that is to have tragic consequences for all concerned.[96]

As their relationship intensifies, it becomes more and more an unstable mixture of the profane and the religious, of mystical exaltation and carnality. They become and behave like lovers, all the while clinging to the belief that they were just "two angels without bodies."[97] Ultimately, their attempt to live on a purely spiritual plane collapses in the face of two very human emotions: lust and jealousy. Like the female saints tempted by visions of vile and lewd men who abuse them sexually, Ana dreams incessantly of Alvaro, and when she meditates on the sacred, Alvaro presents himself instead of God.[98] At the same time, the magistral becomes more possessive of Ana. Like Michelet's confessors, "he was the real owner, the husband . . . the spiritual husband." When he hears that she had actually danced with Alvaro in the casino and fainted in his arms, he becomes intensely jealous and determines to assert his power over her in a decisive and unequivocal manner.[99]

Filled with remorse and determined to make one last desperate attempt to resolve her inner conflict between pure spirituality and erotic desire, Ana returns to Fermín and offers to march barefoot in the Good Friday procession. For the magistral, who eagerly accepts Ana's proposal, the procession represents a seduction so complete that it allows him to exhibit his victim as a "prisoner without chains," naked in front of an admiring multitude. "I have bared the most elegant feet in the city and dragged them through the mud. . . . Who could do anything more?"[100] But this barbaric triumph marks the apogee of the magistral's power over Ana and over Vetustan society. Marching in the procession, Ana felt that she had been submitted to "an unusual form of prostitution" and that baring her feet was the same as baring her body and her soul. For Alvaro, watching the procession from the balcony of the casino, the magistral's victory was only temporary, and he wondered what kinds of lunacy Ana would commit in the transports of love for him now that she had behaved so extravagantly for her confessor.[101]

After the procession Ana suffers a nervous breakdown, and fearing for her sanity, she puts herself completely in the hands of the good confessor, Dr. Benítez. Under his influence, she begins to see her religious exaltation as a form of nervous excitement that is dangerous to her mental and physical health. Ana's religious feeling becomes transformed into a "vague and poetic pantheism," and the stage is set for her seduction by Alvaro Mesía in the bucolic setting of a country house.[102]

When the magistral learns of the affair between Ana and Alvaro, he becomes wild with jealousy. He has been betrayed by Ana, "my wife, the sister of my soul," and he yearns for vengeance.[103] Scheming with Ana's servant Petra, he makes sure that Ana's husband discovers Alvaro leaving his wife's bedroom in the early hours of the morning, then shames him into challenging Alvaro to a duel. Alvaro kills Victor, but the scandal forces him to leave Vetusta so the affair is broken off. Fermín has had a victory of sorts, but the emotional strain of sublimated erotic desire, emotional frustration, and betrayal has taken a deadly toll. Already during the Good Friday procession, the moment of his greatest triumph, he was beginning to feel like "a hollow shell washed up on the beach . . . the husk of a priest."[104] In the gruesome final scene, when Ana returns to the cathedral after her period of mourning hoping to renew her relationship with her erstwhile spiritual brother, the once-proud Fermín has become little more than a "machine to bestow blessings." Deserted by Alvaro, shunned by her friends, Ana has come in a desperate attempt to prove to herself that the magistral is not the "lascivious solicitante" painted by Alvaro. She hopes to renew her relationship with Fermín, to find through him God's mercy and penance for her sins, but all that fills the mind of the burned-out hulk that Fermín has become is an insane desire for revenge. As she moves toward the confessional, an enormous dark figure emerges from inside. It is Fermín, his face pallid, his eyes alight with insane fury, and as he advances toward her with murderous intent, she falls senseless to the floor. Making a herculean effort at self-control, that very self-control that had sapped so much of his vital energy, Fermín stops himself and staggers, almost blind, out of the church.[105]

The tragic failure to integrate the needs of body and soul in *La Regenta* reveals social and institutional pressures that gave rise to solicitation. Unhappy, unfulfilling marriages contracted under extreme pressure, a rigid sexual code, and the increasing constraints on the sexual life of the priesthood made it extremely difficult to realize the confessional ideal. The mixture of the erotic and the spiritual during confession was a powder keg that threatened to blow up priest, penitent, and the sacrament itself. As Ana Ozores lays unconscious on the floor of the cathedral, she is approached by Celedonio, the filthy, effeminate, hideously ugly acolyte in his torn cassock. Carried away by a "miserable desire," he leans over La Regenta and kisses her. Ana awakens, fighting her way through the fog of a terrible delirium during which she imagined that the "viscous, cold belly of a frog" had brushed her lips. Instead of turning into the handsome spiritual companion of Ana's imagination, the frog remains a frog, and the priest remains a man, perverted and destroyed by an inhuman sexual code.

CONCLUSION

From its very beginning, the Counter-Reformation was at once reformatory and repressive. But, as this study has demonstrated, these elements interacted with one another in unexpected ways that are still having an impact on the Catholic world. The stress on sacramentalism at the Council of Trent and in the post-Tridentine Church meant that auricular confession and the role of the confessor underwent a significant transformation. From a sacrament that was barely observed by the laity even in the minimal form set forth at the Lateran Council of 1215, it became central to the religious practice of much of Catholic Europe. At the same time, the Church hierarchy, alarmed at the poor quality of so many parish priests, sought to improve clerical education and morality so that the laity would more readily accept catechizing and confession at their hands.

The intense preoccupation of Church reformers with the moral behavior of the clergy led the Spanish hierarchy to give the Inquisition the responsibility for dealing with sexual solicitation. For 259 years (1561–1820), the Inquisition prosecuted cases of solicitation, but by the middle of the eighteenth century much of the original energy and enthusiasm that drove the Counter-Reformation and generated respect for its institutions had dissipated.[1] All over Catholic Europe, membership in the many confraternities that had organized lay support for charitable and educational projects was declining.[2] In Spain, many of the confraternities of Seville refused to march in religious processions after 1778, and by the end of the century, the Catalan authorities found it difficult to persuade the guilds to participate in liturgical ceremonies.[3]

Even more important from the perspective of the institutional Church was the deterioration of Church-State relations during the eighteenth century. After the Concordat of 1753, the relationship between Church and State shifted in favor of the State, which was able to assert more and more control over the religious orders and harassed and even dismissed bishops who opposed royal policy.[4]

The increasing assertion of regalism in Church-State relations led to growing pressure against the Jesuit order, which was seen as a major supporter of the papacy in its struggle with the secular state. The order was expelled from Portugal in 1759 and France in 1764. In Spain, Jesuit resistance to the regalist measures taken by Charles III and his ministers and suspicion that the order was somehow involved in the Mutiny of Esquilache rioting of March 1766 led to their expulsion in 1767.[5] Unfortunately, the departure of the Jesuits further weakened the Church since the order had been the major force behind the Church's educational efforts among the social elite, as well as providing inspiration and support for lay involvement in many Church-related activities.[6]

The Spanish Inquisition also found itself in a significantly weaker position by the middle of the century. Its strong support for the Bourbons during the War of Succession notwithstanding, it came to be regarded as an enemy of the regime's limited program of modernization. In 1768 Charles III reduced its authority to censor books and two years later warned the Inquisition against imprisoning anyone unless his guilt was fully established. Since imprisonment and interrogation in hopes of forcing the accused to confess was an essential part of inquisitorial procedure, it is little wonder that an increasing number of cases were suspended during the last half of the eighteenth century.[7] Even when there was ample evidence to justify prosecution, the crown's lukewarm support and the increasing administrative lassitude of the Holy Office itself meant prosecutions were initiated after very long delays so that the practices the Inquisition was meant to deter were allowed to continue almost unchecked.[8]

The Inquisition's decline could not have occurred at a worse time for the Church's program to maintain confession at the heart of Counter-Reformation observance. Even though official insistence on certificates of confession, missionary activity, and catechizing had greatly increased popular participation in the sacrament, the clergy themselves were undergoing a crisis of confidence that led many to question its value.[9] José Blanco White's abhorrence of confession, which he termed "one of the most mischievous practices of the Romanist church," was probably typical of many members of the clergy during this period.[10]

At the same time, there was an increasing reluctance to accept the constraints of celibacy among many members of the clergy, which was spurred by a large and growing literature entering Spain through clandestine channels. These works ranged from erotic items like *Vénus dans le cloître ou la religieuse en chemise*, which was published in London in 1740 and circulated in Spain until it was prohibited by the Spanish Inquisition in 1804, to more serious works that attacked celibacy on the grounds that it went against Church tradition, such as Jacques Gaudin's *Les inconvénients du célibat des prêtres*, published in Geneva in 1781 and not prohibited in Spain until 1801.[11]

It is probably fair to assume that the growing frustration at the highest levels of the Inquisition about its failure to check rising levels of solicitation during the eighteenth century is evidence of this revolt against celibacy on the part of many members of the clergy.[12] Antonio Gavin was speaking for many of his fellow priests when he bitterly denounced celibacy as the chief cause of the "misdoings and ill practices of the Romish priests" and assured his readers that "although priests do make a vow of chastity they break it by living loose, lewd, and irregular lives."[13] José Marchena's revolt against traditional Spanish society was more sexual than political. His very first publication attacked clerical celibacy, and he was described later in life as a prodigious lover and a person of "the most incredible immorality" by his French biographer.[14]

The Protestant attack on the sacrament of penance was two sided: an unworthy, sinful priesthood was administering a sacrament of dubious scriptural validity and of no value at all in obtaining justification. In their response, the leaders of the Catholic reform had not only to reaffirm the validity and divine origin of the sacrament, but to create a priesthood worthy of administering it. In their zeal to do this, they embarked on one of the most daring experiments in sexual repression in all of human history. But in spite of more rigorous education and training, the demands of celibacy proved too great for many priests, and with ordinary sexual and social outlets having been largely circumscribed, the confessional was left as the only place where they could make contact with women and talk with them personally and intimately. By sharply repressing the sexual activity of the clergy and placing their moral conduct under the control of episcopal officials, and by insisting that priests demand an exact and detailed accounting of sins, the Church itself had created the objective conditions for solicitation in the confessional.

Consequently, more than two and one-half centuries of persecution by the Holy Office failed to end the problem of solicitation in spite of the fact that few priests could plead ignorance of the laws against it. If anything, by focusing attention on the confessional as a venue for sexual activity, the Inquisition may have eroticized confession. Organized persecution of solicitation ended with the demise of the Holy Office, but the Spanish obsession with an eroticized sacrament of penance remained very much alive. In 1959, a case like the one described above by Llorente was discovered in Málaga. Father Hipólito Lucena, a respected parish priest and theology professor, caused a terrible scandal when it was revealed that a number of his female penitents were accustomed to carrying out a variety of sexual activities with him before the high altar of his church. Father Lucena was quickly spirited out of Spain and spent the rest of his days in an Austrian convent.[15] In November 1992, the police in Santander investigated a complaint from a devout seventy-four-year-old woman who claimed that as she was leaving church at five that afternoon, she was approached by a man of about thirty-five who put his hand over her mouth and dragged her inside one of the confessionals where he raped her.[16] Throughout the post–Civil War period, young Spanish women viewed confession with tremendous anxiety precisely because they felt that they would be questioned more closely about sexual matters than boys of their own age.[17]

The renovation of moral theology in the 1950s, which started with the work of the Germans Tillmann and Häring and the Frenchman Leclerq, was given a strong impetus at the Second Vatican Council (1962–1965). Present-day Roman Catholic theologians have largely abandoned the casuistry and legalism of the post-Tridentine Church and have embraced a more open approach, attempting to relate the notion of individual sin with the dilemmas of living in secular society and the discoveries in psychology, sociology, and anthropology.[18] At the same time, the new penance ritual that was published in 1973 substantially reformed the way the sacrament was administered. Individual confession was retained, but preference was accorded to new forms of community penance, with the priest acting as a kind of presiding officer or moderator. [19] Even where the older form was retained, the priest was no longer expected to carry on an "interrogation" or "investigate the conscience of the sinner."[20] Given the daring and scope of these changes, the Church has gained an unprecedented opportunity to restore the reputation of the sacrament of penance and allow it to play the role in bringing consolation to the spiritually afflicted for which it is so ideally suited. Unfortunately, the evidence from sociological surveys appears to indicate that acceptance of the new communal forms of confession among the laity has failed to stop the rapid decline in the popularity of the sacrament that was already evident by the early 1970s.[21] Much to the chagrin of ecclesiastical conservatives, the mid 1980s saw the virtual abandonment of auricular confession in many parishes. Furthermore, the link between communion and confession, so firmly established in the popular mind after the Council of Trent, was largely broken, with rates of communion far exceeding rates of confession in most places.[22] Ironically enough, indifference to the sacrament of penance by both priests and laity has served to accomplish in a few decades what the Spanish Inquisition had failed to accomplish in several hundred years of persecution: largely to eliminate the problem of sexual solicitation. In the present-day Church, sexual scandals continue, but they stem entirely from the continued insistence on celibacy and take place in locations outside the orbit of confession, in seminaries, schools, or apartments. The wholesale rejection of the sacrament of penance by both clergy and laity in the last few decades stands in sharp contrast to the growing popularity of communion and should be taken into account by the historians of de-christianization. Like the popularity of saint cults and devotions, which rise and fall in accordance with a variety of local and regional conditions, some sacraments can fall from favor without necessarily indicating an overall decline in the importance of the sacraments as a whole. Someday, perhaps in the near future, the sacrament of penance may recover its popularity as the laity rediscovers its very real potential for providing solace, consolation, and spiritual enlightenment.

GLOSSARY

Abjuration de Levi   A renunciation of errors and return to the faith required of those found guilty of lesser offenses by the Inquisition

Abjuration de Vehementi   A renunciation of errors and return to the faith required of those guilty of more serious offenses where suspicion of actual heresy was present

Auto de fe   Public ceremony during which the crimes committed by persons falling under the jurisdiction of the Inquisition were read out along with their punishments

Beata   A laywoman who took a vow of chastity and dedicated her life to God.

Blood libel   The allegation made by anti-Semites that Jews made use of the blood of murdered Christian children in their religious rituals

Carta acordada   Administrative regulation issued to the provincial tribunals by the Suprema

Commissioner   A member of the clergy who represented the inquisition in rural areas. He received information about offenses and sent it to the tribunal

Consulta de fe   The body, including the inquisitors as well as a representative of the bishop and some graduates in law and theology, that pronounced sentence in inquisitorial trials

Converso   A converted Jew or the descendant of converted Jews

Familiar   Unpaid lay assistant to the Inquisition

Mortal sins   The most serious sins involving a loss of grace and the possibility of eternal damnation. These must all be confessed or the confession is considered incomplete and, therefore, useless

Sacramental Penance   An ecclesiastical ritual, carried out by a properly authorized priest, designed to restore Christians who have committed grave sins and fallen from grace to the community of the faithful

Solicitante A priest, secular or regular, accused of seducing or attempting to seduce a penitent by word or deed before, during, or after confession

Suprema The governing council of the Spanish Inquisition, established in 1483

Synod On the level of the diocese, an assembly of the secular clergy and benefice holders led by the bishop at which regulations for the morals and religious life of clergy and laity were set forth

NOTES

Introduction

1. Jaime Contreras and Gustav Henningsen arrive at a total of 1,131 solicitation cases recorded in the relaciones de causas for the period 1560–1700.

2. Thomas Tentler, *Sin and Confession on the Eve of the Reformation* (Princeton: Princeton University Press, 1977).

3. Jean Delumeau, *Le péché et la peur; La culpabilisation en Occident XIII–XVIII siècles* (Paris: Fayard, 1983), 272. But see the extensive discussion of the controversy over sin and penance in *L'aveu et le pardon: Les difficultés de la confession XIII–XVIII siècles* (Paris: Fayard, 1990).

Chapter 1

1. Delumeau, *Le péché et la peur*, 211.

2. Ibid., 212–213.

3. Tentler, *Sin and Confession*, 3.

4. Ibid., 4–5.

5. Ibid., 14.

6. Delumeau, *Le péché et la peur*, 220.

7. Tentler, *Sin and Confession*, 25–27.

8. Mike Hepworth and Bryan S. Turner, eds., *Confession: Studies in Deviance and Religion* (London: Routledge and Kegan Paul, 1982), 52–54.

9. Delumeau, *Le péché et la peur*, 225.

10. Martín de Azpilcueta Navarro, *Manual de confesores y penitentes, que clara y brevemente contiene, la universal y particular decision de quasi todas las dudas, que en las confesiones suelen occurrir de los pecados absoluciones, restituciones, censuras irregularidades* (Salamanca: Andrea de Portonariis, 1556), 137, 138, 174.

11. Ibid., 523–527.

12. Ibid., 129–133, 370.

13. Ibid., 69–71.

14. Ibid., 135, 370.

15. Archivo Histórico Nacional, Sección Inquisición (hereafter AHN, Inq.), January 25, 1531, Legajos (hereafter leg.) 321, expediente (hereafter exp.) 11.

16. José Luis Sánchez Herrero, *Las diócesis del reino de León* (León: Caja de Ahorros y Monte de Piedad, 1978), 305.

17. AHN, Inq., January 24, 1532, leg.231, exp.11. Also see José Luis González Novalín, "Religiosidad y reforma del pueblo cristiano," in Ricardo García-Villoslada, ed., *Historia de la Iglesia en España*, 5 vols. (Madrid: La Editorial Católica, 1979), 3, pt. 1: 361.

18. Alfonso de Valdés, *Diálogo de Mercurio y Caron*, quoted in Marcel Bataillon, *Erasmo y España: Estudios sobre la historia espiritual del siglo XVI* (Mexico: Fondo de Cultura Económica, 1966), 392.

19. Juan de Valdés, *Diálogo de doctrina cristiana* (Madrid: Editoria Nacional, 1979), 96–99, 105.

20. González Novalín, "Religiosidad," in García-Villoslada, *Historia de la Iglesia*, 3:1 355–357.

21. Tarsicio de Azcona, "Reforma del episcopado y del clero de España en tiempo de los Reyes Católicos y de Carlos V," in García-Villoslada, *Historia de la Iglesia* 3/1: 166–167.

22. Sánchez Herrero, *Las diócesis*, 164–165.

23. AHN, Inq., February 26, 1530, leg.233, exp.5.

24. Lewis Spitz, *The Protestant Reformation 1517–1559* (New York: Harper and Row, 1985), 52.

25. AHN, Inq., January 31, 1532, leg.231, exp.11.

26. AHN, Inq., November 13, 1530, January 19, 1532, leg.231, exp.11.

27. Bataillon, *Erasmo y España*, 26.

28. Ibid., 356. Valdés, *Diálogo de doctrina cristiana*, 96–99.

29. Here Valdés rejects the view expressed by Duns Scotus in the fourteenth century. See Louis Braeckmans, *Confession et communion au moyen âge et au concile de Trente* (Gembloux: J. Duculot, 1971), 51–52.

30. Bataillon, *Erasmo y España*, 290.

31. Ibid., 432–434.

32. Spitz, *Protestant Reformation*, 7–13.

33. Martin Luther, *The Sacrament of Penance*, E. Theodore Bachmann, trans., in E. Theodore Bachmann, ed., *Luther's Works*, 55 vols. (Philadelphia: Muhlenberg Press, 1960); Tentler, *Sin and Confession*, 360–361.

34. Spitz, *Protestant Reformation*, 75.

35. Henry Kamen, *Inquisition and Society in Spain* (Bloomington: Indiana University Press, 1985), 73; Fray Casiodoro de Reina, *Confesión de fe cristiana* (Cassel: Wilhelm Wessel, 1602), chapter 11.

36. Bataillon, *Erasmo y España*, 181–182, 471.

37. Kamen, *Inquisition and Society*, 73.

38. AHN, Inq., July 8, 1580, November 26, 1580, leg.110, exp.27.

39. Kamen, *Inquisition and Society*, 76.

40. A. D. Wright, *The Counter-Reformation: Catholic Europe and the Non-Christian World* (New York: St. Martin's Press, 1982), 7–9.

41. Henry Charles Lea, *The History of Sacerdotal Celibacy in the Christian Church* (New York: Russell and Russell, 1957), 450.

42. Hubert Jedin, *A History of the Council of Trent*, Dom Ernest Graf, trans., 2. vols. (St. Louis: B. Herder, 1961), 2: 13–14; Bernardino Llorca, "Carlos V y la intervención de España en el concilio de Trento," in García-Villoslada, *Historia de la Iglesia*, 3/1: 387–393.

43. Jedin, *Council of Trent*, 2: 10.

44. Ibid., 52.

45. Ibid., 177.

46. *Canons and Decrees of the Council of Trent*, H. J. Schroeder, O.P., trans. (St. Louis and London: Herder Books, 1941), 52.

47. Ibid.

48. Jedin, *Council of Trent*, 2: 308.

49. Ibid., 26.

50. Jean Delumeau, *Le Catholicisme entre Luther et Voltaire* (Paris: Presses Universitaires de France, 1971), 57; Schroeder, *Canons and Decrees*, 246–247.

51. Delumeau, *Le Catholicisme*, 58.

52. Ibid., 59.

53. Ibid., 58; Henry Charles Lea, *A History of Auricular Confession and Indulgences in the Latin Church*, 3 vols. (Philadelphia: Lea Brothers, 1896), 1:303.

54. AHN, Inq., August 30, 1717, leg.1826, exp.2.

55. AHN, Inq., June 20, 1719, leg.1826, exp.2.

56. AHN, Inq., December 1, 1747, leg.1827, exp.2.

57. Schroeder, *Canons and Decrees*, 195.

58. Peter Burke, *Popular Culture in Early Modern Europe* (New York: Harper and Row, 1978), 233.

59. Ibid., 233.

60. González Novalín, "Religiosidad y Reforma," in García-Villoslada, *Historia de la Iglesia*, 3/1: 366–367.

61. John Bossy, *Christianity in the West, 1400–1600* (Oxford: Oxford University Press, 1985), 19–25; Schroeder, *Canons and Decrees*, 183–184.

62. Bossy, *Christianity*, 16–18; Schroeder, *Canons and Decrees*, 185–186.

63. Henry Kamen, *The Phoenix and the Flame: Catalonia and the Counter Reformation* (New Haven and London: Yale University Press, 1993), 19–20.

64. Wright, *The Counter-Reformation*, 51; Schroeder, *Canons and Decrees*, 151–152.

65. Peter Burke, "Popular Piety," in John O'Malley, S.J. ed., *Catholicism in Early Modern Europe: A Guide to Research* (St. Louis: Center for Reformation Research, 1988), 121; Wright, *The Counter-Reformation*, 52.

66. Jedin, *Council of Trent*, 321.

67. Tarsicio de Azcona, "Reforma," 160.

68. José Luis González Novalín, *El Inquisidor General Fernando de Valdés 1483–1568* (Oviedo: Universidad de Oviedo, 1968), 70, 93–94, 96.

69. Jedin, *Council of Trent*, 331–332.

70. Jean Pierre Dedieu, *L'Administration de la foi: L'Inquisition de Tolède (XVI–XVIII siècle)* (Madrid: Casa de Velázquez, 1989), 59.

71. Kamen, *The Phoenix and the Flame*, 50.

72. Ibid., 52.

73. Jedin, *Council of Trent*, 358.

74. Schroeder, *Canons and Decrees*, 207.

75. Jedin, *Council of Trent*, 367.

76. Wright, *The Counter-Reformation*, 14.

77. Schroeder, *Canons and Decrees*, 238.

78. Ibid., 208–209. Even though the Spanish monarchy was unable to remove the rights of patronage held by the Benedictines and Augustinians of Catalonia, it did insist that bishops enjoy ecclesiastical jurisdiction over these appointees. Kamen, *The Pheonix and the Flame*, 52.

79. Schroeder, *Canons and Decrees*, 195–196.

80. Ibid., 193–194.

81. Ibid., 192–193.

82. H. Outram Evennett, *The Spirit of the Counter-Reformation*, ed. John Bossy (Cambridge: Cambridge University Press, 1968), 37–39, 40–41.

83. Tentler, *Sin and Confession*, 369.

84. Delumeau, *Le Péché et la peur*, 7.

85. Bernhard Häring, *Das Gesetz Christi*, Spanish trans. Juan de la Cruz Salazar, 2 vols. (Barcelona: Herder, 1961), 1: 58–59.

86. Tentler, *Sin and Confession*, 369–370.

Chapter 2

1. Bossy, *Christianity*, 49. The material from Spain does not seem to bear out Bossy's opinion that most people were fulfilling the annual obligation to confess at Lent.

2. John Bossy, "Moral Arithmetic: Seven Sins into Ten Commandments," in Edmund Leites, ed., *Conscience and Casuistry in Early Modern Europe* (Cambridge: Cambridge University Press, 1988), 215.

3. Schroeder, *Canons and Decrees*, 94.

4. Azpilcueta Navarro, *Manual de confesores*, 371–372.

5. AHN, Inq., December 9, 1580, leg.110, exp.27.

6. Fidèle de Ros, *Un maître de Sainte Thérèse, le père François de Osuna* (Paris: Gabriel Beauchesne, 1936), 122, 130–131, 134.

7. José Luis González Novalín, "La herejía luterana y el nuevo rumbo del Santo Oficio" in García-Villoslada, *Historia de la Iglesia*, 3/2: 193; Virgilio Pinto Crespo, *Inquisición y control ideológico en la España del siglo XVI* (Madrid: Taurus, 1983), 210.

8. AHN, Inq., January 28, 1590, leg.1826, exp.19, 25, 33. Gaspar Lucas was tortured twice and punished by being deprived of his benefice and denied the right to celebrate all the sacraments.

9. Ernesto Zaragoza Pascual, *Los generales de la congregación de San Benito de Valladolid* (Zamora: Ediciones Monte Casino, 1980), 276.

10. Juan Daza y Berrio, *Tesoro de confesores y perla de la conciencia para todos estados* (Madrid: Imprenta Real, 1648), f.2.

11. Manuel Calisbeta, *Enseñanzas espirituales por el mayor provecho de las almas, doce doctrinas a favor de la comunión cotidiana* (Madrid: Pablo de Val, 1663), ffs.3–4v.

12. Ibid., 36.

13. Ibid., 37, 49.

14. Ibid., 38, 43–44.

15. Fray Francisco de Arcos, *Vida del V.Y.R. Fray Simón de Rojas*, 2 vols. (Madrid: Julián de Paredes, 1670), 1: 172.

16. Calisbeta, *Enseñanzas*, 58–59.

17. Diego Pérez de Valdivia, *Tratado de la frecuente comunión y medios para ella principalmente del modo y orden para bien confesar* (Barcelona: Pedro Malo, 1589), f.19.

18. Arcos, *Simón de Rojas*, 1: 193–194.

19. Bernardino de Villegas, S.J., *La esposa de Cristo instruida* (Murcia: Juan Fernández de Fuentes, 1635), 454.

20. AHN, Inq., leg.1952, exp.4, "Relaciones de causas de Granada año de 1635."

21. Pérez de Valdivia, *Tratado*, f.19v.

22. Thomás Reluz, *Vida y virtudes del Señor Fray Thomás Carbonel* (Madrid: Viuda de Francisco Nieto, 1695), 325.

23. AHN, Inq., November 12, 1688, leg.1705, exp.5. Ana Antich y Cerda, the devout widow of a butcher on Menorca, took communion every day with the express permission of her confessor Fray Pedro Joseph Pons, the prior of the Augustinian convent in Ciudadela. AHN, Inq., April 1, 1685, leg.1705, exp. 20.

24. AHN, Inq., leg.1822, exp.20, "Constituciones proprias del convento de San Illdefonso de monjas Bernardas en la ciudad de Las Palmas año de 1638."

25. Alvaro Huerga, *Predicadores, alumbrados y Inquisición en el siglo XVI* (Madrid: Fundación Universitaria Española, 1973), 54.

26. Cristóbal Delgadillo, *Cuestión moral o resolución de algunas dudas acerca de la frecuente confesión* (Madrid: Domingo García Morras, 1660), 22–23, 29v.

27. Francisco Farfan, *Regimiento de castos y remedio de torpes* (Salamanca: Cornelio Bonardo, 1590), ffs.51–51v.

28. Pérez de Valdivia, *Tratado*, 55.

29. Farfan, *Regimiento*, f.51.

30. Francisco de Luque Fajardo, *Fiel desengaño contra la ociosidad y los juegos, utilissimo a los confesores y penitentes, justicias, y los demas a cuyo cargo está limpiar de vagabundos talures y fulleros de la república cristiana* (Madrid: Miguel Serrano de Vargas, 1603), f.5v.

31. Evennett, *Spirit of the Counter-Reformation*, 37. This book consists of lectures given in May 1951.

32. Pedro Galindo, *Parte segundo del directorio de penitentes y práctica de una buena y prudente confesión* (Madrid: Antonio de Zafra, 1680), 478–479.

33. *La confesión ó sea amena controversia entre un joven abogado y un viejo militar sobre la institución divina, del sacramento de la penitencia; su práctica, y necesidad; sus ventajes, y beneficios tanto para la sociedad como para el individuo* (Madrid: Biblioteca Católica Popular, 1845), 17–18.

34. AHN, Inq., May 28, 1731, leg.1825, exp.30.

35. AHN, Inq., April 3, 1784, leg.1825, exp.13.

36. AHN, Inq., June 9, 1787, leg.1828, exp.26.

37. Sara T. Nalle, *God in La Mancha; Religious Reform and the People of Cuenca 1500–1650* (Baltimore and London: John Hopkins University Press, 1992), 131–132.

38. Arcos, *Simón de Rojas*, 1: 185; AHN, Inq., November 7, 1774, leg.1828, exp.25.

39. AHN, Inq., March 26, 1784, leg.231, exp.2.

40. AHN, Inq., May 8, 1815, leg.1867, exp.21.

41. *The Complete Works of Saint Teresa of Jesus*, E. Allison Peers, trans. and ed., 3 vols., 11th ed. (London: Sheed and Ward, 1982), 1: 240–241.

42. AHN, Inq., leg.1953, exp.74, "Relación de la visita que hizo el Dr. Mesa de la Sarte inquisidor apostólico de la ciudad y reino de Granada el año pasado de 1573 y este presente año de 1574 en el obispado de Guadix, Baza y la ciudad de Huesca."

43. *Sínodo diocesano del Arzobispado de Toledo*, April 22, 23, 24, 1682 (Madrid: José de la Peña, 1849), 218.

44. Reluz, *Thomás Carbonel*, 306–307.

45. Vidal Guitart Izquierdo, *Sínodos postridentinos de Segorbe* (Castellón de la Plana: Ayuntamiento de Castellón de la Plana, 1983), 110.

46. AHN, Inq., January 16, 1700, leg.1825, exp.24.

47. William B. Jordon, *Catalogue of the Exhibition El Greco of Toledo* (Boston: Little Brown, 1982), 230, 233.

48. Arcos, *Simón de Rojas*, 1: 57.

49. AHN, Inq., August 3, 1594, leg.228, exp.3.

50. Wright, *The Counter-Reformation*, 77, 183.

51. R. Po-Chia Hsia, *Social Discipline in the Reformation: Central Europe 1500–1750* (London: Routledge, 1989), 56.

52. Isaac Vázquez, "Las controversias doctrinales postridentinas hasta finales del siglo XVII," in García-Villoslada, *Historia de la Iglesia*, 4: 456–460; also see William A. Christian, *Local Religion in Sixteenth-Century Spain* (Princeton: Princeton University Press, 1981), 70–75, 190–199.

53. Antonio Mestre Sanchis, "Religión y cultura en el siglo XVIII Español," in García-Villoslada, *Historia de la Iglesia*, 4: 590; José Fabian, *Disertación histórico-dogmática sobre la sagrada reliquia de la santísima faz de nuestro Señor Jesucristo, venerada en la ciudad de Alicante* (Alicante: Diputación de Alicante, 1979), 67–69, in Mestre Sanchis, "Religión y cultura," 596.

54. Arcos, *Simón de Rojas*, 156–157.

55. The congregation was founded in 1614. AHN, "Inventario de la Real Congregación del Dulce Nombre de María," 2–3.

56. AHN, Inq., March 23, 1689, leg.1825, exp.15.

57. AHN, Inq., November 2, 1681, leg.228, exp.6.

58. Mary Elizabeth Perry, *Gender and Disorder in Early Modern Seville* (Princeton: Princeton University Press, 1990), 98.

59. Mestre Sanchis, "Religión y cultura," 595.

60. Kamen, *The Phoenix and the Flame*, 333–334.

61. Pérez de Valdivia, *Tratado*, 27.

62. Villegas, *La esposa*, 555–556.

63. AHN, Inq., December 17, 1767, leg.1714, exp.13.

64. AHN, Inq., August 10, 1683, leg.1708, exp.32.

65. Delumeau, *L'aveu et le pardon*, 36.

66. Galindo, *Parte segundo del directorio*, 461–462.

67. AHN, Inq., October 19, 1700, May 10, 1704, May 23, 1704, leg.1825, exp.27.

68. AHN, Inq., March 31, 1688, leg.1708, exp.27.

69. AHN, Inq., March 8, 1758, leg.231, exp.14.

70. Perry, *Gender and Disorder*, 98.

71. Ibid., 25.

72. AHN, Inq., May 18, 1765, leg.233, exp.2.

73. AHN, Inq., November 13, 1688, leg.1705, exp.5.

74. Fray Jayme de Corella, *Práctica del confesionario y explicación de los sesenta y cinco proposiciones condenadas por la santidad de N.S.P. Inocencio XI* (Madrid: Marcel Romin, 1717), intro., n.p.

75. Corella, *Práctica*, 144–145.

76. Ibid., 150.

77. AHN, Inq., November 14, 1686, Libro (hereafter lib.) 1266, f.497v.

78. Azpilqueta Navarro, *Manual de confesores*, 55.

79. Arcos, *Simón de Rojas*, 37–39.

80. Ibid., 175.

81. Jodi Bilinkoff, *The Avila of Saint Teresa: Religious Reform in a Sixteenth-Century City* (Ithaca: Cornell University Press, 1989), 92.

82. Reluz, *Thomás Carbonel*, 148–151.

83. Fray Antonio de Lorea, *Bienaventurado El San Pío quinto pontífice máximo de la Iglesia, religioso de la sagrada orden de predicadores* (Valladolid: Imprenta de la Real Chancillería, 1713), 12–13.

84. Bartolomé Bennassar, *L'Homme espagnol: Attitudes et mentalités du XVI au XIX siècles* (Paris: Hachette, 1975), 66.

85. Biblioteca Nacional (hereafter BN), MS 3164 "Un cavallero de la corte de Madrid escrive a un religioso Dominico sobre la novedad que se revele de que el rey nuestro señor D. Felipe V no confiesse con religiosos de dicha orden" (December 1718).

86. Fray Juan de la Cruz, *Crónica de la orden de predicadores* (Lisbon: Manuel Juan, 1567), ffs. 432–42v, 255–256.

87. Quintan Aldea Vaquero, Thomás María Martínez, Juan Vives Gatell, *Diccionario de historia ecclesiástica de España* (Madrid: CSIC, 1972–1975), 4: 2508.

88. Luys Diez de Aux, *Compendio de las fiestas que ha celebrado la imperial ciudad de Zaragoza por haver promovido la magestad católica del Rey Felipe III de Castilla Segundo de Aragón al Señor Fray Luis de Aliaga su confesor y de su Real Consejo de Estado en el oficio y cargo Supremo de Inquisidor-General de España* (Saragossa: Juan de Lanuja y Quartanet, 1619), 143.

89. AHN, Inq., August 19, 1686, leg.1827, exp.20. Luis de Soto's views were shared by other members of the order and many benefice holders in the diocese.

90. AHN, Inq., July 1, 1651, leg.229, exp.11.

91. AHN, Inq., May 26, 1582, leg.1824, exp.2.

92. AHN, Inq., June 16, 1636, leg.1706, exp.5.

93. AHN, Inq., February 28, 1758, leg.232, exp.4.

94. AHN, Inq., October 7, 1722, leg.1715, exp.10.

95. AHN, Inq., September 5, 1625, leg.231, exp.8.

96. AHN, Inq., March 6, 1690, leg.1712, exp.8.

97. AHN, Inq., May 17, 1660, leg.1708, exp.16.

98. AHN, Inq., July 22, 1778, leg.1827, exp.27.

99. AHN, Inq., August 9, 1747, leg.1827, exp.1.

100. Peers, *The Complete Works of Saint Teresa*, 167, 225.

101. Ibid., 200.

102. Fray Angel Manrique, *La venerable Ana de Jesús, discipula y compañera de la S.M. Teresa de Jesús* (Brussels: Lucas de Meerbeek, 1632), 315–316, 318, 338–339. The second papal brief was issued by Gregory XIV.

Chapter 3

1. AHN, Inq., April 27, 1692, lib.1265, ffs.505–505v.

2. AHN, Inq., May 23, 1532, leg.231, exp.11.

3. Lea, *Sacerdotal Celibacy*, 498.

4. Ibid., 500.

5. Juan Machado de Chaves, *Perfecto confesor y cura de almas*, 2 vols. (Barcelona: Pedro de la Cavallería, 1641), 2: 775.

6. Juan de Azevedo, *Tribunal theologicum et Juridicum contra subdolos Confesarios in Sacramento Penitentiae ad venerem sollicitantes ereptum* (Ulissipone: M. Rodig, 1726); R. da Cunha e Silva, *Tractatus de Confesariis Solicitantibus* (Vallisoleti: Ioannum de Rueda, 1620); Juan Escobar del Corro, *De confesariis solicitantibus* (Córdoba, 1642); José Nuño Borgensi, *Medicina moralis tripartita a contagio solicitationis comprehensae in diplomatibus pontificiis et a denunciatione in Sancto Officio confessarios tutius praeservans* (Caesaraugustae: Apud Emmanuelem Roman, 1692).

7. AHN, Inq., June 5, 1687, lib. 1266, ff.438, 442, "Reprehensión de un sacerdote religioso de la Compañía de Jesús por solicitar en acto de la confesión."

8. AHN, Inq., October 13, 1667, lib.1266, f.453, "Reprehensión de un religioso Dominico por solicitante en Valladolid."

9. AHN, Inq., June 5, 1687, lib.1266, f.441v.

10. AHN Inquisition, July 27, 1649, lib.1265, f.174. "Reprehensión de un solicitante." For the continued Protestant attack against confession in the seventeenth century, see John Goodman, *A Discourse Concerning Auricular Confession as Prescribed by the Council of Trent and Practiced in the Church of Rome* (London: H. Hills, 1648), and (Anon.), *A Treatise of Auricular Confession Wherein is Evidently Shown the Authority and Power of Catholic Priests for the Forgery and Remitting of Sins Against the Protestants Bare and Only Preaching of Absolution* (S. Omer: I. Heigham, 1622).

11. AHN, Inq., October 13, 1667, lib.1266, f.450.

12. AHN, Inq., October 23, 1690, lib.1266, ff.509v–510. For the mission of the Trinitarian Order, see Ellen Friedman, *Spanish Captives in North Africa in the Early Modern Age* (Madison: University of Wisconsin Press, 1983), 106–107.

13. AHN, Inq., October 31, 1687, lib.1266, f.444.

14. AHN, Inq., April 27, 1692, lib.1266, f.505v.

15. Schroeder, *Canons and Decrees*, 95.

16. AHN, Inq., June 5, 1687, lib.1266, f.438v, "una mano obscena no es posible labar ni ser instrumento de limpieza."

17. AHN, Inq., February 26, 1684, lib.1266, f.482v.

18. AHN, Inq., February 26, 1684, lib.1266, f.485.

19. Bataillon, *Erasmo y España*, 332–333.

20. Kamen, *The Phoenix and the Flame*, 276–277.

21. Bataillon, *Erasmo y España*, 331–333.

22. AHN, Inq., September 13, 1585, leg.233, exp.7.

23. Dedieu, *L'Administration*, 59.

24. Nalle, *God in La Mancha*, 51–52.

25. Bilinkoff, *The Avila of Saint Teresa*, 30–31, 170–171.

26. AHN, Inq., May 14, 1614, leg.1712, exp.13. Fray Joseph Nuela was cited for solicitation when a formal visitation was carried out to his convent of San Francisco de Paula in the Mallorcan village of Campos.

27. Diez de Aux, *Compendio*, 81–82.

28. Henry Kamen, *Inquisition and Society*, 256–257. For the Valencia tribunal during the allied occupation, see Stephen Haliczer, *Inquisition and Society in the Kingdom of Valencia, 1478–1834* (Berkeley and Los Angeles: University of California Press, 1990), 330–331.

29. AHN, Inq., August 18, 1668, leg.1708, exp.13.

30. Jaime Contreras and Gustav Henningsen, "Forty Four Thousand Cases of the Spanish Inquisition," in Henningsen and John Tedeschi, eds., *The Inquisition in Early*

Modern Europe; Studies on Sources and Methods (DeKalb: Northern Illinois Press, 1986), 114–116.

31. Haliczer, *Inquisition and Society*, 325.

32. AHN, Inq., April 10, 1685, leg.1705, exp.20.

33. AHN, Inq., June 27, 1753, leg.227, exp.6.

34. AHN, Inq., May 11, 1784, leg.1827, exp.27. The case against Cames y Home was suspended by order of the Suprema on September 13, 1784, but he was eventually brought before the tribunal on a charge of solicitation on May 22, 1789, and on June 10, 1789, he confessed to almost all the charges against him.

35. AHN, Inq., June 27, 1753, leg.227, 6.

36. AHN, Inq. February 16, 1644, leg.563, exp.1.

37. Dedieu, *L'Adminsitration*, 210.

38. Haliczer, *Inquisition and Society*, 154–155.

39. Dedieu, *L'Administration*, 193.

40. Jaime Contreras, *El Santo Oficio de la Inquisición de Galicia: Poder, sociedad y cultura* (Madrid: Akal, 1982), 90–91, 142.

41. Henry Charles Lea, *A History of the Inquisition of Spain*, 4 vols. (New York: Macmillan, 1906–1907), 2: 273.

42. Haliczer, *Inquisition and Society*, 205. In Valencia, the commissioners replaced actual subtribunals. Dedieu, *L'Administration*, 205.

43. José Martínez Millán, "La burocracía del Santo Oficio en Valencia durante el siglo XVIII," *Miscelanea Comillas* 40, no. 77 (1982): 153.

44. Dedieu, *L'Administration*, 207–208.

45. Contreras, *El Santo Oficio*, 101.

46. Ibid.

47. AHN, Inq., March 15, 1695, leg.1825, exp.141.

48. AHN, Inq., July 20, 1676, leg.1712, exp.12.

49. AHN, Inq., March 20, 1695, leg.1825, exp.14.

50. Contreras, *El Santo Oficio*, 90, 102.

51. Ibid., 142.

52. Kamen, *Inquisition and Society*, 145.

53. During the last half of the sixteenth century, the inquisitors themselves were spurred to make formal visitations in their districts. Such visitations could turn up evidence of solicitation. AHN, Inq., leg.2022, exp.10, "Relación de la visita que en este año de 1580 a hecho por el districto el lic. Serrano Inquisidor de Murcia." This visitation turned up evidence against four solicitantes.

54. Lea, *A History of the Inquisition*, 2:92, 96–97.

55. Although solicitation was included in the Edict of Faith immediately after the Inquisition gained jurisdiction in 1561, the outcry among the clergy, which did not want to further imperil its reputation, led to its being dropped in 1571, but it was reinstated on March 2, 1576. Lea, *Sacerdotal Celibacy*, 501–502.

56. AHN, Inq., January 9, 1637, leg.1705, exp.12.

57. AHN, Inq., July 27, 1649, lib.1265, ff.360–361.

58. Machado de Chaves, *Perfecto confesor*, 2: 782.

59. AHN, Inq., March 31, 1583, leg.231, exp.9. Request by Fray Francisco López for permission to absolve a penitent whom he had sent to the Holy Office to give evidence in a solicitation case. He expressed the hope that license to absolve would arrive in time for his penitent to celebrate Lent.

60. AHN, Inq., September 23, 1586, leg.231, exp.9.

61. AHN, Inq., March 16, 1698, leg.1825, exp.14.

62. AHN, Inq., March 27, 1670, leg.1708, exp.34.

63. Antonio de Escobar y Mendoza, S.J., *Examen de confesores y práctica de penitentes* (Madrid: María de Quintana, 1650), 424.

64. AHN, Inq., December 12, 1679, March 24, 1680, leg.1710, exp.10.

65. AHN, Inq., August 30, 1741, leg.1764, exp.7.

66. AHN, Inq., December 10, 1688, leg.1712, exp.12.

67. AHN, Inq., August 25, 1688, leg.1708, exp.27.

68. AHN, Inq., March 29, 1689, leg.1712, exp.12.

69. AHN, Inq., February 28, 1688, leg.1709, exp.11.

70. AHN, Inq., June 5, 1632, ff.206–207v, "Libro de testificaciones del tribunal de Toledo."

71. AHN, Inq., May 21, 1759, leg.1714, exp.13.

72. Fray Antonio de Lorea, *David perseguido* (Madrid: Imprenta Real, 1675), 232.

73. AHN, Inq., June 23, 1625, lib.1259, ff.196–204.

74. Lea, *Sacerdotal Celibacy*, 504.

75. AHN, Inq., July 11, 1680, leg.1706, exp.15.

76. AHN, Inq., September 24, 1594, leg.231, exp.3.

77. Lea, *Sacerdotal Celibacy*, 504–505. For the text of the bull of August 30, 1622, see Machado de Chaves, *Perfecto confesor*, 2: 776.

78. AHN, Inq., April 1, 1759, leg.1706, exp.5.

79. See the letters from the Sicily tribunal to Inquisitor-General Andrés Pacheco. AHN, Inq., November 30, December 23, 1624, lib. 1269, ff.258–260. Apparently the Spanish ambassador had intervened at the Vatican to protect the exclusive competence of the Spanish tribunals.

80. AHN, Inq., October 14, 1737, leg.227, exp.7.

81. See Haliczer, *Inquisition and Society*, 296–297, 303, for examples of the way provincial tribunals tended to run ahead of the Suprema in exercising jurisdiction in disputed areas.

82. AHN, Inq., August 18, 1587, leg.231, exp.9.

83. AHN, Inq., December 17, 1602, leg.233, exp.9.

84. AHN, Inq., November 29, 1588, leg.231, exp.7.

85. AHN, Inq., August 7, 1576, leg.233, exp.6.

86. Fray Pedro de Ledesema, *Primera parte de la Summa en la cual se cifra y summa todo lo que pertenece a los sacramentos* (Salamanca: Viuda Antonio Ramírez, 1608), 296.

87. Lea, *Sacerdotal Celibacy*, 506–507.

88. AHN, Inq., February 16, 1682, leg.1712, exp.11.

89. AHN, Inq., May 20, 1768, leg.1714, exp.13.

90. AHN, Inq., September 13, 1721, leg.1715, exp.11. See Machado de Chaves, *Perfecto confesor*, 2: 778, for a discussion of this; and see AHN, Inq., May 6, 1688, leg.1711, exp.22, for an accused confessor's unsuccessful assertion of this point of view during his defense statement.

91. AHN, Inq., lib.1231, ff.367–369v, "carta de Fray Isidoro de Aliaga Arzobispo de Valencia a Fray Luis de Aliaga su hermano Inquisidor-General sobre conocimiento de solicitantes" (1620).

92. AHN, Inq., July 31, 1663, leg.1824, exp.13.

93. AHN, Inq., July 3–August 31, 1814, leg.561, exp.11.

94. AHN, Inq., April 3, 1582, leg.231, exp.4.

95. Lea, *Sacerdotal Celibacy*, 502. AHN, Inq., May 15, 1586, leg.1931, n.f.

96. AHN, Inq., August 12, 1591, lib.101, f.101.

97. AHN, Inq., September 8, 1591, lib.101, ffs.156–156v.

98. AHN, Inq., October 25, 1592, December 15, 1694, lib.101, ffs.230–230v, 704–704v.

99. Lea, *Sacerdotal Celibacy*, 502–504.

100. AHN, Inq., May 2, 1687, leg.1705, exp.20.

101. AHN, Inq., December 15, 1687, leg.1705, exp.20.

102. AHN, Inq., January 15, 1640, Libro de testificaciones, ff.123–124.

103. AHN, Inq., February 3, 1713, leg.230, exp.10.

104. AHN, Inq., October 26, 1713, leg.230, exp.10.

Chapter 4

1. AHN, Inq., April 20, 1697, leg.1713, exp.7.

2. AHN, Inq., March 4, 1732, leg.1825, exp.3.

3. AHN, Inq., April 5, 1625, leg.1705, exp.2.

4. AHN, Inq., February 25, 1681, leg.1712, exp.11.

5. AHN, Inq., January 11, 1706, leg.1825, exp.27.

6. In 1668 the Mallorca tribunal sent secretary Gabriel Fabregues to interview witnesses in Manacor, whose testimony had first been presented by familiar Jayme Nadal y Riera. AHN, Inq., April 18, 1668, leg.1708, exp.13. In the case of Fray Mateo González, the Canaries tribunal appointed the parish priest of La Guía as special commissioner to interview witnesses whose depositions had been previously presented by a Jesuit confessor. AHN, Inq., April 6, 1696, leg.1825, exp.24.

7. AHN, Inq., January 19, 1692, leg.1825, exp.1.

8. AHN, Inq., February 10–April 2, 1693, leg.1825, exp.1.

9. This stage of the proceeding was called the qualification and was carried out by four friars, two Dominicans and two Minims in the case of Fray Pablo Ginart. AHN, Inq., May 20, 1768, leg.1714, exp.13.

10. Jean-Pierre Dedieu, "L'Inquisition et le droit; analyse formelle de la procédure inquisitoriale en cause de foi," *Mélanges de la Casa de Velázquez* 33 (1987): 242.

11. AHN, Inq., August 23, 1694, leg.230, exp.14.

12. AHN, Inq., August 25, 1694, leg.229, exp.7.

13. Dedieu, *L'Administration*, 17.

14. AHN, Inq., September 13, 1676, leg.229, exp.7.

15. AHN, Inq., September 14, 1676, leg.229, exp.7. The unfortunate familiar was even briefly detained by the tribunal, but let go after being admonished to be more diligent in the future. September 15, 1676, leg.229, exp.7.

16. AHN, Inq., May 14, 1605, leg.1821, exp.7.

17. AHN, December 4, 1746, leg.1827, exp.7.

18. AHN, Inq., November 20, 1691, leg.1712, exp.8.

19. AHN, Inq., May 26–June 5, 1698, leg.228, exp.5.

20. AHN, Inq., October 8, 1787, leg.1828, exp.26.

21. Lea, *A History of the Inquisition*, 2: 534.

22. Kamen, *Inquisition and Society*, 171.

23. AHN, Inq., September 18, 1672, leg.1708, exp.34.

24. AHN, Inq., April 5, 1788, leg.1828, exp.26. The inquisitors insisted that he be treated as excommunicate during his trial and did not allow him to see anyone except the friar who had to nurse him.

25. AHN, Inq., February 27, 1756, leg.1827, exp.17.

26. AHN, Inq., February 10, 1691, leg.227, exp.8.

27. AHN, Inq., June 12, 1699, leg.227, exp.11.

28. AHN, Inq., March 15, 1681, leg.1706, exp.15.

29. AHN, Inq., October 1,1731, leg.1825, exp.30.

30. The importance of obtaining full biographical details was underscored by the Suprema when it admonished the inquisitors of the Toledo Tribunal for failing to do so in the case of Fray Juan Bautista de la Resurreción. AHN, Inq., June 25, 1699, leg.227, exp.11.

31. AHN, Inq., November 19, 1619, leg.1705, exp.3.

32. AHN, Inq., April 27, 1722, leg.1715, exp.11.

33. AHN, Inq., January 19, 1686, leg.1827, exp.20.

34. AHN, Inq., September 27, 1731, leg.1825, exp.30.

35. In the ordinary criminal courts, the accused had his choice of local attorneys to represent him. For a discussion of the role of these procuradores, see María Paz Alonso Romero, *El proceso penal en castilla siglo XIII–XVIII* (Salamanca: Ediciones Universidad de Salamanca, 1982), 143–145. During its early years, the Inquisition did not always provide the accused with a defense attorney, and they were frequently required to conduct their own defense. See the case of Antonio de Pareja, AHN, Inq., October 10, 1531, leg.231, exp.11.

36. In the Valencia tribunal, the defense was always carried on by calificadores who were normally of the same religious order as the accused. AHN, Inq., n.d. leg.503, exp.7, ffs. 95v–97.

37. Dedieu, "L'Inquisition et le droit," 244.

38. AHN, Inq., September 5, 1707, leg.230, exp.44.

39. AHN, Inq., October 30, 1686, leg.1827, exp.20. The Suprema took until March 3, 1687, to hand down a final verdict.

40. AHN, Inq., July 11, 1689, leg.1712, exp.12.

41. In the case of Fray Francisco del Rosario defense attorney Marcos Sánchez declared that his guilt had been demonstrated with "written and oral proofs." AHN, Inq., July 6, 1691, leg.1825, exp.16.

42. AHN, Inq., June 21, 1623, leg.1712, exp.15.

43. AHN, Inq., January 10, 1689, leg.1711, exp.22.

44. For the defense statement, see AHN, Inq., August 17, 1693; for the final sentence, see August 25, 1693, leg.1712, exp.8.

45. AHN, Inq., October 26, 1722, leg.1715, exp.10.

46. AHN, Inq., May 22, 1722, leg.1715, exp.11.

47. AHN, Inq., October 30, 1688, leg.1711, exp.22.

48. Tentler, *Sin and Confession*, 99–100.

49. AHN, Inq., May 22, 1722, leg.1715, exp.11.

50. AHN, Inq., October 30, 1688, leg.1711, exp.22.

51. Lea, *A History of the Inquisition*, 2: 539–540. That prosecuting attorneys were under no such constraints is demonstrated by the case of Fray Alonso Pastor, whose defense attorney attempted to get the two chief prosecution witnesses disqualified because they were both former prostitutes. The Mallorca tribunal, to which this petition was addressed, ignored it completely, and Pastor was found guilty.

52. AHN, September 18, 1718, leg.1826, exp.2.

53. AHN, Inq., September 27, 1718, leg.1826, exp.2. According to this document, Nájera was even told that he could not use "intimates or close friends." This would seem to exclude the twelve Franciscan friars that he also presented as defense witnesses.

54. AHN, Inq., March 9, 1594, leg.231, exp.3.

55. AHN, Inq., August 13, 1594, leg.231, exp.3.

56. AHN, Inq., April 22, 1626, leg.1821, exp.12.

57. AHN, Inq., November 15, 1698, leg.228, exp.5.

58. AHN, Inq., March 3, 1692, leg.228, exp.13.

59. For testimony taken in Cuenca, see AHN, Inq., November 18–27, 1694, leg.228, exp.13; for the Suprema's final determination, see February 26, 1695, leg.228, exp.13.

60. Out of 223 cases, only 11 recorded split votes.

61. AHN, Inq., May 27, 1620, leg.229, exp.8.

62. AHN, Inq., October 13, 1667, lib.1266.

63. AHN, Inq., November 7, 1589, leg.228, exp.9.

64. This happened with the tribunal of Toledo at the trial of Fray Manuel de Peraleja. AHN, Inq., August 21, 1758, leg.231, exp.14.

65. See the case of Sebastián de Hontora, where the Suprema increased the period of reclusion from two years to ten and added the humiliation of a circular scourging by the friars of his order. AHN, Inq., October 30, 1582, leg.321, exp.4.

66. AHN, Inq., March 3, 1687, leg.1827, exp.20.

67. AHN, Inq., June 5, 1687, lib.1266, f.444v.

68. AHN, Inq., July 20, 1756, leg.1827, exp.17. The letter goes on to explain that friars who cannot in some way serve the public are denied habits and are not even given enough to eat. The Suprema refused this request.

69. AHN, Inq., August 12, 1676, leg.230, exp.7.

70. AHN, Inq., October 3, 1699, leg.228, exp.5.

71. AHN, Inq., June 15, 1591, leg.233, exp.6. The Suprema did agree to grant this request. The Suprema did the same thing for Fray Manuel de Peraleja on the request of the warden of the Franciscan convent of San Pedro de Alcántara. AHN, Inq., May 7, 1790, leg.231, exp.14.

72. AHN, Inq., December 12, 1690, leg.229, exp.8.

73. AHN, Inq., April 11, 1587, leg.231, exp.9, "inventario de los bienes de D. Gabriel de Osca."

74. For Osca's frantic efforts to gain permission to sell his property, see AHN, Inq., November 20, 1587, leg.231, exp.9.

75. AHN, Inq., June 12, 1789, leg.231, exp.9.

76. AHN, Inq., January 30, 1677, leg.229, exp.7, Circular discipline was administered to Fray Juan Girón in the Franciscan convent of San Juan de los Reyes.

77. AHN, Inq., August 9, 1594, leg.228, exp.3.

78. AHN, Inq., January 26, 1598, October 23, 1601, leg.228, exp.3.

79. Only 4% of those sentenced to confinement in a convent saw their terms reduced, and only 2% were allowed to resume hearing confessions even on a limited basis.

80. AHN, Inq., February 8, 1638, leg.1705, exp.12.

81. AHN, Inq., August 29, 1679, leg.1708, exp.36.

Chapter 5

1. J. H. Elliott, *Imperial Spain 1469–1716* (New York: New American Library, 1963), 363; Téofanes Egido, "La expulsión de los jesuitas de España," in García-Villoslada, *Historia de la Iglesia*, 4: 756.

2. Lea, *A History of the Inquisition*, 4: 136.

3. Evennett, *Spirit of the Counter-Reformation*, 76–83.

4. A labrador imprisoned by the Holy Office in 1567 told his cellmate that "I would rather be the curate of a village than its Señor because the villagers do whatever the curate tells them, while if we fail to confess with them, God will never pardon our sins." AHN, Inq., December 18, 1567, leg.109, exp.1.

5. See the legislation passed at the synod of June 12, 1644, in Guitarte Izquierdo, *Sínodos postridentinos*, 99.

6. In 1791 a young married woman from the village of Moralzarzal in the foothills of the Sierra de Guadarrama accused José de la Virgen, the "limosnero" ("almoner") of a Mercedarian convent of soliciting her while he was in the village begging alms for his order. AHN, Inq., June 13, 1791, leg.233, exp.10.

7. Kamen, *The Phoenix and the Flame*, 162.

8. Felipe Ruiz Martín, "Demografía eclesiástica," in Vaquero et al., *Diccionario de historia eclesiástica;* and Anne Molinié-Bertrand, "Le clergé dans le Royaume de Castille à la fin du XVI siècle," *Revue d'histoire économique et sociale* 51, no. 1: 62–78.

9. Juan Sáez Marín, *Datos sobre la Iglesia española contemporánea* (Madrid: Editorial Nacional, 1975).

10. Antonio Domínguez Ortiz, "Aspectos sociales de la vida eclesiástica en los siglos XVII y XVIII," in García-Villoslada, *Historia de la Iglesia*, 4: 37.

11. AHN, Inq., February 18, 1786, leg.1827, exp.31. The benefice was described by a local observer as "rough and unpleasant" with substantial liens against its income. About a year after his appointment, Estrada had to be removed by the bishop because of complaints about his lewd behavior.

12. AHN, Inq., August 7, 1604, leg.1821, exp.8.

13. Domínguez Ortiz, "Aspectos sociales," 20, 23, 50.

14. Ibid., 20–21.

15. AHN, Inq., January 25, 1651, July 1, 1651, leg.229, exp.11.

16. AHN, Inq., November 14, 1686, lib.1266, ffs. 499v–500.

17. Lea, *Sacerdotal Celibacy*, 526.

18. Domínguez Ortiz, "Aspectos sociales," 55.

19. Testimony by defense witness Simón Martín. AHN, Inq., July 4, 1692, leg.1825, exp.3.

20. In his report to the Suprema, Salazar Frías noted the "pocas letras" (relative ignorance) of so many parish priests in the region and pointed out that the local bishop had recently canceled many confessor's licenses because of the involvement of so many local curates in the witch craze. AHN, Inq., January 28, 1617, leg.1679, exp.2.

21. The anonymous author of a 1689 admonition to a Jesuit solicitante noted that "the nature of certain sins and the eagerness and persistence of certain penitents made the missionaries almost indispensable." AHN, Inq., April 1, 1689, lib.1266, f.87.

22. Joël Saugnieux, *Les jansénistes et le renouveau de la prédication dans l'Espagne de la seconde moitié du XVIIIe siècle* (Lyon: Presses Universitaires de Lyon, 1976), 139–142.

23. Domínguez Ortiz, "Aspectos sociales," 18, 55.

24. Schroeder, *Canons and Decrees*, 224.

25. Ibid., 220–221. In the mid seventeenth century, Philip IV took a special interest in enforcing strict enclosure and attempted to prevent nuns from having contact with anyone but their closest relatives. Domínguez Ortiz, "Aspectos sociales," 44.

26. Villegas, *La esposa*, 588–589, 593–594.

27. Alonso de Andrade, *Libro de guía de la virtud y de la imitación de Nuestra Señora*, 3 vols. (Madrid: Francisco Moroto, 1644), 2: 231–235.

28. AHN, Inq., testimony of Sor Ana de San Miguel, June 29, 1607, leg.233, exp.9.

29. AHN, Inq., August 26, 1603, leg.233, exp.9.

30. AHN, Inq., October 23, 1761, leg.230, exp.3.

31. For the evolution of the Inquisition's attitude toward witchcraft accusations, see Gustav Henningsen, *The Witches' Advocate; Basque Witchcraft and the Spanish Inquisition* (Reno: University of Nevada Press, 1980). However, Henry Kamen is correct in pointing out that witchcraft trials continued in other criminal courts, which freely handed down death sentences. Kamen, *Inquisition and Society*, 214–215.

32. For a brief account of this case, see Marcelino Menéndez y Pelayo, *Historia de los heterodoxos españoles*, 4 vols. (Buenos Aires: Perlado, 1945), 3: 175–176.

33. Lea, *A History of the Inquisition*, 2: 170–171.

34. AHN, Inq., May 11, 1731, leg.1825, exp.30.

35. AHN, Inq., June 18, 1622, leg.1712, exp.15.

36. AHN, Inq., May 15, 1694, leg.1825, exp.21.

37. AHN, Inq., June 30, 1584, leg.233, exp.1.

38. AHN, Inq., November 18, 1747, leg.1827, exp.2.

39. Juan Maldonado *Pastor bonus* in *Opuscula quaedam* (Burgos: Juan de Junta, 1549), fols. cvi–c viii vo., as quoted in Bataillon, *Erasmo y España*, 332–333.

40. AHN, Inq., June 5, 1580, leg.233, exp.7.

41. After he was sentenced, the tribunal refunded him 939 reales. AHN, Inq., December 20, 1670, leg.231, exp.5.

42. AHN, Inq., May 2, 1782, leg.1825, exp.25.

43. AHN, Inq., April 14, 1682, leg.228, exp.6.

44. AHN, Inq., November 2, 1681, leg.228, exp.6.

45. AHN, Inq., August 30, 1663, leg.230, exp.7.

46. AHN, Inq., May 10, 1731, leg.1825, exp.30.

47. Domínguez Ortiz, "Aspectos sociales," 28.

48. AHN, Inq., April 18, 1587, leg.231, exp.9.

49. AHN, Inq., April 10, 1712, leg.1826, exp.6.

50. AHN, Inq., September 28, 1643, leg.1708, exp.36.

51. AHN, Inq., June 20, 1586, leg.229, exp.1.

52. See discussion of Jacome Compana in Chapter 4.

53. AHN, Inq., April 19, 1621, leg.1712, exp.21.

54. The breviary was the only book that Fray Juan Baptista de la Resurreción brought with him when he arrived at the Toledo tribunal. AHN, Inq., February 12, 1699, leg.227, exp.11. Shortly after being incarcerated, Fray Juan de la Olmeda asked the inquisitors, as a special favor, if they would have his breviary sent to him from his convent. AHN, Inq., March 30, 1594, leg.231, exp.3.

55. For the inventory of the library owned by Tomás Matos, see AHN, Inq., May 2, 1782, leg.1828, exp.25. For the books sequestered from Cames y Home, see AHN, Inq., June 14, 1790, leg.1827, exp.27.

56. Gallo was hailed by contemporaries as the leading light of the movement to reform preaching. For a discussion of Gallo's career, see Saugnieux, *Les jansénistes*, 149–156.

57. This positive assessment came from lic. Simón Martín, another priest living in the village who had considerable opportunity to observe Vello at work. AHN, Inq., July 4, 1692, leg.1825, exp.3.

58. Mateo Fernández Vello may have been alluding to this relationship when he told María that "since she made love to other men, she could love him as well." AHN, Inq., April 9, 1688, leg.1825, exp.1.

59. AHN, Inq., December 17, 1691, leg.1825, exp.1.

60. AHN, Inq., January 10, 1688, leg.1827, exp.20.

61. See the case of the Trinitarian Pedro Fiol. AHN, Inq., November 13, 1619, leg.1705, exp.3.

62. As the Franciscan Fray Gaspar de Nájera commented ruefully when asked about this by the inquisitors of the Canaries tribunal, the superiors of his order "no han de decir los motivos que tiene para mudar sus frailes" ("do not have to state their reasons for transferring their friars"). AHN, Inq., April 19, 1719, leg.1826, exp.2.

63. AHN, Inq., September 18, 1694, leg.230, exp.14.

64. Angel García Sanz, *Desarrollo y crisis del antiguo régimen en Castilla la Vieja* (Madrid: Akal, 1977), 82–83.

65. AHN, Inq., November 19, 1699, leg.1825, exp.24.

66. AHN, Inq., June 17, 1602, leg.233, exp.3.

67. AHN, Inq., May 26, 1698, leg.228, exp.5.

68. AHN, Inq., March 5, 1690, leg.229, exp.8.

69. The very low (by modern standards) life expectancy at birth should not be allowed to obscure the fact that early modern Europe did contain numerous middle aged and older persons. Of the 133 soliciting confessors whose ages are recorded, 115 (86%) were aged between 31 and 60, while 16 (12%) were 60 or above. In Venice between 1610 and 1620, 35% of the population was between 30 and 59 and 12.9% over 60. Henry Kamen, *European Society 1500–1700* (London: Hutchinson, 1986), 26.

70. Ruth B. Weg, "Sensuality/Sexuality of the Middle Years," in Ski Hunter and Martin Sundel, eds., *Midlife Myths, Issues, Findings and Practice Implications* (Newbury Park, CA: Sage, 1989), 47.

71. C. G. Jung first identified "stock taking" as part of the individual's process of turning inward as he approaches middle age. C. G. Jung, *Marriage as Psychological Relationship*. In vol. 17, *The Development of Personality*, of *Collected Works*, (New York: Pantheon, 1954), 331. As quoted in David A. Chiriboga, "Mental Health at the Midpoint: Crisis, Challenge or Relief," in Hunter and Sundel, *Midlife Myths*, 121.

72. Norma Haan, "Personality at Midlife," in Hunter and Sundel, *Midlife Myths*, 161.

73. The first instance occurred in 1738. Carrascosa lost his confessor's license for brief periods on both occasions, but when it was restored the second time, he had lost the right to hear the confessions of women. AHN, Inq., October 24, 1749, leg.1827, exp.10.

74. AHN, Inq., July 24, 1804, leg.1827, exp.31.

75. AHN, Inq., May 14, 1614, leg.1712, exp.3.

76. AHN, Inq., October 10, 1716, leg.1826, exp.2.

77. Isabel Vélez testified that Arvelo would tell her "all her sins, both the ones she could remember as well as those she was unaware of." AHN, Inq., May 27, 1782, leg.1828, exp.15.

78. AHN, Inq., February 28, 1784, leg.1825, exp.15.

79. Lea, *Sacerdotal Celibacy*, 499; Tentler, *Sin and Confession*, 82–83.

80. AHN, Inq., April 20–May 2, 1687, leg.1705, exp.20.

81. AHN, Inq., March 19, 1639, leg.229, exp.9.

82. AHN, Inq., September 3, 1689, leg.227, exp.9.

83. AHN, Inq., April 6, 1676, leg.229, exp.7.

84. AHN, Inq., October 2, 1710, leg.1825, exp.32.

85. AHN, Inq., July 21, 1677, leg.228, exp.15.

86. AHN, Inq., November 10, 1677, leg.228, exp.15.

87. AHN, Inq., leg.1822, exp.20, "Constituciones propias del convento de San Illdefonso de monjas Bernardas en la ciudad de Las Palmas año de 1638."

88. AHN, Inq., June 25, 1706, leg.228, exp.8.

89. AHN, Inq., September 23, 1586, October 14, 1586, leg.231, exp.9.

90. AHN, Inq., April 20, 1684, leg.1708, exp.32.

91. AHN, Inq., March 26, 1722, leg.1715, exp.10.

92. AHN, Inq., June 15, 1717, leg.1715, exp.11.

93. AHN, Inq., April 12, 1802, leg.562, exp.5.

94. AHN, Inq., March 24, 1781, leg.233, exp.11.

95. Delumeau, *Le Catholicisme*, 271.

96. The literature on the concept of social stressors and their impact on the individual is discussed in Chiriboga, "Mental Health," in Hunter and Sundel, *Midlife Myths*, 130–139.

Chapter 6

1. Princess Margarita of Austria first summoned Fray Simón de Rojas to the Descalzas Reales without revealing her name. Arcos, *Simón de Rojas*, 188. For Saint Teresa's aristocratic supporters, see *The Letters of Saint Teresa of Jesus*, trans. and ed. E. Allison Peers, 2 vols. (London: Burns, Oates and Washburn, 1951), 1: 99, 104, 125.

2. AHN, Inq., October 29, 1650, leg.229, exp.11.

3. AHN, Inq., February 25, 1681, leg.1712, exp.11, and July 2, 1693, exp.11.

4. AHN, Inq., July 3, 1671, leg.562, exp.11.

5. AHN, Inq., April 6, 1676, leg.229, exp.7.

6. Antonio Domínguez Ortiz, *Sociedad y estado en el siglo XVIII español* (Madrid: Seix y Barral, 1976), 387.

7. Fairchilds estimates that in early modern France, servants, both male and female, might have comprised 15% of the population of Paris and perhaps 8% at Bordeaux, while in rural areas servants comprised anywhere from 2 to 12% of the population. There exists no comparable study of servants for old regime Spain. Cissie Fairchilds, *Domestic Enemies: Servants and Their Masters in Old Regime France* (Baltimore: Johns Hopkins University Press, 1984), 1–2.

8. AHN, Inq., July 4, 1706, leg.1825, exp.30.

9. Domínguez Ortiz, *Sociedad y Estado*, 403.

10. AHN, Inq., February 28, 1758, leg.232, exp.4.

11. AHN, Inq., May 16, 1619, leg.1705, exp.3.

12. AHN, Inq., October 13, 1716, leg.1826, exp.2.

13. Lea, *A History of the Inquisition*, 4: 100.

14. AHN, Inq., June 3, 1762, leg.230, exp.11.

15. Julian Pitt-Rivers, *The Fate of Shechem or the Politics of Sex: Essays in the Anthropology of the Mediterranean* (Cambridge: Cambridge University Press, 1977), 29.

16. Pedro Galindo, *Excelencias de la castidad y virginidad*, 2 vols. (Madrid: Mateo de Espinosa y Arteaga, 1681), 2: 10, 21, 41.

17. AHN, Inq., May 19, 1696, leg.1825, exp.24. When asked by the commissioner why she waited so long, she said that as a single woman she "lived in extreme retirement and was entirely obedient to the will of her parents," who were so restrictive that they would not even allow her to visit the village alone.

18. AHN, Inq., January 17, 1726, leg.562, exp.7.

19. Rafael Carrasco, *Inquisición y represión sexual en Valencia; Historia de los sodomitas* (Barcelona: Laertes, 1985), 171–172.

20. Ibid., 134–135.

21. Ibid., 140–141.

22. Ibid., 178–179.

23. AHN, Inq., December 5, 1795, leg.230, exp.77.

24. AHN, Inq., July 17, 1674, leg.231, exp.15.

25. Fray Luis de León, *La perfecta casada* (1583; reprint, Barcelona: Ediciones Hysma, 1953), 38–39, 242, 245.

26. AHN, Inq., "relación de causes del año de 1635," leg.1952, exp.41, ffs.7–8.

27. Galindo, *Parte segundo del directorio*, 160.

28. Diego Pérez de Valdivia, *Aviso de gente recogida* (1585; reprint, Madrid: Fundación Universitaria Española, 1977), 161.

29. Jodi Bilinkoff, "The Holy Woman and the Urban Community in Sixteenth Century Avila," in Barbara Harris and JoAnn McNamara, eds., *Women and the Structure of Society* (Durham, NC: Duke University Press, 1984), 78–79.

30. Pérez de Valdivia, *Aviso*, 119.

31. Ibid., 231.

32. Ibid., 355.

33. Mariló Vigil, *La vida de las mujeres en los siglos XVI y XVII* (Madrid: Siglo XXI, 1986), 46–49.

34. Peers, *The Letters of Saint Teresa*, 1: 47, 102.

35. María del Rosario had been a nuns' servant for seventeen years and María de Villareal had been a maid of all work in the Augustinian convent of Santa Ursula in Toledo for twenty-four. AHN, Inq., March 5, 1750, leg.1827, exp.11, April 12, 1697, leg.228, exp.12.

36. AHN, Inq., November 12, 1688, leg.1705, exp.5.

37. See the case of Isabel Carion, a literate, upper-class woman whose penchant for devotional books was fed by her confessor, Francisco Bernad. AHN, Inq., October 17, 1780, leg.227, exp.12.

38. See Chapter 2 for the high incidence of frequent confession among victims.

39. AHN, Inq., May 11, 1691, leg.1709, exp.11.

40. Pérez de Valdivia, *Aviso*, 395–396.

41. The tribunal had evidence that she had been solicited from other witnesses with whom she had discussed the matter. AHN, Inq., December 17, 1767, leg.1714, exp.13.

42. AHN, Inq., April 29, 1687, leg.1712, exp.12.

43. Galindo, *Parte segundo del directorio*, 13.

44. Ibid., 541, 543.

45. Ibid., 501–502.

46. Donald Weinstein and Rudolph M. Bell, *Saints and Society: The Two Worlds of Western Christendom, 1000–1700* (Chicago and London: University of Chicago Press, 1982), 238–241.

47. Pérez de Valdivia, *Aviso*, 238–241.

48. AHN, Inq., March 29, 1819, leg.563, exp.8.

49. AHN, Inq., March 15, 1770, August 18, 1785, leg.1827, exp.3.

50. AHN, Inq., June 18, 1783, leg.1827, exp.27.

51. Peers, *The Letters of Saint Teresa*, 1:159.

52. Ibid., 133.

53. Ibid., 138–139.
54. Vigil, *La vida de las mujeres,* 235–236.
55. AHN, Inq., September 6, 1670, leg.231, exp.5.
56. Vigil, *La vida de las mujeres,* 244.
57. Andrade, *Libro de la guía,* 2: 621; quoted in Vigil, *La vida de las mujeres,* 246.
58. AHN, Inq., June 9, 1604, leg.1821, exp.7.
59. AHN, Inq., March 10, 1746, leg.1827, exp.7.
60. AHN, Inq., August 1, 1584, leg.233, exp.6.
61. Vigil, *La vida de las mujeres,* 148.
62. AHN, Inq., March 24, 1680, leg.1706, exp.15.
63. AHN, Inq., April 20, 1768, leg.1714, exp.13.
64. AHN, Inq., August 25, 1688, leg.1711, exp.22.
65. AHN, Inq., leg.1708, exp.28 (n.d.).
66. AHN, Inq., June 13, 1589, leg.231, exp.7.
67. AHN, Inq., August 24, 1764, leg.564, exp.13.
68. AHN, Inq., September 15, 1604, leg.1821, exp.9. Alonso de Castro, Francisca de Jesús' regular confessor may well have been Pedro de Castro's relative not only because they had the same last name but because they were in the same convent. Alonso de Castro's reluctance to see that Pedro was denounced to the Holy Office would seem to indicate an unusual sympathy with him since, as a reader in theology, Alonso could hardly plead ignorance of his obligation to force his penitent to make a deposition by denying her absolution.
69. AHN, Inq., August 1, 1661, leg.1824, exp.10.
70. AHN, Inq., January 26, 1706, leg.1825, exp.24.
71. AHN, Inq., July 24, 1662, leg.1708, exp.18.
72. AHN, Inq., September 23, 1583, leg.231, exp.9.
73. AHN, Inq., August 22, 1629, leg.230, exp.4.
74. AHN, Inq., May 19, 1696, leg.1825, exp.24.
75. AHN, Inq., May 3, 1707, leg.1826, exp.4.

Chapter 7

1. AHN, Inq., November 23, 1635, "Libro de testimonios del tribunal de Toledo."
2. Juan Luis Vives, *Libro llamado instrucción de la mujer cristiana,* Juan Justiniano, trans. (1524; reprint, Madrid: Signo, 1936), 85–86.
3. Andrade, *Libro de la guía de la virtud,* 212.
4. Kamen, *The Phoenix and the Flame,* 299.
5. AHN, Inq., July 26, 1585, leg.231, exp. 7.
6. Galindo, *Excelencias de la castidad,* 25.
7. Ibid., ffs. 5–8v.
8. AHN, Inq., June 21, 1690, leg.564, exp.21.
9. AHN, Inq., April 1, 1636, leg.1705, exp.12.
10. Luis de León, "Avisación a Doña María Pacheco, condesa de Benavente," in *Biblioteca de Autores Españoles,* t. XVI, p. 97, in Joseph Pérez, "La femme et l'amour dans l'Espagne du XVIe siècle," in Augustín Redondo, ed., *Amours légitimes, amours illégitimes en Espagne XVI–XVII siècles* (Paris: Publications de la Sorbonne, 1985), 25.
11. AHN, Inq., December 14, 1622, leg.1705, f. 5. For Isabel Riera, see Chapter 7.
12. AHN, Inq., December 14, 1622, leg.1705, f. 5.
13. Ibid., ffs. 7v–8.

.. AHN, Inq., October 31, 1785, leg.1827, exp.31.

15. Ricardo García Cárcel, "El fracaso matrimonial en la Cataluña del Antiguo égimen," in Redondo, *Amours légitimes, amours illégitimes,* 132.

16. Luis de León, *La perfecta casada,* 89–90.

17. Vives, *Instrucción de la mujer cristiana,* 121–123.

18. Luis de León, *La perfecta casada,* 67.

19. Vicente Pérez Moreda, *Las crisis de mortalidad en la España interior* (Madrid: Siglo Veintiuno de España, 1980), 164.

20. Vives, *Instrucción de la mujer cristiana,* 135–136, 143–144.

21. AHN, Inq., June 3, 1798, leg.564, exp.5.

22. AHN, Inq., December 10, 1795, leg.564, exp.15.

23. AHN, Inq., May 31, 1686, leg.1811, exp.5.

24. AHN, Inq., December 8, 1619, leg.1705, exp.3.

25. AHN, Inq., September 3, 1746, leg.1827, exp.2.

26. James A. Brundage, *Law, Sex, and Christian Society in Medieval Europe* (Chicago and London: University of Chicago Press, 1987), 90–91.

27. Tentler, *Sin and Confession,* 176.

28. AHN, Inq., leg.1952, exp.4B, "Relación de la visita que a hecho el inquisidor Fernando Martínez este año de 1585."

29. Brundage, *Law, Sex, and Christian Society,* 566–567.

30. Vives, *Instrucción de la mujer cristiana,* 118.

31. Pedro de Luxán, *Coloquios Matrimoniales* (Madrid: Atlas, 1943), 21 in Vigil, *La vida de las mujeres,* 100.

32. AHN, Inq., November 28, 1713, leg.230, exp.10.

33. AHN, Inq., November 29, 1713, leg.230, exp.10.

34. Vives, *Instrucción de la mujer cristiana,* 153.

35. Brundage, *Law, Sex, and Christian Society,* 97–98.

36. Galindo, *Excelencias de la castidad,* 26–26v, 29v.

37. In Catalonia widows lost substantial property rights if they remarried. Kamen, *The Phoenix and the Flame,* 314.

38. AHN, Inq., September 25, 1621, leg.1712, exp.15.

39. Jean-Louis Flandrin, *Families in Former Times: Kinship, Household and Sexuality,* Richard Southern, trans. (Cambridge: Cambridge University Press, 1985), 184–185.

40. AHN, Inq., September 3, 1721, leg.1715, exp.11.

41. Flandrin, *Families,* 183–184.

42. AHN, Inq., August 7, 1725, leg.1827, exp.10.

43. AHN, Inq., December 6, 12, 1746, leg.1827, exp.7.

44. AHN, Inq., January 9, 1722, leg.564, exp.1.

45. AHN, Inq., October 15, 1749, leg.1827, exp.11.

46. AHN, Inq., October 11–14, 1690, leg.1709, exp.11. Serre was sentenced on September 6, 1692.

47. For fees paid to friars who preached on important occasions, see Hilary Dansey Smith, *Preaching in the Spanish Golden Age* (Oxford: Oxford University Press, 1978), 21.

48. AHN, Inq., May 19, 1621, leg.1712, exp.21.

49. AHN, Inq., April 10, 1674, leg.1821, exp.11.

50. AHN, Inq., December 9, 1619, leg.1705, exp.3.

51. She admitted this in her spontaneous confession before the Toledo tribunal. AHN, Inq., June 26, 1691, leg.228, exp.13. Although Contreras was able to defend

himself successfully, he was only able to undermine the testimony of the first two witnesses against him and never able to convince the inquisitors that Francisca de Cabreros was lying.

52. AHN, Inq., December 28, 1747, leg.228, exp.16.

53. AHN, Inq., June 17, 1625, leg.1705, exp.2.

54. For the role of clergy in education during the post-Tridentine period, see Paul F. Grendler, "Schools, Seminaries and Catechetical Instruction," in O'Malley, *Catholicism*, 315–326.

55. AHN, Inq., December 30, 1687, leg.1705, exp.20.

56. AHN, Inq., January 22, 1758, leg.231, exp.14.

57. Francisco Pacheco, *Libro de descripción de verdaderos retratos de illustres y memorables varones* (Seville: 1599; reproduction in photochromotype, 1881–1885), quoted in Dansey Smith, *Preaching*, 6.

58. Ibid.

59. AHN, Inq., August 26, 1698, leg.228, exp.5.

60. AHN, Inq., July 5, 1691, leg.1709, exp.11.

61. For an article addressing contemporary concerns about sexual abuse of patients by psychiatrists, see Melinda Beck, Karen Springen, and Donna Foote, "Sex and Psychotherapy," *Newsweek*, 13 April 1992, 53, 54.

62. Freud discusses the negative implications for the therapist-patient relationship in "Further Recommendations in the Technique of Psycho-Analysis: Observations on Transference-Love," in Ernest Jones, ed., *Sigmund Freud, Collected Papers* (New York: Basic Books, 1959), 384–385, 390.

63. Judith Herman, Nanette Gartrell, Silvia Olarte, Michael Feldstein, and Russell Localio, "Psychiatrist-Patient Sexual Contact: Results of a National Survey, II: Psychiatrists' Attitudes," *American Journal of Psychiatry* 144, no. 2. (February 1987): 168.

64. AHN, Inq., December 7, 1802, leg.1867, exp.9.

65. Antonia Bastarda, one of Serre's penitents, commented that even after he began touching her sexual parts during exorcism she remained unconcerned because "she could not persuade herself that such a virtuous person could have any evil intentions." AHN, Inq., May 10, 1691, leg.1709, exp.11.

66. According to J. Herman and her colleagues, "repeat offenders were particularly likely to believe in the therapeutic value of sexual relations with patients." J. Herman et al., "Psychiatrist-Patient Sexual Contact," 166.

67. Serre appeared before the Mallorca tribunal at his own request. AHN, Inq., March 15, 1688, leg.1709, exp.11.

68. Machado de Chaves, *Perfecto confesor*, 2: 792.

69. Lindsey Tanner, "Sex Abuse Scandals Rock the Roman Catholic Church," *The Northern Star*, 20 March 1992, 5.

70. Nanette Gartrell, Judith Herman, Silvia Olarte, Michael Feldstein, and Russell Localio, "Psychiatrist-Patient Sexual Contact: Results of a National Survey, I: Prevalence,"*American Journal of Psychiatry* 143, no. 9. (September 1986): 1128.

71. AHN, Inq., July 26, 1706, September 10, 1712, leg.1826, exp.32.

72. AHN, Inq., February 5, 1693, leg.1825, exp.1.

73. AHN, Inq., November 3, 1696, leg.1825, exp.18.

74. AHN, Inq., July 16, 1729, leg.1825, exp.30. During his fifth audience on September 27, 1731, Quijada del Castillo used the fact that some of the witnesses against him were personal enemies to impugn their motives, blaming his trial on a conspiracy against him and his family.

75. AHN, Inq., September 2, 1625, leg.1705, exp.2.

76. AHN, Inq., October 13, 1690, leg.1709, exp.11.

77. AHN, Inq., January 29, 1692, leg.1708, exp.27.

78. Perry, *Gender and Disorder*, 83–84.

79. Haliczer, *Inquisition and Society*, 278.

80. AHN, Inq., November 5, 1688, leg.1705, exp.5. The order had come directly from the Suprema and was dated May 23, 1688.

81. AHN, Inq., March 6, 1688, leg.1825, exp.15.

82. AHN, Inq., January 8, 1688, leg.1825, exp.15.

83. AHN, Inq., leg.1712, exp.11.

84. AHN, Inq., August 4, 1604, leg.1821, exp.9.

85. Kamen, *European Society*, 109.

86. Perry, *Gender and Disorder*, 91.

87. AHN, Inq., leg.1822, exp.20, "Constituciones propias del convento de San Illdefonso de monjas Bernardas en la ciudad de Las Palmas," (n.d.).

88. Peers, *The Letters of Saint Teresa*, 1: 249.

89. AHN, Inq., July 24, 1680, leg.228, exp.15.

90. Perry, *Gender and Disorder*, 85.

91. AHN, Inq., June 23, 1715, leg.1826, exp.10.

92. AHN, Inq., December 7, 1622, leg.1705, exp.5.

93. Kathryn Norberg, "The Counter-Reformation and Women Religious and Lay," in O'Malley, *Catholicism*, 135.

94. Elizabeth Rapley, *The Dévotes; Women and the Church in Seventeenth-Century France* (Montreal and Kingston: McGill-Queen's University Press, 1990), 38–39.

95. Norberg, "The Counter-Reformation and Women," in O'Malley, *Catholicism*, 135–136.

96. AHN, Inq., October 19, 1582, leg.231, exp.4.

Chapter 8

1. Jonathan Brown, *Images and Ideas in Seventeenth-Century Spanish Painting* (Princeton: Princeton University Press, 1978), 56, 72.

2. For collective rape in fifteenth-century France, see Jacques Rossiaud, "Prostitution, Youth and Society in the Towns of Southeastern France in the Fifteenth Century," in Robert Forster and Orest Ranum, eds., *Deviants and the Abandoned in French Society* (Baltimore: John's Hopkins University Press, 1978), 1–46.

3. Jean-Louis Flandrin, *Le sexe et l'occident* (Paris: Éditions du Seuil, 1981). See the discussion of the easy acceptance of prostitution during the fifteenth century in Jacques Rossiaud, "Prostitution, Sex and Society in French Towns in the Fifteenth Century," in Philippe Ariès and André Béjin, eds., *Western Sexuality: Practice and Precept in Past and Present Times*, (Oxford: Basil Blackwell, 1985), 76–82. This all came to an end by the mid sixteenth century, see pp. 92–94.

4. Perry, *Gender and Disorder*, 139.

5. Ibid., 150.

6. Nalle, *God in La Mancha*, 66–67.

7. Dedieu, *L'Administration*, 300–301.

8. Kamen, *The Phoenix and the Flame*, 282–283.

9. Flandrin, *Le sexe*, 93. For such practices in rural Bavaria and East Friesland, see Hsia, *Social Discipline in the Reformation*, 149–150.

10. Azpilcueta Navarro, *Manual de confesores*, 167.

11. Fray Bartholomé de Medina, *Breve instrucción de como se ha de administrar el sacramento de la penitencia* (Burgos: Juan Baptista Varesio, 1612), 163, 195.

12. Kamen, *The Phoenix and the Flame*, 284. The vicar-general could, however, give permission for the ceremony to be performed.

13. Ibid., 282.

14. Vicente Graullera, "Mujer, amor y moralidad en la Valencia de los siglos XVI y XVII," in Redondo, *Amours légitimes, amours illégitimes*, 118.

15. Delumeau, *Le péché et la peur*, 244.

16. Pierre Darmon, *Le tribunal de l'impuissance: Virilité et défaillances conjugales dans l'Ancienne France*, (Paris: Éditions du Seuil, 1979), 94–95.

17. AHN, Inq., October 24, 1738, leg.1827, exp.10.

18. Kamen, *The Phoenix and the Flame*, 293.

19. Ibid., 294.

20. George Huppert, *Public Schools in Renaissance France* (Urbana: University of Illinois Press, 1984), 77–86.

21. Ibid., 116–129.

22. Paul F. Grendler, *Schooling in Renaissance Italy* (Baltimore: John's Hopkins University Press, 1989), 366, 394.

23. Rapley, *The Dévotes*, 156–158.

24. Brundage, *Law, Sex, and Christian Society*, 568.

25. Nalle, *God in La Mancha*, 27.

26. Jedin, *Council of Trent*, 326.

27. Brundage, *Law, Sex, and Christian Society*, 568.

28. Ibid., 247.

29. Wright, *The Counter-Reformation*, 76.

30. José Ignacio Tellechea Idigoras, *La reforma tridentina en San Sebastián* (San Sebastián: Caja de Ahorros Municipal de San Sebastián, 1970), 18.

31. Ibid., 33.

32. Ibid., 19–20.

33. Ibid., 39–82.

34. Francisco Martín Fernández, "La formación del clero en los siglos XVII y XVIII," in García-Villoslada, *Historia de la Iglesia*, 4: 525–526.

35. Ibid., 528.

36. Nalle, *God in La Mancha*, 89–90.

37. Delumeau, *Le péché et la peur*, 487.

38. BN, MS 872, "Costumbres santas que se guarden en nuestros santos noviciados de descalças de la Santissima Trinidad con extraordinario rigor" (n.d.).

39. AHN, Inq., August 7, 1614, leg.1712, exp.13.

40. Ricardo Saez, "La transgression de l'interdit amoureux: le prêtre, la femme et l'enfant dans l'archevêché de Tolède (1565–1620)," in Redondo, *Amours légitimes, amours illégitimes*, 98.

41. AHN, Inq., May 23, 1718, leg.503, exp.7.

42. AHN, Inq., March 21, 1705, leg.1825, exp.30.

43. AHN, Inq., July 4, 1706, leg.1825, exp.30.

44. AHN, Inq., October 14, 1670, leg.231, exp.5.

45. AHN, Inq., July 7, 1594, leg.231, exp.3.

46. AHN, Inq., August 12, 1712, leg.230, exp.10.

47. Pérez de Valdivia, *Aviso*, 663–667.

48. AHN, Inq., October 18, 1685, leg.1824, exp.9.

49. AHN, Inq., March 24, 1680, leg.1706, exp.15. The legislation excluding the illegitimate sons of priests from their fathers' benefices was passed at the twenty-fifth session on December 3, 1563. Schroeder, *Canons and Decrees*, 248.

50. AHN, Inq., January 2, 1763, leg.563, exp.9.

51. AHN, Inq., May 26, 1582, leg.1824, exp.2.

52. AHN, Inq., April 26, 1819, leg.563, exp.8.

53. AHN, Inq., March 29, 1819, leg.563, exp.8.

54. AHN, Inq., December 4, 1767, leg.1714, exp.3.

55. AHN, Inq., February 23, 1708, leg.564, exp.8.

56. Cunnilingus and fellatio were relatively uncommon even in comparatively recent times. Only 50 percent of the women interviewed by Kinsey for his 1953 report admitted any experience with oral-genital sex. Clifton Bryant, *Sexual Deviancy and Social Proscription: The Social Context of Carnal Behavior* (New York, Human Sciences Press, 1982), 267.

57. AHN, Inq., March 24, 1680, leg.1712, exp.10.

58. Bryant, *Sexual Deviancy*, 22.

59. Azpilcueta Navarro, *Manual de confesores*, 162–163.

60. Jean Leduger, "*Bouquet de la mission composé en faveur des peuples de la campagne*" (1700), in Delumeau, *Le péché et la peur*, 487.

61. AHN, Inq., June 16, 1636, leg.1706, exp.5.

62. AHN, Inq., March 13, 1774, leg.564, exp.20.

63. AHN, Inq., July 10, 1693, February 1, 1694, leg.1708, exp.33.

64. For the relationship between honor and chastity, see Pitt-Rivers, *The Fate of Shechem*, 78–79.

65. AHN, Inq., April 14, 28, 1714, leg.1826, exp.2.

66. AHN, Inq., August 25, 1688, August 2, 1687, leg.1711, exp.22.

67. William Masters and Virginia Johnson, *Human Sexual Response* (New York: Bantam Books, 1981), 123.

68. Tentler, *Sin and Confession*, 208–209.

69. Azpilcueta Navarro, *Manual de confesores*, 175.

70. AHN, Inq., August 24, 1764, leg.564, exp.13.

71. AHN, Inq., March 29, 1819, leg.563, exp.8.

72. Bryant, *Sexual Deviancy*, 243.

73. AHN, Inq., August 30, 1741, leg.1864, exp.7. The tribunal went to extraordinary lengths to find any further evidence against Carrera, but after checking the records of twelve other regional courts, was forced to suspend the case.

74. AHN, Inq., August 8, 1691, leg.1825, exp.15.

75. AHN, Inq., July 6, 1691, leg.1825, exp.15.

76. AHN, Inq., July 6, 1691, leg.1825, exp.15.

77. AHN, Inq., April 11, 1818, leg.563, exp.6.

78. AHN, Inq., April 20–21, 1621, leg.1712, exp.20.

79. Flandrin, *Le sexe*, 265.

80. Sebastián de Covarrubias Orozco, *Tesoro de la lengua castellana o española* (1610; reprint, Madrid: Turner, 1977), 876; Real Academia Española, *Diccionario de la lengua castellana*, 3 vols. (Madrid: Francisco del Hierro, 1726), 2: 314.

81. Azpilcueta Navarro, *Manual de confesores*, 162–164.

82. Bartholomé de Medina, *Breve instrucción*, 119.

83. Delumeau, *Le péché et la peur*, 495.

84. Corella, *Práctica*, 54.

85. Azpilcueta Navarro, *Manual de confesores*, 30. Azpilcueta Navarro merely warns confessors not to question female penitents too closely about sexual sins, but says nothing specific about any consequences. Bartholomé de Medina, *Breve instrucción*, 118v–119.

86. AHN, Inq., February 16, 1682, leg.1712, exp.11.

87. AHN, Inq., leg.1856, exp.43, "Relación de los testificaciones que se recibieron en la visita que yo el Inquisidor lic. Miguel Ximénez Palomino hize este presente año de 1607."

88. AHN, Inq., April 18, 1689, May 21, 1690. leg.1712, exp.8.

89. AHN, Inq., June 19, 1639, leg.229, exp.9.

90. AHN, Inq., August 4, 1678, leg.228, exp.6.

91. AHN, Inq., April 11, 1576, leg.228, exp.7.

92. For the strict prohibition against coitus in a consecrated place, see Azpilcueta Navarro, *Manual de confesores*, 175.

93. AHN, Inq., September 3, 1721, leg.1715, exp.3.

94. AHN, Inq., October 11, 1790, leg.1709, exp.11.

95. Brundage, *Law, Sex, and Christian Society*, 399.

96. Ibid., 534.

97. Haliczer, *Inquisition and Society*, 302.

98. AHN, Inq., March 3, 1788, leg.563, exp.4.

99. Bryant, *Sexual Deviancy*, 215.

100. AHN, Inq., June 17, 1626, leg.1705, exp.2.

101. AHN, Inq., May 24, 1614, and June 2, 1614, leg.1712, exp.13.

102. Haliczer, *Inquisition and Society*, 311.

103. Brundage, *Law, Sex, and Christian Society*, 286.

104. AHN, Inq., May 9, 1705, leg.563, exp.13.

105. Brundage, *Law, Sex, and Christian Society*, 167.

106. Bryant, *Sexual Deviancy*, 266–267.

107. AHN, Inq., January 10, 1673, leg.1708, exp.34.

108. AHN, Inq., April 20, 1768, leg.1714, exp.13. Ginard had previously exposed himself to her and scourged her when she was nude from the waist down.

109. AHN, Inq., April 23, 1768, leg.1714, exp.13.

110. For prohibitions against the use of clerical vestments in theatrical presentations, see Bartholomé de Medina, *Breve Instrucción*, 148.

111. AHN, Inq., July 21, 1677, leg.228, exp.15.

112. Delumeau, *Le Catholicisme*, 280–288. Azpilcueta Navarro, *Manual de confesores*, 175. The Roman ritual of 1612 transplanted the rite of matrimony from the doors of the church to the altar. Bossy, *Christianity*, 25.

113. AHN, Inq., July 11, 1689, leg.1712, exp.12.

114. AHN, Inq., July 7, 1712, leg.1826, exp.6.

115. AHN, Inq., March 24, 1781, leg.233, exp.11.

116. AHN, Inq., June 4, 1804, leg.563, exp.7.

117. AHN, Inq., October 16, 1643, leg.1748, exp.10.

118. AHN, Inq., October 7, 1688, leg.1711, exp.21.

119. AHN, Inq., May 31, 1636, leg.1821, exp.11.

120. AHN, Inq., June 15, 1588, leg.227, exp.8.

121. AHN, Inq., April 7, 1690, leg.564, exp.21.

122. AHN, Inq., April 6, 1605, leg.1821, exp.3.

123. AHN, Inq., March 28, 1758, leg.231, exp.14.

124. AHN, Inq., July 9, 1705, leg.230, exp.44.

125. American Psychiatric Association, *Diagnostic and Statistical Manual of Mental Disorders*, 3d ed. (Washington, D.C.: American Psychiatric Association, 1987), 280.

126. AHN, Inq., July 30, 1705, leg.230, exp.44.

127. AHN, Inq., August 18, 1705, leg.230, exp.44.

128. AHN, Inq., April 4, 1707, leg.230, exp.44.

129. AHN, Inq., October 8, 1707, leg.230, exp.44.

130. Weinstein and Bell, *Saints and Society*, 156.

131. Pérez de Valdivia, *Aviso*, 617.

132. Fray Antonio de Lorea, *Santa Rosa religiosa de la tercera orden de Santo Domingo patrona universal del nuevo mundo* (Madrid: Francisco Nieto, 1671), 61.

133. Sigmund Freud, *Three Contributions to the Theory of Sex: The Sexual Aberrations*, in A. A. Brill, ed. and trans., *The Basic Writings of Sigmund Freud* (New York: Random House, 1938), 569.

134. Arcos, *Simón de Rojas*, 269–271.

135. AHN, Inq., October 12, 1810, leg.564, exp.2.

136. AHN, Inq., July 4, 1767, leg.231, exp.1.

137. AHN, Inq., April 23, 1768, leg.1714, exp.13.

138. Freud, "The Sexual Aberrations," in Brill, *The Basic Writings*, 570.

139. AHN, Inq., April 19, 1674, leg.231, exp.15.

140. AHN, Inq., April 24, 1674, leg.231, exp.15. The confusion between sexuality and mysticism was characteristic of the illuminist movement, which flourished during the early sixteenth century. Certain of its more extreme elements asserted that nothing could be sinful if it came from God. This belief led some devotees to engage in daring sexual experimentation that they believed would aid them in attaining spiritual perfection. Haliczer, *Inquisition and Society*, 276.

141. AHN, Inq., September 2, 1674, leg.231, exp.14.

142. Pérez de Bascones also admitted that there was no valid religious motivation behind his demand that Mariana Serrano scourge him. AHN, Inq., June 13, 1674, leg.231, exp.15.

143. AHN, Inq., June 13, 1750, leg.227, exp.6.

144. AHN, Inq., October 19, 26, 1753, leg.227, exp.6.

145. AHN, Inq. April 12, 1576, leg.228, exp.7.

146. Bryant, *Sexual Deviancy*, 324.

147. In fetishism, a nonliving object (fetish) is necessary or strongly preferred for sexual excitement. American Psychiatric Association, *Diagnostic and Statistical Manual*, 282–283.

148. AHN, Inq., January 10, 1678, leg.228, exp.15.

149. AHN, Inq., August 13, 1640, leg.1931, exp.19.

Chapter 9

1. Lea, *A History of the Inquisition,* 4: 436, 454–455.

2. Delumeau, *L'aveu et le pardon*, 151, 158–159.

3. Ibid., 35–36.

4. Charles Chiniquy, *The Priest, the Woman and the Confessional* (London: Marshall Press, 1882), 85.

5. Anthony Gavin, *The Master Key to Popery*, in *The Great Red Dragon, Or The Master-Key to Popery* (New York: H. Dayton, 1860), 149.

6. Ibid., 9.

7. Ibid., 16.

8. Ibid., 57.

9. Ibid., 30–31.

10. Ibid., 53–58.

11. Ibid., 61–62.

12. Marcelin Defourneaux, *L'Inquisition espagnole et les livres français au XVIII siècle* (Paris: Presses Universitaires de France, 1963), 183. For the failure of the Holy Office to maintain any more than a "mediocre defense" against the ideological threat represented by the French Enlightenment and the long periods during which subversive works were permitted to circulate, see pp. 99, 130–132.

13. José Blanco White, *Cartas de España*, Antonio Garnica, trans. (Madrid: Alianza, 1972), 85–86.

14. Ibid., 123.

15. José Blanco White, *The Preservative Against Popery*, in *The Great Red Dragon, Or The Master Key To Popery* (New York: H. Dayton, 1860), 337.

16. Blanco White, *Cartas de España*, 87.

17. Ibid., 183.

18. Gabriel H. Lovett, Introduction to *A Critical History of the Inquisition of Spain,* by Juan Antonio Llorente (Williamstown, MA: John Lilburne, 1967), vii.

19. Ibid., viii.

20. Juan Antonio Llorente, *Histoire critique de l'Inquisition d'Espagne,* 4 vols. (Paris: Treutiel et Wurtz, Delaunay, Mongie, 1817–1818), 3: 25.

21. Ibid., 44–54.

22. Michel Morphy, *Les mystères de la pornographie cléricale; secrets honteux de la confession, immoralités, obscenités, et guerre aux prêtres, corrupteurs de la jeunesse* (Paris: Librairie Démocratique et Sociale, 1884), 3–7.

23. Leo Taxil, Introduction to *Les livres secrets des confesseurs dévoilés aux pères de famille,* by Gabriel Pagès (Paris: Librairie Anti-Cléricale, 1884), iv.

24. Pierre Longin, *Une passion dans le confessionnal* (Paris: Les Publications Parisiennes, 1935), 14, 64–65.

25. Ibid., 70.

26. Ibid., 121.

27. Fernando García Lara, *El lugar de la novela erótica española* (Granada: Diputación Provincial, 1986), 148–149.

28. Xavier Domingo, *Erótica hispánica* (Paris: Ruedo Ibérico, 1972), 205, 307–308. One of the illustrations on top right of p. 307 clearly shows a priest leaning out of a confessional to fondle the breasts of a naked woman.

29. *Mercedes* (Madrid: Azul y Oro, Biblioteca Pornográfica, 1890), 16, 26–27.

30. This relationship is described in *El cura,* a novel written specifically in opposition to clerical celibacy. Eduardo López Bago, *El cura, caso de incesto* (Madrid: Juan Muñoz Sánchez, [1889?]), 255–256, 259–261.

31. Eduardo López Bago, *El confesionario* (*satiriasis*) (Madrid: Juan Muñoz y Compañía, [1890?]), 41.

32. Ibid., 155.

33. Ibid., 129, 167–169.

34. Ibid., 56–58.

35. Ibid., 190.

36. Ibid., 135.

37. Ibid., 195–203.

38. Ibid., 229–230.

39. Ibid., 232.

40. Domingo, *Erótica hispánica*, 164–165.

41. José Marchena Ruiz de Cueto, *Fragmentum Petronii ex bibliothecae St. Galli antiquissimo mss. exceptum nunc primium in lucem editum gallice vertit ac notis perpetuis illustravit Lallemandus theologiae* (Brussels: A. Mertens, 1865), 23.

42. Domingo, *Erótica hispánica*, 168. José Marchena Ruiz de Cueto, *Lecciones de filosofía moral y elocuencia, ó colección de los trozos más selectos de poesía, elocuencia, historia, religión y filosofía moral y política de los mejores autores castellanos* (Bordeaux: Pedro Beaume, 1820), x–xi.

43. García Lara, *El lugar de la novela*, 50–52.

44. Lily Litvac, ed., *Antología de la novela corta erótica española de entreguerras (1918–1936)* (Madrid: Taurus, 1993), 47.

45. Raymond Carr, *Spain 1808–1939* (Oxford: Oxford University Press, 1966), 492–494; John Devlin, *Spanish Anticlericalism: A Study in Modern Alienation* (New York: Las Americas, 1966), 60–62.

46. Litvak, *Antología*, 55–56.

47. Domingo, *Erótica hispánica*, 168.

48. F. Bullon, *Colegiales adorables* (Madrid: Biblioteca Fauno, 1930), 16.

49. Ibid., 7.

50. José Blanco White, *The Preservative*, 337.

51. Galindo, *Parte segundo del directorio*, 518. Galindo denounces women who think nothing of "appearing in public or even coming to take communion with their back, shoulders, and breasts exposed."

52. Bullon, *Colegiales*, 39–40.

53. Ibid., 68–82.

54. Ibid., 67–68.

55. Catherine Jagoe, "Krausism and the Pygmalion Motif in Galdós's *La familia de León Roch*," *Romance Quarterly* 37, no. 1 (1992), 41.

56. For the gulf between male and female religious practice see Michel Vovelle, *Piété baroque et déchristianisation en Provence au XVIIIe siècle* (Paris: Plon, 1973), 608–609; and Philippe Boutry, *Prêtres et paroisses au pays du curé de Ars* (Paris: Cerf, 1986), 402–403.

57. Jules Michelet, *Le Prêtre, la femme, et la famille* (Paris: Calman Lévy, 1845), 211.

58. Ibid., 208.

59. For the importance of the theme of the dangers of the confessional to the bourgeois family, see René Rémond, *L'Anticléricalisme en France de 1815 à nos jours* (Paris: Fayard, 1976), 26.

60. The Spanish edition was published in Barcelona in 1845 under the title *El sacerdote, la mujer y la familia*.

61. Chiniquy, *The Priest, The Woman and the Confessional*, 92.

62. Ibid., 14–15.

63. Ibid., 14–16.

64. Ibid., 87.

65. Ibid., 91.

66. Alfred Rodríguez, "Algunos aspectos de la elaboracíon literaria de *La familia de León Roch*," *PMLA* 82, no. 1 (March 1967): 122–123, 126.

67. Benito Pérez Galdos, *La familia de León Roch*, in Federico Carlos Sanz de Robles, ed., *Obras Completas*, 6 vols. (Madrid: Aguilar, 1960), 4: 779–781.

68. Jagoe, "Krausism and the Pygmalion Motif," 44–45.

69. Galdos, *La familia*, 782.

70. Ibid., 928–929.

71. Ibid., 899.

72. Ibid., 959.

73. Segismundo Pey Ordeix, *Sor Sicalipsis* (Barcelona: Maucci, 1931), 88–95.

74. Ibid., 232.

75. Michelet, *Le Prêtre, la femme, et la famille*, 2.

76. Vicente Blasco Ibáñez, *El Intruso,* in *Obras Completas* (Madrid: Aguilar, 1969), 1072.

77. Ibid., 1106.

78. Ibid., 1106.

79. Ibid., 1115.

80. Ibid., 1158.

81. Ibid., 1204.

82. Ibid., 1210–1211. This scene is described briefly in Devlin, *Spanish Anti-clericalism*, 105–106.

83. Leopoldo Alas [Clarín], *La Regenta* (Madrid: Alianza Editorial, 1972), 569.

84. Ibid., 189.

85. Ibid., 189–190.

86. José Ortega emphasizes Fermín's lack of autonomy in José Ortega, "Don Fermín de Pas, un estudio de superbia et concupiscentia catholicis," *Revista de Estudios Hispánicos* (October 1975) 9, no. 3: 331.

87. Alas, *La Regenta*, 315.

88. Ibid., 166–167.

89. Ibid., 220.

90. Ibid., 220, 331.

91. Ibid., 331.

92. Francis Wyers Weber, "Ideology and Religious Parody in the Novels of Leopoldo Alas," *Bulletin of Hispanic Studies* 43 (January 1966): 199.

93. Alas, *La Regenta*, 266–267.

94. Ibid., 429.

95. Ibid., 423.

96. Weber, "Ideology and Religious Parody," 201.

97. Alas, *La Regenta*, 461.

98. Ibid., 500.

99. Ibid., 523–524.

100. Ibid., 559.

101. Ibid., 558.

102. Weber, "Ideology and Religious Parody," 202.

103. Alas, *La Regenta*, 625.

104. Ibid., 559.

105. Ibid., 676.

Conclusion

1. Although the earliest case that I have found dates from 1530, the Inquisition did not have formal authority over solicitation until 1561.

2. Louis Chatellier, *The Europe of the Devout; The Catholic Reformation and the Formation of a New Society* (Cambridge: Cambridge University Press, 1989), 175–179.

3. William J. Callahan, "The Spanish Church," in William J. Callahan and David Higgs, eds., *Church and Society in Catholic Europe of the Eighteenth Century* (Cambridge: Cambridge University Press, 1979), 47.

4. Ibid., 48.

5. Richard Herr, *The Eighteenth Century Revolution in Spain* (Princeton: Princeton University Press, 1969), 22.

6. Blanco White, *Cartas de España*, 94.

7. Herr, *The Eighteenth Century Revolution*, 28–29.

8. That this process of decay had begun by the late seventeenth century is demonstrated by the complaint of the Suprema in a letter to the Toledo tribunal regarding the case against Fray Antonio Lloret, who appeared spontaneously in October 1696. The tribunal did not submit this evidence to the Suprema until March 17, 1705. AHN, Inq., May 17, 1705, leg.563, exp.13.

9. The success of the Church's campaign to impose annual confession can be seen from the situation in the diocese of Pamplona in 1801, where annual confession was virtually universal. José Goñi Gaztambide, "El cumplimiento pascual en la diócesis de Pamplona en 1801," *Hispania Sacra*, 26 (1973): 361–372.

10. José Blanco White, *The Life of the Rev. Joseph Blanco White Written By Himself*, John Hamilton Thompson, ed. (London: John Chapman, 1845), 43.

11. Defourneaux, *L'Inquisition espagnole et les livres français*, 185–186. Jacques Gaudin, *Les inconvénients du célibat des prêtres prouvés par des recherches historiques* (Geneva: J. Pellecer, 1781). Gaudin (p. 368) insisted that "it is perfectly clear that according to both the Old and New Testaments, priests were permitted to marry."

12. The increasing level of concern about solicitation can be seen in the extraordinary measures that the Holy Office took to monitor this offense by mandating each tribunal to keep special record books to record evidence about solicitantes. What these books record is not the successful prosecution of offenders, but the increasing difficulty of bringing them to trial, as many eighteenth century cases were suspended.

13. Gavin, *The Master Key to Popery*, 68.

14. Domingo, *Erótica hispánica*, 168.

15. Ibid., 143.

16. Servimedia, "Una piadosa septuagenaria, violada en el confesionario de una iglesia de Santander," *ABC*, Edicion Internacional (25 November–1 December 1992): 23.

17. Carmen Martín Gaite, *Usos amorosos de la postguerra española* (Barcelona: Editorial Anagrama, 1987), 111.

18. Marciano Vidal, "La teología moral en nuestros días" in Agustin Fliche and Victor Martin, eds., *Histoire de l'Eglise*, Spanish translation, Manuela Ureña Pastor, 31 vols., 2 supplements, (Valencia: Edicep, 1978–1982), supplement 1:489, 494.

19. Secretariado Nacional de Liturgia, *Guía para celebrar la penitencia segun el nuevo ritual*, (Madrid: Heroes, 1976), 15–17.

20. Dionisio Borobio, *Penitencia, reconciliacion* (Barcelona: Centre de Pastoral Liturgica, 1982), 54.

21. Rogelio Duocastella, *Actituas i mentalitat religiosa a Granollers* (Barcelona: ISPA, 1972), 79; *Analysis de mentalidad y actitudes religiosas de tres parroquías de Madrid* (Barcelona and Madrid: ISPA, 1972), 128–132.

22. José Luis Gutierrez García, *Diselo a la comunidad; reflexiones sobre la situación de la Iglesia en España hoy* (Avila: Asociación Educativa Signum Christi, 1986), 91.

BIBLIOGRAPHY

Archival Sources

Archivo Histórico Nacional, Sección Inquisición, Legajos 31, 101, 109, 110, 227, 228, 229, 230, 231, 232, 233, 321, 503, 550, 561, 562, 563, 564, 1679, 1705, 1706, 1708, 1709, 1710, 1711, 1712, 1713, 1714, 1715, 1748, 1764, 1784, 1807, 1811, 1814, 1821, 1822, 1824, 1825, 1826, 1827, 1828, 1856, 1864, 1867, 1931, 1952, 1953.

———, Sección Inquisición, Libros 101, 1231, 1259, 1265, 1266, 1269.

Biblioteca Nacional, Madrid MS 3164 "Un cavallero de la corte de Madrid escrive a un religioso Dominico sobre la novedad que se revela de que el rey nuestro señor D. Felipe V no confiesse con religiosos de dicha orden" (December 1718).

——— MS 872 "Costumbres Santas que se guarden en nuestros noviciados de descalças de la Santissima Trinidad con extraordinario rigor" (n.d.).

——— MS 4096 Pedro Calderón de la Barca, "Afectos de un pecador arrepentido hablando con Dios en forma de confesión general estando en el articulo de la muerte" (n.d.).

——— MS 11331 Pedro Galindo, "Discurso sobre las confesiones del Conde Duque de Olivares valido de Felipe IV, dirigido a su confesor el Padre Franco" (1642).

Primary Sources (Printed)

Alas, Leopoldo [Clarín, pseud.]. *La Regenta*. Madrid: Alianza Editorial, 1972.

Andrade, Alonso de. *Libro de la guía de la virtud y de la imitación de Nuestra Señora*. 3 vols. Madrid: Francisco Moroto, 1644.

Ángel, Fray Manrique. *La venerable Ana de Jesús, discipula y compañera de la S. M. Teresa de Jesús*. Brussels: Lucas de Meerbeek, 1632.

Antonio de Lorea, Fray. *Bienaventurado el San Pío quinto pontifice máximo de la*

Iglesia, religioso de la sagrada orden de predicadores. Valladolid: Imprenta de la Real Chancillería, 1713.

———. *La venerable madre Hipolita de Jesús y Rocaberti*. Valencia: Vicente Caprita, 1679.

———. *David perseguido*. Madrid: Imprenta Real, 1675.

———. *Santa Rosa religiosa de la tercera orden de Santo Domingo patrona universal del nuevo mundo*. Madrid: Francisco Nieto, 1671.

Azevedo, Juan de. *Tribunal theologicum et Juridicum contra subdolos Confesarios in Sacramento Penitentiae ad venerem sollicitantes ereptum*. Ulissipone: M. Rodig, 1726.

Azpilcueta Navarro, Martín de. *Manual de confesores y penitentes, que clara y brevemente contiene, la universal y particular decision de quasi todas las dudas, que en las confesiones suelen occurrir de los pecados absoluciones, restituciones, censuras irregularidades*. Salamanca: Andrea de Portonariis, 1556.

Bartholomé de Medina, Fray. *Breve instrucción de como se ha de administrar el sacramento de la penitencia*. Burgos: Juan Baptista Varesio, 1612.

Blanco White, José. *Cartas de España*. Translated by Antonio Garnica. Madrid: Alianza, 1972.

———. *The Preservative Against Popery*. In *The Great Red Dragon or The Master-Key to Popery*. New York: H. Dayton, 1860.

———. *The Life of the Rev. Joseph Blanco White Written By Himself*. Edited by John Hamilton Thompson. London: John Chapman, 1845.

Blasco Ibáñez, Vicente. *El Intruso*. In *Obras Completas*. Madrid: Aguilar, 1969.

Bonilla, Alonso de. *Peregrinos pensamientos de misterios divinos*. Baeza: Pedro de la Cuesta, 1614.

Borda, Andrés de. *Práctica de confesores de monjas*. Mexico City: Francisco de Ribera Calderon, 1788.

Bullon, F. *Colegiales adorables*. Madrid: Biblioteca Fauno, 1930.

Calisbeta, Manuel. *Enseñanzas espirituales para el mayor provecho de las almas, doce doctrinas a favor de la comunión cotidiana*. Madrid: Pablo de Val, 1663.

Canons and Decrees of the Council of Trent. Translated by H. J. Schroeder, O.P. St. Louis and London: Herder Books, 1941.

Carrasco, Francisco de. *Manual de escrupulosos y de los confesores que los goviernan*. Valladolid: Francisco Márquez, 1686.

Casiodoro de Reina, Fray. *Confesión de fe cristiana*. Cassel: Wilhelm Wessel, 1602.

Chiniquy, Charles. *The Priest, the Woman and the Confessional*. London: Marshall Press, 1882.

Ciruelo, Pedro. *Arte de buen confesar*. Sevilla: Dominico de Robertis, 1548.

Contreras, Jaime, and Gustav Henningsen. "Forty-four Thousand Cases of the Spanish Inquisition (1540–1700): Analysis of a Historical Data Bank." In *The Inquisition in Early Modern Europe; Studies on Sources and Methods*, edited by Gustav Henningsen and John Tedeschi. DeKalb: Northern Illinois University Press, 1986.

Covarrubias Orozco, Sebastián de. *Tesoro de la lengua castellana o española*. 1610. Reprint. Madrid: Turner, 1977.

Cunha e Silva, Rodrigo da. *Tractatus de Confessariis Solicitantibus*. Vallisoleti: Ioannem de Rueda, 1620.

Daza y Berrio, Juan. *Tesoro de confesores y perla de conciencia para todos estados*. Madrid: Imprenta Real, 1648.

Delgadillo, Cristóbal. *Cuestión moral o resolución de algunas dudas acerca de la frecuente confesión*. Madrid: Domingo García Morras, 1660.

Diez de Aux, Luys. *Compendio de las fiestas que ha celebrado la imperial ciudad de Zaragoza por haver promovido la magestad católica el Rey Felipe III de Castilla Segundo de Aragón al Señor Fray Luis de Aliaga su confesor y de su Real Consejo de Estado en el oficio y cargo Supremo de Inquisidor General de España*. Saragossa: Juan de Lanuja y Quartanet, 1619.

Domingo López, Fray. *La cándida flor trinitaria; vida prodigiosa y admirable muerte de la Hermana María Cándida de la Santissima Trinidad*. Granada: Imprenta de la SS. Trinidad, 1708.

Escobar del Corro, Juan. *De confesariis solicitantibus*. Córdoba: 1642.

Escobar y Mendoza, Antonio de, S.J. *Examen de confesores y práctica de penitentes*. Madrid: María de Quintana, 1650.

Espinar, Pedro. *El confesor instruido*. Madrid: 1695.

Espinola Baeza, Juan de. *El confesor instruido*. Madrid: Juan García Infançon, 1695.

Farfan, Francisco. *Regimiento de castos y remedio de torpes*. Salamanca: Cornelio Bonardo, 1590.

Felipe de la Gandara, Fray. *El cisne occidental conta las palmas y triunfos eclesiásticos de Galicia ganados por sus hijos insignes, santos, mártires y confesores*. Madrid: Julián de Paredes, 1678.

Felipe de Meneses, Fray. *Luz del alma cristiana en el cual se da la luz así a los confesores como a los penitentes*. Seville: Sebastián Trujillo, 1564.

Fernández, Alonso. *Documentos y avisos que D. Cristóbal de Rojas y Sandoval obispo de Córdoba dio a los rectores y confesores de su obispado acerca de la prudencia que devian guardar consigo mismos*. Córdoba: Juan Bautista Escudero, 1569.

Francisco de Arcos, Fray. *Vida del V.Y.R. Fray Simón de Rojas*. 2 vols. Madrid: Julián de Paredes, 1670.

Galindo, Pedro. *Excelencias de la castidad y virginidad*. 2 vols. Madrid: Mateo de Espinosa y Arteaga, 1681.

———. *Parte segundo del directorio de penitentes y práctica de una buena y prudente confesión*. Madrid: Antonio de Zafra 1680.

Gaudin, Jacques. *Les inconvénients du célibat des prêtres prouvés par des recherches historiques*. Geneva: J. Pellecer, 1781.

Gavarri, José. *Instrucciones predicables y morales que deben saber los padres predicadores y confesores*. Madrid: Antonio Gonçalo de Reyes, 1679.

———. *Noticias singularissimos que saco a la luz de los preguntas necesarios que deben saber los confesores con las personas que oyen de confesar*. Granada: Francisco de Ochoa, 1676.

Gavin, Anthony. *The Master-Key to Popery*. In *The Great Red Dragon or The Master-Key to Popery*. New York: H. Dayton, 1860.

Gómez, Anselmo. *El perfecto examen de confesores matritense*. Madrid: Melchor Alvarez, 1676.

Goodman, John. *A Discourse Concerning Auricular Confession as Prescribed by the Council of Trent and Practiced in the Church of Rome*. London: H. Hills, 1648.

Jaime de Corella, Fray. *Práctica del confesionario y explicación de los sesenta y cinco proposiciones condenadas por la santidad de N.S.P. Inocencio XI*. 2 vols. Madrid: Manuel Román, 1717.

Juan de la Cruz, Fray. *Crónica de la orden de predicadores*. Lisbon: Manuel Juan, 1567.

La confesión ó sea amena controversia entre un joven abogado y un viejo militar sobre la institución divina, del sacramento de la penitencia; su práctica, y necesidad; sus ventajas, y beneficios tanto para la sociedad como por el individuo. Madrid: Biblioteca Católica Popular, 1845.

La Cruz, Felipe de. *Norte de confesores y penitentes.* Valladolid: Jerónimo Morillo, 1629.

Longin, Pierre. *Une passion dans le confessionnal.* Paris: Les Publications Parisiennes, 1935.

López Bago, *Eduardo. El confesionario (satiriasis).* Madrid: Juan Muñoz y Compañía, [1890?]

———. *El cura, caso de incesto.* Madrid: Juan Muñoz Sánchez, [1889?]

Luis de Granada, Fray. *Guía de pecadores.* Buenos Aires: Poblet, 1943.

Luis de León, Fray. *La perfecta casada.* 1583. Reprint. Barcelona: Hymsa, 1953.

Luque Fajardo, Francisco de. *Fiel desengaño contra la ociosidad y los juegos, utilissimo a los confesores y penitentes, justicias, y los demas a cuyo cargo está limpiar de vagabundos talures y fulleros la república cristiana.* Madrid: Miguel Serrano de Vargas, 1603.

Luther, Martin. *The Sacrament of Penance.* In *Luther's Works,* translated by E. Theodore Bachmann. 55 vols. Philadelphia: Muhlenberg Press, 1960.

Machado de Chaves, Juan. *Perfecto confesor y cura de almas.* Barcelona: Pedro la Cavallería, 1641.

Mercedes. Madrid: Azul y Oro, Biblioteca Pornográfica, 1890.

Michelet, Jules. *Le Prêtre, la femme, et la famille.* Paris: Calman Lévy, 1845.

El Motín, Periodico satírico semanal. Barcelona, 1885.

Morphy, Michel. *Les mystères de la pornographie cléricale; secrets honteux de la confession, immoralités, obscenités, et guerre aux prêtres, corrupteurs de la jeunesse.* Paris: Librairie Démocratique et Sociale, 1884.

Nuño Borgensi, José. *Medicina moralis tripartita a contagio solicitationis comprehensae in diplomatibus pontificiis et a denunciatione in Sancto Officio confessarios tutius praeservans.* Caesaraugustae: Apud Emmanuelem Roman, 1692.

Pedro de Ledesema, Fray. *Primera parte de la Summa en la cual se cifra y summa todo lo que pertenece a los sacramentos.* Salamanca: Viuda Antonio Ramírez, 1608.

Pérez de Valdivia, Diego. *Tratado de la frecuente comunión y medios para ella principalmente del modo y orden bien confesar.* Barcelona: Pedro Malo, 1589.

———. *Aviso de gente recogida.* 1585. Reprint. Madrid: Fundación Universitaria Española, 1977.

Pérez Galdos, Benito. *La familia de León Roch.* In *Obras Completas,* edited by Federico Carlos Sanz de Robles. 6 vols. Madrid: Aguilar, 1960.

Pey Ordeix, Segismundo. *Sor Sicalipsis.* Barcelona: Maucci, 1931.

Real Academia Española. *Diccionario de la lengua castellana.* 3 vols. Madrid: Francisco del Hierro, 1726.

Reluz, Thomás. *Vida y virtudes del Señor Fray Thomás Carbonel.* Madrid: Viuda de Francisco Nieto, 1695.

Ruiz de Cueta, José Marchena. *Fragmentum Petronii ex bibliothecae St. Galli antiquissimo mss. exceptum nunc primium in lucem editum gallice vertit ac notis perpetuis illustravit Lallemandus theologiae.* Brussels: A. Mertens et Fils, 1865.

———. *Lecciones de filosofía moral y eloquencia ó collección de los trozos más selectos de la poesía, eloquencia, historia, religión, y filosofía moral y política de los mayores autores castellanos*. Bordeaux: Pedro Beaume, 1820.

San José, Luis. *Luz de sacerdotes y guía de confesores*. Madrid: Juan de la Cuesta, 1622.

Taxil, Leo. Introduction to *Les livres secrets des confesseurs dévoilés aux pères de famille*, by Gabriel Pagès. Paris: Librairie Anti-Cléricale, 1884.

Teresa of Jesus. *The Complete Works of Saint Teresa of Jesus*. 3 vols. Translated and edited by E. A. Peers. 11th ed. London and New York: Sheed and Ward, 1982.

Teresa of Jesus. *The Letters of Saint Teresa*. Translated and edited by E. A. Peers. London: Burns, Oates and Washbourne, 1951.

A Treatise of Auricular Confession Wherein is Evidently Shown the Authority and Power of Catholic Priests for the Forgery and Remitting of Sins Against the Protestants Bare and Only Preaching of Absolution. St. Omer: I. Heigham, 1622.

Valdés, Juan de. *Diálogo de doctrina cristiana*. Madrid: Editorial Nacional, 1979.

Villegas, Bernardo de, S.J. *La esposa de Cristo instruida*. Murcia: Juan Fernández de Fuentes, 1635.

Vives, Juan Luis. *Libro llamado instrucción de la mujer cristiana*. 1524. Reprint. Translated by Juan Justiniano. Madrid: Signo, 1936.

Secondary Sources (Books)

Alonso Romero, María Paz. *El proceso penal en castilla siglo XIII–XVIII*. Salamanca: Ediciones Universidad de Salamanca, 1982.

American Psychiatric Association. *Diagnostic and Statistical Manual of Mental Disorders*. 3d. ed., revised. Washington, D.C.: American Psychiatric Association, 1987.

Ariès, Philippe, and Béjin, André, eds. *Western Sexuality: Practice and Precept in Past and Present Times*. Translated by Anthony Fraser. Oxford: Basil Blackwell, 1985.

Azcona, Tarsicio de. *Isabel la Católica: Estudio crítico de su vida y su reinado*. Madrid: Biblioteca de Autores Cristianos, 1964.

Bataillon, Marcel. *Erasmo y España: Estudios sobre la historia espiritual del siglo XVI*. Mexico and Buenos Aires: Fondo de Cultura Economica, 1966.

Bell, Rudolph. *Holy Anorexia*. Chicago and London: University of Chicago Press, 1985.

Bennassar, Bartolomé. *L'Homme espagnol: Attitudes et mentalités du XVI au XIX siècles*. Paris: Hachette, 1975.

Bilinkoff, Jodi. *The Avila of Saint Teresa: Religious Reform in a Sixteenth-Century City*. Ithaca: Cornell University Press, 1989.

Borobio, Dionisio. *Penitencia, reconciliación*. Barcelona: Centre de Pastoral Liturgica, 1982.

Bossy, John. *Christianity in the West, 1400–1700*. New York: Oxford University Press, 1985.

Boutry, Philippe. *Prêtres et paroisses au pays du curé de Ars*. Paris: Cerf, 1986.

Braeckmans, Louis. *Confession et communion au moyen âge et au concile de Trente*. Gembloux: J. Duculot, 1971.

Brown, Jonathan. *Images and Ideas in Seventeenth-Century Spanish Painting*. Princeton: Princeton University Press, 1978.

Brundage, James A. *Law, Sex, and Christian Society in Medieval Europe*. Chicago and London: University of Chicago Press, 1987.

Bryant, Clifton. *Sexual Deviancy and Social Proscription: The Social Context of Carnal Behavior*. New York: Human Sciences Press, 1982.

Burke, Peter. *Popular Culture in Early Modern Europe*. New York: Harper and Row, 1978.

Callahan, William J., and Higgs, David, eds. *Church and Society in Catholic Europe of the Eighteenth Century*. Cambridge: Cambridge University Press, 1979.

Caro Baroja, Julio. *Las formas complejas de la vida religiosa: Religión, sociedad, y carácter en la España de los siglos XVI y XVII*. Madrid: Akal, 1978.

Carr, Raymond. *Spain 1808–1939*. Oxford: Oxford University Press, 1966.

Carrasco, Rafael. *Inquisición y represión sexual en Valencia: Historia de los sodomitas*. Barcelona: Laertes, 1985.

Chatellier, Louis. *The Europe of the Devout; The Catholic Reformation and the Formation of a New Society*. Cambridge: Cambridge University Press, 1989.

Christian, William A. *Local Religion in Sixteenth-Century Spain*. Princeton: Princeton University Press, 1981.

Contreras, Jaime. *El Santo Oficio de la Inquisición de Galicia: Poder, sociedad y cultura*. Madrid: Akal, 1982.

Dansey Smith, Hilary. *Preaching in the Spanish Golden Age*. Oxford: Oxford University Press, 1978.

Darmon, Pierre. *Le tribunal de l'impuissance: Virilité et défaillances conjugales dans l'Ancienne France*. Paris: Éditions du Seuil, 1979.

Dedieu, Jean-Pierre. *L'Administration de la foi: L'Inquisition de Tolède (XVI– XVIII siècle)*. Madrid: Casa de Velázquez, 1989.

Defourneaux, Marcelin. *L'Inquisition espagnole et les livres français au XVIII siècle*. Paris: Presses Universitaires de France, 1963.

Deleito y Piñuela, José. *La vida religiosa española bajo el quarto Felipe: Santos y pecadores*. Madrid: Espasa-Calpe, 1952.

Delumeau, Jean. *L'aveu et le pardon: Les difficultés de la confession XIII–XVIII siècles*. Paris: Fayard, 1990.

———. *Le péché et la peur: La culpabilisation en Occident XIII–XVIII siècles*. Paris: Fayard, 1983.

———. *Le Catholicisme entre Luther et Voltaire*. Paris: Presses Universitaires de France, 1971.

Devlin, John. *Spanish Anticlericalism: A Study in Modern Alienation*. New York: Las Americas, 1966.

Dickens, A. G. *The Counter-Reformation*. London: Thames and Hudson, 1968.

Domingo, Xavier. *Erótica hispánica*. Gap: Ruedo Ibérico, 1972.

Domínguez Ortiz, Antonio. *Sociedad y estado en el siglo XVIII español*. Madrid: Seix y Barral, 1976.

Duocastella, Rogelio. *Actituas i mentalitat religiosa a Granollers*. Barcelona: ISPA, 1972.

———. *Analysis de mentalidad y actitudes religiosas de tres parroquías de Madrid*. Barcelona and Madrid: ISPA, 1972.

Elliott, J. H. *Imperial Spain 1469–1716*. New York: New American Library, 1963.

Evennett, H. Outram. *The Spirit of the Counter-Reformation*. Edited by John Bossy. Cambridge: Cambridge University Press, 1968.

Fairchilds, Cissie. *Domestic Enemies: Servants and Their Masters in Old Regime France*. Baltimore: Johns Hopkins University Press, 1984.

Flandrin, Jean-Louis. *Le sexe et l'occident*. Paris: Editions du Seuil, 1981.

————. *Families in Former Times: Kinship, Household and Sexuality*. Translated by Richard Southern. Cambridge: Cambridge University Press, 1985.

Forster, Robert, and Ranum, Orest, eds. *Deviants and the Abandoned in French Society*. Baltimore: Johns Hopkins University Press, 1978.

Foucault, Michel. *The Use of Pleasure*. Translated by Robert Hurley. Vol. 2 of *The History of Sexuality*. New York: Pantheon, 1985.

————. *The History of Sexuality: An Introduction*. Translated by Robert Hurley. Vol. 1 of *The History of Sexuality*. New York: Pantheon, 1985.

————. *Discipline and Punish: The Birth of the Prison*. Translated by Alan Sheridan. New York: Pantheon, 1977.

Friedman, Ellen. *Spanish Captives in North Africa in the Early Modern Age*. Madison: University of Wisconsin Press, 1983.

García Lara, Fernando. *El lugar de la novela erótica española*. Granada: Diputación Provincial, 1986.

García Sanz, Ángel. *Desarrollo y crisis del antiguo régimen en Castilla la Vieja*. Madrid: Akal, 1977.

García-Villoslada, Ricardo, ed. *Historia de la Iglesia en España*. 5 vols. Madrid: Editorial Católica, 1979–1982.

González Novalín, José Luis. *El Inquisidor-General Fernando de Valdés 1483–1568*. Oviedo: Universidad de Oviedo, 1968.

Grendler, Paul. *Schooling in Renaissance Italy*. Baltimore: Johns Hopkins University Press, 1989.

Guitart Izquierdo, Vidal. *Sínodos postridentinos de Segorbe*. Castellón de la Plana: Ayuntamiento de Castellón de la Plana, 1983.

Gutiérrez García, José Luis. *Diselo a la comunidad; reflexiones sobre la situación de la Iglesia en España hoy*. Avila: Asociación Educativa Signum Christi, 1986.

Haliczer, Stephen. *Inquisition and Society in the Kingdom of Valencia, 1478–1834*. Berkeley and Los Angeles: University of California Press, 1990.

————, ed. *Inquisition and Society in Early Modern Europe*. London: Croom-Helm, 1986.

Häring, Bernard. *Das Gesetz Christi*. Spanish translation by Juan de la Cruz Salazar. 2 vols. Barcelona: Herder, 1961.

Henningsen, Gustav. *The Witches' Advocate; Basque Witchcraft and the Spanish Inquisition*. Reno: University of Nevada Press, 1980.

Henningsen, Gustav, and Tedeschi, John, eds. *The Inquisition in Early Modern Europe; Studies on Sources and Methods*. DeKalb: Northern Illinois University Press, 1986.

Hepworth, Mike, and Turner, Bryan S., eds. *Confession: Studies of Deviance and Religion*. London: Routledge and Kegan Paul, 1982.

Herr, Richard. *The Eighteenth Century Revolution in Spain*. Princeton: Princeton University Press, 1969.

Hsia, R. Po-Chia. *Social Discipline in the Reformation: Central Europe 1550–1750*. London: Routledge, 1989.

Huerga, Alvaro. *Predicadores, alumbrados y Inquisición en el siglo XVI*. Madrid: Fundación Universitaria Española, 1973.

Hunter, Ski, and Sundel, Martín, eds. *Midlife Myths, Issues, Findings and Practice Implications*. Newbury Park, CA: Sage, 1989.

Huppert, George. *Public Schools in Renaissance France*. Urbana: University of Illinois Press, 1984.

Jedin, Hubert. *A History of the Council of Trent*. Translated by Dom Ernest Graf. 2 vols. St. Louis: B. Herder, 1961.

Jordon, William B. *Catalogue of the Exhibition El Greco of Toledo*. Boston: Little Brown, 1982.

Kagan, Richard L. *Lucrecia's Dreams: Politics and Prophecy in Sixteenth-Century Spain*. Berkeley and Los Angeles: University of California Press, 1990.

Kamen, Henry. *The Phoenix and the Flame: Catalonia and the Counter Reformation*. New Haven and London:Yale University Press, 1993.

————. *European Society 1500–1700*. London: Hutchinson, 1986.

————. *Inquisition and Society in Spain*. Bloomington: Indiana University Press, 1985.

Lea, Henry Charles. *The History of Sacerdotal Celibacy in the Christian Church*. New York: Russell and Russell, 1957.

————. *A History of the Inquisition of Spain*. 4 vols. New York: Macmillan, 1906–1907.

————. *A History of Auricular Confession and Indulgences in the Latin Church*. Philadelphia: Lea Brothers, 1896.

Lezcano, Ricardo. *El divorcio en la segunda república*. Madrid: Akal, 1979.

Litvac, Lily, ed. *Antología de la novela corta érotica española de entreguerras (1918–1936)*. Madrid: Taurus, 1993.

Llorente, Juan Antonio. *Histoire critique de l'Inquisition d' Espagne*. 4 vols. Paris: Treuttel et Wirtz, Delaunay, Mongie aîné, 1817–1818.

Lovett, Gabriel H. Introduction to *A Critical History of the Inquisition of Spain*, by Juan Antonio Llorente. Williamstown, MA: John Lilburne, 1967.

Martín Gaite, Carmen. *Usos amorosos de la postguerra española*. Barcelona: Editorial Anagrama, 1987.

Masters, William, and Johnson, Virginia. *Human Sexual Response*. New York: Bantam Books, 1981.

McKendrick, Melveena. *Woman and Society in the Spanish Drama of the Golden Age: A Study of the Mujer Varonil*. London: Cambridge University Press, 1974.

Menéndez y Pelayo, Marcelino. *Historia de los heterodoxos españoles*. 4 vols. Buenos Aires: Perlado, 1945.

Nalle, Sara T. *God in La Mancha; Religious Reform and the People of Cuenca 1560–1650*. Baltimore and London: Johns Hopkins University Press, 1992.

O'Malley, John, S.J., ed. *Catholicism in Early Modern History: A Guide to Research*. St. Louis: Center for Reformation Research, 1988.

Payne, Stanley. *Spanish Catholicism: An Historical Overview*. Madison: University of Wisconsin Press, 1984.

Pérez Moreda, Vicente. *Las crisis de la mortalidad en la España interior*. Madrid: Siglo Veintiuno de España, 1980.

Perry, Mary Elizabeth. *Gender and Disorder in Early Modern Seville*. Princeton: Princeton University Press, 1990.

Pinto Crespo, Virgilio. *Inquisición y control ideológico en la España del siglo XVI*. Madrid: Taurus, 1983.

Pitt-Rivers, Julian. *The Fate of Shechem or the Politics of Sex: Essays in the Anthropology of the Mediterranean*. Cambridge: Cambridge University Press, 1977.

Quintan Aldea, Vaquero; María Martínez, Thomas; and Vives Gatell, Juan, eds. *Diccionario de historia ecclesiástica de España*. Madrid: CSIC 1972– 1975.

Rapley, Elizabeth. *The Dévotes; Women and the Church in Seventeenth-Century France*. Montreal and Kingston: McGill-Queen's University Press, 1990.

Redondo, Augustín, ed. *Amours légitimes, amours illégitimes en Espagne XVI–XVII siècles*. Paris: Publications de la Sorbonne, 1985.

Rémond, René. *L'Anticléricalisme en France de 1815 à nos jours*. Paris: Fayard, 1976.

Ros, Fidèle de. *Un maître de Sainte Thérèse, le père François de Osuna*. Paris: Gabriel Beauchesne, 1936.

Sáez Marín, Juan. *Datos sobre la Iglesia española contemporánea*. Madrid: Editorial Nacional, 1975.

Sánchez Herrero, José Luis. *Las diócesis del reino de León*. León: Caja de Ahorros y Monte de Piedad, 1978.

Saugnieux, Joël. *Les jansénistes et le renouveau de la prédiction dans l'Espagne de la seconde moitié du XVIIIe siècle*. Lyon: Presses Universitaires de Lyon, 1976.

Secretariado Nacional de Liturgia. *Guía para celebrar la penitencia segun el nuevo ritual*. Madrid: Heroes, 1976.

Sínodo diocesana del Arzobispado de Toledo. Madrid: José de la Peña, 1849.

Spitz, Louis. *The Protestant Reformation 1517–1559*. New York: Harper and Row, 1985.

Tellechea Idigoras, José Ignacio. *La reforma tridentina en San Sebastián*. San Sebastián: Caja de Ahorros Municipal de San Sebastián, 1972.

Tentler, Thomas. *Sin and Confession on the Eve of the Reformation*. Princeton: Princeton University Press, 1977.

Vigil, Mariló. *La vida de las mujeres en los siglos XVI y XVII*. Madrid: Siglo XXI, 1986.

Vovelle, Michel. *Piété baroque et déchristianisation en Provence au XVIIIe siècle*. Paris: Plon, 1973.

Warner, Marina. *Alone of All Her Sex: The Myth and Cult of the Virgin Mary*. New York: Vintage, 1983.

Weinstein, Donald, and Bell, Rudolph M. *Saints and Society: The Two Worlds of Western Christendom, 1000–1700*. Chicago and London: University of Chicago Press, 1982.

Wright, A. D. *The Counter-Reformation: Catholic Europe and the Non-Christian World*. New York: St. Martin's Press, 1982.

Zaragoza Pascual, Ernesto. *Los generales de la congregación de San Benito de Valladolid*. Zamora: Ediciones Monte Cristo, 1980.

Articles and Essays

Arenal, Electa. "The Convent as a Catalyst for Autonomy: Two Hispanic Nuns of the Seventeenth Century." In *Women in Hispanic Literature: Icons and Fallen Idols*, edited by Beth Miller, 147–183.

Azcona, Tarsicio de. "Reforma del episcopado y del clero de España en tiempo de los Reyes Católicos y de Carlos V." In Vol. 3 of *Historia de la Iglesia en España*, edited by Ricardo García-Villoslada, 115–215. Madrid: La Editorial Católica, 1979.

Beck, Melinda; Springen, Karen; and Foote, Donna. "Sex and Psychotherapy." *Newsweek*, 13 April 1992, 53–54.

Bilinkoff, Jodi. "The Holy Woman and the Urban Community in Sixteenth Century Avila." In *Women and the Structure of Society*, edited by Barbara Harris and JoAnn McNamara, 74–80. Durham, NC: Duke University Press, 1984.

Bossy, John. "Moral Arithmetic: Seven Sins into Ten Commandments," in *Conscience and Casuistry in Early Modern Europe*, edited by Edmund Leites, 214–234. Cambridge: Cambridge University Press, 1988.

Burke, Peter. "Popular Piety." In *Catholicism in Early Modern Europe: A Guide to Research*, edited by John O'Malley, S.J., 113–131. St. Louis: Center for Reformation Research, 1988.

Callahan, William J. "The Spanish Church." In *Church and Society in Catholic Europe of the Eighteenth Century*, edited by William J. Callahan and David Higgs, 34–50. Cambridge: Cambridge University Press, 1958.

Casey, James. "Le mariage clandestin en Andalousie à l'époque moderne." In *Amours légitimes, amours illégitimes en Espagne XVI–XVII siècles*, edited by Augustín Redondo, 57–68. Paris: Publications de la Sorbonne, 1985.

Chiriboga, David A. "Mental Health at the Midpoint: Crisis, Challenge or Relief." In *Midlife Myths, Issues, Findings and Practice Implications*, edited by Ski Hunter and Martin Sundel,116–144. Newbury Park, CA: Sage, 1989.

Contreras, Jaime, and Henningsen, Gustav. "Forty Four Thousand Cases of the Spanish Inquisition." In *The Inquisition in Early Modern Europe; Studies on Sources and Methods*, edited by Gustav Henningsen and John Tedeschi, 100–129. DeKalb: Northern Illinois University Press, 1986.

Dedieu, Jean-Pierre. "L'Inquisition et le droit; analyse formelle de la procédure inquisitoriale en cause de foi." *Mélanges de la Casa de Velázquez* 33 (July 1987): 227–251.

Domínguez Ortiz, Antonio. "Aspectos sociales de la vida eclesiástica en los siglos XVII y XVIII." In *Historia de la Iglesia en España*, edited by Ricardo García-Villoslada, 5–72. Madrid: Editorial Católica, 1979– 1982.

Egido, Teófanes. "La expulsión de los jesuitas de España." In vol. 4 of *Historia de la Iglesia de España*, edited by Ricardo García-Villoslada, 745–792. Madrid: La Editorial Católica, 1979.

Freud, Sigmund. "Further Recommendations in the Technique of Psycho-Analysis: Observations on Transference-Love." In Vol. 2 of *Sigmund Freud Collected Papers*, edited by Ernest Jones, 377–391. New York: Basic Books, 1959.

———. "Three Contributions to the Theory of Sex: The Sexual Aberrations." In *The Basic Writings of Sigmund Freud*, edited and translated by A. A. Brill. New York: Random House, 1938.

García Cárcel, Ricardo. "El fracaso matrimonial en la Cataluña del Antiguo Régimen." In *Amours légitimes, amours illégitimes en Espagne XVI– XVII siècles*, edited by Augustín Redondo, 121–132. Paris: Publications de la Sorbonne, 1985.

Gartrell, Nanette; Herman, Judith; Olarte, Silvia; Feldstein, Michael; and Localio, Russell. "Psychiatrist-Patient Sexual Contact: Results of a National Survey, I: Prevalence." *American Journal of Psychiatry* 143 (September 1986): 1126–1131.

Goñi Gaztambide, José. "El cumplimiento pascual en la diócesis de Pamplona en 1801." *Hispania Sacra* 26 (1973): 361–372.

González Novalín, José Luis. "Religiosidad y reforma del pueblo cristiano." In Vol. 3 of *Historia de la Iglesia en España*, edited by Ricardo García Villoslada, 351–384. Madrid: La Editorial Católica, 1979.

———. "La herejía luterana y el nuevo rumbo del Santo Oficio." In Vol. 3 of *Historia de la Iglesia en España*, edited by Ricardo García-Villoslada, 175–202. Madrid: La Editorial Católica, 1979.

Grendler, Paul F. "Schools, Seminaries and Catechetical Instruction." In *Catholicism in Early Modern Europe: A Guide to Research*, edited by John O'Malley, S.J., 315–330. St. Louis: Center for Reformation Research, 1988.

Graullera, Vicente. "Mujer, amor y moralidad en la Valencia de los siglos XVI y XVII."

In *Amours légitimes, amours illégitimes en Espagne XVI– XVII siècles*, edited by Augustín Redondo, 109–119. Paris: Publications de la Sorbonne, 1985.

Haan, Norma. "Personality at Midlife." In *Midlife Myths, Issues, Findings and Practice Implications*, edited by Ski Hunter and Martin Sundel, 145– 156. Newbury Park, CA: Sage, 1989.

Herman, Judith; Gartrell, Nanette; Olarte, Silvia; Feldstein, Michael; and Localio, Russell. "Psychiatrist-Patient Sexual Contact: Results of a National Survey, II: Psychiatrists' Attitudes." *American Journal of Psychiatry* 144 (February 1987): 164–169.

Jagoe, Catherine. "Krausism and the Pygmalion Motif in Galdós's *La familia de León Roch*." *Romance Quarterly* 37, no. 1 (1992): 41–52.

Llorca, Bernardino. "Carlos V y la intervención de España en el concilio de Trento." In Vol. 3 of *Historia de la Iglesia de España*, edited by Ricardo García-Villoslada, 385–452. Madrid: La Editorial Católica, 1979.

Martín Fernández, Francisco. "La formación del clero en los siglos XVII y XVIII." In Vol. 4 of *Historia de la Iglesia de España*, edited by Ricardo García-Villoslada, 523–582. Madrid: La Editorial Católica, 1979.

Martínez Millán, José. "La burocracía del Santo Oficio en Valencia durante el siglo XVIII." *Miscelanea Comillas* 40, no. 77 (May 1982): 147–193.

Mestre Sanchis, Antonio. "Religión y cultura en el siglo XVIII español." In Vol. 4 of *Historia de la Iglesia de España*, edited by Ricardo García-Villoslada, 586–743. Madrid: La Editorial Católica, 1979.

Molinié-Bertrand, Anne. "Le clergé dans le royaume de Castille à la fin du XVIe siècle: approche cartographique." *Revue d'Histoire Economique et Sociale* 51, no. 1 (1973): 5–53.

Norberg, Kathryn. "The Counter-Reformation and Women Religious and Lay." In *Catholicism in Early Modern Europe: A Guide to Research*, edited by John O'Malley, S.J., 133–146. St. Louis: Center for Reformation Research, 1988.

Ortega, José. "Don Fermín de Pas, un estudio de superbia et concupiscentia catholicis." *Revista de Estudios Hispánicos* 9, no. 3 (October 1975): 323–342.

Pérez, Joseph. "La femme et l'amour dans l'Espagne du XVI siècle." In *Amours légitimes, amours illégitimes en Espagne XVI–XVII siecle*, edited by Augustín Redondo, 19–30. Paris: Publications de la Sorbonne, 1985.

Rodriguez, Alfred. "Algunos aspectos de la elaboracíon literaria de *La familia de León Roch*." PMLA 82, no. 1 (March 1967): 121–127.

Rossiaud, Jacques. "Prostitution, Sex and Society in French Towns in the Fifteenth Century." In *Western Sexuality; Practice and Precept in Past and Present Times*, edited by Philippe Ariès and André Béjin, translated by Anthony Forster, 76–94. Oxford: Basil Blackwell, 1985.

———. "Prostitution, Youth and Society in the Towns of Southeastern France in the Fifteenth Century." In *Deviants and the Abandoned in French Society*, edited by Robert Forster and Orest Ranum, 1–46. Baltimore: Johns Hopkins University Press, 1978.

Saez, Ricardo. "La transgression de l'interdit amoureux: le prêtre, la femme et l'enfant dans l'archevêché de Tolède (1565–1620). In *Amours légitimes, amours illégitimes en Espagne XVI–XVII siècles*, edited by Augustín Redondo, 93–100. Paris: Publications de la Sorbonne, 1985.

Vázquez, Isaac. "Las controversias doctrinales postridentinas hasta finales del siglo XVII." In Vol. 4 of *Historia de la Iglesia de España*, edited by Ricardo García-Villoslada, 449–474. Madrid: La Editorial Católica, 1979.

Vidal, Marciano. "La teología moral en nuestros días." In *Histoire de l'Eglise*, edited
    by Augustín Fliche and Victor Martín, translated into Spanish by Manuela
    Ureña Pastor. 31 vols. 2 supplements, supplement 1, 483–499. Valencia:
    Edicep, 1978–1982.

Weber, Francis Wyers. "Ideology and Religious Parody in the Novels of Leopoldo
    Alas." *Bulletin of Hispanic Studies* 43 (January 1966): 197–208.

Weg, Ruth B. "Sensuality/Sexuality of the Middle Years." In *Midlife Myths, Issues,
    Findings and Practice Implications*, edited by Ski Hunter and Martin Sundel,
    31–50. Newbury Park, CA: Sage, 1989.

Wilke, David. *A Selection of the Best Pictures Spanish and Oriental Sketches*. Lon-
    don and New York: George Virtue, 1889.

INDEX

DATE DUE